RED GOD

SUNY series in Chinese Philosophy and Culture

Roger T. Ames, editor

RED GOD

Wei Baqun and His Peasant Revolution in Southern China, 1894–1932

XIAORONG HAN

Published by State University of New York Press, Albany

Printed in the United States of America

For information, contact State University of New York Press, Albany, NY
www.sunypress.edu

Production by Eileen Nizer
Marketing by Michael Campochiaro

Library of Congress Cataloging-in-Publication Data

Han, Xiaorong,
Red God : Wei Baqun and his peasant revolution in southern China, 1894–1932 / Xiaorong Han.
p. cm. — (SUNY series in Chinese philosophy and culture)
Includes bibliographical references and index.
ISBN 978-1-4384-5383-5 (hardcover : alk. paper)
ISBN 978-1-4384-5385-9 (ebook)
1. Wei, Baqun, 1894-1931. 2. Communists—China—Biography. 3. Peasant uprisings—China—Guangxi Zhuangzu Zizhiqu—History—20th century. I. Title. II. Title: Wei Baqun and his peasant revolution in southern China, 1894–1932.

DS777.488.W48H36 2014
951.4'1092—dc23
[B] 2014002041

10 9 8 7 6 5 4 3 2 1

To Ah Meng and Bo Ning

Contents

Illustrations

Maps

Figures

Acknowledgments

It would have been impossible for me to complete this project without the assistance of the many teachers, colleagues, friends, and relatives who made my protracted search for the meanings of Wei Baqun's life and revolution a pleasant and fruitful learning experience.

In Nanning, Fan Honggui and Chen Xinde were very generous in sharing both source materials and insights with me. So did Ya Yuanbo in Hechi. In Baise, the Municipal Office of the CCP History and the Municipal Archives both opened their doors to me and Wei Yongmei was particularly helpful. The Baise Uprising Memorial Hall granted me the right to use the image of a statue of Wei Baqun in this book. In Donglan, the four researchers at the Office of the CCP History, Huang Haoye, Shi Jietai, Wang Honghua, and Wei Hui twice received me and offered me numerous books they had written and edited. Wang Hao of the Political Consultative Conference of Donglan provided some very useful and hard to find locally published books and journals.

Wu Yixiong of Sun Yat-sen University and Pan Jiao of Minzu University granted me valuable opportunitiues to present my research to their colleagues and their very bright students.

Stephen Uhalley Jr., Paul Hansen, Bruce Bigelow, and Li Huaiyin all read the entire manuscript and David Mason read the first two chapters. They all provided very helpful suggestions. I also benefited from conversations with the late Jerry Bentley, Richard L. Davis, Edward Shultz, Huang Xingqiu, and Huang Ying, as well as various forms of assistance from Monte Broaded, Antonio Menendez, Bob Holm, and Scott Swanson.

Susan Berger of the Irwin Library of Butler University was very efficient in acquiring a large number of books and articles I requested through the interlibrary loan service. Matthew Jager of the Butler University Writer's Studio provided editorial assistance for the first draft of the manuscript.

The two grants I received in 2010 from the Butler University Institute for Research and Scholarship and the Chiang Ching-kuo Foundation for International Scholarly Exchange, which were for another project, enabled me to travel to Guangxi and other places to pursue my sideline research for this book.

The two anonymous reviewers for the SUNY Press provided very enlightened and constructive general comments and specific suggestions. Roger Ames and Nancy Ellegate were as helpful this time as they were in the publication of my first book. Eileen Nizer, Jessica Kirschner, Ryan Morris, and Michael Campochiaro were very prompt and patient in offering guidance and assistance with regard to the production of the book.

My former teachers, the late Wu Wenhua in Xiamen, Li Yifu in Beijing, Daniel Kwok, and Truong Buu Lam in Hawaii, were always ready to enrich me with their wise advice and enliven me with their kind encouragement.

Within my family, my wife Liu Meng read both the first and the final draft and made numerous corrections; my brother Yongqing helped purchase a number of very useful old books; and my son Bo Ning read part of the manuscript and also served as a first-class technical assistant.

I am profoundly grateful to all the people and institutions mentioned above as well as to many whose names do not appear here.

Introduction

It was sometime before dawn on October 19, 1932.

Wei Ang, a stout young man, was sitting by a fire at the bottom of the Fragrant Tea Cave (Xiangchadong) on the slope of one of endless mountains in the Western Mountains (Xishan) region of Donglan County, Guangxi Province in southern China. The flickering firelight from time to time lit the pockmarks on Wei Ang's face, a legacy of the smallpox epidemic. Near Wei Ang's feet lay his mother, his second wife, and his younger sister. The four had fled to the cave when the Nationalist troops stormed their village to enforce their most recent military campaign against the Communists. Wei Ang took the cave as a safe haven because its entrance was far away from the nearest road and also hidden behind trees and grasses. The cave was about three meters deep and had a rather narrow bottom. On its innermost wall, a few steps above the bottom, he had found a hollow space large enough to make a small resting place. In that cave within the cave lay a bed made of three pieces of planks and in it were two men in deep sleep. It was quite cold in the cave and both men covered themselves with thick blankets.

Wei Ang had gone through a sleepless night, partly because he had to stand guard over the two men in the bed, and partly because he had a difficult decision to make. One of the two men was his uncle, none other than Wei Baqun, a member of the Central Executive Committee of the Chinese Soviet Republic, the Communist state based in Jiangxi and headed by Mao Zedong. In addition to that symbolic position, Wei Baqun was commander-in-chief of the Right River Independent Division of the Chinese Workers' and Peasants' Red Army as well as one of the most important leaders of the Right River Revolutionary Base Area. In addition to these official titles, since 1921 he had been known as the supreme leader of the Donglan peasant movement, and the most well-known revolutionary in the Right River region as well as in Guangxi Province. For the last two nights, Wei Baqun and his bodyguard Luo Rikuai had camped out with Wei Ang's family, but the two were planning to slip away for neighboring Guizhou Province the next morning to escape from their Nationalist pursuers.

Because Wei Ang lost his father at an early age, Uncle Baqun had been like his father, providing food for him, helping him find a wife, and also bringing him into the revolution and appointing him to various positions. At one time he was even made to serve as Uncle Baqun's bodyguard. The revolution had already changed Wei Ang's status to the extent that this formerly poor peasant had even been able to find himself a second wife, a privilege enjoyed only by the wealthy and powerful, and Wei Ang had expected further changes. Unfortunately, the revolution that Uncle Baqun had launched, which had once been so robust and promising, was now on the brink of collapse. The entire Right River Independent Division had been dispersed, the leaders of the revolution were hiding in caves or had moved to other areas, much of the revolutionary base area had been lost, and the center of the base area had been besieged by Nationalist troops. Wei Ang believed that the revolution was almost over and there would be no hope for Uncle Baqun to rise again. If Wei Ang had been grateful to his uncle for the beneficial changes in his life when the revolution was strong and energetic, he was now somewhat resentful for the difficulties that he believed Uncle Baqun had caused. He thought that continuing the failing revolution would bring about not just inconveniences, but also many deaths. Quite a few of Wei Baqun's relatives had already been killed, and Wei Ang did not want to be the next to die.

In order to completely eliminate the revolution in the Right River region, the provincial government had announced that it would offer monetary rewards for capturing or killing any important Communist leader. The largest reward, of course, was reserved for capturing or killing Wei Baqun—10,000 silver dollars in 1931, upped to 14,000 silver dollars a year later. Such a fortune would allow Wei Ang and his family to live comfortably for the rest of their lives. Besides, Wei Ang believed, if he killed Uncle Baqun, the Nationalists would no longer treat him as a Communist and he would be able not only to survive but also enjoy his freedom as a law-abiding citizen. He did not want to live in the cave any longer.

The pain and indecisiveness that Wei Ang experienced on that cold evening derived from the contradiction between his strong desire for money, survival, and freedom on one side and his residual love for his uncle on the other. Although his second wife had already persuaded him to cut a deal with the Nationalist troops stationed in the nearby town of Wuzhuan, Wei Ang was still hesitant to actually put his plan into action. He was also worried that people would see him as an ungrateful nephew and a coward if he killed his own kin, and that Uncle Baqun's remaining followers would condemn him as a traitor, punishable by death. "But with the silver dollars I can leave Donglan forever and hide in some other place," he thought. Right before dawn, Wei Ang finally decided to act. He knew that in a few hours Uncle Baqun would leave and might not return to Guangxi in the foreseeable future. The morning sun was rising, and uncle or his bodyguard could wake up at any moment. He could not afford to wait any longer.

Wei Ang slowly rose up and threw a few stones into the woods outside the cave, causing some noise. He heard no reactions from the two men in the bed. He then moved slowly toward his uncle and whispered: "Uncle, the enemies are coming!" There were still no responses. Wei Baqun had been seriously sick yesterday, and during the night he had covered his entire head with the thick blanket to protect against the chills, making it difficult for him to hear things even if he was awake. The other man in the bed, Luo Rikuai, had also been exhausted by all the travels they had to make in recent days to outwit their pursuers and was sound asleep. Wei Ang did not take the bodyguard seriously anyway. Luo was only a fifteen-year-old boy and did not even carry a weapon. He was more like a guide than a bodyguard.[1]

Assured that both Uncle Baqun and his bodyguard were in their dreams, Wei Ang quickly took out the handgun from underneath his uncle's head. He knew that the handgun was fully loaded. In the previous evening, right after Wei Baqun went to bed, Wei Ang reminded his uncle to keep his weapon loaded. "The enemies might come at any moment," he warned. Wei Baqun heeded that piece of advice, got up from the bed, and loaded his handgun.[2] Wei Ang now took the same handgun, pulled the trigger with his full strength, and shot two bullets into his uncle's head, killing him instantly.

The gunshots awakened Luo Rikuai. Just as Luo jumped out of the bed, Wei Ang threw back the blanket to reveal Wei Baqun's body. Luo took a glimpse at Wei Baqun's bloody head and knew immediately that his commander was dead. Luo Rikuai began to run toward the entrance of the cave, but Wei Ang quickly caught his arm and forced him at gunpoint to cut off Wei Baqun's head before putting it into a basket. Luo then had to carry the basket on his back and walked toward the town of Wuzhuan, with Wei Ang following him closely and pointing the handgun at him. Once on the road Wei Ang would tell everyone he ran into that "I've chopped off Baqun's head. If you want to take a look then come to Wuzhuan."[3]

By about seven o'clock in the morning, Wei Baqun's head was presented to the Nationalist troops stationed in Wuzhuan, who were thrilled when they confirmed that the head had indeed belonged to Wei Baqun. They decided to hang the grisly trophy atop the gate of the Tower of the Literary Star (Kuixinglou) that housed their regimental headquarters, and more than seven hundred local people immediately gathered outside to watch.[4] The same building had been the seat of Wei Baqun's Soviet government only two years before. The head was then brought to the county seat of Donglan and put on display there. After taking photos of the head, the county authorities had some preservatives applied to it to prevent it from rotting. The provincial government then ordered that Wei Baqun's head be taken to Nanning, the capital of Guangxi Province so that the residents there could "enjoy the pleasure of taking a glimpse at it," and "could see Bandit Wei Baqun's true face."[5] In addition to the provincial capital, Wei Baqun's head was displayed in all other important cities in Guangxi, and the tour and show of the head did not end until late November 1932.[6]

The Nationalists predicted that with Wei Baqun's death, the Communist movement in and around Donglan would die. They knew that many of Wei Baqun's followers were still alive and would try to revive the movement, but they were confident that none of his followers could become as troublesome as Wei Baqun had been. The Communists agreed with the Nationalists that Wei Baqun's death was indeed a great loss for the Communist movement and that as a local revolutionary leader Wei Baqun was irreplaceable. Many of Wei Baqun's supporters completely lost hope in the revolution and stopped fighting after his death, but others, in addition to forever lamenting his death, became ever more hardened in carrying on his cause and avidly enthusiastic about promoting him as a martyr and hero. Thirty years after Wei Baqun's death, his former colleague Deng Xiaoping wrote a long eulogy for his old friend in which he described Wei Baqun as "a hero of the proletariat and working class," "a person who is worthy of the title of people's leader," and "a model Communist." He concluded by affirming that "Comrade Wei Baqun will forever live in our hearts. He will forever be our model as well as a model for our descendants. We will forever remember him!" Mao Zedong was to describe Wei Baqun as "a great son of the Zhuang people and a great leader of the peasants and the Communist Party," and Zhou Enlai would refer to Wei Baqun as "a hero of all the peoples of China."[7]

After the founding of the People's Republic of China (PRC), Chinese historians granted Wei Baqun equal status with supreme party dignitaries Peng Pai and Mao Zedong in describing them collectively as "the three great early peasant movement leaders" of the Chinese Communist Party (CCP).[8] It is arguable that among the three, Wei Baqun was the first to work among the peasants. He began to mobilize the peasants in Donglan as early as late 1921, whereas Peng Pai did not start his peasant work in Haifeng until mid-1922, and Mao Zedong did not discover the power of the peasant until 1925. In Mao's native Hunan province, rural revolutions were preceded by urban movements and did not begin until after the mid-1920s.[9] Wei Baqun was also one of the first to stage a violent peasant revolution. In 1923, he sent shockwaves throughout Guangxi by launching four successive attacks on the county seat of Donglan. It is believed that even Mao Zedong once admitted that in the 1920s he had learned "something" from Wei Baqun about how to stage a peasant movement.[10]

To the local villagers, Wei Baqun was not just a revolutionary, but also a local hero when he was alive and a demi-god after his death. Wei Baqun's enemies hated him so much that they would not allow his headless corpse to lay in peace in the cave. Shortly after Wei Baqun's head reached Wuzhuan, a group of Nationalists went to the Fragrant Tea Cave and burned his body. They left once they were sure that they had completely extinguished Wei Baqun. Some months later, a group of villagers climbed to the cave on a dark evening and collected the few charred bones of Wei Baqun they could retrieve from the ashes. They then buried the remains at the foot of a mountain by Wei Baqun's native village. To prevent the Nationalists from recognizing and destroying Wei Baqun's tomb, the villagers turned it into a shrine that they named the Red God Temple (Hongshenmiao). Wei Baqun's local followers had already begun to spread stories about his supernatural powers when he was alive, and after he died they turned him into a true god, a god in red and a god who had been a revolutionary.

Partly as a result of the process of deification, the local people continued to tell and retell stories about their god, making it difficult for those who are determined to discover the truth to distinguish the historical from the legendary. For instance, since Wei Baqun's death there have arisen many different accounts about what really happened at the Fragrant Tea Cave in the early morning of October 19, 1932. Some believe that Wei Ang's mother, second wife and sister were in the cave when Wei Baqun was murdered, whereas others hold that only his second wife was in the cave or that all three women were not in the cave but spent the night in the town of Wuzhuan. Some claimed that bodyguard Luo Rikuai was on guard duty outside the cave when he heard the gunshots, although Luo himself recalled that he was sleeping by his commander when the shots were fired. Some believe that Wei Ang put only two bullets into his uncle's head, but others argue that he pulled the trigger three times, or even as many as eight times. Some claim that Wei Baqun was woken up when Wei Ang tried to take the handgun from underneath his head and even yelled at Wei Ang ordering him to put down the weapon, but most insist that Wei Baqun was killed while asleep. Some think that it was Wei Ang who cut off Wei Baqun's head, whereas others allege that it was Luo Rikuai who did it, albeit under Wei Ang's command. At the least, however, all accounts agree that Wei Baqun was murdered by his own nephew Wei Ang at the Fragrant Tea Cave on the morning of October 19, 1932. There are similar agreements and disagreements about many other episodes in Wei Baqun's life. Most accounts agree with one another on the major aspects, but disagree on details.

Wei Baqun was one of many peasant movement leaders who rose up in China in the 1920s and 1930s. Judged by the amount of publications, Wei Baqun has been a more popular subject than most other leaders for scholars and general writers in China, but one of the least attractive figures to foreign scholars. Most authors of the Chinese-language publications about Wei Baqun are based in Guangxi, and many of them are historians affiliated with the various levels of the offices of CCP history. They have done a great job in solving the many mysteries about Wei Baqun's life and in compiling and preserving materials about Wei Baqun. Outside China, Diana Lary's nine-page piece published in 1972 has remained the only English article on Wei Baqun and his movement,[11] and Wei Baqun's name has appeared in a few other English articles and books dealing with twentieth century Guangxi and China. My study is the first book-length treatment of Wei Baqun and his revolution ever published in English. My primary goal is to write a biography of Wei Baqun as a person rather than a hero or a deity, and I intend to combine Wei Baqun's personal history with three other levels of history, namely, the history of the Chinese Communist revolution, the local history and ethnohistory of Donglan and Guangxi, and the national history of twentieth-century China.

My study is based on four major categories of source materials. The first consists of contemporary accounts, including Wei Baqun's own writings as well as speeches, letters, poems, diaries, news reports, and political documents left by his followers, enemies, and neutral parties. The second is composed of memoirs and oral histories, most of which were written, collected, and published after 1949. As Gregor Benton has convincingly argued, although Chinese memoirs published since 1949 have many drawbacks, they should not be ruled out as sources because in some cases they are the only sources available and because evidence can be discerned from them if proper techniques are adopted.[12] The third category of sources includes legends and folk tales, most of which were also collected and published after 1949; and the last comprises relevant secondary texts in Chinese and English. Although the source materials contain different and even opposing records and perspectives, they are used here to reconstruct a more or less coherent and unified account of Wei Baqun and his movement.

The most important events in Wei Baqun's life were a few trips he made to places outside Donglan and Guangxi and a few revolts he launched back home. These are the central topics of my study. His journeys to places beyond Donglan and Guangxi were particularly important in his life and career as a revolutionary. They helped to divide his life into distinct major phases because each trip caused him to bring his revolution into a new phase. These journeys allowed Wei Baqun not only to learn new ideas and methods, but also to forge connections and alliances with outside forces that were to play a significant role in the revolution he tried to make in and around Donglan. Through these journeys Wei Baqun turned himself into an active agent in the negotiations between the local, the provincial, and the national; in the transmission of ideas and cultures from the provincial and national centers to the local community; and in the integration of the local into the provincial and national. Wei Baqun's status in his local community partly derived from his role as such an agent, and the trips were a very important factor in his evolution from a village boy to a revolutionary and then to red god.

The connections between Wei Baqun's journeys and his revolution made him comparable to many other revolutionaries in early twentieth-century China. Like Wei Baqun, many other revolutionaries, particularly the Communists among them, were born in villages. They went to small or big cities for education and were exposed to revolutionary ideas there. After becoming politically active, they voluntarily returned or were dispatched to their native villages to make revolutions. For instance, Peng Pai converted to socialism as a student in Waseda University in Japan and then returned to his native Haifeng County of Guangdong Province to start his revolution; Mao Zedong became a Communist during his sojourns in Changsha and Beijing, and was sent back to lead revolution in his native Hunan Province in late 1927; Fang Zhimin transformed himself from a student and a jobless youth to a socialist and Communist during his stays in Nanchang, Jiujiang, and Shanghai, and then went back to his native Yiyang County in Jiangxi Province to organize a peasant movement. The list goes on and on. Wei Baqun's role as an agent between his local community and the national centers, however, was more significant and obvious than that of most others primarily because his community was far more isolated and remote than Haifeng, Hunan, Yiyang, and most other cradles of revolutionary movements. Because of this, his journeys were much more difficult than those of the others. Moreover, although many other revolutionaries went through only one transformative trip in their lives, Wei Baqun experienced as many as three significant journeys.

Wei Baqun shared some other important similarities with other peasant movement leaders of his time. His transition from a reformer to a revolutionary reminds us of similar paths taken by Sun Yat-sen and some other revolutionaries. Like some other Communists, Wei Baqun showed interest in other radical ideologies before settling for Communism, and he went through a process of radicalization, which eventually resulted in his bloody conflicts with powerful local families. Like Peng Pai and many other revolutionaries, Wei Baqun was a son of a landlord who became the leader of a revolution against his own family and class, and his campaigns brought about tremendous losses to his own family. In the constant face of dangerous circumstances and with his voluntary embrace of radical revolutionary ideologies and methods, Wei Baqun developed a kind of brutality and relentlessness that characterize many other revolutionaries. He shared with many other Communist revolutionaries the determination, sacrifice, and commitment, which form what Joseph Esherick has described as "the subjective element of the revolutionary dialectic" that was essential to the success of their revolution.[13]

Wei Baqun went through similar experiments and events as many other Communist revolutionaries, including guerrilla wars, collective farming, intraparty conflicts, and the repeated extermination campaigns launched by the Nationalists. Wei Baqun also had the charisma and popularity of a typical peasant leader of his time and like Peng Pai and some other revolutionaries he eventually emerged as a deity-like figure for the local peasants. His short life and brutal death were also trademarks shared by many revolutionaries of his time.

There are also some important differences between Wei Baqun and most other leaders of Communist and non-Communist peasant movements, making him a rather atypical figure among the prominent revolutionaries and reformers of twentieth-century China. Wei Baqun was from a multiethnic frontier region, whereas most other leaders were from the coastal and interior areas dominated by the Han. Wei Baqun was a Zhuang, and among his supporters were the Zhuang, the Han, and the Yao. He was thus also one of the first peasant movement leaders who had to manage ethnic relations. Whereas most other revolutionaries of his time were familiar with Chinese and Western traditions, Wei Baqun traveled easily between and among four cultures—the Zhuang, the Yao, the Han Chinese, and the Western—and he drew inspiration and wisdom from all four traditions.

Largely because of its remoteness, foreign dominance over the local economy and politics was not as salient a feature for Donglan as for some other communities where radical revolutions took root, and nationalism in the form of anti-imperialism played a less important role in Wei Baqun's conversion to Communism than in the conversion of many other early Communists. Between nationalism and social revolution, the two appeals that many have emphasized in explaining the CCP command of popular support,[14] social revolution played a much more important part in the making of Wei Baqun's movement than nationalism, partly because his revolution began and ended before the beginning of Japan's all out invasion of China in 1937. The defeat of Wei Baqun's revolution and other Communist movements in the early 1930s indicates that the Communist social revolutions in rural China were not yet powerful enough to overwhelm the Nationalist urban centers despite the strong popular support the Communists enjoyed in some regions.

Although a well-educated intellectual, Wei Baqun was more a practitioner than a theorist. Some other peasant movement leaders of both the Communist camp (such as Peng Pai, Mao Zedong, Fang Zhimin, and the early Shen Dingyi) and the non-Communist camp (e.g., Liang Shuming, Yan Yangchu, and the later Shen Dingyi) were prolific writers about their movements, rural China and other national affairs.[15] Some of their works, such as Peng Pai's "Peasant Movement in Haifeng" and Mao Zedong's "Report on an Investigation of the Peasant Movement in Hunan," have become classic texts about the Chinese peasant revolution. Wei Baqun, however, left us only a few brief pieces of formal writing and some folk songs, which contribute to the difficulty of studying his life and thought and the rise of a mystical aura around him. Mao Zedong once jokingly remarked that "Wei Baqun read half of a book about Marxism and then became a big shot in half of China."[16] Obviously, Mao did not see

Wei Baqun as a theoretician, but believed that Wei Baqun was very efficient in applying the Marxist ideas he had learned. It is understandable that studies on Chinese peasant movement leaders have tended to privilege those productive writers, but important practitioners such as Wei Baqun should not be neglected.

Wei Baqun also differs from other early Communist peasant movement leaders in his relations with the CCP. Although he eventually became a member of the CCP and was widely perceived to be a leading Communist by the Nationalists and the public, there is evidence showing that his relationship with the CCP was not always smooth. On the one hand, the CCP leaders saw him as a natural ally and was eager to make use of his fame and influence as well as to reform his movement along the Communist line; on the other hand, some CCP leaders were suspicious of Wei Baqun's past connections and did not always recognize his contributions or approve his practices while he was alive. His popularity among the local people appeared to exceed that within the CCP, and his power over his community also far exceeded that over the local party branch. In his local community, Wei Baqun was a more popular rallying point for mass support than the CCP, and in the eyes of some of his CCP comrades, his popularity among the villagers was both an asset and a burden. Whereas many other Communist peasant movement leaders first converted to Communism and then went to the peasants, Wei Baqun became a famous peasant movement leader long before he formally joined the CCP. Compared with most other Communist revolutionaries, he appeared more like a Robin Hood type folk hero than an orthodox Communist. Partly because of that, there are more folk stories about Wei Baqun than about most other peasant movement leaders. Because of his own fame, he did not depend so much on the CCP for either legitimacy or support during the early phase of his revolution.

Finally, among the famous peasant movement leaders of his time, Wei Baqun's attachment to his local community was much stronger than most others. Despite his national reputation and influence, his connections with the outside world, his interests in external ideas and methods, and his concerns about national and international affairs, his primary interest always lay in changing his native community. The ultimate destination of his several journeys to the interior and coastal areas was always his frontier county. His national fame derived largely from his commitment to his local community and he continued to stay in his local community after attaining national influence. His reluctance to leave his community even after it became extremely dangerous to stay there eventually resulted in his death.

These similarities and differences between Wei Baqun and other peasant movement leaders make his life and movement an opportune case for studying the various topics relevant to the Chinese revolution, such as the modernization of China and its local impact; the transformation of the local elite; the role of intellectuals and organization in the peasant movement and Communist revolution; the interactions between the center and the periphery; the effect of the local tradition, ethnicity, and ecology on the revolution; and the social and economic conditions of rural China.

The focus of this study is on exploring Wei Baqun's life and movement in light of the interactions between his local community and the Chinese nation and his role in such interactions. As an intermediary between the frontier and the center, the important events and moments of Wei Baqun's life can be best understood by inspecting the congruence and conflicts of local, regional, and national forces and perspectives at play during his lifetime. Wei Baqun and his frontier community were in constant interaction with multiple centers at that time. Culturally, there was the division between the center of Han cultural sphere and the periphery of minority cultures; economically, there existed the gap between the center of coastal areas and the periphery formed by interior and frontier regions and between the urban centers and the peripheral villages. Politically, in a divided China, Wei Baqun and his followers had to deal with different centers at different times, and these included the governments of the Old Guangxi Clique and the New Guangxi Clique, the short-lived Yu Zuobai-Li Mingrui regime, Chiang Kai-shek's Nanjing government, and the CCP. Although some of these centers were hostile, others were friendly. Wei Baqun played a significant role in the interactions between Donglan and all the governments.

The study of the interactions between Donglan and the political centers helps illuminate some important differences between Wei Baqun's movement and similar movements in other parts of the country. In comparison with other Communist base areas, the interactions between Donglan and the different political centers had two striking features. One was that the Nationalist enemies of Wei Baqun and his followers were primarily local rather than national. Whereas the Communists in Hailufeng, Jinggangshan, Hubei-Henan-Anhui, and other base areas had to face troops sent directly by Chiang Kai-shek's Nanjing government, Wei Baqun and his followers rarely got to fight the so-called Central Army; their enemies were the troops of local and provincial militarists. Part of the reason was that Chiang Kai-shek's central government did not have effective control over Guangxi during much of the Republican era. In that sense, the relations between revolutionary Donglan and the hostile provincial governments in Guangxi were closely related to center-local relations within the Nationalist system. The second striking feature is that in Donglan and the Right River region the relations between local revolutionaries and outside Communists representing the CCP center were much more peaceful than those in most other base areas. Whereas the integration of local Communist revolutions into the national Communist movement caused brutal killings of local Communists in Jinggangshan, Hubei-Henan-Anhui, Western Hunan and Hubei, Hainan and other base areas, no real purge ever occurred in Donglan and the Right River region.

Analysis of the complicated relations between the center and the periphery also helps locate Wei Baqun and his movement in the larger national setting. Although as remote and isolated as it was, Donglan was never completely secluded from other parts of China and the world. It took a longer time for waves of ideas, policies, technologies, and products emanating from the center to reach Donglan, but the waves eventually would arrive to effect the local society. In responding to the stimuli of change from the outside, some locals were much more sensitive, receptive, and active than others, thus contributing to the split of local society. In that sense, local responses to influences from the center within China are not very different from Chinese responses to Western challenges. The rise and fall of Wei Baqun demonstrates that at crucial moments external factors played a much more important part than local ones in the development and demise of the Donglan peasant movement. The popular local support Wei Baqun commanded was sufficient to enable him to defeat his local rivals, but not the much more powerful external foes. His defeat in 1931 and 1932 confirms that it was very difficult, if not impossible, to build socialism in one county.

Although Wei Baqun's career and movement show clearly that in modern China overall the center or centers had a great transformative or destructive effect on the periphery, it would be wrong to assume that the periphery was always at the receiving end. Successive revolts taking place in Donglan had the effect of changing this frontier county into a political center. The revolutions made Donglan an alternative center to the various levels of hostile governments and a subcenter in the leftist and Communist systems, and in those capacities Donglan exerted great political influence on the surrounding areas.

In addition to the primary theme of center-periphery interactions, this book explores several secondary topics. One is the local culture of violence and its effect on Wei Baqun's movement. Several factors contributed to the prevalence of violence in Donglan and the surrounding areas throughout the historical period. From the Song to the early Qing, Donglan was ruled by hereditary lords known as Tusi whose power rested on honorific titles awarded by the emperors and well-trained private armies. Whereas most other parts of China were ruled by scholar-officials, Donglan as a frontier region had an authentic feudal system dominated by a military class, giving rise to a martial tradition. Ethnic conflicts, especially the clashes between the Yao and the Zhuang, and banditry, which was rampant in Guangxi during the late Qing and early Republican era, were also important factors in shaping the local culture of violence. The deep-rooted tradition of violence served as a double-edged sword to Wei Baqun's revolution. At the beginning of the revolution, this important aspect of the local tradition made it easy for the revolutionaries to acquire weapons, to turn the local villagers into fighters, and to adopt the fighting skills and strategies passed down by feudal lords, rebels, and bandits.

However, the excessive killings conducted by both Wei Baqun and his enemies caused a great loss of human lives and the alienation of the local people, and eventually played an important part in bringing down both the economic production and the revolution.

The role of local ecology in Wei Baqun's movement is also a secondary topic examined in this study. Like the tradition of violence, the ecological setting of Donglan and the surrounding areas also functioned as a double-edged sword to Wei Baqun's revolution. The hilly and mountainous terrain and the large number of hidden caves provided natural shelters and hideouts for Wei Baqun and his followers and made it difficult for his enemies to find the revolutionaries, much less to "exterminate" them. However, these mountainous regions did not provide much arable land and were sparsely populated, and thus could not offer supplies for any large army for a long period. During the last years of the revolution, when the mountains and hills were continuously besieged by the Nationalist troops, Wei Baqun had to disband his forces in order to solve the problem of food shortage. As a result, he was deprived of a fighting force and his defeat became inevitable.

The multiethnic nature of the local population makes ethnicity another pertinent secondary topic for this study. Although there have been suggestions that Wei Baqun's revolution was essentially an ethnic revolt caused by confrontations between the Han and the Zhuang, evidence shows that there was not much hostility between the Han and the Zhuang in Donglan and the surrounding regions. In Wei Baqun's time, the Zhuang were the dominant ethnic group in the area and the Han, most of whom were poor farmers, formed a tiny minority. The Zhuang were so assimilated and their Zhuang identity was so suppressed that local Zhuang like Wei Baqun saw themselves as both Zhuang and Han. It was not until after 1949 that the suppressed Zhuang identity resurfaced and was officially recognized and promoted. As a result, posthumously Wei Baqun was transformed from a Zhuang who was also Han into a Zhuang who was not Han. Besides the Zhuang and the Han, there was a third ethnic group in the region, the Yao, who were the real oppressed minority, and because of that, they became loyal supporters of Wei Baqun and active participants in his movement. In that sense, ethnic conflict was an important factor in Wei Baqun's revolution, although it is not fully justifiable to reduce his revolution to an ethnic revolt.

The book is organized around Wei Baqun's trips and revolts. The first two chapters cover Wei Baqun's pre-revolutionary years, tracing his evolution from a village boy to a rebel and a revolutionary. What distinguished the young Wei Baqun from most other members of his community were his profound contempt for authority and the status quo, his strong desire for change and his intense interest in the outside world and new ideas. He became a rebel at home and in schools long before he entered national politics and began his revolutionary career, and the important factors in the making of Wei Baqun the young rebel and revolutionary included family influence, the local social structure and cultural tradition, the penetration of modernity, the national revolutionary movements, and not least his first trip out of Guangxi.

The three years between 1921 and 1924 represent the first cycle of triumph and defeat in Wei Baqun's life, and this is the topic of chapter Three. After three failed attacks on the county seat in 1923, Wei Baqun finally succeeded in overthrowing the county government later that year with a fourth attack, which brought his first revolt to a high point and made him a well-known revolutionary in the Right River region and Guangxi Province. The first revolt, which was his first attempt at fostering local changes by applying ideas borrowed from the outside, not only demonstrated strong influence of anarchist, nationalist and communist ideologies, but also manifested clear marks of folk and local traditions. However, his power did not last long, and in 1924 he was defeated by his local and external rivals and forced to flee. One crucial factor in his defeat is that although he enjoyed popular local support, he did not have any powerful supporters at the provincial and national levels. In other words, both local and national factors played important roles in the success and failure of his first revolt.

The next two years, which are covered in chapter Four, saw intensive communications between Wei Baqun and national leaders. Although technically he was still a Nationalist, he also began to study and work with the Communists and to familiarize himself further with communist ideas. After all, this was the period of the First United Front, and Wei Baqun was in Guangzhou, the headquarters of the United Front. His past experience of and continuous interest in the peasant movement made him receptive to communist ideas and practices. For him this was a period of recuperation and reeducation and it represented the confirmation and continuation of a very important pattern in his life: Whenever he was defeated in the periphery, he would escape to the center to seek new ideas and methods, to make new contacts, to seek possible supporters, and to wait for new opportunities to implement changes at home.

In early 1925, Wei Baqun realized that the political situation in Guangxi had improved and decided to return to Donglan to stage his second revolt, and thus began the second cycle of triumph and defeat in his life, which is analyzed in chapter Five. It is interesting to note that Wei Baqun's second revolt, which shows stronger communist influence than the first, reached its apogee in middle 1927, precisely when the Communists and radical revolutionaries in coastal and interior areas were suffering defeats and deaths at the hands of Chiang Kai-shek's soldiers. The remoteness of frontier Donglan became an advantage for Wei Baqun. However, the remoteness of Donglan could only delay the anti-Communist campaigns, not block them permanently. When the anti-Communist troops finally reached Donglan in late 1927, Wei Baqun's second revolt seemed to be doomed.

However, this time Wei Baqun's defeat in local Donglan was delayed by dramatic changes taking place at the provincial and national levels. In early 1929, Yu Zuobai and Li Mingrui overthrew the New Guangxi Clique and became the new leaders of Guangxi. They decided to ally with the CCP, and the CCP dispatched such senior revolutionaries as Deng Xiaoping and Zhang Yunyi to work in Guangxi, making Nanning, the provincial capital, a new Communist center. When the Yu-Li regime collapsed in late 1929, the Communists decided to move to Baise, the largest city in northwestern Guangxi, at least in part to get close to Wei Baqun's power base of Donglan. The merging of the revolutionaries from Nanning and those in Donglan delayed the defeat of both groups at the hands of their Nationalist rivals and led to the creation of the large and well-known Left River and Right River Revolutionary Base Area, which was one of the major Soviet base areas in China in the early 1930s. The arrival of outside and senior revolutionaries brought about the fusion of the Communist center and Wei Baqun's local movement and the complete integration of Wei Baqun's political life into the larger Communist movement. This third revolt was the climax in both Wei Baqun's revolutionary career and the revolutionary history of frontier Guangxi. Chapter Six analyzes the making of the third revolt in the light of interactions between the local and external revolutionary and counter-revolutionary forces. It also examines how peripheral Donglan gradually evolved into a revolutionary center as Wei Baqun's fame grew and his movement developed, and how the Donglan peasant movement impacted other regions in the province and the nation.

However, the outside Communist forces did not stay long in the Right River region. After their departure in late 1930, Wei Baqun was left alone to deal with the superior forces of the New Guangxi Clique, which had restored its rule over Guangxi. Deprived of any external support, Wei Baqun's forces were soon dismantled by his enemies. In explaining the defeat of Wei Baqun's movement, chapter Seven focuses on analyzing the ecological and cultural factors.

Wei Baqun's role as an intermediary between his community and the nation did not end with his death. Chapter Eight discusses how in death Wei Baqun was transformed into the Red God, a perfect Communist, and the most prominent member of the Zhuang minority group. The conclusion revisits some central themes of the book and discusses how Wei Baqun's political legacy has been turned into economic assets in the reform era.

CHAPTER ONE

Frontier Youth

1894–1914

Wei Baqun's birthplace, Donglan County of Guangxi Province, was a frontier region in more than one sense. It was not far from China's southern border with Vietnam. In Wei Baqun's time, travelers from Donglan would often choose to pass through Vietnam in order to reach Hong Kong and Guangzhou. Wei Baqun himself took that route at least twice. The border between Guangxi and Vietnam could be easily crossed partly because neither the French colonial government in Vietnam nor the local Guangxi militarists took the area seriously. The French concentrated their attention on Yunnan rather than Guangxi, whereas the leaders of Guangxi thought that the regions to the east and north were much more important than the southern borders.[1] Donglan was also very close to the border dividing Guangxi from three other Chinese provinces: Yunnan, Guizhou, and Hunan, making it a frontier county of a frontier province (Map 1.1).

In the late nineteenth and early twentieth centuries, Donglan fit well the stereotypes of a typical frontier region in China. First of all, it was a multiethnic area. The dominant ethnic group, of which Wei Baqun was a member, was the Turen (which means natives) or Zhuang, whose ancestors, known as Yue, Baiyue, Luoyue, Xi'ou, Wuhu, Liliao, and Lang in different periods and different places, used to occupy a large part of southern China. By the early twentieth century, however, the Zhuang heartland had shrunk so much that it covered only western Guangxi and a small part of Yunnan. The Zhuang area in western Guangxi can be divided into four major regions shaped by and identified with four major rivers, respectively. From the north to the south the four rivers are the Dragon River (Longjiang), the Red Water River (Hongshuihe), the Right River (Youjiang), and the Left River (Zuojiang). All four rivers merge into the

Map 1.1 Location of Donglan in Contemporary China.

West River, which is a major branch of the Pearl River. Donglan is situated in the Red Water River valley, which often is considered part of the greater Right River region (Map 1.2)

The Zhuang people have their own spoken language, but used Chinese characters for writing. Traditionally, they followed many practices that appeared to be exotic or bizarre to the Han. Zhuang women did not bind their feet, and Zhuang men and women were extremely fond of singing and dancing, talents that were very much looked down on by the Han populace in general and the Confucian literati in particular. The Zhuang singing contest could last for days and nights and they would sing about many different themes, ranging from love, family, legendary and historical heroes, rituals, to farming, traveling, fishing, hunting, herding, and construction of houses. It is no wonder that one of the most prominent figures in the folklore of southern China is a Zhuang singer named Third Sister Liu (Liu Sanjie).[2] Han observers also had trouble understanding why in some regions Zhuang women would stay with their parents after getting married and would not live with the husband's family until after giving birth to the first child. Some Han authors believed that Zhuang men were vengeful and violent, and were idlers who made their women do the hard work for them.[3] Although the portrayal of the lazy Zhuang men shows

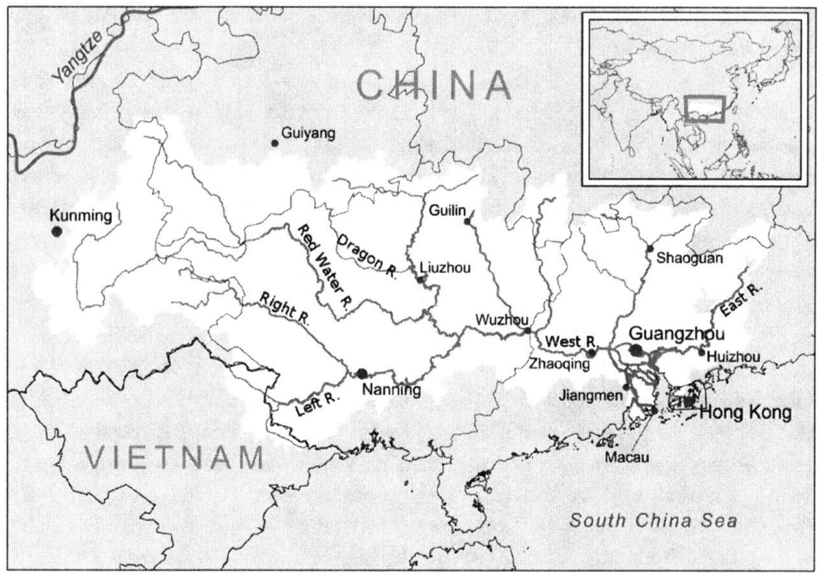

MAP 1.2 The Four Rivers in Northwestern Guangxi.

obvious bias, Zhuang women were indeed very hard working. In Donglan, even before moving into the husband's house, a married woman was supposed to show her skills at farming by planting cotton on the hills near her husband's home in the spring.[4] Extremely unacceptable to some Han commentators was the custom that, after childbirth the husband would stay home with the baby, pretending that he was the one who had given birth to the child, whereas the weakened wife had to go out to take care of the paddy fields.[5]

There are other major and minor differences between the Han and the Zhuang. The Han built their houses on the ground, but the traditional Zhuang houses were built on stilts, with animals staying at the lower level and humans occupying the upper part. Whereas both the Han and the Zhuang worshipped dragons, the Zhuang also worshipped snakes and frogs. The Han followed Confucianism, Daoism, and Buddhism as the three traditional doctrines, whereas the Zhuang embraced Confucianism and Daoism but showed little interest in Buddhism. The Zhuang liked to chew betel nuts and followed some unique burial custom.[6] For ceremonies, the Han used wooden drums, but the Zhuang preferred bronze drums, and Donglan was known as the land of bronze drums. Even today, every village has its own collection of bronze drums, and the villagers living along the Red Water River are particularly fond of them. Often, neighboring villages would hold drum-beating contests on mountaintops that could last for days.[7]

In Donglan, the Sinicized Zhuang elite controlled political and economic power, and the Zhuang commoners were farmers occupying the valleys and basins. Most local officials were Zhuang. Yao and Han were the two minority groups in the county. The Yao in Donglan were divided into two groups. The Tu (indigenous) Yao moved to the county during the Yuan and Ming Dynasties, whereas the Fan ("barbaric") Yao did not arrive until the Qing Dynasty.[8] Although most ethnologists believe that the Zhuang arrived in Donglan much earlier than the Yao, some local people hold that the Yao were the true indigenous people and that they had been driven into the mountains by officers and soldiers from northern China who settled in Donglan and became the ancestors of the Zhuang. There are many folk stories about how the Yao lost the plains to the Zhuang. One popular Yao legend holds that when the Zhuang first came to grab the plain from the Yao, the two groups agreed to ask the plain and let it decide who its owners were. A Yao asked the plain first, but got no answer. A Zhuang then took his turn and received a positive answer from the plain. As a result, the Yao lost the plain. It only became clear later that the Zhuang had cheated by hiding someone near the plain to provide an answer on its behalf.[9]

The Tu Yao lived close to the Zhuang communities and some even lived among the Zhuang. Therefore, they were more assimilated by the Zhuang, and were better off than the Fan Yao. Some Tu Yao were even wealthy enough to qualify as landlords and rented land to the poor Zhuang and Han. The Fan Yao, who scattered on the mountain slopes cultivating dry land crops such as maize, sweet potatoes, and pumpkins using the slash and burn techniques and supplementing agriculture with hunting and gathering, were at the bottom of the local society. They had to provide free labor for the local power holders, and were not allowed to wear white clothes, shoes, hats or other head covers; to use umbrellas; to ride horses; to attend school; to take the civil service examinations; or to live in the plains. Unable to buy enough clothes, in winter the Fan Yao had to sleep by fires to keep warm. Long-time exposure to fire would turn their feet red, giving rise to the derogatory label "Red Feet Yao." They relied on rain for drinking water and during a drought, they traveled long distances to fetch water.[10]

The migration of northerners from China's Central Plains to Guangxi began at the latest during the Qin Dynasty, but the early settlers were small in number and it took only a few generations for them to be assimilated by the ancestors of the Zhuang. The Han people who lived in Donglan in the early twentieth century were recent immigrants or their descendants. They came from Hunan, Guizhou, Sichuan, Guangdong, Jiangxi, and other provinces and spoke various dialects, including Hakka, Cantonese, and various variants of Mandarin. They were traders, officials, and peasants. The Han traders and officials lived in the towns, whereas the peasants lived in the mountains.[11] The saying that "the Zhuang live on riverbanks, the Han live on the streets, and the Yao live on mountains,"[12] which was used to describe the ethnic distribution of a region in the neighboring Yunnan Province, was very much applicable to Donglan, although in Donglan there were Han peasants living in small basins in the mountains. Despite the fact that the Han already made up the majority of the population in Guangxi and controlled both the provincial and central governments, the Han minority in Donglan was not the most powerful local group in the early twentieth century.[13] In fact, because most of the Han settlers who moved into Donglan during the Qing Dynasty were believed to be former anti-Manchu rebels led by Li Dingguo, they were perceived to be renegades and discriminated against by the Zhuang.[14] During the Qing Dynasty, the descendants of these Han rebels in Donglan were not allowed to sit for the civil service examinations, and some of them had to disguise themselves as Zhuang in order to take the exams. It is interesting to note that although many Zhuang identified with the Han of a past era or a faraway place, they were not fond of the real Han around them.

The founding of the Republic of China brought some favorable changes to the Han. Some Han moved from the mountains to the plains, and some even became low-ranking government officials. Overall, the Han occupied a higher position on the local social ladder than the Yao. There was more intermarriage between the Zhuang and the Han than between the Zhuang and the Yao. Economically, most Han were better off than the Yao, but were poorer than the Zhuang. A Zhuang from a village near Wuzhuan commented in 1951 that in his area the Zhuang would eat rice for half the year and corn for the other half, the Han had rice for four months and corn for eight, whereas the Yao had to consume corn, pumpkins, and millet throughout the year. It was estimated in the early 1950s that before the Communist takeover, the Zhuang on average could afford salt for six to ten months every year, whereas the Han could have it for three to four months each year, and the Yao could only have salt for three days every month.[15] Whereas most Han in Donglan were powerless commoners, a few families of Han officials or merchants that moved to Donglan in the late Qing were able to join the local ruling class.

There was some animosity between the three groups. The Zhuang liked to refer to the Han as "Bugun" (base aliens) and the Yao as "Buyou" (monkeys from the mountains); the Han would call the Zhuang "Nitou" (people made of urine soaked earth); and some Yao would call the Zhuang barbarians.[16]

Like some other frontier regions of China, Donglan was sparsely populated in the past, but went through rapid population growth during the Ming and particularly the Qing dynasties. It is estimated that at the beginning of the Ming, there were only about 25,000 people living in the county. The number increased to 72,000 in late Ming and early Qing and 167,000 in late Qing.[17] In the early years of the Republican era, Donglan was about 110 kilometers in both length and width and its land area made up 0.94% of the total land area of Guangxi. Donglan's population density was more than one hundred people per square kilometer at that time, making it the most densely populated county in the Right River and Red Water River region and one of the most densely populated counties in Guangxi.[18]

Nearly forty-three percent of Donglan's land area is mountainous and hilly—the ninth highest percentile among all the counties in Guangxi. The famous seventeenth-century geographer Gu Zuyu described Donglan as "a remote and dangerous area covered with endless stiff mountains."[19] For a magistrate of Donglan in the 1920s, the county was a place hidden "in the middle of many layers of mountains."[20] Most of the mountains and hills are about seven hundred to eight hundred meters above sea level and some are as high as one thousand. The highest mountain in the county is 1,214 meters above sea level.[21] The local people like to divide the mountains of Donglan into two categories: stone mountains and earth mountains. Most of the mountains in the northern part of the county are earth mountains, whereas most of those in the south are stone. For obvious reasons, the stone mountains are much less productive than the earthern ones. The stone mountains in southern Donglan can be divided into three sections, which are known to the local people as Western Mountains, Central Mountains (Zhongshan), and Eastern Mountains (Dongshan). The mountains stand between many stretches of arable plains, which are called Dong in the Zhuang language. Some Dongs are large enough to sustain a small city or a large village, and others are so tiny that they only had enough space for one or two families. On average each farming household in Donglan had only four mu (two-thirds of an acre) of paddy field in the early 1930s, making it the most land-hungry county in Guangxi.[22]

Another striking feature of Donglan as a frontier region was its economic and technological backwardness. Guangxi was among the poorer provinces in China, and during the late Qing the three nearby provinces—Guangdong, Hunan, and Hubei—had to provide annual financial subsidies to Guangxi.[23] Within Guangxi, the counties that are on the coast, close to Guangdong, or that have large plains, were much more advanced and prosperous than Donglan. By the early 1930s, Donglan still did not have any modern industries. Local handicraftsmen could only produce wooden and bamboo goods, pottery, tiles, cloth, and other traditional products. There had been ore mines in the mountains, but they were closed down because of a fuel shortage. Trade was limited to the sale of daily necessities such as cooking oil, salt, liquor, rice, and meat. Dongyuan was the largest town in Donglan. Although it made its first appearance in historical records as early as 1053 AD and had been the county seat since 1730 AD, the town had only four narrow streets up to the 1940s. In the 1920s and 1930s, its population was smaller than that of the largest village of Donglan, which had nearly two thousand residents.[24] Obviously, Dongyuan in the 1930s was still more like a "stockaged village" than a substantial town.[25] Other towns in Donglan included Wuzhuan, Jiangping, Sanshi, Simeng, Changjiang, and Duyi. Local markets in these towns were opened once every five days.[26]

The lack of efficient means of transportation posed a serious obstacle to the development of the economy in general and trade in particular. The Red Water River, which is so named because of the red soil it carries, is the most important watercourse in Donglan. It passes through the county from the north to the south, providing a waterway of about one hundred kilometers. As a major branch of the Pearl River, it was the most convenient means of transportation between Donglan and neighboring regions. However, due to the rugged riverbed, it could only handle the navigation of boats with loads of no more than 1,500 kilograms. Guangxi's mountainous terrain made it difficult and costly to build roads. During the rule of militarist Lu Rongting from 1911 to 1921, only three paved roads totaling 150 kilometers were built in the province, and none of them passed through Donglan. Governor Ma Junwu, who took office in late 1921, had an ambitious plan for road construction, but only paved 2.5 kilometers before stepping down the following year. The New Guangxi Clique, after consolidating their power in Guangxi, began to construct an efficient road network, and by 1928 Guangxi was listed as having more good roads than any other province in China. Unfortunately, this road system had not extended to Donglan by the early 1930s. In Donglan, automobiles were completely absent in Wei Baqun's time because there were no paved roads.[27]

Partly because of the lack of a modern transportation system, the prices of imported commodities were very high in Donglan. Traders had to hire laborers to carry local products such as tung oil from Dongyuan to Tianzhou, which was located about 140 kilometers to the west of Donglan, and then to carry back imported goods such as salt. This long and narrow rugged mountain path between Donglan and Tianzhou was properly called the Salt Road.[28] Another less frequently traveled salt road extended eastward toward Jinchengjiang in Hechi or Huaiyuan in Yishan.[29] Some traders would use boats to ship out medicinal herbs, leathers, and rice and ship in salt, cotton, scissors, needles, and other goods.[30] These trading routes were not only rough but also dangerous because of the presence of bandits in the mountains and along the rivers. All this added to the cost of imported goods. Sometimes half a kilogram of salt was worth a good horse or fifty to one hundred kilograms of grain, and the Yao people living in the mountains at times had to pay 2.5 kilograms of corn for a needle.[31] Even today, of the 3,676 villages in the county, 915 are still not connected to the paved road system.[32]

Agriculture formed the foundation of the local economy, and peasants made up the great majority of the local population. A large number of the peasants were independent but poor. In the early 1930s, among all the peasants in Donglan, sixty-five percent were owner-peasants, thirty-one percent were semi-owners, and only four percent were tenants.[33] However, most owners or semi-owners only possessed a small amount of land. On average, each landlord or rich peasant family owned only between twenty and thirty mu of land, and very few families had more than seventy mu of land (Chinese mu is equal to one-fifteenth of a hectare or one-sixth of an acre).[34] Tenant peasants were even poorer than small-owner peasants. In Donglan, tenants had to submit three-fifths or even two-thirds of their yields to the landlords,[35] and that rate was much higher than the national average.

Politically, Donglan was ruled as a special frontier region during most dynasties. The area was first brought under Chinese control by the First Emperor during the third century BCE. However, the long distance between Donglan and the political centers in the north, the rugged terrain, tropical climate, and epidemic diseases prevented immigration, integration, and efficient administration, so the region was able to maintain its distinctive culture and identity as well as some degree of political autonomy long after the Qin conquest. The Qin used appointed officials to rule the plains, but created a quasi-feudal system for mountainous regions like Donglan. This feudal system permitted the powerful local families hereditary rights to rule their domains as long as they pledged allegiance and paid tributes to the Qin court. During the Tang Dynasty, the imperial court expanded the feudal system to cover the Left River, Right River, and Red Water River region. In the late eighth and early ninth centuries, some powerful local leaders revolted against the Tang court and were able to maintain their control over the Left River and Right River region for about a century.[36] During the Song Dynasty, Nong Zhigao, a powerful local leader from western Guangxi, launched another rebellion with the aim of creating an independent state in the region. Although Donglan never became part of the rebel domain, it was so close to the rebel territory that it was inevitably affected by the rebellion and its suppression. According to one account, after General Di Qing of the Song Dynasty defeated Nong Zhigao, Nong fled to Yunnan and one of his younger brothers moved northward along the Red Water River trying to escape to Guizhou. Di Qing then sent his subordinate Wei Jingdai to pursue Nong's brother. Wei reached Donglan and was then appointed as the ruler of the region. It is believed that Wei Jingdai was from Shandong in northern China, that his descendants ruled Donglan as hereditary lords from the Song until the early twentieth century, and that local families that carry the family name of Wei, including Wei Baqun's family, were all related to this common ancestor.[37]

It is hard to prove both the northern origin claimed of Wei Jingdai as well as the supposed blood relations between him and the Wei families of Donglan. Although it was recorded that imperial troops fighting Nong Zhigao were mostly from Shandong and that some of the troops settled down in Guangxi after the end of the conflict, it was also common among the non-Han people in the south to forge claims about the northern origins of their families,[38] possibly for the purpose of avoiding discrimination. The Wei family that ruled Donglan during the Qing Dynasty could trace its origin to the early Ming, but not as far back as the Song Dynasty.[39] Even if General Wei Jingdai were truly of northern origin, his family would have to be indigenized in a few generations and become just like the previous local powerful families. In other words, the Song conquest, like that of the Qin, did not result in immediate political and cultural integration of the region. Powerful local families were given free hands in collecting taxes, recruiting free labor, maintaining private armies, and passing their positions onto their offspring. As late as the early twentieth century, some local rulers were still demanding the archaic *droit du seigneur* from their subjects, and in some places, this forced people to hold secret wedding ceremonies at midnight.[40]

Unlike the scholar-officials of the Chinese heartland, these local rulers of the frontier region were better known for their military power and skills than for their literary or scholarly achievements, and the Zhuang soldiers from the Right River region were particularly famous for their bravery and the special formations they adopted during battles. One of these formations prescribed the creation of small fighting teams, each consisting of seven soldiers. During battles, four of the seven soldiers would focus on attacking and killing enemies, whereas the other three were responsible for protecting the attackers and chopping off the heads of fallen enemies, which would bring rewards to the team.[41] The Zhuang fighters were so famous that on some occasions even the imperial court would solicit their assistance in dealing with troubles in other parts of the empire. For instance, during the Song and Ming dynasties, the imperial court enrolled Zhuang soldiers to fight against the Vietnamese and the Mongols.[42] In the sixteenth century, the Ming emperors at least three times ordered the lords of Donglan to travel to the southeastern coast with their troops to fight the international pirate groups. The first time occurred in 1509, when the Lord of Donglan, Wei Zhengbao, was dispatched to Guangdong with more than one thousand of his troops plus his son Wei Huchen. The lord and his soldiers fought fiercely and when the lord died of a battle wound a year later, his fifteen-year-old son took over the lordship and defeated the pirates. Wei Huchen then escorted his dead father home. In 1513, the emperor ordered Wei Huchen to take his troops to the southeast coast again to fight the pirates. Huchen was a brilliant commander and repeatedly defeated the bandits and pirates in Jiangxi, Guangdong, and Fujian. Unfortunately, just before he was about to return to Donglan in 1516, some rival officials poisoned him. However, his military achievements eventually earned him an honorary title from the emperor and a status of semi-deity in the local folklore. In 1555, Huchen's son, Wei Qiyun, was sent to Zhejiang by the imperial court with about one thousand of his soldiers and he performed as well as his father.[43] The Ming court also frequently sent the lords of Donglan and their troops to subdue rebellions in neighboring provinces and counties, and in return the lords won monetary rewards and titles, as well as official appointments for their children.[44]

As a frontier county with a strong martial tradition, but not an equally strong literary tradition, Donglan thus stood in stark contrast to the more economically and academically advanced counties in Guangxi, such as Lingui near Guilin, which produced as many as 53 jinshi during the Ming and 190 jinshi during the Qing, but very few generals.[45] The civil service examinations were not introduced in Donglan until 1777. During the late Qing, for every prefectural exam, fourteen students from Donglan and the neighboring Fengshan and Nadi would be awarded the title of xiucai, which was the lowest degree. Among the fourteen, eight were literary xiucai, and the others were martial xiucai. By 1905, when the civil service examinations were abolished, only two students from Donglan had won the title of juren. Guangxi Province produced 173 jinshi during the Ming and 570 jinshi during the Qing, but not a single one of them was from Donglan.[46] The uneven distribution of degree holders in Guangxi is thus comparable to that of Qing Dynasty Zhejiang Province.[47] By 1949, only nine students from Donglan had earned college degrees and six others were studying in college. Altogether they made up 0.01% of the total population of the county.[48] If the Han-dominated areas of Guangxi represented a *semi-periphery*, a term William Rowe adopted to describe the area around Guilin,[49] then Donglan and most other Zhuang-dominated counties in northern and western Guangxi apparently were part of the full periphery of China. Yeh Wen-hsin used a different set of concepts to define the spatial hierarchy in Zhejiang and the Yangtze Delta. She described Jinhua and other middle counties in the Qiantang Valley as the provincial backwaters, Hangzhou as the provincial capital, and Shanghai as the metropolis.[50] If we apply these concepts to Guangxi, then Donglan was definitely part of the provincial backwaters, Guilin and Nanning were the provincial capitals, and Guangzhou, Wuhan, and Shanghai were the nearest metropolises. However, it is important to point out that in the early twentieth century, Donglan was much less "modern" and much farther away from any metropolis than Jinhua.

Despite repeated proposals about replacing the hereditary lords with appointed officials, the emperors of the Ming and Qing dynasties chose to maintain the system in much of the southern frontier mainly for the purposes of appeasing the indigenous people and reducing the administrative cost. In 1730, as a result of the administrative reform initiated by the powerful Manchu official Oertai in southwestern China, southeastern Donglan became a regular county ruled by non-native appointed officials, but northwestern Donglan remained the domain of the Wei family till the early twentieth century, although the Weis now had to submit to the county magistrate. However, the appointed outsiders did not always behave better than the hereditary lords. Part of the reason was that because Guangxi was a remote area replete with tropical diseases, the court would only send second-rate officials or those officials who had made mistakes or committed crimes to the province, and as a result the morale and efficiency of the officials was low. In fact, these officials could be more exploitative than the hereditary lords. Their appointment always came with a time limit, giving them a sense of urgency in making the most profitable use of their power. Besides, they could afford to be brutal because they were outsiders who did not share local and ethnic identities with their subjects and did not have to worry about the safety of their relatives who often chose to stay home. Like their feudal predecessors, these officials must have been familiar with the ancient adage "The heaven is high and the emperor far away" and knew that it was difficult for the emperor to keep a close eye on their behavior.

Surrounded by "barbarians" who were perceived to have a penchant for violence, these appointed officials would attach great importance to defensive measures and would sometimes overreact to a real or imagined threat. One of the first projects initiated by the appointed magistrate was to order the erection of a garrison complex, which was completed in 1732. In 1903, Magistrate Tao Qigan was very brutal in suppressing a secret society whose members were anti-government and refused to pay taxes. He would round up all the suspects and subject them to cruel torture until they confessed. He would then put them to death or release them after collecting fines or bribes. The leaders of the secret society reacted by launching a midnight attack on the county seat and killing the magistrate. Tao's successor, Yi Zhenxing, responded with even greater brutality than his predecessor. He brought in a large number of soldiers and claimed that he wanted to kill all the people in Donglan. Five years later the local elite organized a protest campaign against Yi. After an investigation, the Manchu court discovered that Yi was guilty of "using excessive torture and punishment and was both greedy and atrocious." Yi was demoted and exiled to Xinjiang, a frontier region even more remote than Donglan.[51]

Rebellions were frequent under such repressive hereditary or appointed rulers, and most were not as successful as the movements against Tao Qigan and Yi Zhenxing. The official records of the Ming Dynasty are full of accounts of rebellions launched by the Zhuang and Yao in Guangxi and the imperial campaigns against such rebellions. There were 218 rebellions in Guangxi during the Ming Dynasty, averaging nearly one every year. The Ming ruled China for 276 years, and in Guangxi only 29 of those years were peaceful.[52] Rebellions continued to break out during the Qing period and both Han and minorities participated in the revolts. Secret societies and the so-called roving soldiers—members of Qing army units that had been disbanded—played a large role in many of these rebellions. Some of these uprisings took place in or near Donglan. In 1763, a group of Yao revolted in Donglan and was defeated by government forces after being besieged for forty-six days. In 1858, a secret society leader from neighboring Tianzhou began an attack on the county seat of Donglan. He fought the official forces for two days and then had to withdraw. Three years later, a group of Taiping rebels entered Donglan and many locals joined them. They won some battles, but were eventually crushed by the Manchu forces. In the 1890s, army officer Lu Rongting was promoted by the Qing court for his successful suppression of rebellions launched by secret societies and roving soldiers in Donglan and other places. Mo Rongxin, another army officer, also earned promotions by helping end unrest in Donglan from 1905 to 1910.[53]

Bandits formed a special group among the rebels. In the late Qing, Guangxi was described as a province where "you cannot find a place without mountains, you cannot find a mountain without caves, and you cannot find a cave without bandits."[54] This depiction applied much better to poor and mountainous counties like Donglan than the counties in the prosperous plains. In the Republican era the bandits of Guangxi were often compared with the pirates of Guangdong. Phil Billingsley attributes the prevalence of banditry in Guangxi to both international political factors and a sharp social differentiation. General Li Zongren, a native of Guangxi and the actual ruler of the province during much of the Republican era, emphasized ethnic conflicts, lack of education and poverty as causes of banditry in Guangxi.[55] The bandits in Guangxi sometimes became so powerful that the Qing government had to offer amnesty and official positions to their leaders. Lu Rongting, who ruled Guangxi from 1911 to 1921, was a former bandit who was offered a powerful position in the Qing army, as were many of his subordinates. Their good fortune caused many to see banditry as an easy path to upward mobility.

In 1912, shortly after the founding of the Republic, the Yao in Donglan launched another rebellion that was immediately put down by the provincial government.[56] In 1919, some Yao from Lingyun, Fengshan, Donglan, Enlong, and Tian'e staged a large-scale revolt against compulsory military conscription, forced labor service, and heavy taxation. The rebels demanded freedom and the right to subsistence. Although most leaders were Yao, nearly two-thirds of the rebels were Zhuang and Han. The uprising was crushed in 1921 and Deng Bucai, one of the Yao leaders of the rebellion, was executed in the county seat of Donglan. Many rebels who survived the suppression would later join Wei Baqun's movement.[57]

The recurrent conflicts between local government and the people confirmed the stereotypical impression that in a frontier region like Donglan the officials were brutal and greedy and the people were violent and rebellious. One striking feature of this violent and rebellious society is the popular obsession with weapons. Firearms were one of the most popular commodities in the region. Wealthy families would buy modern weapons, whereas poor people could only afford primitive guns, and sometimes several poor families would collectively buy and own one or more firearms. Guangxi's proximity to Guangdong, Hong Kong, and French Vietnam made arms smuggling easy. A list of weapons confiscated by the government between March and December 1907 shows that more than twenty types of guns were used in the province.[58] Even after 1949, when the Communists ordered all villagers to turn in their weapons, some Yao people in the Western Mountains protested that they needed guns to defend themselves against possible attacks from the Zhuang.[59] It therefore did not require much effort for efficient instigators to turn peasants in this region into bandits, rebels, or revolutionaries.

In the nineteenth and early twentieth centuries, Guangxi as a frontier region was more exposed to foreign influence and more severely affected by foreign encroachment than many interior provinces. In this aspect, frontier Guangxi was similar to coastal areas like Guangdong and Fujian. In Guangxi, foreign influence in both positive and negative forms came from two directions: Guangdong to the east and Vietnam to the south. The opium trade centered in Guangzhou began to affect Guangxi in the early nineteenth century. Initially, foreign opium was brought from Guangzhou to southwestern China by way of Guangxi. Later, as the Chinese began to cultivate poppies in Yunnan, Guizhou, and Sichuan, opium started to flow along the opposite direction, with Guangxi, particularly the Right River region, still making an important link in the trading network. Caravan bands would bring opium from Yunnan and Guizhou to Baise to exchange for salt, cloth, and other goods, turning Baise into the most important economic center and the largest city in western Guangxi.[60] In the early twentieth century, taxes from the opium trade sometimes formed almost half of Guangxi's revenue, and of the taxes from opium trade nearly half came from Baise and the Right River region. Opium smoking became one of the "three grave evils" of Guangxi Province, the other two being banditry and gambling.[61]

Economically, Guangxi became more and more connected to British Hong Kong and French Vietnam. Three cities of Guangxi—Wuzhou, Nanning, and Longzhou—were opened as treaty ports, and currencies issued by the two colonial regimes were widely circulated in Guangxi.[62] The city of Beihai in Guangdong functioned like the fourth treaty port of Guangxi because of its proximity to the latter. Although the Right River region is closer to French Vietnam than to Guangdong, most imported goods sold in the area were brought from Guangdong rather than Vietnam.[63] Foreign religions were also brought to Guangxi and the spread of a distorted form of Christianity contributed to the outbreak of the Taiping Rebellion in southeastern Guangxi in 1851. As the French began to conquer and colonize Vietnam, Guangxi felt the threat of French encroachment and eventually became directly involved in the conflicts between France and Vietnam and between France and China. Liu Yongfu, the fierce leader of the Black Flags who fought the French conquerors in northern

Vietnam in the late nineteenth century, was from Guangxi and most of his soldiers also came from Guangxi.[64] In 1884, Qing China and France fought a war along the border between Guangxi and Vietnam. Although very brief, the war shook Guangxi and further awakened the nationalist consciousness of young scholars and students such as Sun Yat-sen and later Mao Zedong. Twenty years later, Sun Yat-sen would launch rebellions against the Qing court in the same border area and Sun, with his imported Republicanism, had more followers from Guangxi than from many other provinces.

Although Donglan was more isolated than many other counties in Guangxi, it was not immune to foreign influence and threat. Donglan was not very far away from Baise, the most important center of the opium trade in western Guangxi, and some in Donglan later even began to cultivate poppies.[65] Many from Donglan were involved in the Taiping Rebellion, and some Donglan natives also joined Liu Yongfu's Black Flags and participated in the anti-French movement.[66] However, it is true that within Guangxi Donglan was much less exposed to foreign economic, political, and cultural influence than the counties nearer to Guangdong and French Vietnam. The closest treaty port was several hundred kilometers away, and in the late 1920s most people in Donglan still used homemade cloth rather than imported textiles. For lighting they used locally produced tea-seed oil or tung oil rather than imported kerosene.[67] Foreign currencies were not as widely circulated in Donglan as in some other areas, and there were no Catholic or Protestant groups or churches in Donglan. A British Christian arrived in the county seat of Donglan in 1935 to preach his religion, and he was very likely the first Westerner to ever visit Donglan. He played his accordion and sang on the streets to attract people. Once he gathered a crowd, he would begin to preach, and his Chinese companion would translate for him and hand out the pamphlets they had prepared. He spent several days in the county seat, but failed to find any serious followers. The two then traveled to Wuzhuan to repeat what they had done in the county seat. Again they did not get a positive response. Disappointed, they spent only one night at Wuzhuan and then moved to the neighboring county.[68]

It was into this frontier society that Wei Baqun was born on February 6, 1894. His birthplace was the scenic village of Dongli, which was located on the edge of one of the larger plains in the county and had about eighty to ninety families in the early twentieth century.[69] There were mountains near the village and one of the most famous was Mount Yinhaizhou, 747 meters above sea level. Dongli was known for having three beautiful ponds formed by water from mountain springs, which served as the source of the small Dongping River flowing through the village. In front of the village lay the flat paddy fields on which the villagers farmed and lived. A few kilometers away was the town of Wuzhuan, and Dongyuan, the county seat, was about forty kilometers to the east of the village. These were the two most important towns in the county, and both were located on small basins. Not far to the west of the village loomed the Western Mountains, home to a large Yao community. Dongli was on the borderline between the plain around Wuzhuan and the Western Mountains, two areas that would play significant roles in Wei Baqun's peasant movement (Map 1.3).

Some in Dongli village reportedly predicted at the time of Wei Baqun's birth that the boy was not an ordinary human being. They found multiple omens showing that Wei Baqun would grow into a great and powerful person.

Map 1.3 Topography of Contemporary Donglan.

Wei Baqun was born on the new year's day of the year of the horse, which was a lucky day of a lucky year according to folk beliefs. He was much bigger than most other newborn babies at that time, weighing 4.5 kilograms at birth. He was also a handsome boy who was believed to carry the facial features of an extraordinary man. This handsome boy later grew into a handsome man. Wei Baqun's friends, relatives and followers described him as a good-looking man with a medium stature, a stalwart body, a square face, a dark skin, and a full beard.[70] Finally, the boy was the first son of his parents and the first grandson of his grandparents, destined to be the pillar of the Wei family.[71] With the hope and belief that his son would one day become a great man, Wei Baqun's father, Wei Erzhang, decided to name his son Bingji, which means "bearing luck."[72] The name was changed to Bingqian, meaning "to control the world," when Wei Baqun started school at the age of eight. Wei Baqun himself was very likely familiar with all the talk and expectations of his auspicious future and considered himself different from his peers. In 1917, he adopted the new name Cui and styled himself Baqun. Cui means "outstanding" and Baqun, which is the colloquial equivalent of the classical word "Cui," literally means "to stand above the crowd." If the omens heralding Wei Baqun's birth had failed to predetermine his path in life, they probably played a part in shaping and foretelling his character. One of the most striking features of Wei Baqun's personality is that he was a strong-willed person with a strong sense of mission who liked to be in control and who knew how to command people.

FIGURE 1.1 Dongli Village Today. Photograph by the author.

Despite all the folk beliefs regarding Wei Baqun's future power and greatness, few would have been able to foretell that he would attain his power by becoming a rebel. It was hard to find a single reason to envisage Wei Baqun's career as a rebel and revolutionary at the time of his birth. Wei Baqun's family had about ten members when he was born and owned more than two hundred mu (sixty-six acres) of paddy field, making it the wealthiest family in the village. The Wei family had quite a few tenants and nine laborers to cultivate their land.[73] Baqun's father was involved in the tobacco and textile business and had anywhere from three to five wives. Villagers recalled that Wei Baqun's family had not always been wealthy and that it suddenly became rich in the hands of his grandfather. There are at least three different accounts about how the Wei family made its fortune. According to the first account, the family became rich by pure luck. Wei Baqun's grandfather's sister accidentally dug out an urn of silver dollars while laboring in a plot of land on a mountain slope. Baqun's grandfather had only three small pieces of land before that, but he was able to buy one piece of land after another with the silver dollars. He also bought water buffalos and horses and began to involve himself in the usury business.[74] The second account attributes the wealth of the family to the business skills of Wei Baqun's grandfather, who sold firewood and straw sandals in his early years and tobacco and rice wine later in his life.[75] A third account combines the first two.

Villagers also remembered that although Wei Baqun's family was wealthy, it was not politically powerful.[76] There were other wealthy families in Donglan that had produced powerful lords in the feudal era and influential officials in the Qing or Republican governments. Wei Baqun's grandfather became a rich landlord, but held no official positions, and Wei Baqun's father was able to purchase a low-ranking military degree from the Manchu government, but was never able to land any official position. Besides, his father would die at a young age, which was a devastating blow to the family's dream of political power. It is logical to argue that Wei Baqun's grandfather did have a strong aspiration for political power after he acquired wealth, and that might be the reason why he bought an official title for his son. After the son died, it was only natural for him to transfer his hope for power from his son to his eldest grandson, because there is no indication that Wei Baqun's father had any male siblings. The grandfather might have expected Wei Baqun to have an education and then enter the government. Although Wei Baqun would reject that arranged course of life, he may still have inherited his grandfather's dream of influence and prestige. However, contrary to his grandfather's expectations, he would take rebellion and revolution as his path to power.

Most historians in China would discard this familial factor as a motivation for Wei Baqun's rebellion. They argue that Wei Baqun became rebellious at a very young age primarily because of the sufferings of the poor families living around him. There are many stories about how, as a little boy and teenager, Wei

Baqun was already resentful about the inequality he observed and sympathetic toward the poor and the exploited. According to one story, there was a poor villager in Dongli named Wei Nai'en, and her family was so poor that they could only afford to eat thin porridge for almost every meal. One day in 1904, after making sure that there was no one at Nai'en's home, ten-year-old Wei Baqun brought some uncooked rice to Nai'en's home and cooked a solid rice meal for the family. Another story tells that in summer 1905, Wei Baqun went swimming with his friends, one of whom, a poor boy named Chen Qinglian, was wearing tattered clothes. Wei Baqun decided to trade clothes with him. Knowing that it would be hard for him to persuade Qinglian to take the deal, Wei Baqun got out of the pond before the others, put on Qinglian's clothes, and went home. When Qinglian finished swimming he could not find his clothes and had to put on Wei Baqun's new clothes. Qinglian later went to see Wei Baqun to exchange clothes, but Wei Baqun refused. Later that year, as a third story goes, Wei Baqun gave a shirt to another poor friend named Chen Henglong.[77]

There is also a story about a more extraordinary event supposed to have taken place in 1907. On a certain day before the Spring Festival of that year, so the story goes, Wei Baqun was playing with the other kids from the village. His friends were called home by their parents one after another. Their parents told Wei Baqun: "Your family is rich, so you don't have to work and can play all day long, but we are poor and our kids have to work. Otherwise we won't have enough to eat." Wei Baqun was shocked and sad that the other families in the village could not even have a happy Spring Festival because of their poverty, and he decided to do something to help them. He went home and pried open his father's money box. He took more than one hundred dollars from the box to distribute among the poor families, telling them that this was his pocket money. His father soon discovered that someone had stolen his money, but was not sure who the thief was. He then pretended that he had lost the key to his money box and asked people for help. Wei Baqun volunteered and easily unlocked the box with a piece of iron wire. His father then asked him about the lost money, and Wei Baqun admitted what he had done. He was then severely beaten.[78] A different version of this story lists the grandfather as the owner of the money box and the one who punished Wei Baqun. Instead of taking one hundred silver dollars, this account holds that Wei Baqun stole only eighty dollars.[79] The father was a main character in one version of the story, but completely absent in the other, probably because although some people believe that Wei Baqun's father died when he was only nine years old and hence would not be able to be present in this story, others insist that the father did not pass away until Wei Baqun reached sixteen.[80] There are similar stories about how Wei Baqun stole grain from the barn of his own family and gave it to his poor friends and how he disobeyed his grandfather by not collecting rent from a poor tenant who made a living by growing pears.[81] The latter event is supposed to have taken place in 1912 when Wei Baqun was eighteen years old. The story mentions that this event occurred when he was about to attend a school in the county seat. However, most other sources convincingly report that in 1912 Wei Baqun had already dropped out of the school in the county seat and was away from home attending schools in Qingyuan and Guilin.

In some other stories, the young Wei Baqun's sympathy for the poor and the weak caused conflicts not only with his own father and grandfather, but also with other wealthy and powerful local families. There is a story about how in 1905 Wei Baqun and his poor friends stole grain from Liang Shi'e, a landlord.[82] Another frequently cited story features Wei Baqun's conflict with Du Ba, the son of a powerful landlord who liked to bully other kids. According to the story, one day when Wei Baqun was swimming in a river he heard a little girl crying. He jumped to the bank and found that Du Ba was abusing a little girl who was collecting wild plants to feed pigs. Du Ba had kicked her basket away and wanted to "touch" the girl. Wei Baqun ordered Du Ba to pick up the basket and return it to the girl, but Da Ba refused. The two then began to fight and did not stop until Du Ba was defeated and sued for peace. After Du Ba promised not to tell his father about the fight, Wei Baqun let him go. However, Du Ba later broke his promise and asked his father to take revenge for him. His father then complained to Wei Baqun's grandfather who in turn scolded Baqun. Infuriated by Du Ba's betrayal, Wei Baqun and his friends sneaked into Du Ba's house, grabbed three bottles of medicinal liquor that Du Ba's father had stored, poured out the liquor, and replaced it with urine. Since Du Ba had stolen his father's liquor before, the father, after sampling the urine, believed that it was Du Ba who had plotted the mischief, and had him severely beaten.[83]

The problem with this story is that in real life Du Ba and Wei Baqun were not even in the same age group. As a scholar who had taken and passed the lowest level of the civil service examination before the system was abolished in 1905 and who had served for two terms as a county magistrate in Guizhou by 1920,[84] Du Ba was much older than Wei Baqun. Chen Mianshu, a Communist friend of Wei Baqun, met Du Ba in 1926 and reported that Du was in his fifties in that year, which means Du was about twenty years older than Wei Baqun.[85] Although very likely untrue, this story serves as a preamble to a more serious and important conflict between Wei Baqun and Du Ba that would occur later in their lives. The story also foretells one of Wei Baqun's love relationships. In some versions of the story, the little girl bullied by Du Ba was Huang Xiumei, who would become Wei Baqun's fourth wife and loyal supporter.

The story about Wei Baqun fighting Du Ba was probably made up to glorify Wei Baqun. Judging from Wei Baqun's personality and his later deeds, however, the major episodes in these stories could have been real despite some discrepancies, and these stories about Wei Baqun constitute the most recent chapter in a long folk tradition about local rebels and heroes. The earlier chapters in the tradition contain many similar stories about Wei Baqun's predecessors. It often has been suggested that Wei Baqun became rebellious at a very young age not only due to the inequity and sufferings that existed around him, but also because of the existence of moving stories about people fighting inequities and suffering in the past. These stories form an important part of the local culture and Wei Baqun was a very attentive listener of those stories and a product of that culture.

Among all the folk heroes in the local tradition, the aforementioned Nong Zhigao, who rebelled against both the Vietnamese and Chinese court in the mid-eleventh century, was one of the most prominent. As a brilliant military strategist, Nong commanded his army to attack Nanning, Guangzhou and other cities of the region, sending shock waves to both China and Vietnam. Nong was eventually defeated and died a brutal death. Since the Song Dynasty, the Zhuang people of Guangxi and Yunnan who live along the Sino-Vietnamese border have been worshipping Nong as a heroic ancestor, whereas the Zhuang in other areas have tended to condemn Nong as a "rebellious barbarian." Donglan seems to fall into the category of "other areas."[86] It is therefore hard to know whether Wei Baqun identified more with Nong Zhigao, the southern rebel, or Wei Jingdai, the northern general, who helped defeat Nong, and who was believed to be the ancestor of the Weis in Donglan. What is certain is that Wei Baqun was familiar with Nong's stories as all local people were.

Wei Baqun's perception of Lord Wei Huchen should be much less ambivalent than his views on Nong Zhigao. As a local man who managed to attain royal title and national fame with his martial spirit and skills, Wei Huchen was a symbol of the local martial tradition and a source of pride for the local people. He was born in Wuzhuan, the nearest town to Wei Baqun's village. In fact, local people believed that it was Wei Huchen who coined the name Wuzhuan, which means "the seal of Marquis Wuyi,"[87] to celebrate the title he received from the Ming court after defeating the pirates in the Wuyi Mountains in Fujian Province. His tomb was quite close to Wei Baqun's village and ruins of the training facilities he had built still stand on Mount Yinhaizhou.

Wei Baqun would also have been familiar with the stories of the anti-Qing rebels Li Dingguo and Hong Xiuquan. Li was initially a rebel against the Ming Dynasty, but after the collapse of the Ming, he turned against the Manchu invaders. After his movement was crushed, some of his followers settled down in Donglan, becoming the ancestors of some local Han residents. Whereas Li Dingguo's movement began in the north and ended in the south, Hong Xiuquan's Taiping Rebellion took the opposite direction, and both had direct connections with Donglan. A striking feature of the Taiping Rebellion is that it was a multiethnic movement. It is estimated that at the beginning of the rebellion the Zhuang constituted about one-fourth of the 20,000 Taiping troops. The first Taiping martyr was a Zhuang peasant, and among the five early Taiping kings at least two were Zhuang.[88]

One of the stories about Wei Baqun recounts his two encounters with a Yao hunter named Luo Buduo. The first encounter took place on Mount Yinhaizhou sometime before late 1907. Wei Baqun was part of a hunting team and his duty was to hide near an intersection and ambush escaping animals. Suddenly a wounded boar appeared and Wei Baqun was scared, but the animal was soon hit by an arrow in the mouth and killed instantly. The archer was Luo Buduo, whose shining bow deeply impressed Wei Baqun. Baqun was told that the bow had been passed on to Luo by his grandfather, who had joined the Taiping army and fought under General Shi Dakai. Wei Baqun learned quite a few stories about the Taiping rebels from Luo.

Wei Baqun's second encounter with the hunter took place right before the Spring Festival of 1908 during his first trip to the county seat. This time he found Luo Buduo in chains. After being beaten by police, Luo was made to stand in a wooden cage tied to a stone lion sitting in front of the county government, clad only in shorts. Although shivering in the cold wind, he refused to be subdued. Wei Baqun learned that Luo had been accused of banditry and of instigating people to fight against taxation.[89]

In addition to these historical figures, there are also legendary heroes in the folk tradition with whom Wei Baqun would have been familiar. One of these was a young man named King Cengxun, who had green eyes and who grew up on the banks of the Red Water River. Tall, strong, and upright, he traveled to every corner of the Zhuang territory to search for means to subdue the poisonous snakes, ferocious beasts, and destructive floods. He was able to dredge the river to make it navigable; he also moved mountains to build a leeway along the river, preventing floods. Moreover, he turned the land along the river into fertile paddy fields, bringing safety, prosperity, and happiness to the people. Then there came the evil emperor who forced the people to pay exorbitant taxes, causing poverty. King Cengxun reacted by organizing the peasants and launching a revolt against the emperor, and the rebels fought the emperor's troops on the banks of the Red Water River. Although King Cengxun had only a carrying pole as his weapon, he was able to kill hundreds of the emperor's soldiers, whose blood ran into the river, turning the water red, hence the name Red Water River. At this point, the emperor decided to seek help from the Jade Emperor, who offered support to his human counterpart. Hiding himself in a cloud, the Jade Emperor was able to cut down King Cengxun with his sword.[90]

If King Cengxun represents the hero in the folk tradition, then there are also local evildoers in the legends. One of these was a local lord who happened to share the same name as Lord Wei Huchen of the Ming Dynasty. Although both were local lords from Donglan, the Lord Wei in the legend differs greatly from the one in historical records. Whereas the historical Lord Wei attained the status of a national hero by fighting pirates and rebels and brought pride and honor to Donglan, the Lord Wei in the legend was remembered as a brutal ruler. Another difference between the two is in the circumstances of their death. Although both died brutal deaths, the historical lord died of injustice (he was poisoned by his rivals), whereas the lord in the legend was killed by his own subjects and the killing was believed to be morally justifiable. In the legend, Lord Wei imposed a very high tax rate on the peasants, thus making himself the richest man in the area. Fearful of peasant rebellions, he built himself a sturdy fortress on Mount Yinhaizhou where he stored all the silver taels he had collected. All the members of his family lived in the fortress. However, the fortress failed to protect him and his family from the angry peasants, who revolted and burned down the trees and grass, as well as Lord Wei's fortress. All members of Lord Wei's family were burned to death, and the melted silver flew into a crater on the top of Mount Yinhaizhou, forming a beautiful pond that still exists there today.[91] The silver dollars that Wei Baqun's grand-aunt is said to have discovered were believed to be part of Lord Wei's silver collection that survived the fire. In some other versions of this legend, the evil lord was not Wei Huchen but Wei Qianbao, a usurper who attempted to take over the lordship from an ancestor of General Wei Huchen.[92]

According to another version of the legend, the legendary and historical Lord Weis were the same person. While he was away fighting the pirates, the Wei family did not have enough soldiers to protect their fortress back home. A group of bandits seized the opportunity and launched an attack on the fortress. They burned the storehouse, causing all the silver taels to melt.[93] This very likely represents the old and possibly also the accurate account and it was probably transformed into the new version during the era of revolutions. Largely because of the influence of revolutionary ideologies, in the new version the attackers are portrayed as peasant rebels rather than bandits—on many occasions they were the same people anyway. To depict the attackers as the righteous peasants rather than evil bandits, Lord Wei Huchen had to be turned from a patriotic general into an oppressor and exploiter.

In addition to the local folk traditions, Wei Baqun should also have read or heard about some of the stories of rebels and heroes in the Han tradition, which was accessible to him through both an elite and a folk channel. The former was school education, and the latter was the oral tradition. Hence, the young Wei Baqun was enchanted by the stories of the Song Dynasty rebels portrayed in the famous novel, *Outlaws of the Mash*.

It is hard to determine what the young Wei Baqun thought about the various characters in the local and national traditions. What is certain is that he had a good knowledge of these stories of Han, Zhuang, and Yao rebels and heroes and that his deeds and traits resembled those of his predecessors.

Although not all details of all the stories about the young Wei Baqun can be verified, the important components of his character manifested in these stories can be confirmed by his later deeds. These components include a strong sense of justice and mission, generosity, a very strong will, lack of fear of authority, a penchant for conflict, the ability to scheme and organize, and a desire to lead. One anecdote says that Wei Baqun always walked with both of his fists clenched, giving the impression that he was ready to fight at any moment.[94]

Wei Baqun began to stand above the crowd at a very young age by acting as a determined rebel against authorities and a benevolent patron for the poor and weak. The omens that appeared at his birth as well as his status as the first son of the wealthy Wei family made him and those around him feel that he was a special person with a special mission and some special qualities. It is said that even his teachers had to take into consideration his family status when meting out punishments for Wei Baqun.[95]

Although both his grandfather and father attached great importance to Wei Baqun's education, they did not impose on him a very intensive curriculum. His grandfather had to manage a large family and all kinds of business and his father had to distribute his time among his multiple wives, leaving them little time and energy for the young Wei Baqun. Some sources suggest that Wei Baqun's mother or grandfather, or maybe both of them, were very lenient toward him.[96] Such lenience, along with the freedom that Wei Baqun enjoyed, nurtured boldness in the young Wei Baqun.

Unlike typical children of upper-class scholarly families who had to spend most of their time in study rooms and could only play with children of similar social status, Wei Baqun spent a lot of time playing with his poor friends in outdoor settings. He naturally became the leader of his friends because of the status of his family, his generosity, his education, and possibly also his physical strength and attractiveness. Wei Baqun was already a skillful hunter, horse rider, and swimmer when he was young, and would later practice martial arts and running. His friendship and solidarity with the poor children made it easy for him to understand their sufferings and share their concerns. It also contributed a component of "wildness" to his character. Wei Baqun's talent of making and singing folksongs was a result of his interactions with the villagers and this in turn helped earn him admiration from his friends and the villagers. His father's death when he was young, and his grandfather's death a few years later, granted him even more freedom and further boosted his position within and without the family by making him the virtual decision maker for the large and wealthy Wei family when he was only twenty years old.

Like many other revolutionaries of his generation, Wei Baqun began his revolutionary career by fighting against the repressive and old-fashioned patriarch of his family and his teachers. The patriarch of the Wei family was Wei Baqun's grandfather. Despite some dubious references to conflicts between Wei

Baqun and his father, the grandfather was the primary target of Wei Baqun's early rebellions. His father was probably of a more moderate character than his grandfather. Besides, his father died before assuming a leadership role within the family and before Wei Baqun was old enough to pose any real challenge. Wei Baqun's conflicts with his grandfather took several forms. He did not approve the way his grandfather treated the laborers, tenants, and neighbors, believing that his grandfather was too mean and parsimonious. We have already mentioned the occasions when Wei Baqun stole grain and money from his own family to help neighbors, and when he refused to collect rent from his grandfather's tenant. Wei Baqun's sister later recalled that her brother also tried to change the way the family treated the laborers who lived in their house. Quite a few of these laborers were from the Yao minority. It was common for people to use derogatory terms to refer to the Yao, but Wei Baqun told his siblings not to use those terms and that he would punish them if they violated the rule.[97] Wei Baqun himself developed close relations with the children of these Yao laborers as well as with an old Yao woman who had served as his nanny when he was little.

Wei Baqun also did not accept the path of life that his grandfather had designed for him. The grandfather wanted Wei Baqun to learn some profit-making skills so that he would be able to manage the family businesses when he grew up, but Wei Baqun showed little interest in that. His grandfather very likely also hoped that Wei Baqun would do well in school so that one day he could enter the government, but Wei Baqun was never an obedient student. In fact, he was as rebellious in school as he was at home.

Wei Baqun's formal education began in 1902 when he was eight years old. Although the first modern elementary schools had been established in Guangxi in that year,[98] they were located in the more advanced parts of the province, and modern education had not entered Donglan at that time. Wei Baqun had to go to a private academy to study the Confucian classics. He did not like the teaching method of the academy and would occasionally challenge his teacher.[99] Later he moved to the nearby Jiangping village to attend a higher level Confucian academy, and he was as disobedient in his new school as he had been in the previous one. An event that villagers recalled well displayed his daredevil character as well as his love for horses. One day a man came by horseback to visit Wei Baqun's teacher. Upon arriving at the school he tied the horse by the cattle pen. Wei Baqun slipped out from class, jumped on the horse, galloped away at full speed, and did not return until the horse was utterly exhausted.

In 1905, Wei Baqun's father sponsored the creation of a Confucian academy in Dongli and Wei Baqun transferred to this new school to study with a teacher named Wu Jiashu. Wu had more than twenty students in all, and most of them were from well to do families. A year later, Donglan Advanced Elementary School was established in the county seat and Wei Baqun was admitted into that school in 1908. It seemed that Wei Baqun's father created the Confucian academy primarily for Wei Baqun because the academy was closed down as soon as Wei Baqun entered Donglan Advanced Elementary School.[100] The establishment of the advanced elementary school in the county seat was one of the first signs of modernization in Donglan County, and by 1908, seventy-four percent of the counties in Guangxi had created such schools.[101] Another sign of modernization for Donglan was the creation of modern postal service in 1910. During the next decade, a postman would arrive once every five days, keeping Donglan in touch with the outside world.[102] Political reform, including the creation of local assemblies, began after the collapse of the Qing Dynasty, but did not bring about positive political changes in frontier Donglan. For the young Wei Baqun, the establishment of the new school was much more important than the creation of the post office and assemblies.

After six years of training in the Confucian classics, Wei Baqun was now ready for a different kind of education. However, Donglan Advanced Elementary School was not completely modern. Although there were such new subjects as history, geography, science, and English in the curriculum, it retained the old subject of Confucian classics. Moreover, physical punishment was still an important part of everyday life in the school. At least once Wei Baqun went to challenge the principal, asking him to ban physical punishment, and the principal surprisingly agreed. In his study, Wei Baqun showed much more interest in the new subjects than the old ones, and he was particularly fond of sports and often entered sports contests with classmates. He stayed in this school for two years, but had to quit in 1910. According to some, the death of his father was the main reason for him to return home.[103]

Wei Baqun's departure from Donglan Advanced Elementary School, however, was not the end of his student career. In 1911, just before the Wuchang Uprising, which eventually caused the collapse of the Qing Dynasty, Wei Baqun passed the entrance exams of Qingyuan High School, which was one of the first modern high schools in Guangxi Province.[104] Qingyuan was the seat of the prefectural government and a beautiful town sitting on the banks of the Dragon River, more than two hundred kilometers to the east of Donglan. Wei Baqun's insubordination increased as he grew older. Almost every biography or story of Wei Baqun includes the account of a conflict between him and the conservative principal of Qingyuan High School. The principal was a holder of the juren degree and some of the teachers he hired were also degree holders. These Qing loyalists all felt relieved when revolutionary Sun Yat-sen had to hand his presidency to former Qing general, Yuan Shikai, shortly after the 1911 Revolution, and they were supportive of Yuan's call for the revival of Confucian morality. Wei Baqun had followed the national events closely and had read the various popular revolutionary pamphlets authored by Sun Yat-sen's followers. As a firm supporter of Sun Yat-sen and an outspoken critic of the traditional way of teaching, Wei Baqun's conflict with the conservative principal and teachers was inevitable.

The clash occurred right before the 1912 birthday of the principal. The day before the birthday a school official assembled all the students and told them to get ready for the celebration. He wanted each student to donate some money as a present for the principal and to shout blessings to the principal at the party. Wei Baqun bluntly told the official that, "These are not allowed since China is now a Republic!" Embarrassed by this open challenge, the official ordered Wei Baqun to kneel down to express his apology, but Wei refused. The confrontation drew the attention of the principal who made his appearance on the scene. Wei Baqun repeated his argument to the principal, who became very angry. Although some suggested that Wei Baqun be arrested for instigating a riot, the principal decided to settle for a more moderate punishment. He expelled Wei Baqun the next day.[105]

If all the details in this story were true, then Wei Baqun would definitely be a pioneer of the anti-Confucian movement. Although the civil service examination system had been abolished, the Confucian tradition was still the dominant ideology in the country. On the one hand, it was remarkable that Wei Baqun, a youth from the frontier, had already launched an attack on Confucian rituals four years before Chen Duxiu ignited the New Culture Movement. On the other hand, the episodes in this story would become less unbelievable if we consider that the Confucian tradition had never been as deep seated in the frontier regions as it had been in the heartland, that Wei Baqun had already established himself as a rebellious youth, and that many other rebels, including the nearby Hong Xiuquan, had challenged Confucian practices long before Wei Baqun did.[106]

If this rebellious act of Wei Baqun is paired with his next, then both become more believable. His next revolt, which has also been widely covered in his biographies, targeted the principal of another school. After he was expelled from Qingyuan High School, Wei Baqun decided not to return home but to move to Guilin to find a better school. Guilin, located in northern Guangxi, had been the provincial capital for nearly ten centuries, until Nanning became the new capital in 1912. This was the first time for the young Wei Baqun to venture out of the Red Water River culture sphere, which featured very strong non-Han characteristics. Guilin was predominantly a Han city. Wei Baqun should not have felt an unbearable culture shock, however, because he was already familiar with the Han culture through his education and his contacts with the Han people and Sinicized non-Han natives living in the Red Water River area. He should also have learned to speak some variant of the Han language by that time.

With the help of a relative, Wei Baqun was able to enter Guilin College of Law and Politics in 1912. This school was created in 1908 to train officials and judges for the constitutional government planned for China. The principal was a former Qing official who had worked at the court in Beijing and strongly believed that all his students would one day become government officials. It did not take long for Wei Baqun to discover that this was not a suitable school for him and he soon got himself into a serious conflict with the principal. It was a rule of the school that students should wear the official uniform with a hat. Wei Baqun would sometimes violate the rule by wearing only part of the uniform or by putting on the village style outfit that he had brought from home. Another rule of the school stipulated that students should not leave their classrooms during study hours and should not stay overnight outside the school. Wei Baqun would often leave his classroom during study hours to help the cooks at the kitchen and would sometimes sleep in the workers' quarters rather than in the school dormitory. Finally, the principal confronted Wei Baqun one day when he once again broke the dress code.

"How can you become an official with this kind of appearance?" The principal asked.

"I don't want to become an official! . . . I came here to study!" Wei Baqun replied.

"Then you are in the wrong place." The principal answered bluntly. He then ordered Wei Baqun to leave the school.[107]

Wei Baqun's grandfather and other relatives were very hopeful when he was admitted into the college, believing that a degree from the school would ensure him an official position in the government. Once Wei Baqun was expelled, their dreams were crushed. Wei Baqun's rebellious character and acts served to draw him away from a normal path to power and brought him close to the course of revolution. Many other revolutionaries in modern Asia had similar experiences. If Hong Xiuquan had passed the civil service examination, which he took four times, and acquired a position in the Qing government, he probably would not have launched the Taiping Rebellion. If Sun Yat-sen had been granted an audience with Li Hongzhang, as Sun had wished, and been awarded an official position, he probably would not have organized the 1911 revolution. If Ho Chi-minh had entered the school for training colonial officials in Paris, as he had requested, and become an official in the French colonial government in Vietnam, he probably would not have joined the anti-French movement. The list can go on and on.

In Wei Baqun's case, it seems that it was his own decision that he would not enter the government. However, Wei Baqun did not leave the school voluntarily before the clash with the principal. It was the principal who forced Wei Baqun out of the college, making Wei's case more similar to those of Hong Xiuquan, Sun Yat-sen, and Ho Chi-minh than it might otherwise appear to be. It is hard to understand Wei Baqun's claim that he was not interested in becoming an official. If his claim was valid, why did he enter the college in the first place? The kind of career path available to him after graduation should have been obvious the first time he heard the name of the college. He should also have known that holding an official position would offer him power and opportunities to change the society and politics that he was very critical of, not to mention the sense of fulfillment it would bring to him and his family. Nevertheless, it is possible that he had been interested in entering the government before attending the college, but lost his interest after learning more about the school and political realities. Is it possible that by not wearing the official uniform and by working and sleeping with the workers of the college Wei Baqun was trying to make a statement that he wanted to be a different kind of official? There is also evidence showing that Wei Baqun entered the college as a probationary student, and therefore not wearing the complete set of uniform could also be his way to show that he was not yet a formal student of the school. It is not certain whether or not he was still on probationary status when he was expelled from the school.

In early 1914, Wei Baqun returned home. He was now almost twenty years old. He had attended three secondary schools, but had not graduated from any of them. He had experienced conflicts with not only his father and grandfather, but also numerous teachers and at least two principals. His character, which was manifested in his interactions with those around him, combined, sometimes in a contradictory form, the boldness and extravagance of the prodigal son of a wealthy family, the headstrong attitude of a spoiled child, the generosity and good-heartedness of a philanthropist, the sense of mission of a Confucian gentleman and a patriot, the down-to-earth wisdom of a peasant youth, the sophistication of an intellectual, the chivalry of a knight errant, the amiability of a friend, the artistic, romantic and martial predilection of a Zhuang man, and above all the free and undaunted spirit of a rebel from the frontier who detested the way the world was run.

CHAPTER TWO

First Journey

1914–1921

Although he had spent time in the county seat of Donglan, the prefectural town of Qingyuan, and the former provincial capital Guilin, twenty-year-old Wei Baqun had never traveled out of his province. Shortly after returning home in 1914, Wei Baqun decided to make a trip to a few provinces beyond Guangxi. According to one source, his grandfather had died the previous year. Another source holds that his grandfather and father both passed away shortly after he returned from Guilin.[1] As a result, Wei Baqun became the new patriarch of the family, and could now do whatever he wanted. It has been suggested that Wei Baqun's mother was supportive of his decision and let him sell some paddy fields to pay for the travel expenses. Wei Baqun was now married to Huang Fengtao, a woman from his village. It may have been difficult for him to say goodbye to his newly wed wife, but even she could not hold him back.

A third account holds that the grandfather was still alive when Wei Baqun decided to make his trip. It is recalled that his grandfather was disappointed that Wei Baqun had not stayed in the College of Law and Politics and he now wanted Wei Baqun to stay home to take care of the family businesses. Wei Baqun agreed on the condition that he would be granted full authority in making decisions. One of his first decisions after taking over the family businesses was to send three of the hired laborers home and give each of them some money plus a small piece of land as a payment for their service. He also gave money, grain, and land to other poor villagers, causing repeated conflicts with his grandfather. When Wei Baqun decided to leave home and travel to other provinces, the old patriarch vehemently opposed, but to no avail. Wei Baqun collected more than two hundred silver dollars by selling some land and then hit the road. Before his departure, as this account goes, his grandfather had a white chicken killed, cooked, and presented to Wei Baqun. In the Zhuang tradition, this was a way for the grandfather to say that he intended to disown his grandson. Wei Baqun ate the chicken and left home.[2]

It is hard to determine Wei Baqun's motivation for making such a trip. Some scholars have vaguely argued that the purpose of the trip was to seek "revolutionary truth" or "the way to save the nation and the people,"[3] which is hard to confirm. It is likely that Wei Baqun's travels to different areas within the province had aroused his interest in seeing other provinces in the country, and that after reading about different regions of the country he now wanted to see these places with his own eyes. No matter how much Wei Baqun hated the schools he had attended, his teachers must have taught him a great deal about the world beyond Donglan and Guangxi. Finally, it could also be possible that after his unpleasant experiences with schools within Guangxi, he dreamed of finding and attending a better school in a big city. He was still young and had a thirst for new ideas and knowledge. He did not share his dream with his relatives or friends, probably because he was worried that even if he could enter a good school, he would not be able to stay enrolled through graduation.

It is also difficult to verify how long Wei Baqun thought the trip would last and what cities or regions he planned to visit. According to one account, his first stop outside of Guangxi was Guangzhou. This seems an understandable choice because Guangzhou was the closest metropolis to Guangxi and the culture and language of the Guangzhou area were similar to those of the Han regions of southern Guangxi. Wei Baqun should have heard a great deal about Guangzhou since childhood. Accompanied by a man from a neighboring village, as this account goes, Wei Baqun left home for Tianzhou on foot in November 1914. Tianzhou was a large town with about one thousand households sitting on the bank of the Right River.[4] For residents of Donglan, Tianzhou was a stepping-stone to the new provincial capital Nanning. One other source holds that Wei Baqun asked a villager to help take all the silver dollars he had collected for the trip to a man in Tianzhou so that this man could send him money in installments during his journey.[5] In other words, Tianzhou was not only his first major stop after leaving Donglan, but also his financial base during the entire journey.

From Tianzhou, Wei Baqun got on a boat bound for Nanning, and this was probably his first visit to the new capital. Twelve years later, when the Communist Chen Mianshu made his first trip from Nanning to Donglan, he had to spend eight days on the road, including three days from Nanning to Tianzhou on a boat and five days from Tianzhou to Donglan on foot.[6] Wei Baqun most likely covered the distance in a shorter time because the boat from Tianzhou to Nanning sailed with the current and was thus faster than that from Nanning to Tianzhou, and as a local son Wei Baqun could move faster than Chen Mianshu on the mountain paths between Donglan and Tianzhou. Still, it would have been a tiring journey. In Nanning, Wei Baqun transferred onto another boat that took him to Guangzhou. Later he traveled from Guangzhou to Shanghai and several provinces along the Yangtze River, and did not return home until late 1915.[7]

Another account of Wei Baqun's travels lists Guangzhou as the last stop before his return to Guangxi. This source holds that he began his trip by moving eastward instead of westward, but again, on foot. After crossing the Red Water River, he turned northward to reach the town of Hechi near the Dragon River. From there he moved further east to Liuzhou before turning north to hike to Guilin. These were the two largest cities in northern Guangxi. He then trekked eastward and it did not take him long to reach Hunan. He continued to walk toward the east and passed first a small city called Lengshuitan in western Hunan, and then a larger city named Zhuzhou, before entering Changsha the provincial capital. He then turned northward toward the bustling Wuhan, on the banks of the Yangtze River in Hubei Province. From there he turned eastward again to visit the rural but crowded provinces of Jiangxi, Anhui and Jiangsu before arriving in Shanghai. From Shanghai he made a trip to the nearby city of Hangzhou and then went all the way to Guangzhou in the far south. He then returned home from Guangzhou in late 1915.[8] One other source claims that Wei Baqun's itinerary also included Hong Kong, where a sign near the entrance of a garden saying, "No Chinese or dogs are allowed," incensed him.[9] It was quite possible for Wei Baqun to make a trip to Hong Kong from Guangzhou, but it is not certain whether or not a sign with such a message existed in Hong Kong at that time. Most other Chinese who reported being infuriated by such a sign, including Nationalist Sun Yat-sen and Communists Fang Zhimin and Guo Moruo, claimed to have seen it in Shanghai.

Wei Baqun wrote notes and diaries during his trip to record his observations and reflections. However, these were all destroyed in 1926 when his enemies burned down his house.[10] Whereas it is difficult to establish where he actually began and ended his trip, it is certain that he visited large cities such as Shanghai and Guangzhou as well as numerous southern provinces during the trip, which should be an eye-opening experience for him. Li Zongren, who was to become the ruler of Guangxi in the 1920s, also made his first trip out of Guangxi at about this time as a soldier in the Guangxi Army. About his first visit to Guangdong Li later wrote: "I had grown up in a mountainous region and had never traveled out of Guangxi before. Joining the army allowed me to travel to the lower reaches of the Pearl River and to see the moving steamships and trains. It was such a bustling and jolly place! Though I was far away from home and inevitably suffered from homesickness, I was extremely excited to see this new heaven and earth." During his first visit to Hunan, Li noticed the climatic difference between Hunan and Guangxi. He also observed that whereas the women in Guangdong and Guangxi did not bind their feet and played as important a role as their men in farming, the women in Hunan all had bound feet and therefore were not able to perform hard labor.[11]

Huang Shaohong, who would serve as the governor of Guangxi from 1925 to 1929, made his first trip out of Guangxi in early 1912 as a student-soldier. He and his friends from Guangxi were most impressed by the trains they saw in Hubei and the historical sites in and around Nanjing. Although the French made their first proposal about constructing railroads in Guangxi as early as 1888, the first railroad in Guangxi was not completed until 1938.[12]

Wei Baqun, who also grew up in a mountainous region and made his first journey out of Guangxi at the same time, who was about the same age as Li Zongren and Huang Shaohong, and who also visited Hunan, Guangdong, Wuhan, and Nanjing during his trip, might have had feelings and impressions similar to those held by Li and Huang. The trip allowed Wei Baqun to experience his first real winter in central and eastern China. Donglan winters are generally snowless and mild, with temperatures rarely dipping to zero. But winters could be cold in Hunan, Hubei, Shanghai, and some other places that Wei Baqun visited during the journey. Sixteen years later, when many of Wei Baqun's followers from Donglan had to leave home to join Mao Zedong in Jiangxi, some were amazed when they saw snow after entering Hunan. Unfortunately, because they did not have winter clothes, quite a few died from the cold.[13]

In hindsight, Wei Baqun would definitely take it as a pity that he had missed an opportunity to meet the other two leaders of the early Communist peasant movement during his trip. Mao Zedong was a student at the First Normal School of Hunan in Changsha when Wei Baqun roamed through Hunan, and Peng Pai was attending a high school in Haifeng when Wei Baqun passed through the Haifeng coast on a steamship to or from Guangzhou.

The trip gave Wei Baqun a good sense of the gap between his frontier province and the coastal areas, and the vastness and diversity of China despite the fact that he never set foot in northern China during this journey. It has been speculated that during his travel Wei Baqun observed firsthand the serious problems facing China at that time, including class difference, the poverty of the peasants and workers, and foreign invasions. Guangzhou and Shanghai were the two most important treaty ports as well as the most Westernized cities in China at that time. However, in 1915, China's most dangerous enemy was Japan rather than the Western powers that had created the two treaty ports. In that year Japan presented the Twenty One Demands to China with the purpose of turning China into a protectorate of Japan, and that caused a large-scale anti-Japanese movement in the various places Wei Baqun visited. He probably also learned more about domestic politics, particularly the conflicts between Sun Yat-sen, who was determined to protect the Republican system, and President Yuan Shikai, who had been trying to destroy the newly created democratic institutions. Wei Baqun had been a faithful supporter of Sun Yat-sen before making the trip and what he learned during his travel would help affirm his loyalty to Sun. Finally, the travel changed Wei Baqun's appearance. He cut off his ponytail during the trip and returned home with a new hairstyle, causing an uproar in the village.[14] Wei Baqun might have felt pity for his fellow villagers because people in most other parts of the country had already cut off their ponytails, which were perceived to be a symbol of humiliation.

If the conservative villagers disliked Wei Baqun's radical ideas and appearance, his yearlong journey to the more advanced parts of the country won him much admiration from the young people who rushed to his house to listen to his travel stories. Travel, just like education, wealth, or official position, was an important means to earn respect in the village world. For Wei Baqun, this journey served to signal his formal coming of age as the new patriarch of the Wei family and a young but respected member of the local community.

The trip was also a turning point in Wei Baqun's political career. Before the trip, Wei Baqun had been an occasional rebel against his father, grandfather, teachers, principals, and powerful local families, but such acts were spontaneous and personal. Shortly after the trip, Wei Baqun entered national politics by becoming a rebel against Yuan Shikai, the supreme ruler of China, whose attempt at creating a new dynasty caused protests throughout the country. In Yunnan Province, a close neighbor of Guangxi, General Cai E launched an armed rebellion against Yuan and began to march his troops northward toward Beijing. Military commanders in other parts of the country, including the most powerful generals in Guangxi and Guizhou, supported him. Wei Baqun decided to join the anti-Yuan movement in a very ostensible way: He began to recruit villagers to fight for the anti-Yuan army. He also sold some family properties—either twenty to thirty buffaloes or some paddy fields—and used the money to buy weapons and cover travel expenses for the peasant soldiers he recruited. Starting from this point, Wei Baqun's activities became more social and political rather than personal, and hence began to form part of the collective rather than personal memory.

More than one hundred young villagers from Donglan and neighboring Fengshan County formed Wei Baqun's small army. In many ways this was a private army, but Wei Baqun created it for a public purpose. Hearing that fierce battles were going on between Yuan's army and the anti-Yuan troops in Guizhou Province, Wei Baqun decided to march his small army toward Guizhou in early 1916. A more important reason for Wei Baqun and his soldiers to join the Guizhou Army was that a native of Donglan, Xiong Kecheng, was serving as a brigade commander in the Guizhou Army at that time and had set up a recruiting station in a village by the Red Water River.[15] Although they had no automobiles or horses and had to cover the entire distance with their own feet, Wei Baqun and his soldiers were able to reach Guizhou in a short time. There, Wei Baqun's small army was reorganized as a company in the Guizhou Army and Wei Baqun was appointed as its deputy captain. As the battles in Guizhou were already over, the Guizhou Army began to march to southern Sichuan to fight Yuan's troops there. Wei Baqun and his company were involved in battles near Chongqing and this was the first battle experience for Wei Baqun. Fighting stopped in late April when Yuan Shikai decided to abandon his new dynasty and negotiate with the anti-Yuan forces.

If the grandfather was still alive in late 1914, before Wei Baqun set out on his long journey, he must certainly have been dead by late 1915. Otherwise it would have been very difficult for Wei Baqun to sell more land or buffaloes for something that the grandfather would perceive to have nothing to do with his family. Because he had already disowned Wei Baqun, to follow one of the accounts about Wei Baqun's 1915 trip, the grandfather could easily argue that all his properties were off limits to his eldest grandson. According to another source, Wei Baqun sold neither buffaloes nor paddy fields this time, but managed to persuade his mother to hand him the three hundred taels of silver that the grandfather had given to his mother on his death bed,[16] thus confirming the grandfather's death before late 1915. If Wei Baqun was not yet the real patriarch of the Wei family in late 1914, he surely became such in late 1915. Even if the grandfather had indeed disowned Wei Baqun in late 1914, the act was no longer effective after the grandfather's death. The Wei family needed a man to serve as its leader and Wei Baqun was the only adult male in the family at that time. His family now included his father's four or five surviving wives, Brother Wei Jing, who was eleven years old, Brother Wei Jing (a different character with the same pronunciation), six years old, his four younger sisters, and his wife Huang Fengtao and son Wei Shuzu. From this point on, Wei Baqun would have no strong opponents within the family. He now had almost complete freedom to pursue whatever ideas on his mind, no matter how strange or radical they might appear. He was definitely not the type of patriarch that his grandfather and father had expected him to become. He cared little about the family businesses; he spent money on people and projects that would bring no immediate benefits to the family; and he seemed to feel more at home outside than within his own house.

If it is understandable that there was no one from his family who could stop Wei Baqun from embarking on such a military endeavor because he was now the new patriarch of the family, it is not equally understandable why the one hundred or so peasants decided to follow Wei Baqun to a battlefront in another province. Wei Baqun's act was understandable because by now he was already a well-educated and well-traveled man with strong political beliefs, but it would be unfair to expect all his peasant followers to share his level of political understanding and his variant of political beliefs. If we trust the Chinese intellectuals who wrote about the Chinese peasants in the 1910s and 1920s, the general level of political consciousness among the peasants was very low at that time.[17]

It is worth noting that the formation of Wei Baqun's peasant army occurred five years before Lu Xun wrote his famous novel about the ignorant, comic and tragic Ah Q, which many believe reflected Lu Xun's pessimistic assessment of the political consciousness of Chinese peasants in the early twentieth century, an assessment shared by many others. Seen in the larger context, Wei Baqun's creation of a small peasant army in 1916 in frontier Guangxi for the purpose of fighting Emperor Yuan Shikai and protecting the Republic was a remarkable if not unbelievable event that would have shocked many of his contemporaries.

Three of Wei Baqun's followers in the anti-Yuan Shikai movement would remain his lifetime comrades and would die for their common ideals, and two of them would become Wei Baqun's enemies in later years. One of the three comrades was Huang Bangwei, a peasant from a village near Dongli, who was one year younger than Wei Baqun. Huang had studied for one year at a Confucian academy before attending Yucai Advanced Elementary School at Wuzhuan. He learned much about the conflict between Yuan Shikai and Sun Yat-sen in the elementary school and became a supporter of Sun at a young age. There is no indication that he and Wei Baqun were close friends before they joined the Guizhou Army, but the two had definitely known each other long before that. Huang joined the anti-Yuan army with Wei Baqun and stayed in the army until early 1921, when he returned to Donglan and joined Wei Baqun's peasant movement. In 1923, Huang became one of the first martyrs of the Donglan peasant movement. Huang's epitaph states that he despised farming work and was always dreaming of pursuing a military career. It also says that Huang joined the Guizhou Army in 1914 instead of 1915, meaning he was already in the Guizhou Army when Wei Baqun began to organize his small army.[18] If that is true, then it is likely that Huang was another reason why Wei Baqun decided to join the Guizhou Army rather than the Guangxi army, which also opposed Yuan Shikai.

Huang Daquan was another peasant from a neighboring village who joined Wei Baqun's small army and became his lifetime follower. He graduated from Donglan Advanced Elementary School in 1915 at the age of seventeen and then returned to Wuzhuan to teach in a private academy. He stayed in the Guizhou Army till 1917 and then returned home. He spent the next four years teaching at a local school and rejoined Wei Baqun in 1921.[19]

Wei Baqun's third lifetime ally in the group was Liao Yuanfang, a peasant from the neighboring Fengshan County. Liao had also studied first in a Confucian academy and then at an advanced elementary school in Fengshan. He then spent several years in neighboring Guizhou and Yunnan provinces doing small businesses. Born in 1880, he was much older than Wei Baqun, but the two found each other admirable as soon as they met in Fengshan in 1915, and they immediately became sworn brothers. Liao may have been the oldest in the group. After spending some time in the anti-Yuan army, he became a student at Guizhou Military Academy, which Wei Baqun also attended. Liao returned to Donglan after graduating from the academy in 1918, and he joined Wei Baqun again in 1921. Liao's three younger brothers all followed him into the Red Army and were killed one after another.[20]

Chen Shusen and Ya Yufan were the two members of the small army who later became Wei Baqun's enemies. Like Liao Yuanfang, they were also Wei Baqun's sworn brothers. Chen lived in the county seat and was a graduate of Donglan Advanced Elementary School, and Ya was from northern Donglan. Like Liao, the two spent a year in Wei Baqun's company and were then sent to study at Guizhou Military Academy. Shortly after graduating from the school, they both returned to Guangxi to serve in the army of the Old Guangxi Clique. After the fall of the Old Guangxi Clique in the early 1920s, Chen changed sides and joined the army of the New Guangxi Clique. In the early 1930s, he fought against the Communists in Donglan and the Right River region and played a significant part in defeating Wei Baqun. Ya took a similar path and became an officer in the army of the New Guangxi Clique. He was already a regimental commander in early 1926 and offered some cartridges to Wei Baqun's peasant army at that time.[21] In the early 1930s, he also became Wei Baqun's enemy and participated actively in the extermination campaigns against the Communists.

It is arguable that Liao Yuanfang joined the anti-Yuan movement primarily because of his friendship with Wei Baqun, whereas one of the motivations for Huang Bangwei to join the army was his loyalty to Sun Yat-sen and the Republic and his disdain for farming. In fact, quite a few of Wei Baqun's followers were not real peasants but rural intellectuals. To leave farming and earn a respectable position might be a shared incentive for quite many of his followers. Huang Xuchu, one of Wei Baqun's later enemies, would comment that Wei Baqun himself joined the movement because he saw that as a great opportunity for acquiring a good position in the army.[22] The local martial tradition might also have served as a source of inspiration for Wei Baqun and his followers. They could easily identify themselves with either Wei Huchen, if they thought they were helping to protect a rightful government (the Republic), or the Taiping rebels if they believed they were fighting against an illegitimate government (Yuan's dynasty). In organization Wei Baqun's small army was not very different from that of Wei Huchen four hundred years earlier. Edward Friedman has shown that the rural people involved in the 1911 Revolution and the 1916 Anti-Yuan Shikai movement were more like social bandits than revolutionaries, and they participated in these movements with traditional and religious goals.[23] Some of Wei Baqun's followers may have had a similar motivation and outlook.

No matter what prompted the villagers to take part in the anti-Yuan movement, they had to place their trust in Wei Baqun the leader before they decided to follow him, and their trust was built on friendship, common political beliefs, common regional and ethnic ties, Wei Baqun's family status, education, and travel experiences, as well as his reputation as a generous patron, among other factors. It also required the skills of persuasion, mobilization and organization on Wei Baqun's part in the creation of such an army. In that sense this event was Wei Baqun's debut as a revolutionary and political leader.

Not long after the end of the national rebellion against Yuan Shikai in 1916, Wei Baqun became involved in a small-scale rebellion against Lu Yongfen, the captain of his company. Captain Lu was the only outsider in the company, which probably made him feel awkward, at least at the beginning. Partly because he had been in the old army of the militarists for too long and therefore had learned all its practices, and partly because he probably believed that creating fear was the best means to establish his authority, Lu was very brutal to the soldiers and would often subject them to physical punishment. Wei Baqun initially tried to persuade the captain to change his ways but to no avail. One day when the captain once again was about to physically abuse a soldier, Wei Baqun stopped it with his fists. For that intransigent act, Wei Baqun was reduced to the rank of a platoon leader. When his soldiers gathered to protest the punishment, Wei Baqun was discharged and jailed in Chongqing for "inciting a riot."[24]

This was the first time Wei Baqun was imprisoned. For him this was an unexpected reward for his participation in the anti-Yuan movement. Fortunately, Wei Baqun's remarkable deed had earned him quite a few sympathizers, and one of them, a staff officer, brought Wei Baqun's case to the attention of higher authorities.[25] Some high-ranking generals began to speak for Wei Baqun, and one of them, General Lu Tao, became Wei Baqun's true savior. Lu was from Guangxi and his county was not far away from Donglan. Moreover, he was a Zhuang. A graduate of the famous Yunnan Military Academy where he was a classmate of General Zhu De, the founding father of the Chinese Communist Red Army, Lu was one of the very few outsiders who held high-ranking positions in the very provincial Guizhou Army. General Lu Tao obviously felt that he had a special duty to help Wei Baqun because of both regional and ethnic ties and common political views. Lu personally went to plead with the top commander of the Guizhou Army who was his close friend, and the top commander decided not only to release Wei Baqun immediately, but also send him to Guizhou Military Academy for training. In total, Wei Baqun was incarcerated for several months. Unfortunately for him, this would not be his only experience with the prison system.

To make 1917 an even more dramatic year for Wei Baqun, his wife Huang Fengtao died of illness sometime, leaving two young sons for Wei Baqun's mother to take care of.[26] It is not certain when Wei Baqun received the sad news and there is no indication that he went home for the funeral.

Guizhou Military Academy was the fourth secondary school Wei Baqun attended and it turned out to be the only one that he graduated from. The school was created in 1916 for the purpose of training middle- and low-ranking officers for the Guizhou Army. It was also part of the effort at attaining independence for the army and government of Guizhou from the dominance of neighboring Yunnan. The founding principal of the school, He Yingqin, who later became a powerful military commander in Chiang Kai-shek's Nationalist army, was a young officer trained in a Japanese military school. He hired a Japanese officer as his adviser and recruited a group of instructors who were graduates of Japanese military schools like him. Applicants to the school were required to have completed an elementary school level education and to be opium-free. Opium smoking was even more prevalent in Guizhou than in Guangxi at that time, and the troops of the Guizhou Army were widely known as two-gun soldiers because they always carried with them their opium pumps along with their guns.[27] The curriculum of Guizhou Military Academy, which resembled that of Japanese military schools, emphasized both military training and political indoctrination, and it normally took two years for a student to graduate.

Wei Baqun entered the school in 1917 and graduated in 1919. He liked this school much better than the previous two, and he was particularly interested in studying military science. Upon graduation, he became a staff officer in a Guizhou Army unit stationed in Chongqing. It is not certain whether or not General Lu Tao played any role in acquiring this position for him, but the two obviously established contacts with each other after Wei Baqun's release from prison. After General Lu was transferred to Chongqing in August 1920, the two saw each other every day.[28]

It seemed that finally Wei Baqun's grandfather's dream of acquiring power in addition to wealth for the Wei family was about to come true. Now the twenty-four-year old Wei Baqun had a promising position, and the good connections he had in the Guizhou Army meant an excellent prospect of promotion if he followed the rules and stayed close to his patrons. However, Wei Baqun was not the kind of man who would sacrifice his ideals to regulations, and he could not force himself to stay in a designated path just because that would lead to promotion. Strict discipline and intensive political indoctrination failed to prevent him from developing a strong interest in radical ideas spread by popular magazines like *New Youth*. He not only read these magazines himself, but also shared them with his friends in the army and mailed them to his friends back home using the pseudonym of "Fenbuping," meaning "Detest Inequality." He used the same pseudonym to write slogans and pamphlets advocating social revolution and military reform, and to spread them in the army. Eventually, his clandestine activities drew the attention of the high authorities and in October 1920, before the military police came to arrest him, he secretly left the army. It is believed that General Lu Tao saved Wei Baqun one more time by urging him to leave before the impending arrest.[29] The two would never see each other again. A few months after Wei Baqun's departure, Sun Yat-sen appointed General Lu commander-in-chief of the Guizhou Army and governor of Guizhou Province. Although he failed to hold on to these positions for long, Lu Tao remained an influential political and military leader of Guizhou until 1949. In late 1949, he took the leading position in a citizens' organization created by some underground Communists and for that he was executed by the Nationalists a few hours before the Communist troops entered the city of Guiyang, capital of Guizhou Province. In death, Wei Baqun and Lu Tao joined each other again: the Nationalists killed them both and the Communists recognized both as "revolutionary martyrs."[30]

At least two authors have claimed that after leaving the Guizhou Army, Wei Baqun first traveled westward to Yunnan and then from there to Guangzhou.[31] However, Wei Baqun's own account shows clearly that he got to Guangzhou by way of Shanghai, where the headquarters of the Chinese Nationalist Party was based. Wei Baqun wanted to meet Sun Yat-sen there. He did not learn until after arriving in Shanghai that Sun had just moved his headquarters to Guangzhou. Wei Baqun immediately left Shanghai and reached Guangzhou in October. It was during his brief stay in Shanghai in late 1920 that Wei Baqun wrote a letter to his twenty-year-old cousin Chen Bomin, who was a student at the Number Five Provincial High School in Baise. In the letter, Wei Baqun told his cousin that he had left the Guizhou Army, had missed Sun Yat-sen in Shanghai and was about to travel to Guangzhou to find Sun. Attached to the letter was a folksong written in the Zhuang language and style and it goes as follows:

I mail this song-letter to you, Brother Bomin of Nama Village in my hometown;
I have travelled to every corner under heaven, I have seen through the world—
Everywhere, there are evil people devouring innocent souls! This world is full of
devils who pray to Amida Buddha while savouring human flesh.
I mail this song-letter to you, Brother Bomin of Nama Village in my hometown.
How detestable it is that the sun has disappeared from the sky. Cold wind is blowing,
Chilly rain is falling. I have travelled to every corner under heaven, I have
seen through the world— Everywhere, there are evil people devouring innocent souls![32]

The song reaffirmed Wei Baqun's concern with social inequality and the sufferings of the poor and weak. The letter and song moved Chen Bomin so much that he decided to quit school and travel to Guangzhou to meet his cousin and Sun Yat-sen. Unfortunately, he failed to find either of them in Guangzhou and had to return home to teach in an elementary school. One source hints that after making a stay in Guangzhou, Chen proceeded to visit Shanghai and Beijing before returning home.[33] Chen would see his cousin again in a few months but he never got a chance to meet Sun Yat-sen.

Some believe that Wei Baqun got to meet Sun Yat-sen upon arriving in Guangzhou,[34] but others hold that he did not.[35] Even if the meeting did occur, it did not lead to the formation of a strong personal relationship between the two. All agree that Wei Baqun did meet with Sun Yat-sen's close associate Liao Zhongkai, who a few years later would become a crucial supporter of peasant movements in general and Wei Baqun's movement in particular. While in Guangzhou, Wei Baqun joined the Chinese Nationalist Party and befriended some leading Nationalists from Guangxi, among whom the most prominent was Ma Junwu, a scholar from Guilin who had studied in Europe and Japan and was versed in several foreign languages. In fact, he was the first Chinese to earn a PhD from a German university and his field of study was metallurgy.[36] Ma became a follower of Sun Yat-sen while a student in Japan and was a frequent contributor to *Mingbao*, the organ of Tongmenghui, the predecessor to the Chinese Nationalist Party. He was also the first to translate the Communist Manifesto into Chinese. Ma and some other Nationalists from Guangxi had organized the Association for Reforming Guangxi in Shanghai in early 1920, and Wei Baqun immediately joined the association. If Lu Tao had been Wei Baqun's first patron, then Ma Junwu was his second. Both Lu and Ma were natives of Guangxi who had been educated outside their province, were influential in national politics and had wide connections at the local, provincial, and national levels. Through them, Wei Baqun moved a step further toward the center of national political ferment.

The political programs of the Association for Reforming Guangxi called for the rejection of the militarist government in Beijing; elimination of the military governors; free elections; reform of the taxation and budget system; creation of a conscription army; promotion of industry, commerce, agriculture, irrigation, transportation, and education; and the enforcement of a ban on opium and gambling. The association also supported equalizing land rights and equality between men and women. Obviously, the political programs of the association were very similar to those of the Chinese Nationalist Party. The immediate objective of the association was to overthrow the government of militarist Lu Rongting, who had been the actual ruler of Guangxi, and sometimes also Guangdong, since the collapse of the Qing Dynasty. Members of the association were inspired by the achievements of the Association for Reforming Hunan, which had successfully expelled the militarist governor of Hunan. Since Lu Rongting had caused troubles for neighboring Guangdong and Hunan, the Association for Reforming Guangxi easily won the support of many political and military leaders of these two provinces. The association published an organ entitled *New Guangxi Monthly* and was run by a committee consisting of various departments in charge of military and political affairs, propaganda and communications, and so on. Wei Baqun was appointed the deputy head of its department of political affairs at the second congress of the association.[37]

If the Nationalist Party was the most powerful opposition party in the country, then the Association for Reforming Guangxi was the most promising opposition political group in Guangxi. By joining these two organizations, Wei Baqun tied himself closely to the opposition elites at both the provincial and national levels. At the same time, he found some ideologies to follow and some political strategies for future adoption. The connections he made during his stay in Guangzhou were to have great influence on his political career.

Wei Baqun's journey outside of Donglan and Guangxi came to an unexpected end in August 1921. In that month, with the assistance of the revolutionary militarist Chen Jiongming of Guangdong, Sun Yat-sen was able to defeat Lu Rongting and brought both Guangdong and Guangxi under his rule. Lu had been an ally of Sun Yat-sen in 1915 and 1916 when both of them were opposed to Yuan Shikai's founding of a new dynasty, but since then Lu had been acting more and more like a typical warlord. He had promoted gambling and opium smuggling, tried to expand his territory by invading other provinces, practiced military rule, and brutally executed quite a few Nationalists. In August 1920, Sun Yat-sen and Chen Jiongming were able to expel Lu's troops from Guangdong, and a year later they brought war to Guangxi and defeated Lu at his home. Sun Yat-sen then established a headquarters in Guilin and began to prepare for his northern expedition. It was during his stay in Guilin that he met and talked with the Comintern agent Maring (Henk Sneevliet) in December 1921, which contributed to the creation of the First United Front between the Nationalists and Communists.

Ma Junwu and the other Nationalists from Guangxi, including Wei Baqun, moved back to their native province along with Sun Yat-sen. As the most influential Nationalist from Guangxi, Ma was immediately made its governor. He then appointed some members of the Association for Reforming Guangxi as officials in the provincial and county governments. Ma wanted Wei Baqun to serve as the magistrate of Nandan County, situated north of Donglan near the border between Guangxi and Guizhou. Perhaps Ma knew Wei Baqun was familiar with the local conditions of Nandan, and had close relations with Governor Lu Tao of Guizhou. In any case, Wei Baqun turned down the appointment. Ma then offered him the position of the magistrate of Donglan, but again Wei Baqun deferred, knowing that Governor Ma did not have the troops to secure effective control of either Nandan or Donglan. Wei Baqun was not the only candidate who refused to take on positions of county magistrate at that time. Ma's second choice for the position of the magistrate of Nandan did the same.[38]

Not taking Governor Ma's appointment allowed Wei Baqun to spend more time with his friends in Nanning, and he had frequent discussions about how to reform rural Guangxi with his friends in the Association for Reforming Guangxi. Specifically, they tried to find ways to protect people from the oppression of the local powerful families. Wei Baqun's friends believed that to curb the power of the local tyrants, who usually relied on local militias to enforce their power, it was necessary to create a people's police system, which could use force to protect people. They decided to test their theory in a county near Nanning. The magistrate of that county, who was a leading member of the Association for Reforming Guangxi, ordered each township to create a police team consisting of eleven owner-peasants selected by county officials. Villagers would then elect two from the eleven to serve as the leaders of the team.[39]

This experiment, although short-lived, was very significant for Wei Baqun and his future movement because it confirmed his drift toward the conviction that a successful movement was predicated on a loyal armed force. The successful nationwide military campaign against Yuan Shikai, in which he personally participated, and Sun Yat-sen's recent victory over Lu Rongting, which he had closely observed, must have already shown Wei Baqun the importance of an effective military force. Governor Ma also emphasized the importance of military power, arguing that in order to build a new Guangxi it was necessary to create a new Guangxi army to replace the armies of the militarists.[40] In fact, Governor Ma was soon to learn a bloody lesson about the importance of having a loyal military force. In May 1922, Ma had to leave Guangxi, and while retreating from Nanning by steamship, he was attacked at midnight by Yu Zuobai's troops under the command of General Li Zongren, the would-be leader of the New Guangxi Clique, although Li and Yu had pledged their allegiance to Sun Yat-sen and Governor Ma. Yu attacked the steamship for the weapons and money. Ma's small guard unit was no match for Yu's forces, and at least ten guards were killed. Ma's concubine lost her life protecting the governor, and Ma had to surrender all the weapons on the ship to buy his life.[41] It is ironic that a few years later, Yu would become Governor Ma's successor as both the governor of Guangxi and Wei Baqun's patron.

It did not take long for Wei Baqun and others to discover that the warlord army of Guangdong was not necessarily better than that of Guangxi. The soldiers were not well disciplined and the generals liked to interfere in government affairs. Governor Ma admitted that his orders could not go beyond the gates of Nanning and that he had no control over the different armies stationed in various parts of the province. He had to appoint Cantonese who had the support of the Guangdong Army as magistrates and officials in the more prosperous counties of Guangxi, and that was probably one of the reasons he could not offer Wei Baqun any position in or near Nanning.[42] When the *New Guangxi Daily*, which was run by some leading members of the Association for Reforming Guangxi, reported the wrongdoings of the Guangdong soldiers, the officers and soldiers of the Guangdong army reacted by destroying the office of the editors, beating a worker, and threatening the editors-in-chief. A week after this incident, Wei Baqun decided to leave Nanning for Donglan. When asked why he wanted to leave, Wei Baqun replied that he was fed up with the Guangdong Army and could not take it anymore.

"What are you planning to do after leaving us?" The friend asked again.

"Aside from making revolution, what else can I do?" Wei Baqun answered.

Wei Baqun parted with his new patron Ma Junwu and other friends in late 1921. Whereas most scholars believe that he arrived home on the Mid-Autumn Festival which fell on September 16 in that year, meaning that he left Nanning at the latest in early September, there is also evidence suggesting that he was still in Nanning in late November. One source mentions that Wei Baqun returned to Donglan in winter 1921. Still others argue that he first returned to Donglan in September and then came back to Nanning to meet with Sun Yat-sen, who visited the city in late November. Some have claimed that Wei Baqun was among the Guangxi dignitaries who had a photo taken with Sun Yat-sen in Nanning on November 26, 1921.[43] If Wei Baqun was indeed in that photo, then he must have either stayed in Nanning until late November and did not return to Donglan until after that, or he returned earlier and then came back. In any case, if we do not count the brief period he spent in Donglan in late 1915 and early 1916, Wei Baqun had been away from home for nearly seven years by late 1921.

Governor Ma's tenure ended a few months after Wei Baqun's departure from Nanning. In mid-1922, Sun Yat-sen had to return to Guangdong with his troops to suppress a rebellion back home launched by his former friend, Chen Jiongming, thus ending Sun's ten-month occupation and rule of Guangxi. Ma Junwu had to move his government from Nanning to Wuzhou in eastern Guangxi and eventually had to return to Guangdong. His political career ended four years later when he was expelled from the Chinese Nationalist Party for his opposition to the First United Front. It is therefore logical to argue that since Ma did not support class struggle and was not friendly toward the Communists, he would not offer much support to Wei Baqun even if he had stayed on as the governor of Guangxi.[44]

The Association for Reforming Guangxi did not survive long either. Some of its members, Wei Baqun included, would soon become Communists or leftist Nationalists, and Wei Baqun would receive the most substantial support from these leftists a few years later. Specifically, Lei Jingtian was to become the head of the Guangxi branch of the CCP and thus Wei Baqun's direct superior within the party; Chen Xiewu, Chen Mianshu, and others played a crucial part in helping Wei Baqun defeat his enemies in Donglan in 1926, and Chen Mianshu, one of those good friends of Wei Baqun who came to say goodbye before Wei left Nanning for Donglan in late 1921, would play an important role in bringing Wei Baqun into the CCP. On the other hand, some other members of the association would become right-wingers in the Kuomintang (KMT) and therefore Wei Baqun's enemies. The leading member of this group would be Huang Xuchu. A department head in Ma Junwu's provincial government, Huang would emerge as the governor of Guangxi in the late 1920s and early 1930s and would play a significant part in suppressing Wei Baqun's movement. For Wei Baqun, the year in Guangzhou and Nanning was well spent. He made new connections and learned new ideas and methods. Although he did not hold any official position in the government or military when he returned to Donglan, his experiences, connections and ideas made him much more powerful than he had been seven years before when he started his first journey, or five years earlier when he began his political-military career.

One of the unsolved mysteries of Wei Baqun's life is whether he converted to anarchism during this period; if he did, then when and how did he become interested in anarchism? A former follower of Wei Baqun later claimed that Wei became an anarchist in 1919 and 1920 during his stay in the Guizhou Army and remained one until 1927 or 1928. Some of Wei Baqun's CCP comrades shared that belief.[45] Although Wei Baqun did not leave any writings to confirm his connections to anarchism, it is tempting to argue that he very likely did come under the influence of anarchism during this period for three important reasons. First, anarchist writings were accessible to Wei Baqun; second, anarchism might also be attractive to him; and third, some of Wei Baqun's actions and words did reflect anarchist leanings.

Anarchism was quite popular in China at the beginning of the twentieth century. Both Arif Derlik and Peter Zarrow agree that between 1900 and 1920 anarchism was the most influential radical ideology in China partly because it was the only Western radical philosophy translated into Chinese in any detail.[46] Anarchism was so popular among Sun Yat-sen's followers that after the 1911 Revolution Sun even considered making Chongming Island off the shore of Shanghai an experimental zone for the anarchists.[47] Anarchism became even more popular in China after 1912 for two reasons: first, the overthrow of the Qing government allowed many anarchists who had been involved in anti-Qing activities to return to China from Japan, France and other countries; second, their disappointment with the new republic prompted many intellectuals to realize that it was not just the Qing government that should be overthrown. They now believed that government itself was the source of all the problems. Therefore, all governments, including the republican system, should be abolished.

It is estimated that around 1919 there were approximately fifty anarchist organizations in China, which published no less than eighty magazines and pamphlets.[48] It would not have been difficult for Wei Baqun to find some of these magazines in Chongqing, Shanghai, Guangzhou, and other places he visited during this period. He might also have learned about the new village and work-study programs that the anarchists had organized. In Sichuan, the first anarchist organization was created in Daxian County in 1917 or 1918, and Daxian was not very far from Chongqing where Wei Baqun lived until

October 1920. In August 1920, Chongqing had its first anarchist organization.[49] Additionally, Wei Baqun's short-term patron Ma Junwu, although primarily a Nationalist, was interested in and familiar with the various radical ideologies, including anarchism. As early as 1902, Ma had translated an important text on the history of anarchism into Chinese. In his preface to the text he argued that it is legitimate to kill all the despots in the world. As a trained scientist, he had a hand in making the explosives used by the revolutionaries to assassinate Manchu officials, and he was also a close friend of such prominent Chinese anarchists as Liu Shipei and Cai Yuanpei. Ma could have helped further familiarize Wei Baqun with anarchism. On the other hand, because Wei Baqun could not read any foreign language, it was not easy for him to learn about other radical ideologies in China during the first two decades of the twentieth century because most of their works had not been translated into Chinese.

There are elements in anarchism that suited Wei Baqun's personality and conformed to his beliefs. For Wei Baqun, the most appealing anarchist idea was probably the contempt for authority. As Arif Derlik explains, in the Chinese context authority could mean government, family or tradition,[50] and Wei Baqun had butted heads against all of the above. He would also have liked the anarchist ideas of communal solidarity, individual autonomy, and the sanctity of labor, its condemnation of imperialism and capitalism, and its concerns about the conditions of the peasants and workers. The Chinese anarchists were the first political group in China to seriously advocate and engage in the study of the conditions of Chinese peasants, to educate and mobilize the peasants, and to work out a theory that would allow the peasants to play an important role in the revolution.[51] When Wei Baqun began his peasant work in late 1921 neither the KMT nor the newly founded CCP had shown serious interest in the peasant movement. If Wei Baqun had to be reminded or inspired by someone about the importance of the peasant in 1921, that someone was much more likely to be an anarchist than a Nationalist or Communist.

Sometimes Wei Baqun's actions, decisions, and speeches showed some anarchist tendencies. It is arguable that anarchist teachings factored into his decision against assuming the position of county magistrate that Governor Ma offered him in 1921. Later, once he created a revolutionary government in Donglan, he did not make himself its leader as many would have expected, but gave the position of magistrate to one of his followers. In 1926, Communist Yan Min discovered in the notebook of one of Wei Baqun's local followers the questions, "how can there be equality if there is a government? and how can there be freedom if there are laws?" Yan saw the questions as indications of anarchist influence, and he explained to that follower that not all governments and laws were dreadful and that the influence of anarchism should be eradicated. Obviously, Yan Min would see Wei Baqun as the source of anarchist influence in Donglan.[52]

It is one thing to argue that anarchism had some influence on Wei Baqun, but quite another to claim that Wei Baqun was an ardent anarchist. Although anarchism was very popular in China in the early twentieth century, not many Chinese intellectuals would identify themselves as anarchists. To many of them, anarchism was one element constituting their overall political philosophies, but not the only or even the most important component in their thought. It is believed that prominent Chinese political and cultural leaders of that time, including Sun Yat-sen, Li Dazhao, Liang Shuming, Mao Zedong, Zhou Enlai, and Peng Pai, were all influenced by anarchism.[53] According to one estimate, among the fifty-two members of the CCP at the time of its founding in 1921, twenty-two showed anarchist tendencies. In 1920, seven of the nine members of the Communist executive committee in Guangzhou were anarchists.[54] These individuals were influenced by anarchism or would even call themselves anarchists, but they also embraced other ideologies. In this aspect, these early Chinese intellectuals were not very different from the traditional Chinese literati who could be Confucian, Taoist, and Buddhist at one and the same time. Later intellectuals, particularly Communist revolutionaries, moved away from this tradition when they began to emphasize the purity of thought and an exclusive conversion to one ideology.

In Wei Baqun's case, although he might have come under the influence of anarchism, it is hard to prove that he was a genuine or loyal anarchist. There is no indication that he ever joined any anarchist organization or contributed to any anarchist journal. Like his patron Ma Junwu, anarchism was probably one of the ideologies that he was interested in. A leading Communist from Guangxi reported in early 1929 that Wei Baqun "had read some anarchist books and magazines, liked to talk about anarchism, but was actually a leftist Nationalist."[55]

It is also likely that he was interested in some, but not all, anarchist ideas. As his movement began and grew, it became more and more obvious that Wei Baqun did not follow all the major anarchist principles. For instance, the Chinese anarchists were the ones who popularized the phrase social revolution in China and Wei Baqun began to use that phrase in the late 1910s. Whereas for the anarchists, social revolution primarily meant education and the spread of a new morality, it meant something quite different to Wei Baqun. It has been suggested that the most popular variant of anarchism in China was that advocated by the Russian anarchist Pyotr Kropotkin, which emphasized mutual aid, laborism, and pacifism.[56] Wei Baqun would support laborism and would also accept mutual aid if it was class-based, but he was hardly a pacifist. Finally, the anarchists were against any kind of government. Although Wei Baqun was against Yuan Shikai's government, the governments of the old and new militarists, and Chiang Kai-shek's Nationalist government, he was not against all governments. He was actually deeply involved in the creation of a new type of government.

If it is relatively easy to prove the anarchist influence on Wei Baqun during this period, it is much harder to confirm that Marxism had also become an important element in his thought during his first journey. Some historians in China have argued that during his years in Sichuan Wei Baqun had already begun to read magazines like *New Youth* and the *Guide Weekly*, which was the organ of the CCP, and that during Wei Baqun's stay in Guangzhou, "he was greatly inspired and stimulated by the Hailufeng peasant movement led by Communist Peng Pai."[57] Such claims are problematic because Wei Baqun was in Sichuan from early 1916 to August 1920, but the *Guide Weekly* did not begin to publish until September 1922. It was also impossible for Wei Baqun to be inspired by the Hailufeng peasant movement during his stay in Guangzhou in 1920 and 1921 because that movement did not begin until mid-1922 and did not become influential until 1923 and 1924. It is possible that Wei Baqun had read or heard about Marxism or Communism, as Li Dazhao had already edited a special issue on Marxism for *New Youth* and because Wei Baqun was so close to Ma Junwu, the first translator of *The Communist Manifesto*, but it is hard to verify that Marxism had already had a strong influence on Wei Baqun during this early stage.

CHAPTER THREE

The First Revolt

1921–1924

Wei Baqun's first journey consisted of two trips separated by a brief stay in his home village. The first was a personal excursion and the second a political and military undertaking that lasted much longer than the first. If his first trip won him admiration from the young people in Donglan, then the second gave them reasons to worship him. During his first tour, Wei Baqun did not accomplish anything substantial other than seeing and experiencing the wider world. His second outing was much more fruitful. Back in his village, Wei Baqun could now share all his achievements with his young friends: He had helped bring down Emperor Yuan Shikai from his throne; he had not only attended but more importantly graduated from Guizhou Military Academy; he had served as a staff officer in the Guizhou Army and lived for a while in the large city of Chongqing; he had revisited Shanghai and Guangzhou, which were even larger and more important than Chongqing; he had joined the Chinese Nationalist Party and become an official follower of the revered leader Sun Yat-sen; he had become a friend of two provincial governors—Governor Lu Tao of Guizhou and Governor Ma Junwu of Guangxi; and he had twice turned down offers of the position of county magistrate, a gesture that generated more respect than if he had taken the offers.

He shared with his friends not only his achievements, but also the ideas acquired during his long journey, particularly those about social revolution. It did not take long for him to persuade his friends that Donglan needed a revolution. Although forces loyal to Sun Yat-sen had taken Nanning and the area around it, Sun had no control over a remote area like Donglan, which was under the rule of General Liu Rifu of Baise and General Meng Renqian of Hechi. Both generals were former subordinates of Lu Rongting. They collected exorbitant taxes from the people, but did not provide much protection. On the day Wei Baqun returned home, a group of bandits sacked the county seat and occupied the town for more than a month.

Among those young people who now gathered around Wei Baqun were his cousin Chen Bomin, and three of those who followed him into the Guizhou Army in 1916: Huang Bangwei, Huang Daquan, and Liao Yuanfang. Also included in this group were Ya Sumin, a graduate of Nanning School of Law and Politics; Qin Kongxian, who had studied at the Number Two Normal School in Guilin; and Huang Shuxiang and Wei Mingzhou, two other educated young villagers from Wuzhuan. Almost all of them, except Liao Yuanfang, were from Donglan, and all had received at least an elementary school level education and can be thought of as rural intellectuals. Finally, they were all old friends of Wei Baqun.

In October 1921 or later, Wei Baqun gathered his friends in Dongli and together they decided to create an organization named the Association for Reforming Donglan. Obviously, it was Wei Baqun who coined the name and in many ways this association was a replica of the Association for Reforming Guangxi. With only about twenty founding members, its organization was simpler than that of its model. Like the Association for Reforming Guangxi, most members of the Association for Reforming Donglan were educated people, although on average their level of education was lower than that of the members of its model. This was a group of determined young men who shared a strong desire for change and resistance as well as a spirit of solidarity and militancy. They were similar to the dissident elites who had led or were leading revolutions in other parts of the world.[1] In later years, most would die for the revolutions they helped bring about. A few would be branded traitors, and at least three would suffer death at Wei Baqun's hands.

The political programs of the Association for Reforming Donglan, which resembled those of its model, called for the overthrow of warlords, corrupt officials, local tyrants, and evil gentry, and the reform of the old politics, old economy, and old culture of Donglan. It is apparent that Wei Baqun was trying to transplant what he had learned from his friends in Guangzhou and Nanning to Donglan. If the small anti-Yuan army was the first military unit Wei Baqun created, then the Association for Reforming Donglan was the first political organization he founded, and this move signaled the beginning of local revolution in Donglan.

What distinguished the Association for Reforming Donglan from the Association for Reforming Guangxi is that from the very beginning Wei Baqun and his friends attached great importance to winning the support of the local people, including the peasants. Members of the Association for Reforming Guangxi tended to work harder on winning the support of friendly militarists than that of the masses. Wei Baqun and his friends in Donglan, however, were much closer to the people physically and the people were the only source of support they could exploit, because there were no friendly militarists in or near Donglan for them to work on. On market days, Wei Baqun and his friends would go to Wuzhuan and other towns in Donglan to make speeches to people on the streets, and Wei Baqun's favorite topics were "social revolution" and "Guangxi is miserable."[2]

The various taxes imposed by the local militarists caused the greatest resentment among the local people, and this conforms to Philip Kuhn's assessment that in China at that time the most hated of the new taxes were those levied by "warlord regimes of doubtful legitimacy."[3] In 1921, peasants in the Right River region had to pay no less than thirty types of taxes. The peasants in Donglan had to pay taxes to both General Liu Rifu in Baise and General Meng Renqian in Hechi, and in 1922 the taxes for Donglan were more than ten times higher than before.[4] Wei Baqun and his friends decided to focus their first movement on the tax issue, and in early 1922 they called for a citizens' assembly at the newly created Yucai Advanced Elementary School in Wuzhuan to discuss the issue of taxation. People were particularly unhappy about a special tax that General Liu Rifu was collecting to pay for the movement of his troops.

It was decided at the assembly that Wei Baqun and Chen Bomin would travel to Baise to plead with General Liu as delegates of the Donglan people. Surprisingly, once they arrived in Baise, General Liu agreed to meet with them. They explained to the general how the special tax had become a huge burden for the people of Donglan, whose lives were already miserable because of natural disasters and the "exploitation of evil gentry and corrupt officials." Unexpectedly, the general immediately agreed to abolish the special tax. Liu Rifu even refused to admit that it had been his idea to collect such a tax. The general was probably awed by Wei Baqun's military experiences and powerful connections, particularly his relations with Governor Ma, but it could also be true that General Liu was not a typical brutal and greedy militarist. Huang Shaohong, a rival of General Liu who became Liu's boss in 1924, later described Liu as "an honest person without ambition who enjoyed the popular support in the Baise area."[5] To seal this first victory, Wei Baqun and Chen Bomin asked the general to put his words on paper and the general agreed. Wei and Chen then rushed home with the general's order that the special tax be abolished. For the people of Donglan, this written order from General Liu not only removed an unpopular tax, but also evinced how powerful Wei Baqun had become. Now even the local powerful families had to recognize the change of Wei Baqun's status. They might be wondering why the powerful general would be willing to listen to this former villager who did not command a single soldier or possess any official position.[6]

Shortly after this victory, Wei Baqun launched his attack on Du Ba, a landlord and former official in Wuzhuan. If Wei Baqun's family was wealthy but not powerful, then the Du family was both wealthy and powerful. Du's ancestors came from a place near Nanning. Whereas most sources fail to mention his ethnicity, there is one account holding that the Dus were of Han origin.[7] However, this does not mean that he was not Zhuang, since many Zhuang families claimed Han heritage. Du's father had served as the commander of the official militia organization of Donglan; his brother had served as a county-level official, and so had Du Ba himself.[8] In 1919, Du Ba and a group of local dignitaries had formed a committee for the construction of Yucai Advanced Elementary School in Wuzhuan, which was Donglan's second advanced elementary school. The fact that Wei Baqun's family was not represented on the committee further confirms that the Wei family was wealthy but not prestigious.

The committee collected eight hundred silver dollars from the residents of Wuzhuan to build the school. The construction was completed in late 1920 and the school began to operate that same year.[9] Yucai stood not far from the Tower of the Literary Star, which was the symbol of Wuzhuan at that time. The tower was a three-story structure constructed between 1905 and 1907 with public funds raised by some local elites who were upset that their district had produced very few higher-level degree holders. They hoped that bringing literary deities to the town would better the chance of local students in the civil service examinations. On the top floor of the tower was a statue of Cang Jie, the legendary inventor of the Chinese characters, on the second floor was a portrait of the Literary Star, and the first floor housed the memorial tablet of Chen Hongmou, a famous eighteenth-century Confucian scholar-official from Guangxi.[10] Obviously, the tower could have no effect on the fortunes of the degree candidates from Wuzhuan since the civil service examinations had already been abolished before the tower was fully constructed. Again, Du Ba was one of the elites involved in the construction of the tower, whereas Wei Baqun's family was not represented in that group.

It became clear later that the construction of the school did not cost as much as eight hundred silver dollars, but Du Ba was reluctant to pay back the surplus. In early 1922, Wei Baqun and his friends from the Association for Reforming Donglan gathered delegates from Yucai and various villages, and together they confronted Du Ba and demanded an explanation. One account holds that more than one hundred people followed Wei Baqun in this movement and the confrontation took place at the school, but according to another source, as many as four hundred people went with Wei Baqun to Du Ba's house and confronted him there.[11] A third report claims in excess of two hundred participated.[12] Most sources agree that Du Ba, who was deeply embarrassed, immediately gave back the surplus. Wei Baqun and his followers also confronted two other local power holders and forced them to hand out several guns that had been purchased with public funds. Wei Baqun's close comrades Chen Bomin, Liao Yuanfang, Huang Daquan, and Huang Bangwei were all standing by him during the confrontation.[13] The three student delegates from Yucai who participated in the confrontation, Chen Hongtao, Bai Hanyun, and Huang Fangri,[14] later became Wei Baqun's loyal supporters and would all die for the peasant revolution.

This was one of many cases occurring in China at that time showing that modernization often went hand in hand with corruption. The clash with Du Ba, together with the earlier confrontation with General Liu Rifu, supports Lucien Bianco's argument that taxation and the oppression of the weak by the powerful were more prominent causes of peasant discontent and spontaneous peasant resistance than rent, debt and some other factors.[15] Although the incident involving Du Ba was caused by the construction of the new school, it is different from the anti-modernization movements targeting new schools and other modernizing reforms that were prevalent in China about a decade before.[16] Wei Baqun and his followers were against corruption, but not the new school and modernization.

The two conflicts with Du Ba and General Liu Rifu efficiently illustrate that Wei Baqun was quick at grasping popular sentiment and very adept at using moral power in fighting the local rulers. In both cases, Wei Baqun managed to accumulate mass support before the confrontation. He went to challenge General Liu and Du Ba not as an individual or a member of a small group like the Association for Reforming Donglan, but as a delegate or leader of the masses. The power holders were frightened because they thought that Wei Baqun had support from provincial and national leaders such as Sun Yat-sen, Governors Ma Junwu and Lu Tao, as well as the local people. This was the incipient and moderate phase of Wei Baqun's movement when his approach was primarily reformist and peaceful.

There are conflicting accounts of Wei Baqun's activities from late 1921 to early 1923. For example, different dates have been proposed for the founding of the Association for Reforming Donglan and Wei Baqun's first confrontation with General Liu. As for the conflict with Du Ba, we have already noted the disagreements about the number of people involved. Whereas some believe that this conflict took place in March 1922, others have argued that it occurred in August 1922. Although most concur that Du Ba immediately paid back the three hundred silver dollars, there are also suggestions that Du Ba initially was very angry with Wei Baqun and others and refused to submit his account book. He did not pay back the money until Wei Baqun and his followers challenged him for a second time, which, according to one account, did not take place until 1923![17] Again, in most cases the different accounts agree on major issues and aspects and only disagree on details.

Another controversial event is Wei Baqun's imprisonment in late 1922. According to some sources, on the lunar day of September 9, 1922, which was a festival, Wei Baqun invited at least 180 friends from different districts of

Donglan as well as neighboring counties to his home for a gathering. Together they climbed to the top of Mount Yinhaizhou, where they took an oath by drinking wine mixed with chicken blood and passing through a gate of knives. Some claimed that in their oath Wei Baqun and his new allies pledged to join the fight against imperialism, warlords, corrupt officials, and evil gentry. Some scholars went as far as to argue that at the meeting Wei Baqun and his friends also expressed their support for the Russian Communists and their hope of organizing peasant associations and citizens' self-defense forces.[18] However, many other sources show that it was impossible for such a gathering to take place in September 1922 because Wei Baqun was in jail in that month.

This personal danger was a result of the political disorder besetting Guangxi at that time. After the departure of Sun Yat-sen and Governor Ma Junwu in 1922, there emerged many autonomous armies in Guangxi to fill the political vacuum. These were either remnants of former armies of the Old Guangxi Clique or bandit groups, and some of them had even been affiliated with Sun Yat-sen's Nationalist Party before. Nanning, the provincial capital, was taken over by General Lin Junting, a subordinate of former Governor Lu Rongting. When Lu was defeated by Sun Yat-sen in 1921, Lin survived the attack by escaping to northern Guangxi with his troops. A close friend of General Lu Tao, who was then governor of Guizhou, Lin had Governor Lu's permission to subsist on the opium trade between Guizhou and Guangxi. General Lu was obviously double-dealing at that moment. It was Sun Yat-sen who appointed him as the governor of Guizhou, yet he was secretly protecting and supporting Sun Yat-sen's enemy Lin Junting. After occupying Nanning, Lin was recognized as the commander-in-chief of all the autonomous armies in Guangxi, although he had actual control over only the area around Nanning.[19] General Liu Rifu in Baise also pledged allegiance to General Lin.

One of these autonomous armies temporarily occupied Donglan in 1922, and its commander was General Huang Qi. In April 1922, a squad of General Huang's soldiers spent a night at Wei Baqun's house, and Wei had a chat with the soldiers. After hearing their complaints about abuses in the army, Wei Baqun encouraged them to desert. The soldiers took his advice and ran away that very evening. General Huang was infuriated and he sent soldiers to take Wei Baqun, who escaped shortly before the soldiers reached his house. Wei Baqun first fled to Liuzhou because he had heard that a unit of the Guizhou Army had arrived there and thought his old friends in the Guizhou Army would offer him protection. After reaching Liuzhou he was disappointed to find that the Guizhou Army had left. He then went to Nanning and hid with a friend. General Huang and his soldiers later also arrived in Nanning and the general even became a deputy commander-in-chief of the united autonomous army.

According to some sources, Wei Baqun stayed in hiding for eight months, but was then recognized on the street of Nanning and arrested.[20] A more believable account holds that Wei Baqun was in hiding for only two months. He was arrested in June 1922 and released in December 1922.[21] The Nationalist Huang Xuchu reported that one day, as Wei Baqun was about to be taken out for execution under Huang Qi's order, Wei Hongqing, the former hereditary lord of Fengshan County, who was a close friend of General Huang, happened to be on the spot, and he appealed on behalf of Wei Baqun. General Huang then decided to spare Wei Baqun's life in exchange for six hundred silver dollars. This was a huge amount of money at that time considering that it cost only five hundred silver dollars to build Yucai Advanced Elementary School. Later, Wei Baqun's followers would kill Wei Hongqing's entire family.[22] To Huang Xuchu this shows how ungrateful Wei Baqun was to his savior. Unfortunately for Wei Baqun, this was not his last dangerous encounter with General Huang Qi.

Wei Baqun's imprisonment in 1922 was more painful than his previous incarceration because he actually faced the possibility of execution and the Wei family had to pay a large sum of money to buy his life. Wei Baqun wrote an autobiography during his imprisonment, but unfortunately it is no longer extant.[23] All third-party accounts agree that Wei Baqun was indeed arrested and imprisoned and that the Wei family had to pay six hundred silver dollars to have him released, but most accounts completely omit former lord Wei Hongqing and disagree on the dates of Wei Baqun's arrest and release. It is possible that if Wei Hongqing indeed saved Wei Baqun's life, then his presence in Nanning on Wei Baqun's execution day was very likely not entirely accidental. He probably went to see General Huang at the request of Wei Baqun's family. In theory, at least, Wei Baqun was a blood relative of Wei Hongqing because they were both related to the former lords of Donglan. It is also possible that General Huang Qi was more interested in earning some cash than killing Wei Baqun, so he invited Wei Hongqing to Nanning to help extort money from Wei Baqun's family.

The accounts also disagree on the role of Wei Baqun in the soldiers' desertion, the reason for his presence in Nanning, and the role of Du Ba in Wei Baqun's arrest. Huang Xuchu and some others thought that the desertion did occur, that Wei Baqun did play a significant role in instigating the desertion, that Wei had to travel to Nanning to escape from his pursuers, and that Du Ba had nothing to do with Wei Baqun's imprisonment. Some other accounts, however, hold that if a desertion did occur, then Wei Baqun had nothing to do with it, that Wei Baqun was in Nanning to discuss with an old friend "how to save the country and the people," and that the cause of his imprisonment was Du Ba's false accusation. It is suggested that Wei Baqun himself believed that Du Ba was the one who got him arrested.[24] Although it is quite apparent that Du Ba did have a strong motivation to put Wei Baqun behind bars, or to make Wei Baqun feel the pain of losing several hundred silver dollars, or even to put Wei Baqun to death, it is not certain whether or not Du Ba had the power to persuade General Huang to do any of these things if the latter had no grudge at all against Wei Baqun.

The argument that Wei Baqun was in Nanning to discuss revolution and national affairs with his friends is not very convincing. His Nationalist friends, including Governor Ma Junwu, had all left Nanning, and there was nothing for him to do in a city under the control of the old-fashioned militarists. Another reason why Wei Baqun's trip to Nanning in 1922 was more likely to escape from a danger rather than for visiting some friends was that sometime during that year he had taken a new wife, after being a widower for five years. His second wife was Chen Lanfen, and like his first wife Lanfen was also from Dongli Village. Wei Baqun's marriage with his first wife, Huang Fengtao, could have been an arranged one since his grandfather was certainly alive and his father was also probably alive when the two were married, but the Zhuang men and women had much more freedom to court and choose a spouse than their Han counterparts, and overall the arranged marriages of the Zhuang were not as arbitrary and forced as those practiced in the Han areas. The fact that Huang Fengtao and Wei Baqun were from the same village indicates that the two had known each other for a long time before the marriage. According to folk stories, Wei Baqun's marriage with his second wife Chen Lanfen was purely a love match, partly because by 1922, Wei Baqun had been the patriarch of the Wei family for a number of years, and therefore had full freedom in arranging his own marriage. His new love would make him more reluctant to take a long journey to Nanning without a serious reason.

Despite claims that Wei Baqun and his friends had already collected quite a few weapons, had begun to recruit young peasants for military training, and had created a citizens' self-defense army by 1922,[25] there is no indication that Wei Baqun had already created an armed force before his second imprisonment. His confrontations with both General Liu Rifu and Du Ba were entirely peaceful. There is no doubt that Wei Baqun had already realized the importance of creating an armed force before his second imprisonment, but he was probably too busy in the months before his imprisonment to focus his attention on such a matter. Or perhaps he needed a little more stimuli to prompt him on to the path of armed revolution.

His second imprisonment provided that stimulus. At the moment he was set free, Wei Baqun told his friends that, "These troops are all bandits and I'll wipe them out."[26] Before the second imprisonment, his experience with Liu Rifu and Du Ba seemed to convince Wei Baqun that his connections with powerful provincial and national leaders as well as his popular local support would serve to protect him. But by late 1922 he had come to realize that because Governor Ma and the Nationalists had handed power back to the Old Guangxi Clique, he no longer had any powerful patrons, and therefore the only way for him to subdue these corrupt power holders was to use collective violence. His second imprisonment had made this crystal clear to him.

After being released from prison in late 1922, Wei Baqun immediately returned to Donglan to resume and expand his movement. His first move was to transform the Association for Reforming Donglan from a small elite group into a mass organization, which he decided to name the Citizens' Assembly. Before his second imprisonment he had relied mostly on the small opposition elite in Wuzhuan and other places. His strongest supporters had been the teachers, graduates, and students of local schools and the delegates of the villages, who were also people with some education. Following his release from prison, he began to mobilize the peasants and tried to bring them into permanent organizations. In addition to having a much wider social base, the Citizens' Assembly also had its armed wing in the form of a Citizens' Self-defense Army. Members of the Association for Reforming Donglan naturally became leaders of both Citizens' Assembly and the Citizens' Self-defense Army, and Wei Baqun himself became the commander-in-chief of that army. Wei Baqun dispatched Huang Daquan and Huang Bangwei to organize the peasants in Wuzhuan and the Western Mountains in western Donglan, and he sent Ya Sumin, Qin Kongxian, and some other followers to northern, southeastern, and southern Donglan to create citizens' self-defense units.[27]

It was during this period that Wei Baqun began to pay serious attention to the Western Mountains of Donglan. The region consisted of a cluster of high stony mountains with large and small caves and many small plains. For outsiders the region was not easily accessible. Wei Baqun's battle experience, military training, and his plan to wage war led him to recognize the strategic importance of the region. The residents of the area were the poorest among the local population and therefore easily agitated. The Yao, who made up the majority of the population and who had been living under miserable conditions, were particularly receptive to Wei Baqun's revolutionary messages about economic, political, and ethnic equality. Wei Baqun personally visited some villages in the region and made speeches to the villagers. In order to win the trust of the poor Yao residents in the area, he wore straw sandals and bamboo hat.[28] This was the beginning of his alliance with the Yao people. He also visited other important settlements in the county to help his comrades with mobilization and organization. His skills at speaking Zhuang, Yao, Cantonese, and Mandarin, and his talent at composing and singing folksongs made it easy for him to communicate with the villagers. Gradually he became known among the villagers as "Bage" (Elder Brother Ba).

The weapons of the citizens' self-defense army came from various sources. Wei Baqun and his followers forced local power holders to turn in the weapons they had purchased with public funds.[29] Some peasants already owned weapons and would take them into the army. Wei Baqun also invited a blacksmith to help make guns and organized a team to produce hand grenades and land mines.

The violent phase of Wei Baqun's revolution formally began on June 16, 1923. On that day, Wei Baqun took a group of armed peasants to the county seat to attack Wei Longfu, a powerful landlord and the brutal commander of the Donglan militia. Wei Longfu was a descendant of the hereditary lords of Donglan and owned more than two hundred mu of land.[30] Wei Baqun picked him as the first target because among all the powerful local rulers Wei Longfu had incurred the greatest popular indignation. The Citizens' Assembly received at least five hundred letters of complaints against him shortly after its creation, and he was accused of all kinds of crimes, including looting, raping, and killing innocent people.[31] On one occasion, he killed six of the seven members of one family just because the family had failed to pay an extra tax of ten silver dollars. He had eight private guards who also served as his messengers. Families that were visited by any of these guards had to pay a straw sandal fee calculated according to the distance between the family and Wei Longfu's residence. These families also had to provide meals for these guards, who liked to tell the villagers that they preferred a fancy meal with meat dishes because, "we are townsfolk and we don't eat vegetables."[32] Wei Longfu even maintained a private prison in his residence and partly because of that he became known as "the second magistrate."[33]

Wei Baqun might have preferred to make Du Ba the first target of his armed force, but Wei Longfu was obviously a better choice simply because he was more powerful and brutal than Du Ba. The Self-defense Army would earn more prestige and win more popular support if it could demonstrate to the people that it was willing and able to take on the most powerful and most hated local ruler. Although public opinion was the most important factor prompting Wei Baqun to attack Wei Longfu, his personal feelings likely also played a significant part in his decision. In the previous year, Wei Longfu had offended Wei Baqun by trying to stop members of the Association for Reforming Donglan from making revolutionary speeches. Wei Baqun's loyal follower, Huang Bangwei, also had a burning hatred toward Wei Longfu, which would surely further strengthen Wei Baqun's ill feelings toward the latter. Wei Longfu had attempted to take Bangwei's sister as his concubine, leading her to commit suicide. Later, Wei Longfu forced Bangwei's father to pay a poll tax, causing the old man to lose his mind. Huang Bangwei also confirmed that Wei Longfu and Du Ba were close collaborators.[34]

Wei Baqun's armed group took a two-front approach upon entering the county seat. Wei Baqun went to visit the county council of representatives, the county magistrate Meng Yuanliang, and Commander Luo Wenjian of a battalion of General Liu Rifu's troops, to ask for approval to attack Wei Longfu, or at least to ensure that they would not act to protect Wei Longfu. Meanwhile, a group of armed peasants secretly surrounded Wei Longfu's house, making sure that he would not be able to escape. They were ordered not to attack before Wei Baqun finished his negotiations with the political and military leaders.

One source holds that the attack was a great success: Wei Baqun's men stormed Wei Longfu's house, found him trembling underneath his bed, drew him out, tied him up, and carried him triumphantly back to Dongli.[35] However, most other sources concur that the attack did not go well. The soldiers were so eager to punish Wei Longfu that they attacked while Wei Baqun was still negotiating. They easily put Wei Longfu under control and also seized some of his treasures, but Wei Longfu's concubine was able to sneak out through the backdoor. She went directly to Magistrate Meng and Commander Luo, telling them that bandits had attacked her home and asking for their help. She promised them monetary reward if they took quick actions. Meng and Luo reacted immediately by sending soldiers to Wei Longfu's house. A fight broke out and Wei Baqun's followers were defeated. According to these accounts, which are more believable than the one claiming an easy victory, Wei Longfu was set free, the treasures were returned, and seven of Wei Baqun's followers were captured by Commander Luo's soldiers.

Wei Baqun's naiveté arguably contributed to the failure. It was impossible to get official approval to attack the commander of the county militia forces and to neutralize the army unit. Wei Baqun had awed General Liu Rifu and Du Ba with powerful connections, popular support and moral power, and he thought he could do the same with the power holders in the county. He knew that his small group of peasant soldiers was no match for Commander Luo's troops, but he reckoned maybe he could neutralize these troops through moral persuasion.

According to some sources, when Wei Baqun learned that the attack had aborted and seven of his followers had been detained, his reactions were quite dramatic. He took the rest of the group out of the county seat and asked them to find a place to rest. He then returned to the county seat and went directly to see Magistrate Meng, asking him to release his seven soldiers. The magistrate refused, arguing that the seven were bandits. Wei Baqun then took out his handgun and pointed it at the magistrate, threatening to kill him if he did not obey. The magistrate, fearing for his life, asked the county police to release the seven. Under Wei Baqun's demand the magistrate then escorted the group out of the town and was permitted to return only after the rebels reached a safe place.[36]

Other sources provide more credible scenarios. One account simply says that the seven peasant soldiers were held for three days and then released.[37] A participant in the attack recalled that the day after the defeat, Wei Baqun wrote a letter to a prominent resident of the county seat asking him to inform the other townspeople to stay home the next day because his soldiers would attack the town if the government failed to release the seven peasants. This warning generated fear among the residents, who gathered in front of the government office building and demanded the release of the peasants. The magistrate yielded and the peasants were set free the next morning.[38] Another account holds that Wei Baqun first threatened the magistrate that he would use bombs to destroy the entire town, and when that threat failed, he mobilized the townspeople to put pressure on the magistrate, which resulted in the release of his followers.[39] Although the attack on Wei Longfu failed, Wei Baqun was able to take everyone back to the village.

The failed attack on Wei Longfu convinced Wei Baqun that the county magistrate and the army commander were all linked up with local power holders like Wei Longfu and should all be treated as targets of the revolution. Only two weeks after his armed group returned to Wuzhuan, Wei Baqun launched a large-scale attack on the county seat, with the purpose of expelling the magistrate, defeating the army, and capturing Wei Longfu. To prepare for this attack, Wei Baqun sold nine buffaloes of his family to buy weapons and ammunitions. He also went to the Western Mountains to invite the Yao people to join the attack and the Yao villagers responded enthusiastically. Peasant soldiers from various districts in the county, including Wuzhuan and Lansi in the west, Changjiang in the north and Duyi in the southeast, formed the bulk of the attacking force, which had between 300 and 1,000 soldiers in total. The soldiers had more than two hundred guns and many knives and spears. As the commander-in-chief of the Self-defense army, Wei Baqun divided the soldiers into four groups, which were commanded by Huang Bangwei, Huang Daquan, Ya Sumin and Qin Kongxian, respectively.[40]

The attack began on the morning of July 1, 1923, and the four groups assaulted from four directions. Unfortunately, the enemy had built three barricades in strategic locations, making it difficult for Wei Baqun's soldiers to pass through the narrow roads leading to the county seat. The four groups also failed to arrive at the same time, which affected greatly the strength of the attack. The most destructive factor turned out to be the weather. It began to rain heavily in the morning, rendering useless most of their weapons, which were of the primitive type that had to be ignited using a fuse. The rain also caused the water level of the Jiuqu River that flowed through the town to rise rapidly. Huang Bangwei's group was one of those that failed to arrive on time. When they finally reached the town around noon, they struggled to ford the river under enemy fire, and Huang Bangwei was shot dead along with four Yao peasants.[41] To avoid further casualties, Wei Baqun ordered his soldiers to retreat. Huang Bangwei became the first founding member of the Association for Reforming Donglan to die for the revolution.

Although the attack failed, Wei Baqun's forces did not suffer great losses. He realized that in order to defeat the enemies in the county seat he needed more and better weapons. He called on his followers to donate money to buy guns and volunteered to purchase six guns himself. In total he and his followers donated enough money to buy at least twenty guns.[42] About a month later, he was able to launch a third attack on the county seat. This time around eight hundred peasants joined the action. They were no match for the enemy force, which consisted of the county police, militia forces under Wei Longfu, and the battalion of troops under Commander Luo Wenjian. The assault failed again.

After three failed attacks, Wei Baqun decided that new measures had to be adopted in order to defeat his enemies in the county seat. He managed to expand his Self-defense Army by recruiting more villagers; he ordered that the local landlords of all six districts in the county be put under strict surveillance so that they would not be able to serve as informants for their allies in the county seat; he tried to cut off the grain supply for the county seat; finally, he sent messengers to neighboring counties to seek support. In September 1923, Commander Luo's battalion was moved back to Baise, thus removing the core of the enemy forces. Wei Baqun and his friends saw a window of opportunity and decided to initiate their fourth attack on the county seat. On October 18, which was September 9 in the lunar calendar and a festival, Wei Baqun organized an oath-taking ceremony near his village. Attending the ceremony were his leading followers from different districts of Donglan as well as more than one hundred young revolutionaries from Fengshan, including Liao Yuanfang and his twenty to thirty followers.[43] The fourth attack on the county seat, which occurred just after the oath-taking ceremony, turned out to be a great victory. Between 1,000 and 1,500 peasants gathered around and sacked the county seat on that day. Magistrate Meng Yuanliang and Wei Longfu were not able to resist the attacking force without the support of Commander Luo's battalion, and they both escaped before the armed peasants could find them. Their subordinates then surrendered and Wei Longfu's son was captured.

This was the second time in two years that the county seat of Donglan was taken by rebel forces. The first occurred on the day Wei Baqun returned from Nanning to Donglan in late 1921. Bandit Chen the Six seized the town on that day, and his men looted, burned, and killed, causing much fear among the residents. From the perspective of the wealthy and powerful residents of the town and the entire county, Wei Baqun and his followers were not very different from the bandits. In subsequent years, they would keep calling Wei Baqun a bandit and try very hard to persuade others that Wei Baqun was no more than a bandit. However, if we follow the argument that the presence of a bureaucratic revolutionary organization is the sole feature distinguishing a modern revolution from a pre-modern rebellion, then Chen the Six's attack on the county seat was a genuine premodern rebellion, but Wei Baqun's movement was obviously a modern revolution.[44]

The easy success of the fourth attack and the fact that the county seat had fallen into the hands of rebels twice within two years demonstrates how weak the government was at that time. Studies of revolutions have frequently listed the decline and breakdown of the state as an important factor causing modern revolutions,[45] and such a factor was clearly present in this situation. Guangxi in 1923 did not have a unified and efficient provincial government. At the beginning of the year there were seventeen separate major military commands in the province, and each had more than 1,000 troops.[46] The division made it difficult for any of the major commands to subdue Wei Baqun's movement, allowing Wei Baqun to develop a minor military command in Donglan. Whereas the presence of Commander Luo's battalion was the main reason for Wei Baqun's defeat during the first three attacks, the absence of any external troops was the primary factor in his victory during the last attack. As would be shown repeatedly in subsequent years the results of local conflicts in Donglan were often determined by the presence or absence of external forces. Although Wei Baqun had become a member of the KMT and very likely saw his movement as a part of the Nationalist revolution led by Sun Yat-sen, he did not receive any support or instructions from the KMT authorities during this period. Strictly speaking, participants of the first uprising fell somewhere between the "peasants without the party" defined and analyzed by Lucien Bianco,[47] and the revolutionary peasants that would emerge after the Communists launched their rural revolution.

For Wei Baqun and his followers, the occupation of the county seat signaled a great step forward. Their center of influence had been based in Wuzhuan, which was located in the southwestern corner of the county and was only one of the six districts that made up Donglan County. By taking the county seat they had established their control over the entire county. When Wei Baqun refused to take Governor Ma Junwu's offer of the position of magistrate of Donglan in 1921, he explained to the governor that it was because he did not have the backing of a revolutionary army. It took him two years to build himself such an army. Even Wei Baqun himself must have been amazed at the change that two years had made in his fortunes.

Now Wei Baqun and his comrades were able to enforce some of the programs of the Association for Reforming Donglan. They unlocked the county jail and released all the criminals; they confiscated Wei Longfu's properties and gave them to the poor; they also redistributed among the poor grain and money collected by the county government; they abolished taxes and called for ethnic and gender equality. Defending against exorbitant taxation and other corrupt practices of the local officials and powerful families was the most important rallying point for the movement. The day after they took the city, Wei Baqun presided over a large mass meeting to celebrate the victory and commemorate the fallen soldiers, and he wrote a moving elegiac couplet for his close friend and comrade Huang Bangwei, praising his loyalty to the community, the people, and the nation. The peasants celebrated the victory with singing, dancing, and reveling that lasted several nights.[48]

It was much more difficult to maintain control over the county seat than it had been to take it. The neighboring counties and the entire province were under the control of militarists who were hostile to revolutionaries like Wei Baqun, and would try every means to suppress his movement. A new governor named Zhang Qihuang had taken office in Nanning, and he was a Guangxi native appointed by the militarist government in Beijing with the approval of the militarists in Guangxi. He reacted to Wei Baqun's movement with a policy of appeasement. He announced the demotion of Magistrate Meng Yuanliang and the dispatch of a new magistrate named Huang Qiongyao, who was a close associate of General Liu Rifu.[49] It is not certain whether or not Wei Baqun had expected to be appointed as the new magistrate. After arriving in Donglan, Huang Qiongyao tried to mediate between what he called the "new party," Wei Baqun and his group of young opposition elites, and the "old party," the faction of Wei Longfu, Du Ba and other powerful local men. He then declared the reorganization of the council of representatives and invited Wei Baqun to serve as its chairman. Wei Baqun refused, but sent some of his followers to serve in the council. The council thus included members of both parties, giving the impression that Magistrate Huang was a successful peacemaker.

However, the peace between the magistrate and Wei Baqun's group, and between the two parties did not last long. In winter 1923, one of Wei Baqun's followers in the Citizens' Assembly was brutally murdered by Huang Qiongyao's county police for accusing Magistrate Huang of exploiting the people in collusion with the old party. Wei Baqun's group reacted by lodging a protest against the magistrate, sending people to Nanning to file a complaint, and also starting to prepare for a military showdown. Magistrate Huang then asked for help from General Liu Rifu, who decided to send Commander Luo Wenjian's battalion back to Donglan to protect the magistrate. Wei Baqun's peasant-soldiers fought several battles with the Luo Battalion and suffered some losses. Some of his soldiers had already been disbanded after the fourth attack on the county seat, and some of his sworn brothers simply disappeared at the moment of fierce fighting. Commander Luo then took back the county seat and Wei Baqun had to retreat to Wuzhuan. The provincial government also stood behind Magistrate Huang. In early 1924, Governor Zhang Qihuang listed Wei Baqun and some of his followers as wanted criminals for "organizing a laborist party, confronting the government, and disturbing the society."[50]

Wei Baqun's defeat was apparent, and it had come not by the hands of enemy forces within Donglan, but of outside forces from Baise and Nanning. He knew now that external support was crucial for the success and survival of his movement. Although he knew that General Liu Rifu and Governor Zhang were both hostile, Wei Baqun still sent four delegates to Nanning to plead with the governor because that was his only hope for keeping his movement alive.

The sudden defeat of his first revolt disappointed Wei Baqun, but he was still hopeful. While waiting for the four delegates to return, he wrote a letter to Qin Ruiwu, who was head of the educational bureau of Donglan and a teacher at Donglan Advanced Elementary School, in addition to being another sworn brother of Wei Baqun's.[51] The letter reads as follows:

> I have received your letter and am very grateful for your meticulous instructions. The local tyrants and evil gentry have colluded with the warlord bandits to oppress and trample on our peasants, students and members of the Nationalist Party. Their purpose is to deprive the people of their lawful rights and expand the power of the officials so that they can maintain their hereditary privileges. What they do not understand is that the mind of the people has changed along with global trends and the people of the new era will no longer be as obedient as the people of the autocratic period who would tolerate the oppression of corrupt officials and evil gentry. Science has proved that the stronger the pressure is the more powerful the reaction will be.
>
> Our people have suffered great losses in this past war because the government resorted to brute force to subdue us. However, our hearts are not dead and the revolution will continue. Though brute force is frightening, justice is even more indomitable. I dare to predict that as long as the Republic is alive, the people of Donglan will definitely be able to raise their heads one day.
>
> I will surely follow the five suggestions you laid out for me in your letter, but I cannot leave Donglan before the four delegates (Xiangqing, Huanting, Changsheng, and Bomin) return home. If none of them comes back, I will go out before the end of this month. The purpose of my trip will be to study. It is so true that you only regret how little you have learnt when it's time for you to apply what you have learnt! If we stop learning, then we are humans who compete with chickens and dogs for food.

Brother Ruiwu had suggested that Wei Baqun leave Donglan and Wei Baqun liked the idea. Shortly after writing the letter, Wei Baqun left home and embarked on his second trip to the place of hope. As he expected, this would be another long journey of learning.

CHAPTER FOUR

Second Journey

1924–1925

Although Wei Baqun had told his friend Qin Ruiwu that he planned to begin his trip before the end of April, he did not leave Donglan until August 1924. It is interesting to note that from February 1924, when Wei Baqun was declared a wanted criminal by the provincial government, to August 1924, the provincial and county governments made no effort to arrest him. It shows that local officials still did not take him seriously. It seemed that the government would allow him to live freely if he did not make more trouble despite his status as a criminal, or that it was waiting for Wei Baqun to venture out of his power base to have him arrested. It would be much easier to subdue Wei Baqun while he was away from his large numbers of supporters.

Meanwhile, Wei Baqun was eager to get out of Donglan and Guangxi after losing the county seat. Part of the reason was that there was not much he could do in Donglan after the retreat. He had spent three years trying to transform Donglan using the ideas and methods he learned in the large cities, had created several organizations and staged numerous confrontations, and had taken control over the county but then lost it. Defeated and disappointed, he was not sure which road he should take, although he was still confident about the future of the revolution. He thought that once outside the province he would have complete freedom of movement; he also wanted to make new connections, learn new ideas and tactics and then come back to restart. He wanted to go to Guangzhou, where the Nationalists and Communists had recently formed a united front. The news of the new revolutionary movement very likely had penetrated even into remote Donglan. Wei Baqun might also have heard or read about the powerful peasant movements that were emerging in Guangdong, particularly the one Peng Pai had helped bring about in Hailufeng, which was not very far from Guangzhou.

The four delegates returned to Wuzhuan shortly after Wei Baqun wrote his letter to Qin Ruiwu. Wei Baqun had hoped that the delegates could persuade the provincial government to reverse its policy toward his movement, but the four failed to accomplish their mission. This helped affirm his determination to make a trip to Guangzhou. According to Huang Hongyi, a student from Donglan who was studying in Nanning at that time, as soon as the four delegates returned to Donglan, Wei Baqun called for meetings of the leaders of the Citizen's Assembly, at which it was decided that four of the leaders, Wei Baqun, Chen Bomin, Huang Daquan, and Huang Shulin, would make a study trip to Guangzhou. Although it has been suggested that the group selected the four, it seems more likely that they volunteered. These meetings were rather informal, as only a small number of leaders were invited. It was hard to take a formal vote at such meetings. Because each traveler was responsible for his own expenses, the final decision had to be made by the travelers themselves. The journey had to be postponed to August to give Huang Daquan and Huang Shulin enough time to raise money.[1]

Huang Hongyi recalled that Wei Baqun and his three comrades began their trip on an evening in August 1924 disguised as students. Huang Shuzhu, a local villager and martial artist who served as their carrier and guard accompanied them. Traveling with them were two real students, Huang Hongyi and Huang Hongfu. They were Wuzhuan natives who were attending the Number Three Normal School of Guangxi in Nanning. The plan of the group was to travel from Wuzhuan to Tianzhou on foot, and then from Tianzhou to Nanning by boat. In Nanning they would stay briefly at the dormitory room of the two students, and then get on another boat bound for Guangzhou.

Unfortunately, shortly before they reached Tianzhou the group ran into three soldiers, Donglan natives serving in General Liu Rifu's army based in Baise, all of whom knew Wei Baqun. Seeing Wei Baqun in a student uniform naturally raised their suspicions. But Wei Baqun had a plan. He invited the three for dinner and they happily accepted the offer. At dinner, Wei Baqun sent people to buy tickets for a steamship going to Nanning and told the soldiers that they would stay at the dormitory of the Number Three Normal School in Nanning. After dinner, Wei Baqun arranged for the three soldiers to have a room in the same hotel where the seven of them were staying. To ensure safety, after making sure that the soldiers had all fallen into sleep, Wei Baqun, his three comrades, and Huang Shuzhu rushed back to Wuzhuan, leaving only the two students to continue the journey to Nanning. The five covered 110 kilometers in less than twenty-four hours and then hid for two days at the Beidi Cave near Dongli before going home. When the three soldiers woke up the next morning they found that the entire group of seven had left and believed that they all had gone on to Nanning. A few days later, a group of soldiers went to search for Wei Baqun at the dormitory of the Number Three Normal

School, but failed to find him. Despite the delicious dinner and a small bribe Wei Baqun had given them, the soldiers still reported to General Liu about Wei Baqun's trip to Nanning, and General Liu in turn passed on the information to the provincial authorities.[2]

This account is problematic, because two months before Wei Baqun's chance meeting with the three soldiers in August 1924, General Li Zongren, the emerging leader of the New Guangxi Clique, had already taken Nanning. Governor Zhang Qihuang, who had been in office for barely a year, and his supporter General Lin Junting were overthrown.[3] In fact, this was one of the most important turning points in the modern history of Guangxi. Lu Rongting, the leader of the Old Guangxi Clique, completely lost control over Guangxi and went into retirement after this event, and his former subordinates, Li Zongren, Huang Shaohong and Bai Chongxi, rose as the leaders of the New Guangxi Clique that would rule the province for the next twenty-five years with only a brief interruption. James Sheridan argues that Li Zongren was a "reformist warlord" and was different from Lu Rongting of the Old Guangxi Clique, who might fall into Sheridan's category of "conservative warlords."[4] Diana Lary also points out that the leaders of the New Guangxi Clique differed from those of the Old Guangxi Clique in that they had received modern military training, were more exposed to modern ideas, and possessed a broader vision and a sense of higher identity. However, Lary is quick to add that the distinction between the two groups is a very loose one and she convincingly argues that although the leaders of the New Guangxi Clique were attracted to the revolutionary ideology of Sun Yat-sen, they became part of the Nationalist establishment without undergoing any real political transformation.[5] The lack of fundamental differences between the Old Guangxi Clique and New Guangxi Clique was to have tremendous effect on the politics of China and Guangxi in general and Wei Baqun's movement in Donglan in particular.

It was Governor Zhang's government of the Old Guangxi Clique that had declared Wei Baqun a criminal, and there was no reason for the new government of the New Guangxi Clique to be so eager in enforcing an order issued by its predecessor and rival. Besides, as a subordinate of Lin Junting and Zhang Qihuang, General Liu Rifu was an enemy of the New Guangxi Clique until August 1924 or later, when he decided to surrender to General Li Zongren and received an appointment from the New Guangxi Clique. Even if Liu Rifu had already submitted to the New Guangxi Clique when Wei Baqun and his friends made the trip, it would still be difficult for Liu to persuade his new bosses to enforce an order issued by his former bosses.

Huang Hongfu, the other student of the Number Three Normal School mentioned in the above account, provided a different version of the story. He recalled that in January 1924 (lunar calendar), after spending the winter vacation at home, he and Huang Hongyi were on their way back to their school in Nanning. When they arrived at a place in Enlong County one evening, they saw Wei Baqun and Chen Bomin, and the four decided to spend the night in the same hotel room. Wei and Chen told the two Huangs that they were on their way to Guangzhou. The next day, the four of them traveled to Tianzhou. They had dinner at a small hotel and planned to spend the night there. After dinner, they ran into two policemen from Donglan who had checked into the same hotel and who planned to travel to Baise the following day. Both policemen knew Wei Baqun. Wei and Chen grew wary and decided to return to Donglan that very evening. The two Huangs stayed at the hotel for the night and left for Nanning on a boat the next morning.[6]

Huang Hongfu's account is more believable because there were many more convincing reasons for Wei Baqun and Chen Bomin to be wary of the police and be cautious about passing through Nanning in early 1924 than in August 1924. Governor Zhang Qihuang and Lin Junting were still in power in early 1924. Chen Bomin was probably not on the list of the most wanted, since shortly after this failed attempt to travel to Guangzhou, he went to Nanning as one of the four delegates of the Donglan Citizens' Assembly.

Both accounts agree that Wei Baqun's first attempt to travel to Guangzhou failed and that his second try succeeded. Huang Hongfu admitted that he had no idea of when and how Wei Baqun resumed his journey to Guangzhou.[7] Huang Hongyi claimed that Wei Baqun and Chen Bomin set off in August 1924, which would be a few months away from their first attempt if we accept Huang Hongfu's account, but only a few days away from the first attempt if we trust Huang Hongyi. Huang Hongyi recalled that although disappointed by their unexpected meeting with the three soldiers, Wei Baqun and his friends were not ready to give up the idea of traveling to Guangzhou. Realizing that passing through Nanning would be dangerous, the group decided to take a different route. Instead of taking the southern road via Tianzhou, Nanning, and Wuzhou, they would now first travel northward to Guizhou, and then turn westward to Yunnan. From Yunnan they would take the train to Vietnam and then go to Hong Kong from Vietnam by steamship. They would then take a Guangzhou-bound ship from Hong Kong.[8]

Although this route was considerably longer, it would take the group out of Guangxi much sooner. It was probably as dangerous as the other route, though it would be a different kind of danger. It is very unlikely that the Guangxi government would be able to do any harm to them once they moved into Guizhou and Yunnan, but bandits were rampant in the remote areas of these two provinces. This was probably the reason for Wei Baqun to expand the group. The four let their friends know that they wanted to take more people with them, and soon Liang Shishu and three others decided to join.[9] Most of the eight travelers were founding members of the Association for Reforming Donglan.

Again it is hard to understand why Wei Baqun was so cautious about avoiding Nanning in August 1924. He should have been aware of the political change in Nanning that had taken place two months before. Although Li Zongren and his generals later would become the most deadly enemies of Wei Baqun, there was no reason for Wei Baqun to see Li Zongren as an enemy in August 1924. It is likely that Wei Baqun and his friends decided to travel through Guizhou, Yunnan and Vietnam rather than Tianzhou and Nanning not because of their fear of a possible arrest by the New Guangxi Clique, but because they wanted to avoid the war between the New Guangxi Clique and its various enemies that was going on in many parts of Guangxi at that time. The fact that after the change of provincial government Wei Baqun still decided to leave Guangxi for Guangzhou and still saw Nanning as a very dangerous place maybe also indicates that he had already realized that the leaders of the New Guangxi Clique would be hostile to the peasant movement. Maybe the four delegates he had sent to Nanning had already approached the new leaders and tried to win their support but failed. It is also possible that they began their trip before June 1924, when the Old Guangxi Clique was still in power.

According to Huang Hongyi's account, the now enlarged group first walked from Donglan to Guiyang, the capital of Guizhou Province, and from there they trekked further to Kunming. After reaching Kunming they found that they did not have enough money left to pay for the remaining portion of the journey for the entire group. It is not clear what caused the problem. Maybe they had underestimated the cost, or maybe they had overspent on their way from Wuzhuan to Kunming. The group then decided that only two of them, Wei Baqun and Chen Bomin, would continue the journey to Guangzhou, while the others had to walk all the way back to Wuzhuan. Those who had to turn back must have been extremely disappointed. Their only accomplishment was to have escorted Wei Baqun and Chen Bomin to a safe place.

Wei Baqun probably had visited Yunnan during the years he spent in the Guizhou Army, since the Guizhou Army was a lesser partner of the Yunnan Army at that time, and the two provinces were neighbors. Even if he had never been there he would not have felt much of a cultural shock in Yunnan since like Guangxi, Yunnan had diverse ethnic groups, an evergreen natural setting, and a rather mountainous topography, although it is much cooler than Guangxi because of its high altitude. Yunnan and Guangxi also shared a strong French influence at that time. Since 1910, Kunming had been directly connected to Hanoi by a narrow gauge railway designed and run by the French. Wei and Chen traveled from Kunming to Vietnam by train. It should have been an exciting journey as it was their first time traveling to a foreign country. They were probably somewhat disappointed after reaching the destination because, after all, Vietnam did not appear very foreign to people from Guangxi. The climate and natural setting are similar, the Vietnamese look like southern Chinese, and the Vietnamese language sounds like Cantonese and Zhuang. One difference was that in Vietnam they would be able to find a much stronger French presence. Guangxi and Yunnan were part of a French sphere of influence, whereas the three regions of Vietnam had become French protectorates and colonies.

Although the train could take them directly to Haiphong and the distance between Haiphong and Hong Kong was much shorter than that between Saigon and Hong Kong, Wei Baqun and Chen Bomin traveled all the way to Saigon and then boarded a steamship bound for Hong Kong. Maybe they wanted to see more of Vietnam. After arriving in Hong Kong they found that they had once again used up their money. They checked into a hotel and Wei Baqun wrote a letter to his wife asking for money. Chen Lanfen then sent some money to Huang Hongyi, the student at the Number Three Normal School, and Huang then remitted the money to Wei Baqun at the hotel in Hong Kong using Wei's former name.[10]

It appears that for Wei Baqun money was no longer as easy to come by as it had been before. Since taking over the family from his grandfather, he had spent a great amount of money on his first tour to the coastal and interior provinces, to cover the expenses of the small anti-Yuan Shikai army that he raised, to buy his life and freedom from General Huang Qi, and to purchase weapons used for attacking the county seat. His household income was likely lower than before because he was much more lenient to the tenants and laborers than his grandfather and father. A reduction in income and overspending would cause financial problems for the Wei family sooner or later. Wei Baqun ran into financial difficulties at least three times during his journey to Guangzhou: first in Wuzhuan, then in Kunming, and finally in Hong Kong. By now Wei Baqun must have realized that revolution was a rather costly undertaking. Many other revolutionaries had to face serious family conflicts when their activism began to take a toll on the fortunes of their own families. Peng Pai, for instance, was scolded by his mother and very much hated by most of his other relatives for giving his family's land away.[11] On the other hand, as the patriarch of the Wei family, Wei Baqun met little resistance from his relatives for his free spending habits. His new wife, Chen Lanfen, seemed to be supportive of his actions, and for that Wei Baqun was grateful to her. It was probably in 1924, right before he began his second journey, that Wei Baqun crafted a folksong dedicated to Lanfen. The song later became popular in Donglan and its lyrics are as follows:

Mother is old and weak,
You are the caretaker of the family.
Keep your husband in your heart,
Keep his words on your mind.
The two sons are little,
Please be patient in guiding them.
I work for the people day and night,
And to you I entrust the entire family.[12]

In October 1924 or a bit later, Wei Baqun and Chen Bomin finally arrived in Guangzhou. They went to see Liao Zhongkai, the leader of the left wing of the KMT, shortly after their arrival. Wei Baqun had met Liao in Guangzhou in 1921. A strong supporter of the United Front and the peasant movement, Liao suggested that Wei Baqun and Chen Bomin attend Guangzhou Peasant Movement Institute, which had been created jointly by the Communists and Nationalists. Communists Lin Boqu and Peng Pai first established the institute in July 1924, and Peng served as the director of the first class, which had thirty-eight students and lasted for about two months. Sun Yat-sen was very supportive of the institute and in August 1924 he even paid a visit to give a talk about the equalization of land rights. The second class began in late August 1924 with 225 students and it ran until late October. Its director was Luo Yiyuan, another famous Communist peasant movement leader. Wei Baqun and Chen Bomin arrived too late to join the second class, and so became members of the third class, which began on January 1, 1925 and ended on April 1 of the same year. The director of the third class was Ruan Xiaoxian. Like his two predecessors, Ruan was also Cantonese, Communist, and a famous supporter and leader of the peasant movement. All of the students in the first two classes were from Guangdong. The third class had 128 students when it began and among them only Wei Baqun, Chen Bomin and a Sichuanese student were not Guangdong natives.[13]

The regular curriculum of the institute consisted of courses on peasant movements, workers movements, socialism, imperialism, social theories, the Soviet Union, the history of the Chinese revolution, and revolutions in the world. In addition to class instruction, students also had to go through military training and field study related to peasant movements. In fact, military training took about one-third of the time and the second class was even directly involved in military actions by playing an important part in helping Sun Yat-sen put down the rebellion of the Guangzhou Chamber of Commerce in October 1924.

The teachers of the third class included Ruan Xiaoxian, Liao Zhongkai, Peng Pai, Chen Yannian, Michael Borodin, General Galen (V. K. Bluecher), and others.[14] It is rather certain that Wei Baqun did meet Peng Pai at the institute as Peng was an instructor there, but it is very unlikely that the two developed a close relationship, as some scholars have argued. As the leaders of the most influential peasant movements in their respective provinces, Peng Pai and Wei Baqun probably had heard of each other and they should have had a great deal to talk about, but they did not have much time to spend together. In late 1924 and early 1925, Peng Pai was very busy organizing peasant movements in Hailufeng and other places in Guangdong and participating in the two expeditions against militarist Chen Jiongming. He had to spend most of his time outside Guangzhou, and that was one of the reasons he had to let his colleagues take over the institute. It should not have been very difficult for Wei

Baqun and Chen Bomin to make a trip to Hailufeng to observe the movement Peng Pai had created, but there is no indication that they ever traveled there. Although they did not go to Hailufeng, they did spend some time in the villages around Guangzhou to investigate local class relations and peasant movements.[15]

The claim that Wei Baqun was a student of Mao Zedong at Guangzhou Peasant Movement Institute was once very popular, but has been proved wrong. Mao served as the director of the sixth class of the institute which began in May 1926 and Wei Baqun was already back in Guangxi at that time. Mao visited Guangzhou in January1924 and revisited the city in September 1925, but was not there in late 1924 and early 1925. The two never had an opportunity to meet each other in their lifetime. In the 1950s, Mao commented that "Wei Baqun was the most outstanding student of Guangzhou Peasant Movement Institute,"[16] but it is not certain whether he had already heard about Wei Baqun in 1925. It is equally uncertain whether or not Wei Baqun had heard about Mao in that year.

Another person Wei Baqun missed during his stay in Guangzhou in late 1924 and early 1925 was Sun Yat-sen. In late 1924, Sun Yat-sen was preoccupied with the issue of the reunification of the country. Although a United Front government had been established in Guangzhou, much of China was still under the control of various militarists, each of whom was waiting for the next opportunity to expand his territory, by force if necessary. From 1922 to 1924, the two largest military groups in northern China, the Zhili Clique and the Manchurian Clique, fought two wars with each other over the control of northern China. During their second war, General Feng Yuxiang of the Zhili Clique turned against his bosses and overthrew the military government in Beijing led by Wu Peifu and Cao Kun. Feng then allied himself with two other powerful militarists, Zhang Zuolin of the Manchurian Clique and Duan Qirui of the Anhui Clique. These three enemies of the Zhili Clique created a provisional government in Beijing with Duan Qirui as its leader. On October 25, 1924, the provisional government issued a joint declaration in which they suggested that Sun Yat-sen and leaders of other powerful groups travel to Beijing to discuss national affairs with the ultimate goal of setting up a unified government. A few days later they extended a formal invitation to Sun. On November 13, 1924, Sun Yat-sen left Guangzhou for Beijing. On March 12, 1925, while in Beijing and before reaching any agreement with the militarists, he died of liver cancer. Sun was probably still in Guangzhou when Wei Baqun and Chen Bomin arrived there, but the two did not get a chance to meet with him.

Despite claims that the two stayed in Guangzhou until the end of the training program in April 1925, it has been convincingly shown that they were already back in Guangxi in March 1925.[17] Since the third class of Guangzhou Peasant Movement Institute did not end until April 1925, the institute became yet another school that Wei Baqun attended but failed to graduate from. Among the 128 students of the third class, only 113 graduated.[18] Wei Baqun and Chen Bomin were among the fifteen dropouts. Why did they not wait for a few more weeks to complete their study at the institute? There are several possible reasons. One of them was that neither Wei Baqun nor Chen Bomin cared much about degrees and diplomas. They knew that a diploma was not necessary for one to become a revolutionary. They would stay in a school only if they found its curriculum interesting and useful or if they did not have more meaningful work to do.

At least from Wei Baqun's perspective, the curriculum of the institute was not very novel or useful. Thanks to Director Ruan Xiaoxian's revision of the curriculum, the third class of Guangzhou Peasant Movement Institute attached greater importance to the training of military and organizational skills than the first two. Students were made to wear army uniforms, form a company, and live like soldiers. They were also taught how to organize peasant associations and experimented with actual organizational work.[19] These programs probably were not very attractive to Wei Baqun. As a graduate of Guizhou Military Academy, a veteran of the Guizhou Army, a local leader who had created the Association for Reforming Donglan, the Citizens' Assembly as well as the Citizens' Self-defense Army in Donglan and who had organized and commanded four attacks on the county seat, Wei Baqun obviously no longer needed such basic training. In fact, he had sufficient experience and qualities to serve as an instructor for such programs. One of these qualities was his age. Although it was specified that all applicants to the institute must be under the age of twenty-eight,[20] the thirty-year-old Wei Baqun was still admitted, possibly based on Liao Zhongkai's recommendation. Wei Baqun was very likely the oldest student in his class, and he was also older than some of his teachers. He was three years older than Ruan Xiaoxian and two years older than Peng Pai. In an age-conscious society like China, Wei Baqun might have felt some discomfort sitting among his classmates.

Wei Baqun found the courses on political theories and tactics for developing peasant movements more interesting than those on military skills. Ruan Xiaoxian taught a course titled, "Peasant Movements in Guangdong"; Peng Pai taught "How to Organize Peasant Associations and Peasant Self-Defense Armies"; Liao Zhongkai spoke on the three principles of the people; and Chen Yannian talked about imperialism. One source holds that Wei Baqun was a very attentive student in these classes and his notes filled a thick notebook.[21]

Another possible reason for their early departure from Guangzhou was their failure to acquire concrete financial, military, and political support from the United Front government. Wei Baqun made the arduous trip to Guangzhou not only to learn new ideas and methods, but also to make new connections and seek support for his movement. He hoped that with external support he would be able to defeat his enemies back home. But although he did learn some new ideas and methods in Guangzhou, his attempt at gaining immediate support from the United Front government came to near complete failure. The political situation in Guangxi and southern China at that time was quite byzantine. General Li Zongren had taken over the provincial government, but he had not unified the entire province and did not have real control over Donglan. General Li had pledged his allegiance to Sun Yat-sen's United Front government in late 1924, but Guangdong and Guangxi had not been well integrated, and General Li was very much independent in handling affairs within Guangxi. In other words, even if the Guangzhou government ordered General Li to support Wei Baqun and his movement, General Li might choose not to follow that order; and even if General Li did sincerely support Wei Baqun and his movement, there was not much he could do about Wei Baqun's enemies in Donglan because he did not have actual control over Donglan at that time. If there was no hope for them to get real support from the Guangzhou government, then Wei Baqun and Chen Bomin might decide that it did not make much sense for them to extend their stay in Guangzhou.

The thriving peasant movements in Guangdong might also serve to prompt them to go back to Guangxi earlier rather than later. Some of their classmates at Guangzhou Peasant Movement Institute were peasant movement activists and they should have been able to tell their two friends from Guangxi what had happened and what was happening in rural Guangdong, particularly in the Hailufeng area. By early 1925, peasant associations had been created in as many as twenty-two counties in Guangdong. About 200,000 peasants had joined peasant associations, and the Guangdong provincial peasant association had been created.[22] The success of the peasant movements in Guangdong and the new ideas and methods Wei Baqun and Chen Bomin had learned helped boost their confidence, but it might also have generated in them a sense of shame and urgency, which in turn impelled them to return to Donglan as soon as they could to revive their movement.

However, the immediate reason for their early departure from Guangzhou was probably a new war that broke out in early 1925 between the New Guangxi Clique and the Yunnan Clique led by General Tang Jiyao. Nominally, both cliques were allies of the United Front government at that time, but both were independent of the Guangzhou government and of each other. There were three factors that led Tang Jiyao to believe that he was the only one who had the power to reunify southern China: Sun Yat-sen was seriously ill, he had not been able to create a powerful military force of his own, and both Guangdong and Guangxi were riven by conflicts between different military groups. Tang Jiyao had already established full control over Yunnan and had turned Guizhou into his sphere of influence. His next target was Guangxi, and then, Guangxi would serve as his stepping-stone to Guangdong. Before invading Guangxi, Tang sent an envoy there to deliver a letter to General Li Zongren. Tang's message was that he only wanted to borrow a road to Guangdong, and that if General Li was to cooperate and offer him such a road, there would be no war between the two provinces. General Li saw that as a ruse and refused to collaborate, and the Yunnan Army then invaded Guangxi. By late February 1925, Nanning had fallen to the hands of General Long Yun of the Yunnan Army.

In order to ensure his victory over the New Guangxi Clique, General Tang Jiyao made contact with his old friends within the armed forces of the Guangzhou government and asked for their support. Two of his old friends responded positively. One was General Yang Ximin, who had served in the Yunnan Army before, and the other was Liu Zhenhuan, a native of Guangxi who had been a veteran Nationalist as well as a member of the Old Guangxi Clique. Both of them held high-ranking military positions in the United Front government. General Liu Zhenhuan sent his subordinate, General Li Dingjian, to Guangxi to work with the Yunnan Army. General Li was also a native of Guangxi and had been in Donglan briefly in the early 1920s.[23] Wei Baqun and Chen Bomin returned to Guangxi in the employ of General Li.

It is not clear how the two got in touch with General Li Dingjian. Perhaps it was done through some networks of Guangxi expatriates in Guangzhou, but it was also possible that Liao Zhongkai was the one who introduced Wei Baqun and Chen Bomin to Generals Liu Zhenhuan and Li Dingjian. In November 1924, Sun Yat-sen's government, of which Liao was a powerful official, had appointed General Liu Zhenhuan as the governor of Guangxi, but because of the opposition of the New Guangxi Clique, Liu was not able to return to Guangxi to assume office. Li Zongren had played a part in expelling General Liu from Guangxi in 1922, and did not want him to return.[24] Li's deputy, Huang Shaohong, had been a subordinate of Liu Zhenhuan for a brief period, but did not have a happy relationship with him. Generals Li Zongren and Huang Shaohong had invited a senior civilian official in Lu Rongting's former government to serve as the governor.[25] This illustrates how independent the New Guangxi Clique was and how little respect they had for Sun Yat-sen and his government. In order to become the governor of Guangxi, General Liu had to recruit supporters from among the Guangxi expatriates in Guangzhou, and it was natural for Liao Zhongkai, the mutual friend and boss, to recommend Wei Baqun and Chen Bomin to Generals Liu and Li. Once back in Guangxi, Wei Baqun and Chen Bomin told their friends that it was Liao Zhongkai who had sent them back to Guangxi as special agents of Sun Yat-sen's government. At the same time, they also made it known that they were friends of General Li Dingjian. Wei Baqun told a friend that General Li Dingjian had paid for all their travel and living expenses.[26]

The first stop of the three in Guangxi was Longzhou near the Sino-Vietnamese border,[27] which means that they probably had traveled through Vietnam. They arrived in Nanning shortly after the city fell to the Yunnan

Army. General Li's mission was to set up a divisional commanding office in Nanning, but his ultimate goal was to pave the way for General Liu Zhenhuan to come to Nanning to assume the office of governor. The Yunnan Army had appointed Lu Rongting's former subordinate Lin Junting as the governor of Guangxi and Lin made Li Dingjian the head of the department of political affairs in his government.[28] The political situation in Guangxi was rather chaotic at that time. The New Guangxi Clique wanted to unify the province and maintain their control over it. The Yunnan Army wanted to establish its control over the entire southern China, including Guangxi. And General Liu Zhenhuan wanted to return to Guangxi to take the office of governor. The New Guangxi Clique saw Generals Tang and Liu as real or potential threats and wanted to keep them out of Guangxi. General Liu supported General Tang because the New Guangxi Clique had been hostile toward him and because he believed that General Tang would make him the governor of Guangxi. In May 1925, Tang Jiyao did appoint Liu Zhenhuan as the governor of Guangxi.[29] Thus, General Liu Zhenhuan was appointed as governor by both the Guangzhou government and its rival Tang Jiyao.

All three groups, the New Guangxi Clique, the Yunnan Army, and General Liu, were nominal allies of Sun Yat-sen's government, which tried not to take sides as long as the three groups did not expand their conflict to Guangdong. For instance, General Tang began to invade Guangxi in early 1925, but Sun's government did not do much to stop him. Sun's government remained silent when the Yunnan Army took Nanning in late February 1925. It did not declare General Tang an enemy until March 1925, when it was discovered that Tang had a secret plan to occupy Guangzhou and reorganize Sun's government there. Although Sun's government had appointed General Liu Zhenhuan as the governor of Guangxi, it did not condemn the New Guangxi Clique when it appointed someone else as the governor and refused to let General Liu enter Guangxi to assume his duty. Technically, General Liu was closer to Sun's government than the other two cliques, mainly because Liu was stationed in Guangdong and his army was under the direct command of Sun Yat-sen.

Among the three groups, Wei Baqun and Chen Bomin supported General Liu Zhenhuan. They saw Liu as the legitimate governor of Guangxi because he had been appointed by Sun Yat-sen's government. They also thought that he would take his office soon because the New Guangxi Clique had been defeated by the Yunnan Army, and that once General Liu became governor, he would be supportive of the peasant movement and would help them defeat their enemies back home. They were not supportive of the New Guangxi Clique because of its real or imagined hostility or indifference to the peasant movement.

It is likely that Wei Baqun and Chen Bomin were not aware that Generals Liu Zhenhuan and Tang Jiyao were already planning to overthrow or take over Sun Yat-sen's government in February 1925. They did not see any problem with working for General Liu Zhenhuan even after Tang Jiyao was declared an enemy by the Guangzhou government because the same government still saw General Liu as a loyal supporter. General Liu did not openly revolt against the Guangzhou government until June 1925, and by that time Wei Baqun and Chen Bomin were already back in Donglan and no longer had any contact with the general. A year later, the leaders of the New Guangxi Clique, now back in power in Nanning, would claim that during the Yunnan Army's invasion of Guangxi in 1925, Wei Baqun and Chen Bomin had worked for the enemy troops.[30] This claim is true only in the sense that Generals Tang Jiyao and Liu Zhenhuan were secret allies at that time. Wei Baqun and Chen Bomin could have refuted that accusation by arguing that they were working directly for General Liu Zhenhuan, but ultimately for the Guangzhou government, because Liu was the governor of Guangxi appointed by the Guangzhou government. They never consciously worked for the Yunnan Army, which was the primary enemy of the New Guangxi Clique. In any case, it is not certain what kind of service Wei Baqun and Chen Bomin actually provided for Generals Liu Zhenhuan and Li Dingjian. In Nanning there was not much they could do for the two generals.

Most scholars agree that during his brief stay in Guangzhou in late 1924 and early 1925 Wei Baqun went through a change of his worldview or a great leap in his political consciousness, meaning that he either formally and fully converted to Communism or came under its strong influence during this period.[31] Although it is hard to determine whether or not Wei Baqun had begun to see himself as a Communist during his stay in Guangzhou, there is no doubt that he received much more exposure to Communism this time than during his previous stay. At Guangzhou Peasant Movement Institute, he was surrounded by teachers and classmates who were Communists or Communist sympathizers. Wei Baqun was not resistant to Communist ideas, as he later would work hard to spread these ideas in Donglan. In fact, it is arguable that what he had been doing and planned to do in Donglan conforms more to the Communist than the Nationalist ideology and therefore he should have had no problem recognizing the Communists as his natural allies and accepting Communism as his new guiding ideology. It would have been equally natural for the Communists to recognize Wei Baqun as a comrade-in-arms and invite him to join their party. Some students did join the CCP during their stay at the institute. It is therefore worthwhile to examine why Wei Baqun did not join the CCP during this period. He had the opportunity of becoming the first Zhuang Communist from the Right River area, but he did not or could not take the opportunity.

One possible explanation is that Wei Baqun had no strong motivation to join the CCP at that time. Because he had already joined the KMT, and the KMT and the CCP had become close allies to the extent that they were perceived by many to be one unified party, it was not necessary for him to join the CCP. The differences and conflicts between the two parties were not yet apparent at that time, and to support the peasant movement was the official policy of the United Front government created by both parties. The Communists at Guangzhou Peasant Movement Institute were also Nationalists and they did their work in the name of the KMT. Officially, the institute was created by the KMT rather than the CCP. Besides, as a veteran Nationalist, Wei Baqun was likely aware that Sun Yat-sen and other leaders of the KMT were willing to accept the Communists into the KMT, with the hope that eventually all Communists would become Nationalists, but were not willing to allow Nationalists to join the CCP.

On the other hand, the Communists were probably not eager to bring Wei Baqun into their party either. There were at least two reasons for the Communists to be cautious about recruiting Wei Baqun. The first reason was that Wei Baqun was not only already a member of the KMT, but also a friend of Liao Zhongkai. The Communists thus felt that recruiting Wei Baqun would offend the KMT. The second reason was that they probably knew that Wei Baqun was a landlord. The policies of the institute specified that people from landlord families were not eligible to apply.[32] Wei Baqun was admitted probably because he told no one of his landholdings, but it is also likely that the institute already knew that Wei Baqun was from a wealthy family and admitted him only because of Liao Zhongkai's intervention. The admission officers had already shown lenience about Wei Baqun's age, and they may have adopted the same outlook on his family status. The CCP, however, adopted a stricter admission criterion than the institute. Since the Communist leader Chen Duxiu was obsessed with the idea of maintaining the purity of the CCP, the Communists were very careful about admitting people with dubious backgrounds at that time. When Zhu De, later the founding father of the Communist Red Army, told Chen Duxiu in person in summer 1922 that he wanted to join the CCP, Chen refused to take him in. Several months later, when Chen finally approved Zhu De's membership, he told Zhu to keep his CCP membership a secret. Chen Duxiu's hesitance showed his concerns about Zhu De's background as a former militarist and his worries that admitting Zhu De, who was already a member of the KMT, would upset the Nationalist leaders.[33] The Communists at Guangzhou Peasant Movement Institute probably had similar concerns and worries about recruiting Wei Baqun. Zhu De eventually was able to join the party because he found two strong supporters, Zhou Enlai and Zhang Shenfu, who were founding members of the CCP, but there were no senior Communists who knew Wei Baqun well enough to recommend him for party membership.

It is apparent that the Communists had not yet realized how important and influential Wei Baqun had already become. In many senses, what Wei Baqun had accomplished in Donglan was very similar to what Peng Pai had done in Hailufeng, but Peng Pai was much more well known in Guangzhou than Wei Baqun because of Hailufeng's proximity to Guangzhou, as well as due to Peng Pai's high rank within the CCP and KMT. Despite Wei Baqun's popularity and influence in Donglan, he was nobody in Guangzhou in late 1924 and early 1925. More than a year later, Ruan Xiaoxian commented, "there were two students from Donglan who had studied at the Peasant Movement Institute. They have only achieved some success after working very hard for a long time."[34] Obviously, in late 1924 and early 1925 the Communist leaders in Guangzhou were far less impressed by Wei Baqun's movement in Donglan than by Peng Pai's movement in Hailufeng. Otherwise, they would have worked much harder to convert him.

CHAPTER FIVE

Second Revolt

1925–1929

In late 1924, Wei Baqun left Guangxi as a wanted criminal, and in early 1925, he returned a free man. As a friend of General Li Dingjian, who in March 1925 became head of the Department of Political Affairs of the provincial government supported by the Yunnan Army, Wei Baqun was not only free, but also ascendant. Wei Baqun and Chen Bomin must have been baffled by the new political makeup in Nanning. General Lin Junting, a supporter of the militarist government in Beijing and thus an enemy of Sun Yat-sen's government in Guangzhou, was now cooperating with the Yunnan Army, which was supposed to be an ally of the Guangzhou government; the Yunnan Army and the New Guangxi Clique, both allies of the Guangzhou government, were fighting against each other; General Li Dingjian, an officer in Sun Yat-sen's revolutionary army, was now serving under General Lin Junting, a rival of Sun Yat-sen. Wei Baqun must have been happy to have such a powerful friend in the provincial government and he should also have been aware that such a confused political situation could be a blessing for revolutionaries like himself. It would allow them to find their space between and among different factions and to expand their freedom and power.

Unfortunately, neither the political confusion nor General Li Dingjian's power lasted long. In July 1925, the Yunnan Army that had occupied Nanning for nearly five months was defeated by the New Guangxi Clique, which had also nearly eliminated the major rival militarist groups within Guangxi. The province was finally reunified and order was restored. Generals Lin Junting and Li Dingjian fled with the Yunnan Army, and in September 1925, General Huang Shaohong of the New Guangxi Clique was sworn in as the new governor. Four years before becoming governor, Huang, then a battalion commander, had made a brief stay in Donglan.[1] Although Wei Baqun was at home at that time, it seems that the two never met.

Resurgence

Wei Baqun and Chen Bomin were eager to get back to Donglan, and they had already left Nanning before the city fell to the army of the New Guangxi Clique in July 1925. Although they acquired no concrete financial, political, or military support during their brief second journey, they returned with new ideas and restored confidence. The trip also helped reaffirm old connections and establish new ones. They were ready for a fresh restart.

On their way home, the two made a stop at Shanglin County to visit Huang Daquan, who had escorted them to Kunming the previous summer. Since returning from Kunming, Huang had organized an armed band, named it an autonomous army, and appointed himself its commander-in-chief. He chose to move his small army to Shanglin, located to the northeast of Nanning, where high mountains covered with thick forests stood next to some fertile and prosperous plains, making an ideal setting for small predatory bands. In Shanglin, Huang Daquan befriended some local notables, who introduced him to Meng Renqian, a former officer in Lu Rongting's army. Meng had briefly served as governor following Ma Junwu's departure. Huang Daquan then merged his band into Meng's larger army and became an officer under Meng. It did not take Wei Baqun and Chen Bomin much effort to persuade Huang Daquan to return to Donglan to help revive the peasant movement.[2]

From Shanglin they went to Enlong County to visit Huang Bangcheng, who was also a founding member of the Association for Reforming Donglan. As a graduate of the Number Three Normal School in Nanning, the proctor of Donglan Advanced Elementary School and someone who had traveled to such large cities as Beijing, Shanghai, Guangzhou, and Hong Kong, as well as neighboring provinces like Yunnan and Guizhou, Bangcheng was one of the best educated, most capable and influential members of the association. Partly because of that, he became an important leader of the first revolt and was one of the four delegates who traveled to Nanning to seek support after the defeat of the first revolt. After Wei Baqun and Chen Bomin left for Guangzhou, Huang Bangcheng also left Donglan and traveled to several different counties before settling down in a small town in Enlong, where he also organized a small, armed band. Like Huang Daquan, Huang Bangcheng also agreed to return to Donglan.[3]

After visiting Huang Bangcheng, Wei Baqun and Chen Bomin made a stop in Lunxu of Fengyi County to meet some friends. The meeting took place at the home of Li Zhengru, a high school graduate who was to become one of the earliest CCP members in the Right River region. Li and a few others who attended the meeting would soon become Wei Baqun's strong allies, and together they would turn Lunxu into a reliable base for the peasant movement. Li himself would act as a messenger between Wei Baqun and the CCP in 1927 and still later served as a Red Army officer under Wei Baqun. In early 1931, he was taken by the Nationalist troops at a cave in Donglan and executed in Wuzhuan.[4]

It was probably during their journey back to Donglan that Wei Baqun and Chen Bomin began to circulate copies of "To the Compatriots," a document they had drafted and printed in Guangzhou or Nanning. The document, which was issued in the name of the Guangxi special branch of the KMT, called for a national revolution against warlords and imperialists, and the creation of associations and self-defense armies for the students, peasants, and workers, respectively.[5] A copy of the document was later discovered in the Right River region, but unfortunately it was not dated. Some have claimed that this document was written as early as 1916,[6] whereas others have argued that it was created on the March 3 Festival of 1922, May 1924, summer or fall 1924, September to October 1924, or March 1925. The content of the document shows that it could not have been created before the formation of the First United Front in 1924. National revolution defined as a war against imperialists and warlords was the political program of the First United Front; organizations such as peasant associations and armed forces for peasants and workers also first appeared during the First United Front. The only existing copy of the document indicates that it was produced with a rather advanced printing technique, which was not available in Donglan and Guangxi in the early 1920s.[7] Most likely the document was produced during or after Wei Baqun's second journey to Guangzhou in late 1924 and early 1925. It could not have been written before that because during his first revolt Wei Baqun was too preoccupied with pressing local issues to worry much about the wider world, which was the primary concern of the declaration. Wei Baqun's close associates Chen Bomin, Ya Sumin and Qin Kongxian indirectly confirmed in 1927 that "To Our Compatriots" was created during the First United Front. In a report about the KMT affairs in Donglan, the three affirmed that the political messages of the KMT were first brought to Donglan by Wei Baqun and Chen Bomin after they graduated from Guangzhou Peasant Movement Institute.[8]

Many of Wei Baqun's followers had to leave Donglan after the defeat of the first revolt, but they did not waste their time. People like Huang Daquan and Huang Bangcheng worked hard in other places to create networks and organize peasants. In some sense what they did during this period was not very different from what Wei Baqun and Chen Bomin were trying to do. They all took their defeat as an opportunity to enrich and strengthen themselves by traveling, meeting new people, and learning new ideas and methods. Both

Huang Daquan and Huang Bangcheng had developed new attachments in Shanglin and Enlong, respectively, and the fact that they were willing to leave their new safe havens and return to dangerous Donglan showed their confidence in their leader and their common cause. For Huang Daquan, this was at least his third time to become a follower of Wei Baqun. The first occurred in late 1915 when he gave up his position as a teacher to join Wei Baqun's small anti-Yuan Shikai army; the second time took place in 1921, when he again quit teaching to become a founding member of the Association for Reforming Donglan and a leader of the first revolt. Like Wei Baqun, Huang Daquan also sold some of his family's paddy fields to buy weapons for the peasant army during the first revolt.[9] Huang Bangcheng had much more to lose than most of his comrades when he joined the revolution. He had a well-paid and respectable position as a schoolteacher, which he lost once he began to work with Wei Baqun. After the collapse of the first revolt, he was driven out of his home. Now he was ready to work for Wei Baqun again!

There was a whole stratum of rural intellectuals like Huang Daquan and Huang Bangcheng who were just waiting to be agitated and organized. Political failures, military defeats, and death threats failed to deter them. They seemed to recognize Wei Baqun as the leader they had been waiting for. Wei Baqun's visits to Huang Daquan and Huang Bangcheng before his return to Donglan show how much Wei Baqun appreciated the talents, will, and work of his comrades. He knew clearly that without the support of rural intellectuals like Huang Daquan and Huang Bangcheng his revolution would never succeed. Just as he had laid the groundwork for his first revolt by organizing the rural elites, he would prepare for the second revolt by recruiting rural intellectuals like Huang Daquan and Haung Bangcheng. Most of his former comrades came to gather around Wei Baqun as soon as he returned to Wuzhuan.

In addition to calling back his old comrades, Wei Baqun also began to recruit new followers from among the younger students and scholars. Huang Hongfu, one of the two students who Wei Baqun and Chen Bomin met during their aborted trip to Guangzhou in 1924, joined Wei Baqun as soon as Wei returned from Guangzhou to Nanning in early 1925. Huang Hongfu recalled that in March 1925 he and his classmate, Chen Gutao, also a native of Wuzhuan, accidentally ran into Chen Bomin on a street in Nanning. Chen immediately took them to see Wei Baqun, who in turn introduced them to General Li Dingjian. A few days later, Wei Baqun invited Huang Hongfu and Chen Gutao to return to Donglan to "make revolution," and the two agreed, partly because their school had been closed due to the war between the Yunnan Army and the New Guangxi Clique. Huang Hongfu and Chen Gutao ended up spending the entire summer helping Wei Baqun organize peasant associations. With Wei Baqun's permission, they went back to school in the fall. A year later, both of them were sent to attend the sixth class of Guangzhou Peasant

Movement Institute directed by Mao Zedong. Chen Gutao paid a visit to Peng Pai's base area Hailufeng and joined the CCP during his stay at the institute, and the two returned to Donglan to work for Wei Baqun in late 1926.[10]

Two students from the Number Five Provincial High School of Guangxi in Baise also joined Wei Baqun at this time. One was Chen Hongtao, who was from the same village as Chen Gutao; and the other was Huang Songjian, who hailed from Fengshan. Both of them became admirers of Wei Baqun when they were still in elementary school, and during their stay in Baise, they served as leaders of a student association that was supportive of Wei Baqun's peasant movement. While Wei Baqun and his comrades were fighting the power holders in Donglan, Chen Hongtao and Huang Songjian were involved in a confrontation against the children of these power holders who were attending the Number Five High School. Chen Hongtao was so active in mobilizing support for Wei Baqun that the school authorities began to make trouble for him. In 1925 he quit school and returned to Donglan to work for Wei Baqun. In late 1925, Wei Baqun sent Chen to Wuzhou in eastern Guangxi to attend a training program, and Chen joined the CCP there. He was the first Zhuang Communist from the Right River region and the first Communist in Donglan. Later he was to emerge as the head of the Communist organization in Donglan and the Right River region as well as Wei Baqun's right-hand man.[11]

Huang Songjian stayed at the Number Five Provincial High School after Chen's departure. In late 1926, with Wei Baqun's encouragement, he returned to Fengshan County as a KMT special agent. Three years later, Wei Baqun brought him into the CCP. He was to play an important role in expanding the Donglan peasant movement into Fengshan. By 1932, he had emerged as the third most important leader of the Communist movement in the Right River region, next only to Wei Baqun and Chen Hongtao.[12]

Closer to home Wei Baqun was able to attract some new followers from Donglan Advanced Elementary School. Huang Juping, who became a student at the school in 1924 at the age of twenty, joined Wei Baqun in late 1925. Other young students who joined Wei Baqun after he returned to Donglan in 1925 included Bai Hanyun, a classmate of Chen Hongtao and Huang Songjian at the Number Five Provincial High School; Huang Fangri, who came from the Sanshi district and was a graduate of Guangxi Military and Political School; Lu Haoren, who also hailed from Sanshi and joined the peasant movement after graduating from Donglan Advanced Elementary School in 1926; and Huang Wentong, a young man from Fengshan who joined the peasant movement in late 1925 while studying at the Number Five Provincial High School.[13] They would all grow into important leaders of the peasant movements and most would die in its service. These new cohorts were about ten years younger than Wei Baqun. Overall, the younger group was better educated and tended to be more radical than Wei Baqun's older comrades partly because of their age and partly because they were more familiar with the radical ideologies. Stories about Wei Baqun were part of their childhood education and they grew up believing that Wei Baqun was the great local hero, which helped generate and affirm their loyalty to him.

After making connections with his old and new intellectual friends, Wei Baqun began to work on revitalizing and reforming the Citizens' Assemblies, with the purpose of changing them into peasant associations modeled on similar organizations in Guangdong. He traveled to different places to mobilize the peasants. Wei Jie, who later became Wei Baqun's follower, was eleven when he first caught sight of Wei Baqun. Wei Jie's village was near the town of Sanshi east of Wuzhuan. One day in 1925, he saw a huge crowd at the market of Sanshi. He went over and saw a circle formed by more than a dozen young men wearing red armbands and holding knives and spears. Inside the circle were five to six red square tables, and on the tables were laid silver dollars and copper coins. There were clothes, quilts, grain, and farming tools around the tables. There were also several men holding the reins of more than a dozen buffaloes. Soon a stout man entered the circle, and he also wore a red armband in addition to a pair of straw sandals and an old gray hat. Following him were a group of poor villagers. The man handed some silver dollars and coins to each poor villager, and some in the group even got buffaloes. The man then told people that their lives would be greatly improved once peasant associations were created. Wei Jie later learned that this man was none other than Wei Baqun. This scenario illustrates that Wei Baqun knew what the poor villagers wanted and how to win their trust. He was also good at choosing the time and location for his show. His performance at the market of Sanshi was quite successful. Wei Jie confirmed that not long after the show peasant associations were created in his district.[14]

Wei Baqun was not able to travel to every town and village to talk to people or to stage such a show. He therefore had to rely on his educated friends to help organize peasant associations in various towns and villages. To make use of the several dozen students around him he organized them into a student army and sent them to various districts to help spread the message and organize the peasants. Huang Hongfu and Chen Gutao spent a month in Bohao in southeastern Donglan with Chen Hongtao and a few others to help mobilize the peasants.[15] It is estimated that by September and October of 1925 more than seventy peasant associations had been created in Donglan and together they had a membership in excess of 20,000. In September 1925, the Donglan Peasant Association was established, with Chen Bomin as its president and Wei Baqun as the head of its military department. Huang Daquan served as a committee member,[16] and most other committee members of the Donglan Peasant Association were also founding members of the Association for Reforming Donglan.

Wei Baqun's reputation among the villagers as a brave and wise leader who dared challenge the brutal and corrupt power holders and who was always willing to offer protection to the poor and weak helped attract villagers to form or join the peasant associations. The folklore about Wei Baqun's greatness continued to grow despite the defeat of the first revolt. Shortly after returning to Wuzhuan, Wei Baqun impressed the villagers by helping to drive away a group of roving soldiers. These soldiers were part of the invading Yunnan Army that had been defeated by the New Guangxi Clique. On their way back to Yunnan they would often loot the villages and towns they passed through and also kidnap villagers. When a group of such soldiers was approaching Wuzhuan, the local people panicked and went to see Wei Baqun for advice. Wei Baqun told the villagers to make a red banner and hang it on the top of a nearby mountain. When the soldiers saw the banner they immediately decided not to enter Wuzhuan but to take another route. The villagers were amazed by the mysterious power the red banner embodied and Wei Baqun explained to them that when the soldiers saw the red banner they had been scared away because they thought there were troops of the New Guangxi Clique stationed near the town.[17]

The peasant associations that sprang into being in Donglan in 1925 were different from the citizens' assemblies that Wei Baqun created during his first revolt in several aspects. The most obvious difference is that they had different names. Although there are claims that the name "peasant association" had already been used during the first revolt, there is no evidence showing that this was the case. The new term indicates a new focus. If the citizens' assembly was meant to be a tool of the national revolution in the old definition, which posed all citizens of China against foreign invaders, then the peasant associations were created for a new type of national revolution that was more class based. Although Wei Baqun had not yet joined the CCP, he was obviously receptive to the Communist theory of class struggle, which he had already practiced during the first revolt. The name peasant association was one of the new concepts he acquired during his second journey.

The peasant associations also were better organized than the citizens' assemblies. In Donglan there developed three levels of peasant association. The lowest was the township-level peasant association. Each of these was formed by peasants from a handful of villages. Several township peasant associations formed a district peasant association, and all the district peasant associations in Donglan constituted the unified county-level peasant association. The membership of the peasant associations was more permanent than that of the citizens' assemblies. In late 1926, there were eleven district peasant associations and 134 township peasant associations in Donglan, with a total membership of nearly 80,000. The district and township peasant associations as well as members of peasant associations in Donglan far outnumbered those in any other county in Guangxi at that time. In fact, peasant association members in Donglan made up nearly half of the total number of peasant association members in the entire province, which stood at 150,822 in late 1926.[18]

Moreover, the peasant associations were more legitimate than the citizens' assemblies, which were spontaneous organizations that had no legal basis and government support. The creation of peasant associations was part of the political program of the United Front government, and the Guangzhou government had even clearly defined the status and power of peasant associations. Wei Baqun was a private citizen when he created the Association for Reforming Donglan in 1921 and the citizens' assemblies during the first revolt, but when he organized the peasant associations in 1925 he and Chen Bomin were both special agents of the Department of Peasant Affairs of the KMT.

Finally, the peasant associations were larger than the citizens' assemblies. Although exact statistics are not available, it seems that the members of the citizens' assemblies had never exceeded 20,000, and the number of peasant association members was several times higher than that. Obviously, the Donglan peasant associations were modeled more on the peasant associations of Guangdong than on the citizens' assemblies Wei Baqun had created during the first revolt, although the citizens' assemblies can still be seen as predecessors of the peasant associations in the sense that the former had helped train leaders and create useful networks for the latter.

The peasant associations required the members to follow a set of orders and regulations, to pay a monthly membership fee, to break barriers between regions and lineages, to stop feuds and give up corrupt behavior, and to unite to fight imperialists and warlords. All members were required to memorize and abide by these rules.[19] This code shows clearly a strong interest in transforming the peasants, which was a shared concern of many revolutionary intellectuals at that time. The ultimate goal of these revolutionary intellectuals was to turn the peasants into a political force against the enemies of the nation, namely, the imperialists and warlords. In order to achieve that goal, they believed that they had to first reform and unite the peasants.

The creation and expansion of the peasant associations required a large number of leaders, and in order to train leaders for the peasant associations Wei Baqun decided to adopt another method he had learned during his stay in Guangzhou, that is, to establish a peasant movement institute. The problem, however, was that he did not have the resources that the Nationalists and Communists in Guangzhou possessed. The most devastating obstacle was that he did not even have classrooms, nor the time and money to build them. Fortunately, it soon occurred to him that he could put his entire school in the Beidi Cave (Fig. 5.1), which was not far from Dongli and was located on the slope of the Lajia Mountain sitting on the edge of the Wuzhuan Basin. Forty meters high, 64 meters wide and 137 meters deep, the cave could provide living space for nearly two thousand people. At that time, the cave was used to house some

Buddhist and Daoist statues and there was an old man living there to take care of the gods. Wei Baqun easily persuaded the old man to make space for his comrades and students who would not only take classes at the cave, but also live there. Wei Baqun and his followers remodeled the cave by dividing the space into classrooms, a library, a meeting room, living quarters for students and teachers, offices for teachers, and a kitchen. They made chairs, desks and beds using bamboo and trees they found near the cave. They also collected some stones from the mountain and built an arched gate at the entrance of the cave.[20] Wei Baqun decided to name his cave school Guangxi Peasant Movement Institute. To distinguish his school from another Guangxi Peasant Movement Institute that appeared later in Nanning, I will hereafter refer to it as Donglan Peasant Movement Institute.

To ensure that students and visitors were constantly reminded that this was a revolutionary school, revolutionary messages were displayed at every corner of the cave. On the arched gate was pasted a couplet written by Wei Baqun: "Come and join us if you support the revolution, go away if you are not a revolutionary." This was apparently a replica of a similar couplet Wei Baqun had seen at Whampoa Military Academy in Guangzhou. On the front wall of the classroom hung the portraits of Lenin and Sun Yat-sen, which had probably been brought back from Guangzhou or Nanning. Near the portrait was

FIGURE 5.1 The Beidi Cave. Photograph by the author.

another couplet written by Wei Baqun, which read: "The local tyrants and evil gentry treat the poor people like food on their dinner plates, and the working masses take the local tyrants and evil gentry as their shooting targets." Near the bulletin board was a slogan reading "Nothing is happier than revolution," which was supposed to be a teaching from Karl Marx. On the wall was also a famous classical poem about the sufferings of the peasants, and slogans like "Down with local tyrants and evil gentry," and "Down with feudal warlords!" The motto of the school was "Work, mutual aid, struggle, and sacrifice," and that was on the wall, too. In front of the cave was a piece of land that the students chose to name Revolutionary Garden, and around the cave was a creek that the students decided to call Revolutionary River. In the evening, Wei Baqun and the students had to cover themselves with "Revolutionary Quilts," which were actually made of rice straw.[21]

The first class of Donglan Peasant Movement Institute began in November 1925. With 276 students, it was much larger than the class Wei Baqun and Chen Bomin had attended in Guangzhou. Although most of the students were from Donglan, there were also people from neighboring counties. Most of the students were Zhuang, but there were also a few Han. Wei Baqun reserved some spots for the Yao, but these spots were not filled.[22] Some of the students were teachers and students from local schools, whereas others were peasants, but all were literate. The oldest were around thirty, and the youngest were only eleven to twelve. Most of them were sent by the peasant associations. The students were divided into teams based on their hometowns. The number of the students and the number of counties they represented confirmed how successful Wei Baqun and his friends had been in organizing the peasants and creating networks. Wei Baqun served as the director of the institute, Chen Bomin was the manager, and Wei Mingzhou was the secretary. Several other founding members of the Association for Reforming Donglan, including Huang Daquan, Huang Bangcheng, and Huang Shuxiang, were teachers at the institute.[23]

The curriculum of the institute was modeled on that of Guangzhou Peasant Movement Institute. Courses offered included History of World Revolutions, Soviet Russia, Basics of Economics, and Organization and Principles of Peasant Associations.[24] Wei Baqun and Chen Bomin had brought back two mimeographs. Initially they set up a secret printing office at a cave near Dongli, and after the founding of the institute they moved the mimeographs to the cave. They simply reprinted some of the books they had brought back from Guangzhou and used them as textbooks for their students. Military instruction was an important part of the curriculum, and the first class had at least two military instructors, one of whom was a young officer Wei Baqun befriended during his stay in Guangzhou in 1925. Students took three classes in the morning, and two sessions of military training plus one session of labor work in the afternoon. In the evening they held discussion sessions or went to the villages to talk with the peasants. On market days the students would go to the towns to make speeches and stage shows.[25]

Like Guangzhou Peasant Movement Institute, Donglan Peasant Movement Institute was primarily a political organization rather than an academic one. The teachers and students of the institute did not just teach or study the revolutionary messages; they were eager to apply their lessons, and these soon led them into direct confrontation with the local authorities. Clashes with local authorities were inevitable because some of the rules of the institute directly violated the laws of the government. For instance, students of the institute were taught to oppose rent and debt payment, military conscription, gambling, opium, greed, fear of death and taxes.[26] Besides, Wei Baqun did not seek permission from any local institution before creating the institute and his associations and he did not want his associations and institute to become part of the local government or to be put under its control. He wanted them to become an alternative government, and eventually to replace the existing government.

The institute and peasant associations began to act as an alternative government not long after their creation. One governmental function they performed was to serve as a mediator in disputes between peasants. Chen Mianshu, a county magistrate dispatched to Donglan in October 1926, lamented that he did not judge a single case during his first month in Donglan because the peasant associations could solve all the minor disputes among peasants.[27] The associations and the institute also served as the judge for disputes between landlords and tenants. A Yao peasant and his sons forced two of their landlords to come with them to the peasant movement institute one day. His family had been paying debt to the landlords for generations and had to give their land to the landlords as a pledge, but the landlords kept telling them that they had more debt to pay. He wanted the institute to try the case. The institute took the case and reached an immediate verdict: the debt was cleared and the land should be returned to the peasant. The landlords had tried to prevent the peasant from bringing the case to the institute but failed. They were aware that although the county government often favored the rich and powerful over the poor and weak, the peasant movement institute was just the opposite. One day after the trial, the Yao peasant and his sons returned to the cave with many bundles of firewood for the institute, and he wanted all his five sons to work for Wei Baqun and the revolution.[28] To assume the duty and power of an alternative government that provided protection and support to the weak and poor became one of the most important means of drawing the peasants into the peasant associations and peasant revolution.

Another governmental function the peasant associations assumed was to provide public security and help eliminate crimes and unhealthy customs. Chen Mianshu reported in late 1926 that gambling and opium smoking had completely disappeared from the five districts of Donglan that were under the control of the peasant associations since these were prohibited. The boy scouts, who were teenage revolutionaries, played an important role in eliminating opium smoking. They were entrusted with the power of confiscating opium paraphernalia, and they were very enthusiastic in applying their power.[29] Banditry was also eliminated. As a result, people could travel safely and could "sleep without closing their doors."[30] The many positive changes Chen Mianshu observed in Donglan in late 1926 are very similar to those Mao Zedong and others observed in rural Hunan at about the same time.[31]

Although the classrooms and furniture of the peasant movement institute were all free, it still cost some money to run the school. Even with provisions of grain and vegetables from local peasant associations, student contributions, and foraging expeditions for wild plants, mountain fruits, and fishes and crabs from the rivers, students only ate twice a day and still went hungry. To pay for the meals and other expenses, Wei Baqun managed to secure some money from the chairman of the county council of representatives as well as from Qin Ruiwu, head of the educational bureau of the county. Both officials were his friends. In addition, he sold seven to eight mu of family land plus the dowry of his wife. Other teachers and leaders also made donations.[32] Still, after two months the institute ran out of money. To solve the problem Wei Baqun and his friends decided to take on another duty of the government: tax collection. This was a government function they had hated and tried to abolish. Their plan was to take over not all the taxes, but only the commercial tax of the Wuzhuan market. This caused a direct conflict between Wei Baqun and his enemy Du Ba because Du was the one who had been collecting that tax. Du Ba was the chairman of the board of directors of Yucai Advanced Elementary School, and his son was the principal of the school. The commercial tax of Wuzhuan had been used to support the school. Wei Baqun and his supporters argued that the tax should be used to support the peasant movement institute rather than the elementary school. As Wei Baqun had more supporters than Du Ba, he easily won the argument. Wei Baqun and his followers also set up a new market, which was 1.5 kilometers away from the old one at Wuzhuan. To attract villagers they collected lower sales taxes there.[33]

Whereas the confrontation with Du Ba was peaceful, that with Long Xianyun was not. Long was a landlord living at the village of Jiangping, about four kilometers to the south of the Beidi Cave and eight kilometers to the south of Wuzhuan. Long Xianyun became a target partly because he was nearby and therefore relatively easy to attack, and partly because his family was wealthy and therefore a successful attack on him would help solve the financial problem of the institute. Besides, Long was quite brutal toward the peasants and thus in the eyes of the revolutionaries qualified as a local tyrant and evil gentry. Finally, Long had close relations with fellow landlords like Du Ba as well as with the county government, and was not friendly toward the peasant associations and the peasant movement institute. In the recent past, Wei Baqun and his friends had butted heads with Long Xianyun about some public funds he had been managing. To express his anger at Wei Baqun, Long Xianyun had robbed some salt merchants and then put the blame on the peasant movement institute. He had also tried to prevent villagers from going to the new market that the institute had set up.[34] Long was therefore perceived to be a serious threat to the peasant movement and the leaders believed that it was necessary and justifiable to eliminate him. One source holds that Chen Bomin sent the two military instructors of the peasant movement institute to kill Long Xianyun, and the leaders themselves did not participate in the attack; but according to another source, Wei Baqun himself led the attack at night. Both accounts agreed that the leaders planned to kill Long, but Long managed to escape. The revolutionaries seized his properties. They redistributed the clothes and grain to the villagers and then burned down Long's mansion.[35]

These local conflicts finally drew the attention of the county government. Magistrate Huang Qiongyao, who took office after Wei Baqun's fourth attack on the county seat in 1923 and successfully put down Wei Baqun's first revolt in 1924, had left Donglan in October 1924 after his boss, Governor Zhang Qihuang, was overthrown by the New Guangxi Clique. He was replaced by Magistrate Huang Shouxian, who was appointed by the New Guangxi Clique. In fact, some believed that the new magistrate was the uncle of Governor Huang Shaohong.[36] Huang Shouxian turned out to be as hostile to Wei Baqun and his movement as his predecessor. He saw powerful landlords like Du Ba and Long Xianyun as his strong allies and together they tried to defeat and destroy the peasant associations and the peasant movement institute. In late December 1925, Magistrate Huang and the head of the county militia forces made a trip to Baise to talk with General Liu Rifu, and they returned with General Liu's approval to launch attacks on the peasant movement institute. One of Magistrate Huang's accusations against Wei Baqun and his followers was that they had listed the magistrate as one of the corrupt officials and General Liu Rifu as one of the warlords that deserved to be overthrown.[37]

Despite having approved Magistrate Huang's planned attack on the institute, General Liu did not provide the magistrate with troops. The magistrate had to rely on the county police, some militia forces and a friendly bandit group for military support. Both Du Ba and Long Xianyun offered their help. Altogether the magistrate managed to gather more than two hundred armed men, and the attack was planned for December 21, 1925. Wei Baqun and his supporters were well prepared because they had learned about the attack in advance. They decided to close their cave school. Thus the first class, which should have lasted for six months according to the original plan, ended after less than three months. Some students returned home, and others were organized into an armed band. As the peasant army did not have many weapons, Wei Baqun decided to leave a few men to pose a token resistance at the cave, but withdrew most of his soldiers to a nearby village. Magistrate Huang's men easily took the cave and they destroyed everything they found there. They then went to Chen Bomin's and Huang Daquan's villages and burned down their houses. They also destroyed the house of Huang Hanying, one of the military instructors of the peasant movement institute. That evening the magistrate and his men held a huge feast in a village to celebrate their victory. After they got drunk and went to sleep, Wei Baqun's soldiers attacked. The magistrate had to run back to the county seat with his men, and the peasant soldiers were able to injure more than twenty of their enemies and seize five rifles.[38]

The attack on the peasant movement institute and the abrupt dismissal of the first class of the institute signaled the end of the first phase of Wei Baqun's second revolt. Within about six months, Wei Baqun, Chen Bomin, and their friends were able to apply the ideas and methods Wei and Chen had brought back from Guangzhou and successfully revive the peasant movement in Donglan. Magistrate Huang's attack on the peasant movement institute forced an early closure of the institute, but failed to eliminate the peasant associations and peasant armies. The lines were now clearly drawn and both sides knew that neither could easily defeat the other without external support. Outsiders held the power to determine the result of the local contest in Donglan.

Massacre and Contest

Three weeks before Magistrate Huang's attack on the peasant movement institute, Wei Baqun and Chen Bomin had organized the Donglan Congress of the KMT and created the Donglan branch of the KMT. It was decided at the congress that Huang Bangcheng would serve as the delegate of Donglan at the First Guangxi Provincial Congress of the KMT to be held in Nanning in January 1926. The congress was another factor prompting Magistrate Huang to attack the institute because in order to show their support of the congress, students from Yucai Advanced Elementary School and the peasant movement institute held a joint demonstration in front of the county government office. They shouted slogans like "down with imperialism, warlords, corrupt officials, and others," and again Magistrate Huang believed that the students counted him as one of the corrupt officials.[39]

About a week after Magistrate Huang's attack on the cave school, he sent his brother Huang Zhiyuan, who was the head of the county police, to a village to collect grain from a member of the peasant association. Wei Baqun led a group of his men to the village and captured the police chief. The magistrate then sent some militia forces to attack Wei Baqun, trying to rescue his brother, but Wei Baqun's band was able to defeat the militias and chase them all the way to a village near the county seat. Unable to crush Wei Baqun, the magistrate reported to the provincial government that a bandit group led by

Wei Baqun was attacking the county seat and asked the governor to send troops to Donglan to help exterminate the bandits. Governor Huang Shaohong, who believed that Wei Baqun's movement had not been approved by the provincial government and was therefore illegal,[40] endorsed the request and ordered General Liu Rifu to send troops to Donglan to help Magistrate Huang. General Liu responded by sending his subordinate Gong Shouyi to Donglan with a whole regiment of troops.[41]

Although the leaders of the New Guangxi Clique had pledged allegiance to the revolutionary government in Guangzhou, they were not strong supporters of the peasant movement that the Guangzhou government had been trying to promote. Governor Huang Shaohong later explained that although from Wei Baqun's Marxist point of view his actions and policies were justifiable, the provincial government had to stop him because what he was doing in Donglan contradicted and harmed the political system the New Guangxi Clique was trying to create. Huang's position was supported by his colleague and superior General Li Zongren, who was never enthusiastic about the peasant movements and the United Front.[42]

At the same time, Magistrate Huang sent a telegram to the First Guangxi Provincial Congress of the KMT, arguing that because Wei Baqun was a bandit, his delegate Huang Bangcheng should not be allowed to attend the congress. The magistrate's demand was turned down by the Communists and left-wing Nationalists in the congress.[43] However, Wei Baqun's supporters in Nanning failed to prevent the governor from sending troops to Donglan. The conflict between Wei Baqun and his enemies in Donglan now became a confrontation between the Communists and left-wing Nationalists on one side and the right-wing Nationalists on the other in the provincial government.

Wei Baqun was not the only reason for Governor Huang Shaohong to send troops to Donglan. Former Governor Meng Renqian had recently entered Donglan after being defeated in Nanning. He had been a subordinate of Lu Rongting and had collaborated with the Yunnan Army during its invasion of Guangxi, and was thus an enemy of the New Guangxi Clique in multiple senses. He was passing through Donglan to reach Yunnan. Meng still saw himself as the legitimate ruler of Guangxi and as soon as he arrived in Donglan, he appointed Du Ba as the new county magistrate.[44] However, Magistrate Huang refused to hand his position to Du Ba and again asked Governor Huang Shaohong for help.

Although both Wei Baqun and former governor Meng Renqian were perceived to be enemies by Magistrate Huang as well as Governor Huang, this did not automatically make Wei Baqun and Meng Renqian allies. Wei Baqun probably did not care much about Meng's collaboration with the Yunnan Army, but would definitely not approve Meng's decision to appoint Du Ba as the new magistrate of Donglan. Wei Baqun's friend, Huang Daquan, had served briefly under Meng Renqian in early 1925, but both Wei Baqun and Huang Daquan decided to ignore that personal tie. Realizing that Meng's troops were still reeling from defeat and were not that powerful, Wei Baqun and his friends decided to make a stand, with the hope that they might be able to seize some weapons from Meng. They fought Meng in a village and defeated his soldiers. Meng escaped to Fengshan, but was captured by Wei Baqun's peasant soldiers, who seized more than 120 rifles. Unfortunately, General Liu's regiment under Gong Shouyi arrived just after Wei Baqun's victory over Meng Renqian. The Gong Regiment attacked and easily defeated the peasant soldiers. They took Meng Renqian and seized no less than seventy rifles from Wei Baqun's men.[45] Meng was executed shortly after that.

Thus began a disaster for Wei Baqun's supporters in Donglan that later became known as the Donglan Massacre. After the capture of former governor Meng, Wei Baqun and his movement became the only target of the Gong Regiment. Guided by Wei Baqun's local enemies Magistrate Huang, Du Ba, Long Xianyun and others, the Gong Regiment destroyed many families and villages. Villagers around Wuzhuan remembered February 5, 1926 with horror. On that day alone Gong's soldiers looted and burned down eleven villages in Wuzhuan, including Dongli. Two hundred fifty-five families were looted and their houses destroyed. The soldiers took money, grain, clothes, pigs, sheep, plus 335 buffaloes and horses. They kidnapped some peasants, burned one to death, and took the others to Wuzhuan for execution.[46]

Over the next few months, Gong's soldiers attacked many other villages in Donglan. According to one report, more than seven thousand families were looted and among them six hundred had their houses burned down. The soldiers confiscated large sums of money and nearly 2,500 horses and buffaloes. Above all this, they killed 140 villagers. Wei Baqun and his supporters claimed that in excess of five hundred peasants were killed during the massacre, and another source holds that that number exceeded seven hundred.[47] On some occasions, the soldiers would kill villagers and then force their relatives to pay for the bullets. Many villagers were driven to live in mountain caves. Wei Baqun's house was burned down and his wife, Chen Lanfen, was jailed. His son, who was only three days old, was jailed with the mother. Wei Baqun had named his son Geming, meaning revolution, and the son indeed became part of the revolution as soon as he was born. It was very cold in the jail, and Lanfen had to ask for rice straw to cover the baby, which her jailers refused. The government and army told the villagers that Wei Baqun was the source of all their troubles, implying that if they killed Wei Baqun or turned him in, then everything would be fine, but no one responded to that call.[48]

After two months of brutal looting, burning, and killing, the army and the government began to classify the local residents as "good people"—those who did not support the peasant movement—or "members of the Ba Party"—Wei

Baqun's supporters. In order to be recognized as good people, villagers had to buy certificates from local power holders such as Long Xianyun and Du Ba. For those who had been involved in the peasant movement, the certificates could be much more expensive than for others. Those who could not afford the certificates would remain members of the Ba Party and targets of further persecution.[49]

This was but one of a rash of violent conflicts between mobilized peasants led or supported by revolutionaries, and their local and non-local enemies who preferred to maintain the status quo. Similar conflicts occurred across southern China during the First United Front in Haifeng, Huaxian, and Wuhua in Guangdong, some counties in Hunan and Hubei, and other places.[50] In many cases, both sides claimed to be supporters of the same United Front government, and the results of such conflicts were largely determined by the negotiation between the leftists and rightists within the United Front government.

The arrival of the Gong Regiment completely changed the balance of power in Donglan. To respond to the brutal suppression imposed by the government and the army, Wei Baqun and his friends retreated to the Western Mountains where they created the Donglan Revolutionary Committee to direct battles against their enemies. The committee also served as the alternative government of Donglan. They began to turn their armed bands into more formal peasant self-defense armies and fought several battles against the Gong Regiment, although they were defeated most of the time. They also resorted to assassination as a weapon against their powerful enemies. Most of their targets were local power holders who supported the government and the army. From late 1924 to early 1925, the revolutionaries made twenty-one assassination attempts and killed eight people. Two attempts were made on Long Xianyun, but he survived on both occasions. Du Ba's brother, Du Qi, also survived one assassination attempt.[51] However, these violent responses failed to stop the aggressive actions of the magistrate and the Gong Regiment.

In May 1926, realizing that it would be impossible for the Donglan peasants to defeat their enemies, Wei Baqun and his friends began to seek external support. Their first move was to draft an announcement addressed to the Guangzhou government, the Central Committee of the KMT, the leaders of the New Guangxi Clique, the Guangxi Provincial Committee of the KMT, KMT branches in the counties, and mass associations and newspapers. In the announcement they reported the growth of peasant movements in Donglan and neighboring areas since the return of Wei Baqun and Chen Bomin from Guangzhou in 1925, including the creation of local KMT branches, peasant associations and the peasant movement institute. They emphasized that the students at Donglan Peasant Movement Institute were recruited and registered according to the policies enacted by the Central Committee of the KMT, and that the students had made efforts at teaching the peasants about the national revolution. They then described the atrocities committed in Donglan by Magistrate Huang and his local supporters as well as Commander Gong and his regiment. They demanded that Magistrate Huang be demoted; that local tyrants such as Du Ba and Long Xianyun be punished and made to repay the losses of the peasants; that Commander Gong be ordered to return all the weapons his soldiers had taken from the peasants; and that the new county magistrate should help reopen the peasant movement institute. This public announcement was issued in the name of the Donglan Peasant Association.[52]

In the same month, Wei Baqun sent Chen Bomin, president of the Donglan Peasant Association, and Chen Shouhe, committee member of the peasant association, to Nanning to seek support from provincial leaders. The two delegates were both well educated and very articulate. They distributed printed copies of the announcement of the Donglan peasant association and made speeches at meetings and gatherings in Nanning. Their call for outside support came at an opportune moment. In mid-1926 peasant movements were on the rise in southern China, particularly in Guangdong, where the United Front government was based. In Guangzhou, Communists and left-wing Nationalists, who were the strongest supporters of the peasant movements, were enjoying their brief moment of dominance over the Guangzhou government and the KMT, and they made it an official policy of the Guangzhou government to support peasant movements. "The national revolution is the revolution of the peasants" became a cliché among the leaders of the Guangzhou government at that time.

In Nanning, the two most powerful leaders of the New Guangxi Clique, Li Zongren and Huang Shaohong, were no friends of the peasants, but they had to at least tolerate the peasant movement, because they were part of the United Front government and had to support the official policy of that government. Moreover, the United Front policy had allowed some Communists and left-wing Nationalists to take up important positions in the provincial government of Guangxi. Governor Huang Shaohong later recalled that among the nine members of the executive committee of the Guangxi Branch of the KMT, seven were leftists. Since the Guangzhou government was supportive of the peasant movements, Li and Huang sometimes had to yield to their Communist and left-wing Nationalist subordinates in the provincial government. Governor Huang later admitted that he thought it would be easy to put down Wei Baqun's movement at that time, but did not do so mainly because of the opposition of his colleagues in Nanning and superiors in Guangzhou.[53] In the county seat of Donglan and Baise, Wei Baqun and his friends could find few supporters among government officials, but Nanning and Guangzhou were very different and the political atmosphere and trend in Nanning and Guangzhou was to have immediate impact on the peasant movement in Donglan.

Chen Bomin and Chen Shouhe immediately won the support of leftist officials and organizations in Nanning. The Workers' Association, the Women's

Association and the Students' Association, which were all under the control of leftists, offered their joint support to the peasants of Donglan by holding demonstrations and assemblies and releasing posters. Leading leftists in Nanning all stood behind Wei Baqun and his movement.[54] Among the leftists, Chen Xiewu and Chen Mianshu were particularly enthusiastic about supporting the Donglan peasant movement. Chen Xiewu was a left-wing Nationalist serving as the director of the Department of Peasant Affairs of the Guangxi Branch of the KMT. He was a well-trained Confucian scholar, who earned a juren degree after passing the civil service examination. He then went to study at Japan's Waseda University and became a follower of Sun Yat-sen during his stay in Japan. After returning to Guangxi, he worked for Governor Lu Rongting for a while. In 1920 and 1921 he was involved in the Association for Reforming Guangxi, of which Wei Baqun was also a member, although it is not certain whether the two ever met at that time. Since becoming the head of the Department of Peasant Affairs of the Guangxi Branch of the KMT in early 1926, Chen had been actively promoting the policy of rent reduction and because of that had alienated Governor Huang Shaohong. He had also been involved in creating peasant associations in various counties. Above all, he had founded Guangxi Peasant Movement Institute in Nanning, which was similar to Wei Baqun's Donglan Peasant Movement Institute. It was therefore natural for Chen Xiewu to see Wei Baqun as an ally. In his perspective, what Wei Baqun had been doing conformed completely to the policies of his department and the KMT. Wei Baqun's confrontations with the magistrate and the army might remind Chen of his own clashes with the governor. After hearing a report made by Chen Bomin and Chen Shouhe at a gathering, Chen Xiewu invited one of them to attend the meeting of the executive committee of the Guangxi Branch of the KMT and reported their case to the committee.[55]

Chen Mianshu, head of the Department of Youth Affairs of the Guangxi Branch of the KMT, became another strong supporter of Wei Baqun and his movement. Chen was a descendant of a Taiping rebel. Like Chen Xiewu, Chen Mianshu was from southern Guangxi and had been a long-time member of the KMT. He had also been involved in the Association for Reforming Guangxi. A graduate of Beijing Advanced Normal School (later Beijing Normal University), he had assisted Chen Duxiu with the publication of *New Youth* and had participated actively in the May Fourth Movement. In late 1921, both Wei Baqun and Chen Mianshu were in Nanning and the two became close friends. Since their parting in 1921, Chen Mianshu had joined the CCP and had worked for a time for the revolutionary government in Guangzhou. In early 1926, he supported Chen Xiewu in creating Guangxi Peasant Movement Institute. In addition to heading the Department of Youth Affairs, he was also the leader of the Nanning branch of the CCP and president of the *Nanning Republican Daily*, the major newspaper of the city.[56] He later recalled that he became "extremely interested in" the dispute over the Donglan peasant movement after hearing a report made by Chen Bomin and Chen Shouhe. He also attended the meeting of the executive committee of the Guangxi Branch of the KMT to hear Chen Bomin talk about the case.

After hearing and discussing Chen Bomin's report, the executive committee, which was dominated by the Communists and left-wing Nationalists, made two decisions. One was to move the Gong Regiment out of Donglan immediately, and the other was to send Chen Xiewu to Donglan to investigate the case.[57] A third decision was made either during or after the meeting, which involved replacing Magistrate Huang Shouxian with a new magistrate appointed by Governor Huang. Obviously, all three decisions favored Wei Baqun and his supporters, although they failed to meet all the demands laid out in the public announcement of the Donglan Peasant Association. The right-wing Nationalists represented by Governor Huang were defeated by the leftists at the executive meeting and this would inevitably lead to the defeat of Governor Huang's representatives in Donglan.

The Gong Regiment left Donglan for Baise in June 1926 after receiving the order from the provincial government, and Magistrate Huang Shouxian left with the regiment. Wei Baqun sent his peasant soldiers to ambush the regiment and the magistrate, but failed to find them. The local supporters of Magistrate Huang and the Gong Regiment either left for Baise or moved to live in the county seat. But Long Xianyun and Du Ba, Wei Baqun's two most prominent local enemies, decided to stay in or near home. Du Ba turned his house in Wuzhuan into a fortress and Long Xianyun hid himself in the mountains. Wei Baqun immediately sent his men to attack the two, forcing Du Ba to move to the county seat and Long Xianyun to flee to Baise, where he later died.[58] The county seat soon fell into Wei Baqun's hands, forcing Du Ba to move to a village and hide with a former student.

Wei Baqun was surprised to discover after taking the county seat that his wife, Chen Lanfen, and baby son were still alive. Not long after they were taken away in February 1926, Wei Baqun thought that they had both been killed and decided to take Wang Juqiu as his new wife. Juqiu was from a village in Wuzhuan and was one of Wei Baqun's followers at that time.[59] When Lanfen returned home, Wei Baqun did not want to divorce either of the wives and thus became a polygamist. This did not cause an uproar among his followers, because polygamy was still widely practiced by wealthy men at that time. However, it was definitely an awkward arrangement for a revolutionary who had been an outspoken critic of the tradition and who had pledged his support for equality between men and women.

Soon after the departure of the Gong Regiment and Magistrate Huang Shouxian, Chen Xiewu arrived in Donglan to investigate the conflict between Wei Baqun's group and its enemies. Accompanying him was Huang Zuyu, the new magistrate of Donglan appointed by Governor Huang. Wei Baqun gathered more than five thousand people in Wuzhuan to welcome the investigator and the new magistrate and also to present their demands.[60] From June 14 to July 18, 1926, Chen Xiewu paid visits to 103 hamlets in forty-six villages scattered across four districts in the county. Wei Baqun sent Chen Bomin and Chen Shouhe to escort Chen Xiewu during his stay in Donglan. In every hamlet, Chen would carefully record the names of the victims and the attackers, the amount of money and properties taken, and the number of houses destroyed.[61] Chen Xiewu made no effort to conceal his sympathy and support for the peasant movement, and for that the peasants nicknamed him "the nanny of the Donglan peasants."[62] When Chen Xiewu decided to leave, Wei Baqun ordered Chen Bomin and Chen Shouhe to accompany him to Nanning. Back in Nanning, Chen Xiewu told Governor Huang that Wei Baqun was very popular in Donglan and was a true believer in Sun Yat-sen's Three Principles of the People. Chen suggested that the governor disregard the rumors about Wei Baqun spread by the landlords and "tyrants," and that the governor make a trip to Donglan to see for himself what was happening there. Governor Huang did not accept any of Chen's suggestions, which actually helped set the two further apart.[63]

Shortly after returning to Nanning, Chen Xiewu wrote a report entitled "The Massacre of the Peasants in Donglan of Guangxi," in which he condemned Magistrate Huang Shouxian and the Gong Regiment for their atrocities against the peasants and defended the violent actions of Wei Baqun and his followers. He also issued an open telegram expressing his sympathy and support for the Donglan peasant movement.[64] When Chen Xiewu submitted his report to the *Nanning Republican Daily* for publication, it caused a clash between the president and the editor-in-chief of the newspaper. Huang Huabiao, the editor-in-chief, was a leading right-wing Nationalist in Guangxi and a supporter of Governor Huang Shaohong. Naturally he did not want to have Chen's report published in his newspaper. Communist Chen Mianshu, the president of the newspaper, strongly supported the publication of the report. He went to argue with the editor-in-chief, but to no avail. Chen Xiewu then sent his report to Guangzhou and it was immediately published in *Peasant Movement*, a weekly created by the Department of Peasant Affairs of the KMT, although edited by Communists.[65] The Guangzhou government now began to get involved in the dispute over the Donglan peasant movement.

Even before the publication of Chen Xiewu's report, many in Guangzhou had already learned about the conflict in Donglan through public telegrams sent by Wei Baqun and his supporters. One of these telegrams claimed that in Wuzhuan alone Magistrate Huang Shouxian and the Gong Regiment had killed more than two hundred people and caused no less than six thousand people to become homeless. Those killed included people as old as seventy and as young as three. The telegrams also claimed that the prices for the certificates for the so-called good people could be as low as twenty silver dollars for those who did not support the peasant movement or as high as two thousand silver dollars for those who had been involved in the peasant movement.[66] *Guide Weekly*, the organ of the CCP, also covered the conflict in Donglan. Some in Guangzhou had already expressed their support for the peasants in Donglan before reading Chen Xiewu's report.

Very active in publicizing the incident and mobilizing support for Wei Baqun and his movement was a group of students from Guangxi who were waiting in Guangzhou to be sent to the Soviet Union to study. One of them argued that the conflict in Donglan was a replica of similar conflicts in rural Guangdong and that revolutionary forces in different parts of the country should be united, that the attack on the Donglan peasants should be taken as an attack on the national revolutionary movement.[67] Another student, Liao Mengqiao, was Magistrate Huang Shouxian's cousin. He wrote an open letter to Magistrate Huang accusing him of betraying his own promise to support the revolution and serve the people. He declared at the end of the letter that "my conscience does not allow me to stand on your side. I will join the peasants and organize other forces to attack you so as to take revenge for the victims. You used to be my beloved brother, but now you have become my enemy."[68]

Ruan Xiaoxian, Wei Baqun's teacher at Guangzhou Peasant Movement Institute, who was now a member of the executive committee of the Peasant Association of Guangdong as well as a member of the Committee on Peasant Movements of the KMT, expressed his concerns over the "brutal massacre" in Donglan at a meeting held in August 1926.[69] Wei Baqun's affiliations with Guangzhou Peasant Movement Institute helped connect his local revolution to the national movement. Because he was a student of the institute, because he returned to Donglan as a special agent for the peasant movement representing the KMT, and because what he had done in Donglan conformed to what he had been taught at the institute, the Donglan peasant movement was logically seen as an integral part of the national revolution. Whereas Magistrate Huang Shouxian and the local power holders claimed that Wei Baqun and his supporters were bandits that should be eliminated, the revolutionaries in Guangzhou and Nanning argued that Wei Baqun was a revolutionary and his movement should be supported.

Much of the debate centered around who had the legitimate right to use violence. Governor Huang Shaohong and his rightist supporters believed that only the government had the power to use violence and that it was illegal for peasants to use violence without official approval. Radical revolutionaries like Peng Pai, Mao Zedong, and Wei Baqun, however, argued that revolutionary peasants had the legitimate right to use violence against the "local tyrants and evil gentry." When commenting on the peasant movement in his native Hunan Province in late 1926, Mao went as far as to assert that "anyone with land is a bully; and all members of the gentry are evil" and "in correcting a wrong, we must be excessive in upholding the right."[70] The argument of the revolutionaries is reminiscent of Mencius' teaching, more than two thousand years before, that the people had the heaven-given right to revolt against an unjust ruler.

Chen Xiewu's firsthand report helped further publicize the conflict in Donglan. More and more peasant associations in other parts of the country expressed their moral support for the peasants of Donglan. Students from Guangxi who were studying in the Soviet Union (or were on their way to the Soviet Union) continued to express their sympathy for the Donglan peasants. One of them praised the Donglan peasants as the vanguards of peasant liberation in Guangxi.[71]

The external moral and political support, although helping remove Wei Baqun's two most powerful enemies, Magistrate Huang Shouxian and the Gong Regiment, did not completely resolve the conflict in Donglan. Huang Zuyu, the new magistrate who came to Donglan with Chen Xiewu, shared his predecessor's attitude toward the peasant movement. If Chen Xiewu was representing the Communists and left wing Nationalists, then Huang Zuyu was a member of the right wing faction led by Governor Huang. Whereas Chen Xiewu spent most of his time with Wei Baqun's supporters in the villages during his stay in Donglan, Huang Zuyu stayed in the county seat surrounding himself with Wei Baqun's enemies. Wei Baqun sent his peasant soldiers to besiege the county seat shortly after the arrival of the new magistrate and announced that the peasant associations would break off economic relations with the "local tyrants and evil gentry" living in the county seat, causing the price of rice to skyrocket.[72] Wei Baqun and his peasant soldiers wanted the magistrate to respond to their demands, which included punishing those who had carried out the massacre, compensating the losses of the peasants, and reopening the peasant movement institute. From June to September 1926 the magistrate gave no response to any of the demands. Wei Baqun or one of his supporters then composed a folksong to ridicule the magistrate as a false revolutionary who talked about supporting the peasants while in Nanning, but actually suppressed them upon arrival in Donglan. The magistrate then reported to Governor Huang that the peasants were planning another attack on the county seat, and Governor Huang gave him permission to use militia forces and the county police to defend the town.[73]

The expected attack came in September 1926. Wei Baqun's men easily took the town, and the magistrate fled to Hechi in the east, from where he sent a report to Governor Huang Shaohong, asking him to send troops to Donglan to crack down on the "bandits" led by Wei Baqun. Meanwhile, Wei Baqun reported directly to the Guangzhou government and the KMT leaders that Magistrate Huang Zuyu was no better than his predecessor and asked for a revolutionary magistrate. At the same time, he made Ya Sumin the provisional magistrate and sent Chen Bomin and Huang Daquan's brother, Huang Daye, to Nanning to seek support.[74]

This new development caused a second round of confrontation and negotiation between the left and the right in Nanning. Governor Huang insisted that "mass associations should not resort to the use of violence." He condemned Wei Baqun for using violence and Chen Xiewu for his support of the Donglan peasant movement. Chen was forced to resign, but the leftists managed to have another leftist, Yu Zuobai, appointed as Chen's successor. Although his colleagues such as Li Zongren, Bai Chongxi and Huang Xuchu liked to describe Yu as a selfish opportunist who would often change sides to serve his own interest,[75] Yu's friendship with the Leftists seemed to be quite consistent and persistent. To respond to Governor Huang's criticism, the Communists organized a mass assembly in Nanning to show popular support for the peasants of Donglan. Several thousand peasants came to the assembly and they demanded that the provincial government send officials to Donglan to investigate the situation.[76]

The Communist leaders of Guangxi saw this as a great opportunity to bring Wei Baqun and his movement under the control of the CCP. A report submitted to the CCP Central Committee by the leading Communists in Guangxi testified that:

> When the government was considering sending a new magistrate to deal with the problems arising from the conflict in Donglan, we seized the opportunity and tried to penetrate into the Donglan peasant movement (at that time there was not a single comrade in Donglan). We did three things: the first was to send Chen Mianshu to serve as the magistrate (he was acceptable to all sides); the second was to organize the Committee for Supporting the Peasant Friends in Donglan to mobilize public support; and the third was to organize an investigation committee. . . . Two thirds of the committee members were our comrades. Our purpose was twofold: on the one hand, we wanted to enhance our influence on public opinions; on the other hand, we hoped to take the opportunity to examine the peasant associations and peasant armies [in Donglan], and to help improve these institutions and strengthen their organization.

The report also confirmed that it was part of their plan to bring Wei Baqun into the CCP and to send more Communists to work in Donglan.[77] The Communists did not show much interest in Wei Baqun during his stay at Guangzhou Peasant Movement Institute, but they now realized how important and influential he had become and were very eager to recruit him. The actions taken by the Communist leaders of Guangxi obviously conformed to the policies of the CCP Central Committee, which showed strong interest in promoting peasant movements during the Northern Expedition.[78] In a document about peasant movements drafted in November 1926, the CCP Central Committee listed Guangxi as one of the provinces deserving special attention. It specifically called for the integration of the peasant movement in Donglan and similar movements in other counties along the Right River.[79] A Nationalist observer argued that the Comintern adviser Darhanov was the one who gave the order to incorporate Wei Baqun's movement. Darhanov was in Nanning and was a close friend of Yu Zuobai's at that time. According to this observer, Darhanov suggested that Yu Zuobai send a team of Communists to Donglan to recruit Wei Baqun and other leaders, to organize a CCP branch, and to expand and strengthen peasant associations. He wanted the team to accomplish its tasks in three months.[80]

The Communists managed to get Governor Huang Shaohong's approval to dispatch the investigation committee to Donglan. Chen Mianshu became the leader of the committee, which consisted of seven members. Among the seven were at least three Communists and one Communist Youth League Member, and there were only one or two right wing Nationalists on the committee. The Youth League member was also the only female member of the team. Undoubtedly the most important member of the team was Chen Mianshu, the Communist. The governor also asked him to serve as the magistrate of Donglan, and Chen Mianshu believed that Yu Zuobai played an important part in securing the position for him.[81] Governor Huang was willing to support Chen Mianshu's appointment partly because none of the right-wingers would accept that position. The right-wing officials knew that even the right-wing governor would not be able to protect them once they were in Donglan. Governor Huang had failed to protect two magistrates of Donglan he had appointed!

Wei Baqun's delegates, Chen Bomin and Huang Daye, returned to Donglan with the investigation committee, and the team arrived in Donglan in late October 1926. Wei Baqun organized a huge assembly to welcome the delegates. Peasants formed long lines by the road, each holding a red flag, and together they sang a revolutionary song about fighting imperialists and warlords that Wei Baqun had brought back from Guangzhou. Wei Baqun presided over the welcome party and also delivered a speech. At the end of the meeting Du Ba's elder brother Du Qi and a nephew were executed. Du Ba was still in hiding. Also executed was Wei Baqun's former friend, Chen Yuzao, a founding member of the Association for Reforming Donglan. Chen was from a wealthy family in the Western Mountains that hired farm hands, rented out land, and made profits from usury. He began to disassociate himself from Wei Baqun when the latter called for the elimination of tenancy and usury. In 1923, Chen decided not to participate in the attacks on the county seat, and during the second revolt the peasants in the Western Mountains began to attack him. He reacted by offering service to the Gong Regiment during the Donglan Massacre.[82] Chen was the first founding member of the Association for Reforming Donglan to be liquidated by Wei Baqun.

Five years had passed since Chen Mianshu and Wei Baqun parted with each other in Nanning in late 1921. The two old friends should be very excited to see each other again in Donglan. Like Chen Xiewu, Chen Mianshu and the other leftist members of the investigation committee sided with Wei Baqun and his supporters. Their findings naturally confirmed what had been described in Chen Xiewu's report. In November 1926, Chen Mianshu sent some members of his team back to Nanning to report to the provincial leaders about their investigation. To put pressure on the provincial government, the Communists organized another mass assembly in Nanning and invited a leftist member of Chen Mianshu's team to report about the conditions in Donglan. On November 28, 1926 the Guangxi provincial government issued a public telegram in which it pledged its support for the Donglan peasant movement and announced its decisions to hand Magistrate Huang Shouxian to the court for inquiry, to demote Huang Shouxian's successor Magistrate Huang Zuyu, to demand the army to check the behavior of Commander Gong Shouyi, to list five local tyrants, including Du Ba and Long Xianyun, as wanted criminals and give their properties to the Donglan Peasant Association, and to exempt the peasants of Donglan of their grain tax for the year of 1926. The telegram also accused Wei Baqun of assisting the Yunnan Army in the previous year and of failing to get official approval before launching his peasant movement, but meted out no punishment for him.[83] Finally, the leftists in the provincial government won their battle over the rightists in Nanning and they also helped their ally Wei Baqun to win his battle against his enemies in Donglan.

Triumph

Chen Mianshu's arrival signaled the triumph of Wei Baqun's forces over their enemies and it was the beginning of the high point of Wei Baqun's second revolt. The victory was brought about primarily because of the strong external support provided by the Communists and left-wing Nationalists in Nanning and Guangzhou. The right-wing Nationalist leaders in Nanning, who held the most powerful positions in the provincial government and army, had to yield to their leftist colleagues mainly because the leftists, in addition to holding important positions in the Guangzhou government and the provincial government in Nanning, were very efficient in mobilizing public support for their cause. Rightist leaders such as Li Zongren and Huang Shaohong did not change their minds about the peasant movement, but they felt that it was wise to make a concession to the leftists. The leftists decided to offer their support to Wei Baqun and his followers because they recognized Wei Baqun as a fellow revolutionary and his movement as the type they were trying to promote. Wei Baqun's previous connections with revolutionaries like Liao Zhongkai, Chen

Mianshu, Ruan Xiaoxian and others, and organizations such as the KMT, the Association for Reforming Guangxi, and Guangzhou Peasant Movement Institute, certainly helped solidify his alliance with the outside leftists. The triumph of the Donglan peasant movement was a victory for the Communists in Guangxi and it was the beginning of the integration of the Donglan peasant movement into the larger Communist movement in China. Until October 1926 there were no Communists in Donglan. Afterward, the number of Communists would increase gradually, and they would finally turn the Donglan peasant movement into an important part of the Communist revolution.

Communist Chen Mianshu became the most powerful official in Donglan in October 1926. In addition to serving as the magistrate, he was also the leader of the Donglan branch of the KMT. He had the support of the provincial government, and with Wei Baqun as a strong ally, Chen now also enjoyed the support of the peasant association. There are even suggestions that Chen Mianshu also served as the president of the Donglan Peasant Association during his stay there.[84] Since their birth, the peasant associations and their predecessors, the citizens' assemblies, had always been in opposition to the county government, and Wei Baqun and his supporters had experienced conflicts with quite a few magistrates, including Meng Yuanliang (February to September 1923), Huang Qiongyao (September 1923 to June 1924), Huang Shouxian (June 1924 to June 1926), and Huang Zuyu (June to October 1926). Chen Mianshu became the first magistrate of Donglan to enjoy the full support of the peasant associations. Chen Mianshu and Wei Baqun now entered a symbiotic relationship. Chen established tight control over the Donglan branch of the KMT by expelling all the rightists from the party through a procedure of re-registration. By March 1927, the reorganized KMT branch of Donglan had admitted more than three thousand members, most of whom were peasants.[85] Chen Mianshu thus established himself as the first officially approved revolutionary magistrate of Donglan.

Shortly after taking the county seat in September 1926, Wei Baqun began to work on reopening the peasant movement institute. The arrival of Chen Mianshu made it certain that the new county government would support the move. In November 1926 the second class of Donglan Peasant Movement Institute formally started. The second class was different from the first in several aspects. Whereas the first class had to be held in a cave, the second class was moved to Yucai Advanced Elementary School in Wuzhuan, which had been previously controlled by Du Ba and his family. The first class admitted students from Donglan and more than ten neighboring counties, but the second class recruited more students from Donglan and fewer from other counties. The first class admitted male students only, whereas the second class also took in female students. In total the second class had about 120 students, including 81 men and 48 women. Most of the female students were around eighteen years old, and some of them were already married. Wei Baqun's two wives Chen Lanfen and Wang Juqiu, his youngest sister Wei Zhenglun, Huang Shuxiang's younger sister Huang Meilun, who later became Wei Baqun's sister-in-law, and Wei Baqun's two younger brothers Wei Jing (the elder) and Wei Jing (the younger), were all students of the second class. Men and women were organized into different classes, and the women's class was also named the Women's Movement Institute.[86]

The curriculum for the men was similar to that of the first class. Teachers included some younger followers of Wei Baqun who had joined him at the beginning of the second revolt. Chen Gutao and Huang Hongfu had just graduated from the sixth class of Guangzhou Peasant Movement Institute and both taught in the second class. Chen Hongtao, who had recently attended a training program in Wuzhou, taught courses about the Russian Revolution and the Three Principles of the People and was in charge of political education.[87]

Female students in the second class followed a different curriculum, partly because their level of education was, on average, much lower than that of the male students. Among the forty female students, only four had received elementary level education and the rest were illiterate. Their curriculum therefore had to focus on literacy education. They were taught how to read and write their own names as well as the names of their teachers and relatives. They also learned to read and write popular political messages and slogans, particularly those about the liberation of women. When Wei Baqun came to teach a class one day, he taught the women how to read and write phrases meaning "enforcing the liberation of women," and "freedom of marriage, freedom of love, education and awareness, inheritance of property, right to political participation, elimination of oppression, group solidarity, independent life, and equality between men and women." Because the female students were trained to serve as instigators, they also took lessons on how to make speeches and sing folksongs. To ensure that these women would be able to protect themselves, Wei Baqun invited a master from a neighboring county to teach martial arts to the female students every evening.[88]

Women not only were brought into the peasant movement institute, but also had their own organizations and became part of the power structure. The first women's association in Donglan was created in the Western Mountains in 1925. Initially it had only 9 members, but by early 1926 its membership increased to nearly 2700. In November 1926, with Chen Mianshu's support, the Second Peasant Congress of Donglan was held in the county seat. Among the 268 delegates attending the congress, there were 21 women.[89] In late 1926, with the assistance of Huang Ruoshan, the only female member on the investigation committee headed by Chen Mianshu, the First Women's Congress of Donglan was held in the county seat, which resulted in the transformation of the earlier women's association into the Donglan Association for the Liberation of Women.

There were nearly 3700 members in the new association.[90] By late 1926 in excess of 2600 women had joined the peasant associations in Donglan and some of them held official positions in the associations. There was a Department of Women's Affairs in each peasant association. Huang Zhengxiu, wife of revolutionary Bai Hanyun, served as the director of the Department of Women's Affairs of the Donglan Peasant Association, and Huang Meilun was the deputy director. Women also became active in party affairs. By March 1927 no less than two hundred women from Donglan had joined the KMT, making women a visible minority among the 3117 KMT members in the county. Some women, such as Chen Hongtao's future wife, Pan Xiaomei, even became targets for CCP recruitment.[91]

Encouraged by all the messages about liberation and equality, women became more and more assertive in social and personal affairs. Chen Mianshu was excited to report that more than one thousand women in Donglan had cut their hair short and adopted the new hairstyle that was popular in coastal areas.[92] In early 1927, the Donglan Peasant Association approved the first divorce case, which involved a woman named Huang Yumei who wanted to leave her abusive husband. The peasant association made great efforts to publicize the case in order to educate other women. Increasingly more women then came out to divorce their husbands, prompting the peasant association to announce that it would approve only those cases that met one of ten conditions, including the husband often physically abused the wife; the husband prevented the wife from joining the revolution; the husband was a reactionary who was against the peasant association; the husband was involved in gambling, stealing, or banditry; the husband was lazy and did not do much farming; and the husband had physical disabilities.[93]

Politically, women played a particularly important role in making propaganda for the revolution, and they were adroit at bringing revolutionary messages to the peasants through folksongs. These made them comparable to the female revolutionaries in some other places, including Haifeng in Guangdong and Macheng in Hubei, who also used folksongs and other forms of popular culture to make connections with the peasants. Both Wei Baqun and Peng Pai personally composed quite a few revolutionary folksongs that became popular among their followers, and at least one revolutionary folksong from Haifeng was brought to Donglan and became popular there.[94] Some women served as messengers for the leaders.[95]

In addition to the peasant movement institute run by the Donglan Peasant Association, every township set up a school for adult peasants and a school for children from poor families, and these were all free. There was a speech platform at every market and some leaders of the peasant associations or students from the peasant movement institute would come to make speeches on market days.

Literacy education and political education became the striking features of the new educational system in Donglan.[96] Education became another governmental function the peasant association undertook in Donglan.

With Chen Mianshu as magistrate, the county government began to do what other revolutionary governments were doing in Guangdong, Hunan, and other provinces. Chen made it manifest that "I came to Donglan not to serve as an official but to make a revolution." Taxes were reduced or abolished and he allowed the peasant associations to collect and use some of the taxes; some notorious bandits were executed; and former power holders who were branded local tyrants and evil gentry were put on trial and some were executed.[97] Du Ba was one of those denounced and tried at a mass meeting. After being labeled a most wanted criminal by the provincial government, he went to hide in a former student's house. The student then decided to cooperate with the new county government and turned his teacher in. At the denunciation meeting, Du Ba was made to wear hat and gown made of paper and a pair of wooden glasses, and after the meeting he was paraded through the streets.[98] These were methods adopted by radical peasants throughout southern China at that time to humiliate their former masters. Forty years later the Red Guards would use these same techniques against many of the senior revolutionaries who had invented these tactics. The county government wanted to put Du Ba to death, but it failed to get approval from the provincial government. Du Ba soon died in jail. The revolutionaries claimed that he committed suicide, but Du Ba's sons later reported to the government that their father had died of torture and starvation.[99]

One assignment Chen Mianshu had received from the leaders of the Guangxi branch of the CCP was to expand Communist influence in Donglan. In the same month that Chen Mianshu arrived in Donglan, three other Communists also came to Donglan—Chen Hongtao, Chen Gutao, and Yan Min. Chen Hongtao and Chen Gutao were the first two Donglan natives to join the CCP, and both of them had joined Wei Baqun's peasant movement before becoming Communists. Yan Min was from Guangdong. A graduate of Guangdong University, which was created by the KMT, he joined the CCP in 1925. The CCP leaders had planned to send him to the Soviet Union for training, and when that failed to happen they dispatched him to Guangxi to help spread communism. He arrived in Nanning in early 1926 and the Right River region in July 1926. In late 1926, the four Communists formed the first CCP cell in Donglan with Chen Hongtao as its head.[100] According to one source, the cell had a fifth member, Huang Hongyi, who had been brought into the CCP by Yan Min while a student in Nanning.[101] Most other sources omit him, possibly because he later left the party.

As mentioned previously, another assignment Chen Mianshu had received from his CCP superiors before leaving for Donglan was to bring Wei Baqun into the CCP. That did not happen immediately. One account holds that shortly after the creation of the CCP cell in Donglan, Wei Baqun submitted a letter to the cell, which read: "I, Baqun, am willing to dedicate my body to the party, to follow the party in the elimination of inequality in the world and the creation of an equal society, and to live a spectacular life and die a spectacular death."[102] Although there are claims that Wei Baqun joined the CCP in late 1926 or late 1928, there is solid evidence showing that Wei Baqun was admitted into the party in late 1926 or early 1927 on Chen Mianshu's recommendation as a probationary member, but his membership was not formally approved until August 1929.[103] Several factors contributed to the delay. In April 1927, the Nationalists turned against the Communists, causing the collapse of the United Front in all places and at all levels. In Guangxi the purge led to the fall of the CCP network, which was only partially revived in early 1928 and not completely restored until July 1929. During the months between April 1927 and early 1928, there still existed CCP organizations in the Right River region, but these organizations probably did not have the authority to finalize Wei Baqun's party membership.

The purge and the ensuing collapse of the Communist system in Guangxi could only cause a delay after April 1927, but not before that. What had prevented the CCP from admitting Wei Baqun as a formal party member before April 1927 was probably a policy enacted by the party in early 1925, according to which new party members had to go through a probationary period before they could become formal members, and the length of the probationary period was three months for workers and six months for nonworkers. But the party gave local branches the power to shorten or prolong the probationary period of applicants. For applicants from wealthy families, the probationary period could be as long as one to two years.[104] It seemed that both Chen Hongtao and Chen Gutao did not go through a long probationary period, but Wei Baqun was likely made to endure a probationary period of six months or even longer partly because he was a landlord, but more importantly because the Communists believed that he had some major weaknesses. Reports made by Communist leaders during that period show that the Communists did not recognize Wei Baqun's movement as a real Communist land revolution. They saw Wei Baqun as a peasant leader with some serious flaws, one of which was that he "was surrounded by the anarchists,"[105] although it is not certain who these anarchists were. Another flaw, which is related to the anarchist accusation, was that "the CCP has had little influence on him [Wei Baqun]. . . . He always lead the people like a hero would lead his worshippers."[106]

The Communists were interested not just in bringing Wei Baqun into their party, but also in changing both Wei Baqun the person and the movement he was leading. Chen Mianshu, while praising Wei Baqun for his bravery and courage as well as for his dedication to the interest of the peasants, argued that the Donglan Massacre had occurred because Wei Baqun's movement was primarily based on sympathy and chivalry, that Wei had failed to apply correct theories and tactics in leading the peasants, and that he had also failed to find allies among other worker-peasant associations, resulting in isolationism.[107] Chen Mianshu had the impression that Wei Baqun had attached too much importance to building up military power, but had not paid enough attention to political work. He suggested that Wei Baqun and the other leaders take defensive positions in military affairs, but be more aggressive in promoting their political cause.[108] Wei Baqun's secretary claimed that Chen Mianshu also felt that Wei Baqun was too unruly and brutal.[109] Another leading Communist remarked that before the CCP fully established itself in Donglan in 1929, Wei Baqun was the only person the peasants in Donglan would follow. What he implied was that the peasants were following an individual rather than an organization, or a cause. He echoed Chen Mianshu's criticism about Wei Baqun's negligence of political work by arguing that at that time the peasants in Donglan had a deep hatred toward the ruling class, but possessed little political consciousness.[110] The Communists wanted to incorporate the Donglan peasant movement into the Communist revolution, but Wei Baqun and his supporters were probably resistant to the Communist takeover. Wei Baqun and the Communists became allies during this period, but a complete integration was not yet achieved.

The Guangxi Special Committee of the CCP created in early 1928 continued the policy adopted before April 1927 regarding Wei Baqun's party membership. In May 1928 the committee sent Yan Min to Donglan to inform Wei Baqun of the new policies of the party and help him to reorganize the revolutionary government.[111] But it did not offer formal party membership to Wei Baqun. In October 1928, after Yan Min became the head of the CCP organization in the Right River region he immediately admitted Huang Zhifeng, the leader of the peasant movement of Fengyi County, into the CCP,[112] which indicates that he had the authority to bring people into the party. Yan Min kept in touch with Wei Baqun, but did not offer him formal CCP membership, possibly because he still believed that Wei Baqun did not meet the standards of a CCP member. Later the CCP special committee of the Right River region would criticize itself for adopting a mechanistic approach in regard to the issue of Wei Baqun's party membership,[113] suggesting that it was the CCP's fault that Wei Baqun did not become a full member of the party sooner and that despite the suspicions and delay, Wei Baqun never lost his interest in joining the CCP.

In early 1927, Chen Mianshu left Donglan. One account claims that Chen was called back by the provincial government because the right-wing leaders did not want him to "pour fuel onto the fire" in Donglan,[114] but some CCP documents vaguely mention that the Communists had to leave Donglan because of conflicts with local peasant movement leaders led by Wei Baqun. One of the documents reveals that the secret activities of the CCP members in Donglan caused some misunderstandings, and therefore they had to stop and leave.[115] A Nationalist source asserts that Chen Mianshu became unhappy about Wei Baqun's unruliness and began to scheme to remove Wei Baqun and put in his place younger leaders such as Chen Gutao. The scheme was discovered by Wei Baqun and so Chen Mianshu had to leave. This argument is supported by Wei Libo, who was Wei Baqun's secretary at that time.[116] This claim might be at least partially true because not long after Chen Mianshu's departure, Chen Gutao and Chen Hongtao also left Donglan. Chen Gutao would never return to Donglan to work with Wei Baqun again. Chen Hongtao spent two years in the counties along the Right River and would become a close ally of Wei Baqun again in 1929. The other outside Communist, Yan Min, also left.[117] Wei Libo mentioned a conflict between Chen Mianshu and Chen Xiewu and cited that as a reason for Chen Mianshu's departure.[118] This was very unlikely because Chen Xiewu had lost power even before Chen Mianshu left Nanning for Donglan.

Gao Yaoguang, Chen Mianshu's assistant at that time, confirmed that it was Chen Mianshu himself who decided that it was time for him to leave Donglan and that his departure did not have much to do with his alleged conflicts with Wei Baqun. Chen told Gao that the Comintern adviser, Michael Borodin, and the leaders of the Guangxi branch of the CCP had instructed him to work in Donglan for four months and then return to Nanning. Before leaving Donglan, Chen told Gao that there was a possibility for him to return. After arriving in Nanning, Chen informed Gao that a new magistrate had been appointed and therefore he would not return to Donglan. Gao also recalled that before leaving Donglan, Chen Mianshu held meetings with Wei Baqun, Chen Bomin and others for several days, and on his way to Nanning, Chen made a stop in Wuzhuan to say goodbye to Wei Baqun. It was at that point that Wei Baqun told Chen Mianshu that the right-wing Nationalists had begun to purge the Communists and leftists and warned Chen to be cautious. Wei probably had learned about the purge from the anarchist Ye Yimao, who had just arrived in Donglan from Nanning to escape from his pursuers. Before Chen Mianshu left Nanning for Donglan in late 1926, Yu Zuobai gave him a revolver as a gift, and Chen left the revolver for Wei Baqun before leaving Donglan. Gao's impression was that there were no misgivings of any sort between the two old friends.[119]

During the second revolt, Wei Baqun developed close connections with three political forces: Communists represented by Chen Mianshu, Yan Min, Chen Hongtao and Chen Gutao, left wing Nationalists such as Chen Xiewu and Yu Zuobai, and anarchists like Ye Yimao. The three groups were both allies and competitors and they all tried to win Wei Baqun's loyalty. Communist Lei Jingtian would recall later that both Nationalist Chen Xiewu and anarchist Ye Yimao wanted to establish control over the peasant movement in Donglan, Fengshan and the Right River region.[120] It seemed that Wei Baqun was willing to work with all three groups and tried to maintain a balance among them. In so doing he was able to maintain his independence.

If it is true that Chen Mianshu did have conflicts with Wei Baqun, then they would have been much less serious than Chen's confrontations with the right-wing Nationalists. In December 1926, Chen wrote a report about the Donglan peasant movement in which he confirmed that Wei Baqun and his followers were not bandits, but revolutionaries who were fighting for the interests of the peasants, and that the local tyrants and evil gentry, the militia forces and the Gong Regiment were oppressive and exploitative. He agreed with Chen Xiewu that the violent actions of the peasants were justifiable and urged the provincial government to stand behind Wei Baqun and the peasants.[121] Chen's report was approved by the leftist members of the investigation team, but not by the right-wing members, who drafted a separate report condemning Wei Baqun and his followers. These caused further conflict between the leftists and the rightists in the provincial party branch, which decided to publish both reports in the *Nanning Republican Daily*. However, the workers at the printing shop, who were supporters of the Donglan peasants, replaced the rightist report with a public telegram endorsing the Donglan peasants. Two workers were arrested after this incident.[122]

In all major aspects, Chen Mianshu completely agreed with Chen Xiewu. If the right-wing Nationalists could not stand Chen Xiewu, then they would like Chen Mianshu even less. Chen Xiewu merely submitted a report, but did not try to make changes in Donglan. Chen Mianshu did not just present a report, but was also directly involved in changing Donglan in favor of Wei Baqun and his supporters. It was fortunate for him that he managed to sneak out of Guangxi before the right-wingers began their purge. Otherwise, he would have certainly become a victim of the white terror.

Decline

Chen Mianshu's departure from Donglan was permanent. He would never return, and he and Wei Baqun would never see each other again. Although he was a prolific writer and outlived Wei Baqun by six years, he did not write anything about Wei Baqun and his movement other than the report he submitted in 1926. The decline of the second revolt began as soon as Chen Mianshu left Donglan. Two months after Chen's departure, Chiang Kai-shek launched the purge of the Communists. The leaders of the New Guangxi Clique, who had been in clashes with the leftists for a long time, participated enthusiastically in enforcing the white terror against the Communists. The three supreme leaders of the clique, Li Zongren, Huang Shaohong, and Bai Chongxi, were all present at the meeting presided over by Chiang Kai-shek that made the decision about the purge and all supported the decision. Diana Lary argues that without the support of the New Guangxi Clique, it would have been virtually impossible for Chiang Kai-shek to carry out the purge. Huang Xianfan, a Zhuang historian from Guangxi, agrees.[123] Bai Chongxi directly masterminded the purge in Shanghai, which was very bloody. Years later he would be proud to admit that people of that time often interpreted the phrase "white terror" as "Bai terror" since his family name Bai happened to mean white.[124] Huang Shaohong later recalled that he had conflicts with the leftists on several issues, including the status of Confucianism, the workers movements, and the peasant movements, but his primary motivation for supporting the purge was his fear of the peasant movements, particularly the Donglan peasant movement led by Wei Baqun. His friend, Governor Li Jishen of Guangdong, had similar fears of the peasant movement in Hailufeng led by Peng Pai. Huang admitted that he did not support the peasant movement partly because he was from a landlord family that collected annual rent of more than five hundred piculs.[125]

The right-wing Nationalists began to arrest the leftists in Nanning on the same day that Chiang Kai-shek and Bai Chongxi started to kill the Communists in Shanghai. In April 1927 alone, more than 390 suspected leftists were arrested and among them 27 were executed. Those killed included not only Communists, but also left-wing Nationalists. All critics of the right-wing policies were rounded up no matter whether they were Communists or Nationalists. Only the natives of Rong County were spared, because Governor Huang Shaohong and many of his subordinates in the provincial government were from that county. Governor Huang later explained that the only reason for Wei Baqun's ally Chen Xiewu to be spared was because he was a native of Rong County. The right-wingers did not even spare Li Zhengfeng, cousin of General Li Zongren, or Lei Peitao, younger brother of an important official in the provincial government.[126] Both Li and Lei were leading Communists in Guangxi. Most of those who were killed during the purge were strong supporters of Wei Baqun and his movement in Donglan.

In the Left River and Right River area several important peasant movement leaders were arrested and executed during the purge. Because Donglan was so far away from political centers such as Nanning, Nanjing, and Wuhan, the wave of the anti-Communist campaign did not arrive there immediately. It is ironic that although the Communist leaders in Guangxi had reservations about admitting Wei Baqun into their party, the right-wing Nationalists had no problem identifying Wei Baqun as a true Communist. To them, those who were engaged in peasant movements or workers' movements were Communists, or at least leftists. Governor Huang Shaohong believed that Wei Baqun had joined the CCP during his stay at Guangzhou Peasant Movement Institute in 1925, which was not true. His successor, Huang Xuchu, saw Wei Baqun as the "most reckless Communist" in Guangxi in 1927.[127] In late 1927 and early 1928, the provincial government decided to clean the names of former magistrate Huang Shouxian and the five local power holders who had been punished for their involvement in the making of the Donglan Massacre. The confiscated properties of the five families were returned. Magistrate Huang returned to Donglan to fight Wei Baqun as an officer in the government army and at least two of the five local leaders became commanders of local anti-Communist militia units. At the same time the government listed Wei Baqun and some of his followers as most wanted criminals and ordered the confiscation of the family properties of some of them.[128]

Governor Huang ordered his generals to attack the county seat of Donglan as early as April 1927, but his generals did not take immediate actions against Wei Baqun. They probably knew that they were not yet ready to deal with Wei Baqun, who lived in a faraway place, could hide himself in many different places, and had many local supporters. Although there were no formal and large enemy forces in Donglan, Wei Baqun was still very cautious about his safety, fearing assassins. He would not sleep in the same place for more than one night and sometimes he would move two or three times during a single evening.[129]

The safe haven of Donglan allowed Wei Baqun to create his third class of Donglan Peasant Movement Institute in early July 1927, nearly three months after the Nationalists began the purge. The third class, like the second, was housed in Yucai Advanced Elementary School in Wuzhuan. There were 127 students coming from Donglan, Fengshan, Baise, Hechi, Du'an, and other counties. All the students were men, and they were sent to the institute by their peasant associations. Students all had meals in the institute, but had to pay for their food. Those from well-to-do families paid out of their own pockets, whereas students from poor families received subsidies from their peasant associations. The curriculum and extracurricular activities were similar to those of the first two classes.[130]

Wei Baqun served as the director of the third class as he did for the first two. The three most important teachers, Ye Yimao, Bi Xueping, and Zhao Shijun, were all non-native revolutionaries who would not have been in Donglan had there not been a white terror. The most controversial among the teachers was Ye Yimao, the academic officer and instructor of the third class. According to one source, Ye had accompanied Chen Xiewu to Donglan in early 1926 and therefore was an old friend of Wei Baqun's.[131] He had been one of the most well-known anarchists in Guangxi, and a close friend of the famous anarchist writer Ba Jin. To some Communists his presence at the institute further confirmed Wei Baqun's connections with the anarchists. However, by 1927 the Communists had completely overwhelmed the anarchists and the distinctions between the two groups had been minimized. Nationalists like Governor Huang Shaohong did not believe that there was any substantial difference between them.[132] In Nanning Ye had worked alongside some Communists and at the peasant movement institute he continued to work closely with some Communists, and the right-wing Nationalists saw him as an enemy.

It is interesting to note that Wei Baqun always made sure that he hired the people with the most up to date revolutionary ideas to serve as the instructors of the peasant movement institute. Most of the instructors for the first class were his old comrades from the Association for Reforming Donglan. For the second class the most important instructors were Chen Hongtao, Chen Gutao, and Huang Hongfu. These were younger revolutionaries who had just attended training programs in Wuzhou and Guangzhou. The teaching staff of the third class was dominated by refugee revolutionaries who had recently arrived from Nanning.

At the end of the third class Wei Baqun asked Ye Yimao to accompany Wei's brother Wei Jing (the elder) to Wuhan to gather information about the political situation.[133] Wei Baqun knew that with the New Guangxi Clique in power, Baise and Nanning would remain hostile toward his movement in the foreseeable future. He wanted to learn more about what was happening between Chiang Kai-shek's Nanjing government and Wang Jingwei's Wuhan government and see whether or not he could find some supporters in Wuhan who would be able and willing to help him defeat his enemies. Unfortunately, the trip proved unsuccessful. When Wei Jing and Ye Yimao left Donglan for Wuhan in September 1927, the alliance of the Communists and left-wing Nationalists had collapsed for over a month, and Wuhan had become as hostile to the Communists and real leftists as had Nanjing. Wei Baqun apparently knew nothing about this new development. He was aware that Chiang Kai-shek had turned against the Communists, but did not know that Wang Jingwei had also become an enemy of the Communists. Ye would never return to Donglan and would never see his friend Wei Baqun again.

In July and August 1927, just before the white terror reached Donglan, Wei Baqun launched another round of red terror against the local wealthy families. The Liang family in Wuzhuan became the primary target. The family was of Hakka origin and had migrated to Donglan from Guangdong. The Liangs owned a large amount of land (estimates of their land property ranges from two hundred to four hundred or even more than one thousand mu) plus a pawnshop, and the family was also involved in usury. The Liang family had produced some local officials in the past, and therefore was another family that was not just wealthy, but also powerful. They even had private armed guards. In previous years the Liangs had been spared, possibly because one of the Liang brothers, Liang Shishu, who taught at Yucai Advanced Elementary School, was a close friend of Wei Baqun's. He was a founding member of the Association for Reforming Donglan and was involved in managing Donglan Peasant Movement Institute. Some sources vaguely mention that Liang Shishu later betrayed the revolution, but do not specify how he did that, or whether his betrayal was the cause or the result of the downfall of his family.

Wei Baqun decided to attack the Liang family mainly because it violated the policy of "no rent, no taxes and no payment for debt" by continuing to collect rent and debts from the poor peasants. It was believed that the Liangs had also been secretly colluding with other "local tyrants" and the enemy troops. Liang Shixun, the leader of the family, became the primary target, charged with as many as sixteen crimes. The revolutionaries put the leading members of the family to death, distributed their properties to the poor, and kept their grain for the officials of peasant associations and the peasant army and their houses as offices of the Wuzhuan peasant association. The students at the third class of the peasant movement institute participated in destroying the Liang family. Liang Shishu, who had been working for the third class of the peasant movement institute, was executed along with his elder brother and some other relatives.[134]

Wei Baqun's conflict with the Liang family took a different form from his clashes with Du Ba's family. One was protracted, whereas the other was rather abrupt. The attack on the Liang family was a sudden decision. Liang Shishu was the second founding member of the Association for Reforming Donglan to be executed by Wei Baqun. During the first revolt, many local power holders were threatened but not killed; the second revolt, however, almost wiped out the former ruling class of Donglan. The Dus and the Liangs were both destroyed during the second revolt. Both the Du and Liang families were relatively new immigrants to Wuzhuan, and in a way their elimination can be seen as a result of conflicts between indigenous strongmen and non-native power holders or between the village elites and the wealthy town dwellers.

Before launching a new extermination campaign against Wei Baqun, Governor Huang Shaohong sent Huang Yun, a native of Wuzhuan and a senior staff officer in the Nationalist army, to negotiate with Wei Baqun. The governor wanted to turn Wei Baqun's peasant army into a brigade in the Nationalist army, with Wei Baqun as the brigade commander.[135] From the governor's perspective, this was a wise scheme that would serve to eliminate a potential threat while at the same time strengthening his own military power. Wei Baqun turned down the offer, making him the target of an imminent military attack.

The Nationalist attack on Wei Baqun's movement began in August 1927, nearly four months after Chiang Kai-shek first launched his anti-Communist campaign. This put an abrupt end to the third class of the peasant movement institute, which was supposed to last six months. In that month General Liu Rifu dispatched Huang Mingyuan and his battalion to attack Fengshan where fierce fighting between local militia forces and the peasant army under Liao Yuanfang had been going on since April. Wei Baqun took most of his troops to Fengshan to help. The peasant army failed to prevent the well-equipped Huang Battalion from taking the county seat of Fengshan, but the Huang Battalion was not able to do much damage to the peasant army. In fact, Wei Baqun's forces efficiently besieged the county seat so that the Huang Battalion did not dare to venture out of the town.[136] This was a strategy that Wei Baqun had used in Donglan earlier.

In October 1927, realizing that one battalion of troops would not be sufficient for the task of defeating Wei Baqun and his forces, Governor Huang decided to send two regiments to the Right River region. One of the two was none other than the Gong Regiment under General Liu Rifu, which had committed the Donglan Massacre in early 1926. Their strategy was for the Gong Regiment to attack the western front of Wei Baqun's base area, whereas the second regiment, commanded by Lin Huating, would attack the eastern front of Wei Baqun's base area from Hechi. Both regiments were part of the Seventh Army, the war machine of the New Guangxi Clique, which was in turn part of the Nationalist Army under Chiang Kai-shek. Wei Baqun's force suffered initial defeats at the hands of the two powerful regiments. October 12, 1927 was a black day for Wei Baqun, because two of his close followers were killed on that day. One was his half-brother, Wei Jing. A graduate of Yucai Advanced Elementary School and the second class of the peasant movement institute, Wei Jing joined Wei Baqun's movement in 1925 and was a lower ranking officer in the peasant army. He was only eighteen years old when he was killed by a traitor. The other follower killed on that day was Huang Shulin, who had been a founding member of the Association for Reforming Donglan and an instructor of the first class of the peasant movement institute. Huang and Chen Bomin were traveling from the county seat to Wuzhuan when they ran into enemy forces on their way. Chen survived, but Huang did not.[137]

The Nationalist troops easily took the county seat and other towns. Wei Baqun and his forces retreated to the Western, Central and Eastern mountains, and the Nationalists soon followed them into the mountains. The Nationalists could take whatever village or town they wanted, but they were not able to destroy Wei Baqun's troops or capture Wei Baqun and the other leaders. Wei Baqun dispersed his troops and created small assassination and bombing teams, launching a guerrilla war against his enemies.

By late 1927, the Nationalists had come to the conclusion that they had defeated Wei Baqun's forces and there was not much else they could do in Donglan and the surrounding areas. At the same time conflicts in other parts of Guangxi made it urgent for them to move their troops elsewhere. Peasant armies in other counties in the Right River region had launched counterattacks against the Nationalists, and they were so aggressive that in late 1927 the provincial government had to move the Huang Battalion out of Donglan and the Lin Regiment back to Hechi.[138] The Gong Regiment stayed in Donglan and Fengshan.

It was nevertheless a great pity for the provincial government that Wei Baqun and most of the peasant movement leaders were still at large. In December 1927 the provincial government issued a list of twenty-three most wanted criminals and offered monetary rewards for capturing or killing any of them. Among these twenty-three peasant movement leaders from the

Right River region, eleven were from Donglan, five were from Fengshan, four were from Fengyi, one each was from Enlong, Liuzhou, and Guangdong. Wei Baqun was at the top of the list with the highest reward: five thousand silver dollars, dead or alive. The reward for Chen Shouhe was three thousand silver dollars, and the rewards for Chen Bomin, Huang Daquan, and Huang Shuxiang were one thousand, respectively. Wei Baqun's sworn brother, Liao Yuanfang from Fengshan, was also worth one thousand silver dollars. Three other young followers of Wei Baqun were worth only five hundred silver dollars each, which was the lowest reward. Ye Yimao, Wei Baqun's anarchist friend, was also on the list, although he had left Donglan for Wuhan a few months before. He was worth three thousand silver dollars.[139] It is ironic that none of the twenty-three was a formal member of the CCP at that time, although the Nationalists considered all of them to be Communists. The real Communists who were active in the Right River region at that time included Yu Shaojie, Yan Min, Chen Hongtao, and Chen Gutao, and none of them was on the list, which indicates that the Nationalists did not know much about the relations between the CCP and the peasant movements in the Right River region.

Chen Shouhe's name appeared next to that of Wei Baqun on the list of most wanted criminals. What the Nationalists did not know was that Chen had died at the hands of his own comrades shortly before the release of the list. Chen was a village intellectual from Wuzhuan and had been one of Wei Baqun's most loyal and capable followers since 1922. He and Chen Bomin had played an important part in winning external support for the Donglan peasant movement. He was one of the four delegates Wei Baqun sent to Nanning to report to the provincial government in early 1924, and in early 1926 Chen Shouhe again accompanied Chen Bomin to Nanning to report about the Donglan Massacre. Later that year, with Wei Baqun's strong recommendation, the provincial government sent Chen Shouhe to Enlong and Fengyi to help lead peasant movements there. During the fierce conflict between the peasant army and the Nationalists in late 1927, Chen was executed for defection and betrayal. He was officially branded a "traitor" in 1927 and then rehabilitated by the Guangxi Provincial Committee of the CCP in 1984.[140] Chen was the third founding member of the Association for Reforming Donglan who was executed for betrayal, after Chen Yuzao and Liang Shishu. The radicalization of Wei Baqun's movement caused a split among his followers. Some of his comrades supported a movement against local tyrants and evil gentry as well as heavy taxation and other corrupt practices, but were reluctant to endorse an all-out class war.

During the difficult years of 1927 and 1928 each of Wei Baqun's two wives bore him a son. Wei Baqun named his fourth son, born in 1927 by Wang Juqiu, Jianchi, meaning "perseverance," and his fifth son, born the following year by Chen Lanfen, Daodi, or "to the end."[141] It seems that "perseverance" did help Wei Baqun and his followers survive "to the end" of the second revolt. Six months after their release of the list, the Nationalists had failed to capture or kill any of the twenty-three most wanted criminals. In June 1928, the Gong Regiment was moved back to Baise, and after that there were no more formal government troops in or near Donglan. Both sides had reasons to claim victory. The Nationalists had defeated and dispersed Wei Baqun's army and had caused a great deal of economic losses for Wei Baqun and his followers, but most of the leaders, soldiers, and participants of the peasant movement survived. The movement could be easily revived once the Nationalist troops retreated.

The Nationalist attack helped bring Wei Baqun and the Communists together. Wei Baqun began to work on reestablishing contact with the CCP and restoring his movement immediately after the withdrawal of the Gong Regiment. In July 1928, he dispatched two of his young followers, Huang Songjian and Liang Fuzhen, to Jiangxi to study guerilla tactics with the Red Army commanded by Mao Zedong and Zhu De. The two got into a confrontation with the police in Wuzhou and Liang was killed. Huang Songjian reached Jiangxi, stayed with the Red Army for a few months, and returned to Donglan in February 1929.[142] It seems that Huang Songjian did not bring back any important instructions from Mao or any other Communist leader in Jiangxi and his trip did not lead to the creation of regular communications between Wei Baqun and the Communists in Jiangxi.

Six months after the withdrawal of the Gong Regiment, Wei Baqun was able to resume his contact with the CCP leaders in Guangxi, reestablish his revolutionary committee in the Western Mountains and also hold a political military training program for his followers. Shortly after that he moved back to Wuzhuan and began to send his followers to neighboring counties to mobilize the peasants. By spring 1929, Wei Baqun's forces had reoccupied most villages in Donglan, leaving only the county seat and a few major towns in the hands of his enemies. At the same time he also reestablished his control over some areas of the neighboring counties, including Fengshan, Lingyun, and Enlong. In August 1929, he called for a meeting of the peasant soldiers of Donglan and Fengshan, and between one thousand and two thousand people showed up. By December 1929, on the eve of the Baise Uprising, the number of peasant soldiers under Wei Baqun's command had increased to more than three thousand.[143]

There are some important similarities between Wei Baqun's first and second revolts. In both Wei Baqun tried to adopt ideas and methods he had learned during his journeys and tried to seek external support from various political groups. In both, Wei Baqun and his followers engaged in fierce fighting with their local enemies, forcing them to seek outside support. The result of the two revolts was primarily determined by which side had stronger external support.

There are also obvious differences between the two revolts. The first was primarily against the exorbitant taxes of the militarists and repressive practices of the local tyrants; during the second revolt, the revolutionaries called for the rejection of not only taxes, but also rent and debt. The United Front government supported the reduction of rent and interest, but Wei Baqun and his followers went further and advocated the policy of nonpayment of rent and nondischarge of debt obligations. Similar radical moves occurred in Hunan and other places.[144] During the first revolt the local ruling class was challenged and threatened, but not eliminated. In the second revolt, however, many members of the former ruling class were physically annihilated. Although both revolutions were radical and violent, the second was much more so than the first.

The second revolt was better organized and had a broader social base than the first. Part of the reason is that in the second revolt Wei Baqun and his followers attached great importance to the training of organizers. Following the example of Guangzhou Peasant Movement Institute, Wei Baqun created a peasant movement institute in Donglan and trained three classes of students, many of whom became important leaders or active participants of local peasant movements. The liberation of women also became an important aspect of the second revolt, and as a result, more and more women joined the peasant movement.

During the first revolt, Wei Baqun's outside allies such as Governor Ma Junwu provided nominal, moral, and temporary support. In the second Wei Baqun and his followers received strong political, organizational, public, and military support from the left-wing Nationalists and Communists. The leftists were willing to offer support to Wei Baqun because they believed that Wei Baqun' movement conformed to the principles of their revolution and that it would be beneficial to incorporate Wei Baqun's movement into the national revolution. The Communists showed special interest in integrating Wei Baqun's movement. As a result of the expansion of both his local base and external connections, Wei Baqun's influence and prestige were much greater during the second revolt than in the first.

The second revolt covered a much larger geographical area than the first. The first revolt was based primarily in Donglan and Fengshan, but the second involved more counties in the Right River region. The second revolt also lasted much longer than the first.

Finally, the peasant army under Wei Baqun's control during the second revolt was much stronger than the armed force he had created during the first revolt. In late 1923 and early 1924 it took General Liu Rifu one battalion of troops to suppress the first revolt; in early 1926 General Liu had to send one regiment to put down the first phase of the second revolt, and in late 1927 and early 1928 it took Governor Huang Shaohong nearly three regiments of troops to defeat Wei Baqun's peasant army. In the first revolt Wei Baqun's enemies were the militarists of the Old Guangxi Clique, including Lin Junting, Huang Qi, and Liu Rifu. During the second revolt his enemies were members of the

New Guangxi Clique led by Li Zongren, Bai Chongxi and Huang Shaohong. In their attitude toward the radical peasant movement the New Guangxi Clique was not very different from the Old Guangxi Clique. Part of the reason was that the two cliques were closely related to each other. People like Li Zongren, Bai Chongxi, Huang Shaohong, Huang Qi, and Liu Rifu were members of both cliques at different times and they did not go through any mental transformation when leaving the old for the new.

Some sources claim that the first revolt was designed and enforced by an anarchist organization led by Wei Baqun and Huang Daquan, and that many participants later recalled that anarchism was very influential in Donglan at that time.[145] However, there is no evidence to prove the existence of an anarchist organization in Donglan during that period. Even if Wei Baqun indeed considered himself an anarchist at that time, his first revolt was not a pure anarchist movement. He was informed not only by anarchism, but also by Communism and the theory of national revolution as defined by Sun Yat-sen before his collaboration with the Communists. His second revolt closely followed the principles of the new national revolution advocated by the left wing Nationalists and Communists during the First United Front.

CHAPTER SIX

Third Revolt

Integration of the Local and National Revolutions, 1929–1930

Since 1921, Wei Baqun and his supporters had demonstrated repeatedly that if there was no external intervention, they could easily defeat their local enemies within Donglan. They proved that by sacking the county seat numerous times after 1923. Donglan was an impoverished county where poor peasants far outnumbered the wealthy landlords and the officials. Wei Baqun and his supporters mobilized and organized these poor peasants and drew a line between them and their enemies, including the so-called local tyrants and evil gentry, the militia forces, and the county police. If Donglan had been sealed off from the outside, Wei Baqun would have easily made himself the red king of the county.

It is unfortunate for Wei Baqun that even remote Donglan was not isolated enough to escape the attention of outside forces inimical to his movement. Every time a conflict arose between Wei Baqun and his local enemies, external forces from Baise, Hechi, Nanning, and other places would get involved. When the external forces supporting Wei Baqun overwhelmed those backing his enemies, Wei Baqun would win, and this happened in late 1926 and early 1927. Otherwise, he would lose. Wei Baqun had suffered defeats at the hands of hostile outsiders in 1924, in early 1926 and late 1927, and again in early 1928. The result of local conflict in Donglan was determined by the contest between rival external forces. Wei Baqun came to realize the importance of winning external allies following his first defeat in 1924. In order to make connections with outside supporters, he traveled to Guangzhou in late 1924, sent Chen Bomin and Chen Shouhe to Nanning in 1926 to report about the Donglan Massacre, and dispatched his younger brother Wei Jing and Ye Yimao to Wuhan in 1927 to investigate the political situation there. Wei Baqun and his followers also learned to issue announcements to influence public opinions, to mobilize the support of Donglan students studying in the cities, to win over investigators sent to Donglan by the provincial government, to acquire weapons from their outside allies, and to solicit support from their friends in neighboring counties.

When the Gong Regiment withdrew from Donglan in June 1928, it seemed that Wei Baqun and his movement had been defeated one more time by external enemies. However, despite the killings, lootings, and burnings the regiment conducted, the enemy failed to capture or kill Wei Baqun and most other leaders of his movement. After the retreat of their enemies, these leaders immediately came out of their hiding places to revive their movement.

To date, Wei Baqun's external allies had never managed to send regular troops to Donglan to help fight his enemies. Armed peasants from other counties had fought on Wei Baqun's side in Donglan numerous times, but these ill-equipped and ill-trained fighters were no match for the battalions and regiments of enemy forces from Baise, Hechi, and elsewhere. A fully mobilized revolutionary army had never come to Donglan and the Right River region to support Wei Baqun and his movement, but that would change in 1929.

Baise Uprising

Since the early 1920s the New Guangxi Clique had achieved exceptional political and military success both within Guangxi and beyond. The three top leaders, Li Zongren, Bai Chongxi, and Huang Shaohong, were all natives of Guangxi who had been trained in modern military schools. They were young and energetic, and their mindset reflected both traditional and modern influences. Together they formed a trio that combined the qualities of a brave soldier and commander (Li), a wise military strategist (Bai), and a shrewd politician (Huang). By 1925, they had eliminated all the rival militarist forces in Guangxi, expelled all the invading troops of neighboring provinces, and reunified the province. After that, the New Guangxi Clique participated actively in national political and military affairs. Their Seventh Army fought fiercely under Chiang Kai-shek during the Northern Expedition. After April 1927 the clique became a strong ally of Chiang Kai-shek in his war against the Communists. Whereas Huang Shaohong stayed in Guangxi to rule the province, Li Zongren, Bai Chongxi and most commanders and soldiers of the New Guangxi Clique stayed outside Guangxi fighting the larger civil war.

By 1928, the New Guangxi Clique had emerged as one of the five major non-Communist military groups in China along with Chiang Kai-shek's Nanjing government, the Manchurian Clique, the Shanxi Clique, and Feng Yuxiang's army in northwestern China. The Seventh Army of the New Guangxi

Clique had grown quickly into the Fourth Group Army, and the number of troops under the control of the clique had increased from 40,000 to more than 200,000. At the beginning of the Northern Expedition in 1926, the clique had control over only Guangxi, but in 1928, in addition to Guangxi, it had also established rule over Guangdong, Hunan, Hubei, Beijing, Tianjin, and Hebei.[1] As Chiang Kai-shek pushed for his grand plan of reunifying China, which would ultimately lead to the elimination of powerful regional military groups, conflicts inevitably arose between Chiang's central government and the New Guangxi Clique. In March 1929, a war broke out between the two sides. It turned out that the New Guangxi Clique was not as powerful as it had appeared, and it took Chiang Kai-shek only two months to defeat it. By May 1929, the three generals had lost most of their troops as well as the provinces under their control, including their home province Guangxi. All three were forced to flee to Hong Kong.

General Yu Zuobai played a key role in the defeat of the New Guangxi Clique in 1929. Yu had been a long-time subordinate of the ruling trio of Guangxi. Among the important leaders of the New Guangxi Clique, Yu was one of the few left-wing Nationalists who sincerely supported the United Front policy and the mass movements, including peasant movements. He once remarked that "Guangxi should follow Peng Pai and Wei Baqun, and China should follow the Soviet Union."[2] When serving as the head of the Department of Peasant Affairs in Nanning in 1926 and 1927, Yu supported the appointment of Chen Mianshu as the magistrate of Donglan, secretly offered Chen Bomin more than thirty pistols,[3] and overall was one of Wei Baqun's most powerful supporters during his second revolt. When the New Guangxi Clique began to purge the Communists and left-wing Nationalists in April 1927, Yu moved to Hong Kong, where he lived with Chen Mianshu and was in touch with other important Communists, and served as the leader of a committee formed by exiled left-wing Nationalists and Communists from Guangxi. The committee publicly condemned Governor Huang Shaohong for suppressing the peasant and worker movements in Guangxi. Yu Zuobai's younger brother, Yu Zuoyu, who had also been an officer in the army of the New Guangxi Clique, became a CCP member in 1928 thanks to Chen Mianshu's recommendation and was the head of the CCP branch in his native Beiliu County in 1929. Their cousin Li Mingrui was a powerful general in the army of the New Guangxi Clique, and his troops were stationed in the strategic Hubei Province. Li had served under Yu Zuobai and earned a reputation as a brave general during the Northern Expedition. Like his two cousins, Li was sympathetic toward the Communists, and he once complained openly that the purge of the Communists had affected the morale of his troops. Li Mingrui was upset with the three leaders of Guangxi in 1929 because his close relations with Yu Zuobai had cost him a promotion he thought he deserved.

Chiang Kai-shek was aware of the conflict between Yu Zuobai and the top leaders of Guangxi. He decided to temporarily ignore the fact that Yu was a left-wing Nationalist and Communist sympathizer and tried to make an efficient use of Yu's clashes with his former superiors. In early 1929, Chiang sent a delegate to visit Yu in Hong Kong and asked him to persuade Li Mingrui not to fight for the New Guangxi Clique, but to take his troops back to Guangxi. In return Chiang promised to appoint Yu and Li as the new rulers of Guangxi once the New Guangxi Clique was defeated. Both cousins saw Chiang Kai-shek as a political enemy rather than an ally, but at the same time they considered the Generalissimo a lesser evil than the New Guangxi Clique. Yu Zuobai thus secured permission from his Communist friends to help Chiang Kai-shek, promising the Communists that he would turn against Chiang after eliminating the New Guangxi Clique. He also sent messengers to persuade Li Mingrui not to fight against Chiang. After the war between Chiang Kai-shek and the New Guangxi Clique erupted in March 1929, Li Mingrui declared that his two divisions would remain neutral, a defection that caused the immediate collapse of the clique. With Chiang Kai-shek's help, Li then shipped his two divisions back to Guangxi. Chiang kept his promise, and in June 1929 appointed Yu Zuobai as the governor of Guangxi and Li Mingrui as the commander-in-chief of all the troops in Guangxi. In early July 1929, Yu and Li arrived in Nanning to assume their duties.

After taking over the province, Yu Zuobai and Li Mingrui decided to cooperate with the Communists. As mentioned earlier, they had been sympathetic toward the Communists since the early 1920s. Besides, they were short of allies at that moment. Chiang Kai-shek offered the two high positions, but nothing else. Large numbers of officials and officers loyal to the New Guangxi Clique remained in Guangxi and kept their positions, and they could revolt at any moment. Yu and Li needed a group of military and political leaders who could help them control the army and government as well as win the support of the peasants and workers. They approached the Communists for help and the CCP responded by sending more than forty experienced Communist leaders to Guangxi. Most of these leaders had military experience, and at least twenty-five were graduates of Whampoa Military Academy or had studied in foreign countries. Quite a few had participated in the Nanchang Uprising and Guangzhou Uprising in 1927. Some of them came to Guangxi as Communists sent by the CCP, and others kept their CCP membership secret and entered Guangxi through personal channels. Most of these Communists were southerners, and the large percentage of military commanders among them betrays a strong desire on the part of the CCP to influence and reform the armed forces of Yu Zuobai and Li Mingrui.

The leader of this group was the twenty-five-year-old Deng Xiaoping, who had spent several years in France and the Soviet Union as a worker, student, and Communist, and had held important positions within the CCP.[4] In Nanning, Deng used the pseudonym Deng Bin, and his official position was secretary of the provincial government. Secretly Deng was the head of the military committee of the CCP Guangxi branch. Deng's deputy was the twenty-two-year-old Chen Haoren, who had been the leader of the Fujian provincial branch of the CCP before being transferred to Guangxi. Chen held the same position as Deng in the provincial government. Another important member of the group was the Hainanese Zhang Yunyi, a veteran army officer who had fought for Sun Yat-sen for many years before joining the CCP in 1926. A former high-ranking officer in the National Revolutionary Army of the United Front government, he was the most experienced military commander within the group. At age thirty-seven, he was also one of the oldest in the group. Zhang kept his party membership secret and was recommended to Yu Zuobai by a mutual friend. Yu and Li appointed him to important positions in their army.[5] Gong Chu, who had been a CCP member since 1925 and an important peasant movement leader in Guangdong, and who had participated in the Nanchang Uprising and fought in Jinggangshan under Mao Zedong and Zhu De, also arrived in Nanning at this time.[6] He had been a classmate of Li Mingrui at a military school and partly because of that was appointed as the police chief of Nanning. The most powerful CCP member in Guangxi during this period was probably Yu Zuoyu, who served as the direct link between the CCP group and the Yu-Li clique. He helped secure important positions for the Communists and established CCP control over three military units.[7] These developments led Li Zongren to make the bitter comment that "Guangxi had almost become the Communist base area in southwestern China since Yu and Li took over the province."[8]

Under the rule of Yu Zuobai and Li Mingrui, Guangxi became the only province in China that tried to revive the United Front. Yu and Li ordered the release of all political prisoners. As a result, the Communists and left-wing Nationalists who had been imprisoned since the purge in April 1927 were all set free. At the same time holdouts loyal to the New Guangxi Clique were arrested, and former KMT party branches across the province were disbanded. Yu and Li also encouraged the development of peasant and worker movements. The provincial government created the Office of Conveying Appreciation to the Peasants, and Yu Zuobai appointed his old friend, Chen Xiewu, as its director. The New Guangxi Clique had declared Chen a wanted criminal following the collapse of the First United Front. In early 1928, his son, Chen Mengwu, was killed while trying to stage a peasant rebellion in southern Guangxi.[9]

In August 1929, with Yu Zuobai's approval, the First Peasant Congress of Guangxi was held in Nanning. The congress was organized by the Communists, who decided to create the Preparatory Committee of the Guangxi Provincial Peasant Association, with Communist Lei Jingtian as its director and Wei Baqun as its deputy director. To attend the congress, Wei Baqun, who adopted the pseudonym Nong Yousan, traveled to Nanning. It was during this visit that the CCP finally approved Wei Baqun's formal party membership. Shortly after that, Wei Baqun's close followers such as Chen Bomin and Huang Daquan all joined the CCP.

Wei Baqun got to meet Governor Yu Zuobai during his stay in Nanning. The meeting took place in Yu's office, which was not far from Deng Xiaoping's. Although both Deng Xiaoping and Wei Baqun were in Nanning from August to mid-September 1929, the two very likely never met. Deng adopted a secretive lifestyle during that period. The Communists in Nanning were aware that Deng Bin was their leader, but very few of them had the opportunity to meet him. Even Zhang Yunyi did not get to meet Deng in Nanning. For Wei Baqun, Yu Zuobai appeared to be a much more important contact than Deng Xiaoping at that moment. After his meeting with Wei Baqun, Yu offered Wei more than 300 rifles and 20,000 cartridges, and Wei Baqun immediately arranged for three hundred of his soldiers to travel to Nanning to receive the weapons. These fighters from Donglan stayed in Nanning for a while for some military training and did not return to Wuzhuan until mid-September 1929.[10]

In addition to appointing leftists to important positions in Nanning, Yu Zuobai and Li Mingrui also put a number of leftists in charge of some county governments. Three of Wei Baqun's followers were appointed to positions of county magistrate. Chen Bomin became the magistrate of Hechi, Huang Daquan the magistrate of Enlong, and Huang Shuxiang the magistrate of Guode. Later, Yu Zuobai's enemies were to accuse him of committing a long list of crimes during his tenure as governor, and one of the items on their list was that Yu offered important positions to "Communist bandits" like Wei Baqun.[11]

Nominally Yu and Li were part of Chiang Kai-shek's Nanjing government and therefore their cooperation with the Communists had to be handled cautiously. The Communists were permitted to join the government, but not allowed to keep their organization. This was also a practice adopted by the First United Front. The Communists did not heed the rule and secretly kept their organization. Overall, the Communists were hardly sincere in cooperating with Yu and Li. In a letter to the Guangxi Special Committee of the CCP issued in early October 1929, the CCP Central Committee described Yu and Li as warlords, reformists and followers of Wang Jingwei, arguing that they were not different from the leaders of the New Guangxi Clique. The CCP Central Committee ordered the Communists in Guangxi to work to destroy the Yu-Li regime and to publicly champion the CCP line in order to confront the Yu-Li government.[12] In a report submitted to the Guangdong Provincial Committee of the CCP, the Communists in Guangxi responded to the above instructions by confirming that Yu Zuobai was indeed a reformist rather than a revolutionary and that his policies had been exploitative and inefficient. They reported that the people of Guangxi hated the Yu-Li regime even more than they did the New Guangxi Clique.[13] The cynicism of the Communists is understandable considering their unhappy experience with other Nationalists such as Chiang Kai-shek and Wang Jingwei. The CCP leaders were aware that Yu and Li were also seeking support from Wang's Reorganization Faction, which was an enemy to the Communists. Wang Jingwei and Chiang Kai-shek were rivals at that time, and Yu Zuobai had also promised his friends in the Reorganization Faction that he would revolt against Chiang as soon as he eliminated the New Guangxi Clique.

Yu and Li managed to destroy themselves before the Communists could do them any harm. Encouraged by their friends in the Reorganization Faction, the two hastily declared war on Chiang Kai-shek in early October 1929 and moved their troops toward Guangdong, which was controlled by a general loyal to Chiang at that time. The two believed that occupying prosperous Guangdong would not only put them in a stronger position against Chiang, but also help solve the financial problem they had been facing. Chiang Kai-shek destroyed Yu and Li in the same way he had defeated the New Guangxi Clique. He offered money and promotions to some key generals under Yu and Li, and several of them revolted against their bosses. As a result, the Yu-Li regime collapsed less than ten days after they launched their anti-Chiang Kai-shek campaign.

The Communists had tried to prevent Yu and Li from staging a reckless war against Chiang Kai-shek. When that failed, they managed to persuade Yu and Li to allow the more than four thousand troops under Communist control to stay in Nanning rather than move toward Guangdong. They argued that these troops would help protect the provincial capital and the rear base. After the collapse of the Yu-Li government, the Communists moved these troops to the Left River and Right River region in mid-October 1929. They also took with them in excess of five thousand rifles and a large amount of ammunition stored in the Nanning arsenal. On their way from Nanning to Baise, the Communists offered some of these weapons to the peasant armies in the Right River region, and Wei Baqun received more than one thousand rifles, twelve machine guns, and other weapons, which greatly upgraded the armory of the Donglan peasant army. With these weapons, Wei Baqun and his peasant soldiers were able to reconquer Wuzhuan and the county seat of Donglan in October 1929. In fighting the enemies in the county seat, Wei Baqun's troops used their newly acquired machine guns and mortars, and their enemies were utterly overwhelmed in just a few hours.[14]

Having lost most of their troops to Chiang Kai-shek and the remaining ones to the Communists, Yu Zuobai and Li Mingrui now became guests of their guests. The Communists, who they had invited into Guangxi two months before, now became their hosts. One of the Communist controlled units, under the command of Yu Zuoyu, moved to Longzhou, the largest town in the Left River region, and Yu Zuobai and Li Mingrui traveled with this unit. From

Longzhou Yu Zuobai traveled to Hong Kong by way of Vietnam. After he moved to Hong Kong, the Communists continued to ask him for money, but when Yu suggested that he travel back to Guangxi to lead the revolution, the Communists rejected the idea. Li Mingrui wanted to go to Hong Kong with his cousin, but the French believed that he had connections with the Communists and did not permit him to enter Vietnam.[15] Chiang Kai-shek had sent a long telegram to Li Mingrui before Li's revolt trying to persuade Li to remain loyal to the Nanjing government. After the fall of the Yu-Li regime, Chiang worried that the New Guangxi Clique would reestablish its rule over Guangxi. He offered Li Mingrui the office of governor along with a high-ranking military position. Chiang believed that Li still wielded some influence over the armies in Guangxi. Li ignored Chiang's offer and decided to stay with the Communists. But when he tried to move his former troops to the more prosperous southern Guangxi, the Communists did not allow it. It was only then that he realized that the troops were no longer his. He then joined the CCP and became a probationary Communist. The other two military units under Communist control were commanded by Zhang Yunyi and Deng Xiaoping, who moved their troops to the Right River region and set up their headquarters in the city of Baise.

The Communists decided to move to the Left River and Right River region partly because these were remote areas where there was not a large number of Nationalist troops, partly because of the thriving opium trade that was going on along the Right River which would make it easy to make money, and partly because there had been rather robust peasant movements in these places. Among all the peasant movements in this region, Wei Baqun's movement in Donglan was the earliest and the most influential and powerful. In other words, Wei Baqun's Donglan peasant movement was one of the factors prompting the Communists to move from Nanning to the Left River and Right River region. Deng Xiaoping recalled in 1968 that

> the Right River region of Guangxi was a place where there was strong mass support for the Communist movement, and there were such outstanding and prestigious peasant leaders as Wei Baqun in the region. Comrade Wei Baqun had been working in Donglan and Fengshan for a long time, turning these two counties into a very good revolutionary base area. This provided great convenience for the creation and development of the Seventh Red Army.[16]

Another leading Communist later commented that the Red Army would not have been able to exist and expand in the Right River region if it had not integrated with the local revolution and relied on the existing base area.[17] Deng Xiaoping and the other leaders were apparently familiar with the strategy adopted by the leaders of the Nanchang Uprising, who decided after taking

Nanchang in early August 1927 that they should move to the Chaoshan area in eastern Guangdong. One of their reasons was that Chaoshan was adjacent to Hailufeng, where Peng Pai had built up a powerful peasant movement. In December 1927, after losing their battle in Guangzhou, the Communist survivors of the Guangzhou Uprising also moved to eastern Guangdong, believing that they would be able to get support from the peasants of Hailufeng.

The ultimate goal of the Communists, which was already set when they first entered Guangxi, was to create a red army and a revolutionary base area in the province. Occupying the Left River and Right River region represented a substantial step toward realizing that goal. In the Right River region, it took the Communists nearly two months to eliminate local enemies and to reorganize their armed units. On December 11, 1929, which was the second anniversary of the Guangzhou Uprising, the Communists formally announced the creation of "the Seventh Army of the Chinese Red Army," with Zhang Yunyi as its commander-in-chief and Deng Xiaoping the political commissar. On that day, every officer and soldier received a new uniform, including a hat with the symbol of a red five-point star. Each of them also put on a red band. The Communists had confiscated all the opium they could find in the various towns and collected taxes from opium trade, and they were therefore able to pay each soldier and officer a generous monthly stipend of twenty silver dollars. The first payment was made on December 11, 1929.[18]

At its birth the Seventh Red Army consisted of three columns. The first was formed by soldiers from some former units under Yu Zuobai and Li Mingrui, the second was a mix of former Yu-Li troops and peasant soldiers from the lower reaches of the Right River, including at least two hundred peasant soldiers from Donglan, and the third was primarily composed of peasant soldiers from Donglan and neighboring counties. Each column had more than one thousand soldiers and all together the three columns numbered about four thousand soldiers. About half of the soldiers were Zhuang and more than two-thirds of them were from the Right River region. Wei Baqun was appointed as the commander of the third column, and Li Pu, a Communist from Sichuan who had studied in the Soviet Union, became the head of the political department of the third column. There were some other non-natives serving in the column, including the commanders of the machine gun company, the mortar company, the mountain gun company, and the medical team.[19] The first column was stationed in Pingma, located seventy-five kilometers to the southeast of Baise; the second column was deployed in Baise; and Wei Baqun's third column was placed in Donglan.

In addition to this regular army, the Communists also created a militia system known as the Red Guards. Every county had a Red Guard unit and together there were about 10,000 militiamen and women in the Right River region. In Donglan there were about 400 Red Guards in early 1930, but by July 1930 the number had increased to between 1,400 and 2,000. The entire Donglan society was further militarized as a result of the arrival of the Communists from outside. For instance, among the 3800 residents of the fifty-nine villages in one part of the Western Mountains, nearly 700, or twenty percent of the local population, joined the Red Army and the Red Guards. Throughout the county, villagers who did not join the Red Army or the Red Guards were organized into various teams performing different paramilitary or logistical functions. Some specialized in making explosives, land mines, and straw sandals. Others were responsible for moving supplies and wounded soldiers. There was a sewing-washing team, a team of medical assistants, and a sabotage team whose duty it was to destroy the defense facilities of the enemy.[20]

With better weapons and the support of the other two columns and the Red Guard units, Wei Baqun launched attacks on rival militia groups in Donglan. Within Donglan, the districts on the eastern bank of the Red Water River had been beyond Wei Baqun's control most of the time, and now he was able to wipe out his enemies there. He also took his third column to Enlong, Nadi, Baise, and Du'an to defeat rival militia groups and set up Soviet governments.[21]

On the same day that the Seventh Red Army was created the Right River Soviet Government announced its birth in Pingma, and the new government held a huge banquet for 50,000 people that evening to celebrate. Wei Baqun was very busy on that day. He first attended the founding ceremony of the Seventh Red Army in Baise and then rushed to Pingma by steamboat to celebrate the creation of the Soviet government. Lei Jingtian, the veteran Communist, became the chairman of the Soviet government, and Wei Baqun and Chen Hongtao served as committee members of the government. Among the eleven top leaders of the government, six were Zhuang and Yao from the Right River region.[22] Wei Baqun thus became an important leader of both the Red Army and the Soviet government. Communist governments were established in about ten counties in the Right River region, and Donglan was one of the ten.

What happened in Pingma and Baise on December 11, 1929 later became known as the Baise Uprising, considered one of the major Communist uprisings that occurred following the collapse of the First United Front in 1927. The CCP Central Committee had ordered that the uprising be staged on November 7, 1929, which was the twelfth anniversary of the Russian Revolution, but the Communists in Guangxi were not ready at that time. December 11, the anniversary of the Guangzhou Uprising, probably meant much more than November 7 to the leaders of the Baise Uprising, since several of them were participants in that revolt. Besides, the Guangxi CCP branch was under the direct control of the Guangdong Provincial Committee of the CCP at that time. Unlike the Guangzhou Uprising, which was very bloody and short-lived, the Baise Uprising began rather peacefully and lasted much longer. The

Communists, who had had to keep their party membership and organization secret in Nanning, now all came "out of the closet" and began to openly champion the communist cause.

In February 1930, a similar uprising occurred in Longzhou, leading to the creation of the Eighth Red Army, the Left River Soviet Government, as well as Soviet governments in eight counties in the Left River region. Yu Zuoyu became the commander of the Eighth Red Army, and Deng Xiaoping was later appointed as its political commissar. Li Mingrui was made the commander-in-chief of the Seventh and Eighth Red Armies, with Deng Xiaoping as the political commissar of both. At its zenith, the combined Right River and Left River base area consisted of more than twenty counties with a land area of 50,000 square kilometers and a population of about 1.5 million. The Communists thus occupied nearly one-fourth of the total land area of Guangxi.[23] The Left River and Right River Revolutionary Base Area was one of the largest Communist revolutionary base areas in the late 1920s and early 1930s (Map 6.1).

As soon as the Baise Uprising became known, the Guangdong Provincial Committee of the CCP encouraged the Seventh and Eighth Red Armies to attack major cities for the purpose of "exerting great political influence and creating a huge revolutionary wave."[24] The collapse of the Yu-Li regime had paved the way for the revival of the New Guangxi Clique. In late 1929, only weeks after it came back to power in Guangxi, the New Guangxi Clique was involved in another war with Chiang Kai-shek's supporters in Guangdong, making the Communists in Guangxi believe that Nanning was undermanned and vulnerable, and they began to move their troops toward that city. Li Mingrui and Yu Zuoyu were extremely eager to move back to Nanning to attack their enemies. The Communists decided to march toward Nanning from the Right River and Left River valleys, respectively, and to meet somewhere near Nanning in February 1930.[25]

However, the war between the New Guangxi Clique and Guangdong ended soon, and before the Communists could attack Nanning, General Li Zongren's troops had arrived in the Right River region to fight the Communists. In February 1930, the Seventh Red Army fought against Li's troops in three places along the Right River, and the Communists were defeated in all three battles. As a result they lost all the towns along the Right River, and had to retreat to the Panyang region, which was on the border between Donglan and Fengshan and was part of the Western Mountains. Wei Baqun's third column participated in all three battles. Although not as well trained as the soldiers from Nanning, Wei Baqun's peasant soldiers fought bravely and efficiently and greatly impressed the outside Communists. Mo Wenhua, a Communist from Nanning who witnessed the performance of Wei Baqun's troops in one of the battles, recalled that they attacked enemy troops like "fierce tigers jumping down from the mountains."[26]

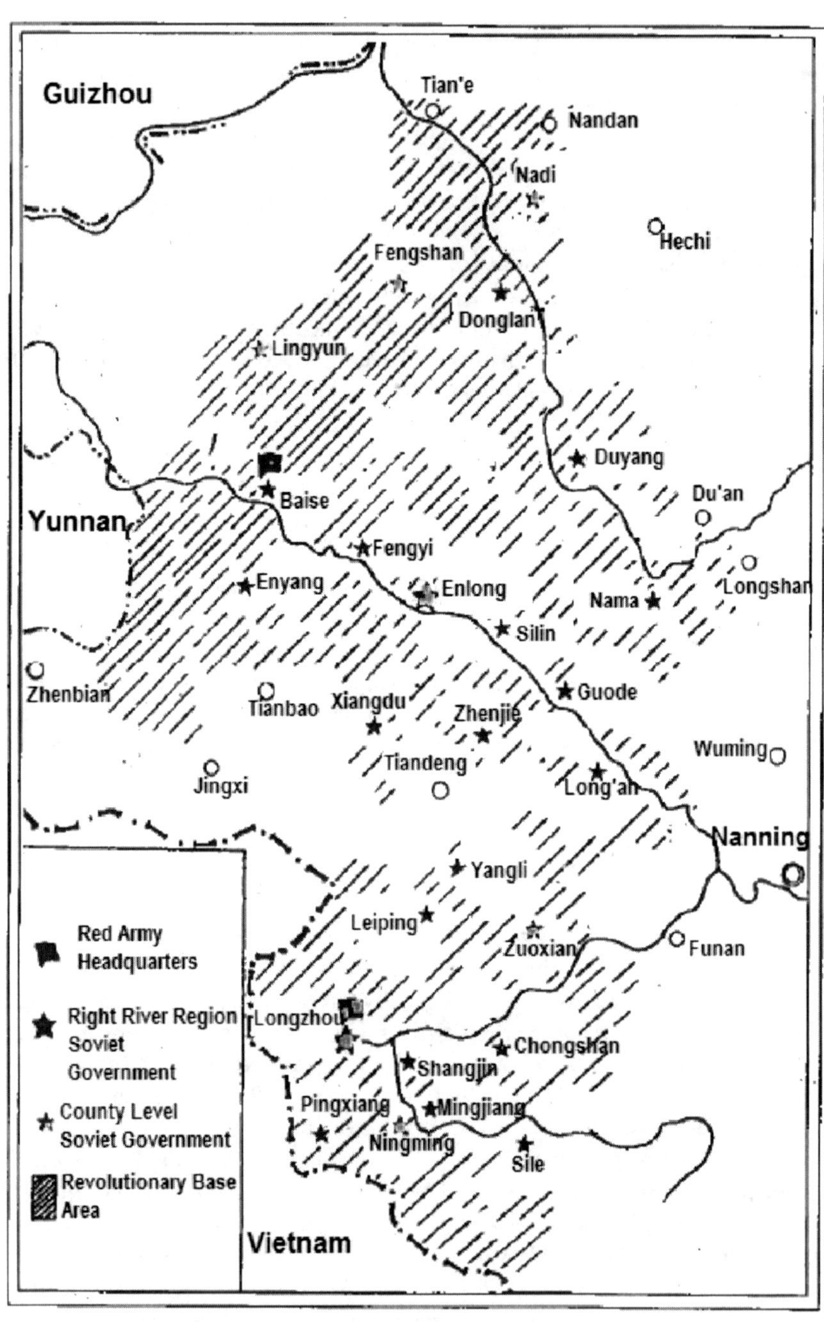

Map 6.1 The Left River and Right River Revolutionary Base Area.

Panyang provided safety, but not subsistence. It was an impoverished region where peasants were not even able to feed themselves, much less to supply an army of several thousand soldiers. In early March 1930, the leaders decided that they had to move out of the Western Mountains to acquire supplies, but they could not reach an agreement about where to go. Some proposed to move into areas controlled by the Nationalists, and others supported the idea of fighting guerrilla wars along the border of the Right River region.[27] In early April, it was decided that the first two columns would leave the Western Mountains and move eastward toward Hechi, while Wei Baqun's third column would stay in Donglan and Fengshan to protect the rear base and to wait for the Eighth Red Army, which had been ordered to move to Donglan to join the Seventh Red Army. The Right River Special Committee of the CCP and the Right River Soviet Government would also stay in Donglan. Most of the leading Communists from Nanning would move with the first two columns, but Lei Jingtian, Chairman of the Right River Soviet Government, stayed in Donglan. Three to four hundred wounded soldiers were left in the Red Army hospital near Wuzhuan.[28]

The first two columns moved to Hechi and easily defeated the local militias. They acquired a large quantity of supplies there, but they arrived too late to rescue Chen Bomin. Through his various visits to Nanning during the second revolt, Chen developed a close relationship with Yu Zuobai, who appointed Chen as the magistrate of Hechi in late 1929. After the collapse of the Yu-Li regime, Chen had to leave Hechi for his former base Du'an, but was soon defeated there by local militias. On his way back to Donglan, he was captured by some anti-Communist militias. Wei Baqun sent a company of troops to attack the fortress where Chen and his seventeen comrades were kept, but failed to take it. The enemy militias then transferred all eighteen prisoners to the county seat of Du'an where they were summarily executed.[29] At about the same time, Wei Baqun lost two other close friends. One was Chen Enshen, a young man from the Western Mountains who served as a battalion commander in the third column in early 1930. After the departure of the first two columns, Wei Baqun sent Chen to defend the western border of the base area, and Chen got killed in Pingma. The other was Ya Sumin, who had been with Wei Baqun since 1921. In early 1930, he was the commander of the Red Guards in Donglan. Ya was killed while defending the eastern border of the base area. To mourn Ya Sumin's death, Wei Baqun wrote a eulogy for him that read, "Whether we are in the Red Army or the Red Guards, we all fight to save the people; whether we die now or later, we all die for the revolution."[30]

The first two columns of the Seventh Red Army, after taking Hechi, moved northward and entered Guizhou Province, where they defeated the local forces and acquired more weapons and other materials. They returned to Donglan in May 1930. Since the New Guangxi Clique had joined another war against Chiang Kai-shek and had moved most of their troops into Hunan, the Communists decided to move westward to re-conquer Baise and the other towns along the Right River. By June 1930 the Seventh Red Army had defeated the one thousand or so enemy troops along the Right River and retaken Baise and the other towns. Shortly after that they lost Baise to the invading Yunnan Army, but managed to keep most of their other conquests.[31] Wei Baqun took two battalions of his third column to participate in the battles along the Right River, but he returned to Donglan soon after the Seventh Red Army reached the banks of the Right River.

Land Revolution

The Communist support of the land revolution, or the confiscation and redistribution of land properties of wealthy families, accompanied by the persecution or execution of "local tyrants and evil gentry," was an important factor causing the collapse of the First United Front in 1927.[32] After the split, land revolution became the official policy of the CCP and was carried out in almost all revolutionary base areas. The Resolution on Recent Peasant Struggles, passed at the meeting of the CCP leaders held in Wuhan on August 7, 1927, supported the policy of confiscating the landed property of the large and middle landlords and of peasant uprising. The Resolution on the Peasant Movement, passed at the Sixth National Congress of the CCP held in early 1928 in Moscow, reaffirmed the party's support for peasant demands for land. It specified that in places where the poor peasants formed the majority of the population, the Communists should support the policy of equal redistribution of land, but in places where the owner peasants were in dominant position the Communists should be cautious in endorsing such a radical policy. The CCP leaders considered land revolution an efficient means of maintaining the morale of the peasants. After learning that the peasants in Donglan were no longer as enthusiastic about the revolution as before because they had nothing to do after defeating the local tyrants in late 1929, the CCP Central Committee remarked that the local leaders should have launched land revolution to boost morale.[33]

The Communists in Guangxi obviously agreed that overall Guangxi was one of the places where the poor peasants made up the majority of the population, and where tenants endured a rent rate as high as fifty percent and had to provide free labor for the landlords. They made land revolution one of their primary objectives soon after they entered Guangxi. The First Guangxi Provincial Congress of the CCP, held secretly at Lei Jingtian's native village near Nanning, listed land revolution as one of the tasks for the Communists in Guangxi.[34]

Within Guangxi Wei Baqun was probably the first to enforce land redistribution. He confiscated the property of some of his enemies even before he became a full member of the CCP. The land revolution advocated by the CCP after 1927 consisted of several steps, including classification of the rural population, creation of peasant organizations, denunciation or even elimination of the landlords, destruction of land deeds, and confiscation and redistribution of land and other properties of the landlords and rich peasants. Wei Baqun had done some but not all of these steps. Lei Jingtian believed that land confiscation and redistribution began in Donglan at the latest in March 1929. Wei Baqun offered the confiscated land to peasants who were willing to take it, and those receiving land had to pay part of the yield to the peasant associations.[35] However, Wei Baqun never created a uniform policy regarding land revolution, and his practice of land revolution before 1929 was selective and fragmentary. Some CCP members argued that what Wei Baqun had been doing was not real land revolution, but the Guangxi Special Committee of the CCP officially confirmed in late 1929 that Wei Baqun's practices actually conformed to the policy of land revolution. The committee argued that what had happened in Donglan could at least be described as a form of spontaneous land revolution.[36]

A systematic land revolution as defined by the CCP did not begin in Donglan and the Right River region until after the Baise Uprising. A week after the founding of the Right River Soviet, an editorial of the Communist newspaper the *Right River Daily* listed land revolution as one of the four major tasks of the Red Army and the Soviet government, and the other three were to develop the Soviet base area, to expand the Red Guards, and to develop mass organizations. Ten days after the creation of the Seventh Red Army, its political department issued a pamphlet entitled *Land Revolution*, which argued that the lack of land was the source of all sufferings for the peasants. It urged the peasants of the Right River region to follow the examples of peasants in other provinces who had risen up to seize the land of the landlords and create Soviet governments. The document laid out specific policies about how to confiscate and redistribute land.[37] At about the same time the Soviet government created a list of fifteen official slogans, and at least five of these were directly related to the land revolution. These included: "Down with Local Tyrants and Evil Gentry," "Down with Landlords and Capitalists," "Implement Land Revolution," "Burning the Deeds," and "Pay No Rent or Debt!"[38] The Seventh Red Army also left posters in various places calling for land revolution, and even the literacy textbooks compiled by the Communists contained several lessons about land revolution.[39]

Deng Xiaoping played an important role in designing the policies of land revolution for the Right River Soviet Government. Some historians in China like to emphasize Deng's role in creating the overall strategies for the Communists in Guangxi, in winning over Yu Zuobai and Li Mingrui, in acquiring important positions for the Communists in Guangxi, and in determining the location and date of the Baise Uprising. Although Deng himself confirmed in

1984, after all the other top leaders of the Baise Uprising had died, that "I led the Baise Uprising and founded the Seventh Red Army when I was 25,"[40] not all these claims can be corroborated.

Although Deng was the top CCP leader in Guangxi at that time, his political and military connections and experiences were inferior to other Communists such as Zhang Yunyi and Yu Zuoyu, and he knew much less about Guangxi than natives like Lei Jingtian and Yu Zuoyu. Deng was one of the decision makers, but not the only one, possibly also not the most influential one. Benjamin Yang's assessment that before September 1930 "Deng's role was mainly to communicate the Party Centre's line in principle and did not therefore involve much practical operation" is a fair one.[41] Deng recalled in the 1960s that "the Central Committee sent me to Guangxi to promote a united front. I met Yu Zuobai a few times and preformed my duty according to the guidelines of the Central Committee. At the same time, I tried to help appoint the comrades that the Central Committee had dispatched to Guangxi to appropriate positions." He also admitted that he knew little about military affairs when he was in Guangxi.[42] In fact, although holding important positions in the Seventh and Eighth Red Armies, Deng was not even present in the Left River and Right River region when the Baise and Longzhou Uprisings occurred. He left Baise for Shanghai in November 1929, shortly before the Baise Uprising, to report to the CCP Central Committee, and did not return to Guangxi until February 1930, just after the Longzhou Uprising. He also had a personal reason for making the trip since his wife, who was living in Shanghai, was due to give birth in early 1930. Tragically, the childbirth killed both his wife and their baby. Deng was not with either the Seventh or Eighth Red Army during much of the time and he missed most of the battles the two armies fought in Guangxi and Guizhou. Gong Chu, who later defected to the Nationalists, made the dubious claim that before the Baise Uprising he was the leader of all the Communists in Guangxi, and during and after the uprising Chen Haoren was put in charge of political affairs in the Right River region, whereas Zhang Yunyi and Gong Chu were responsible for military affairs. On the other hand, Chen Haoren's descendants claim that Chen was the "number one leader of the Baise Uprising."[43]

If Deng Xiaoping's contributions to some other aspects of the Right River revolution are uncertain, the rather important role he played in making the policies of land revolution is beyond doubt. In early February 1930, Deng returned to Longzhou from Shanghai by way of Hong Kong and Vietnam. He spent some time in the Left River region and then embarked on a journey to the Right River valley. From mid-March to early April he visited several counties along the Right River and talked to leading revolutionaries there. He left Enlong for Donglan on April 1 and arrived in Wuzhuan a few days later. After reaching Wuzhuan he went directly to look for Wei Baqun and found him in Huang Shuxiang's house.[44] This should not have been the first meeting between the two because they would have had opportunities to meet each other in the previous fall in or near Baise. Eager to find the main force of the Seventh Red Army, Deng left for Hechi the next morning, and Wei Baqun sent two companies of soldiers to protect him.[45] After arriving in Hechi, Deng learned that the Seventh Red Army was not there and decided to turn back to Wuzhuan. He spent the next two months in Donglan, working primarily on training party members and land revolution. During his stay there he lived together with Wei Baqun on the second floor of the Tower of the Literary Star at Wuzhuan (Fig. 6.1) and the two became close friends.

Deng Xiaoping also created a training program for the local revolutionaries. Deng delivered lectures on the organization and tasks of the Soviet, the Communist Party, and policies and slogans of land revolution. These lectures were printed and distributed to the students. Together with Lei Jingtian, Wei Baqun, and Chen Hongtao, Deng Xiaoping worked on drafting the agrarian law, which was promulgated on May Day 1930 in the form of the Provisional Regulations of the Agrarian Law. The document offered guidelines about how to classify the rural population, confiscate land and other properties, and collect taxes. According to these regulations, the entire rural population should be divided into six major classes: landlords, despotic gentry, rich peasants, middle peasants, poor peasants, and rural laborers; and the land of the landlords,

FIGURE 6.1 The Tower of the Literary Star. Photograph by the author.

despotic gentry, and counter-revolutionaries should be completely confiscated. The regulations also ordered the confiscation of land owned by family temples and Buddhist temples as well as public land and wasteland. The confiscated land would be redistributed among the poor peasants and rural laborers based on the size of their families. The rich peasants would be permitted to keep their land for cultivation, but the ownership of their land would be transferred to the Soviet government. The regulations made the Soviet government the sole landowner in the revolutionary base area and made it illegal to buy or sell land. The policy of progressive taxation was adopted. Peasants were required to pay five percent of their yield to the Soviet as taxes, and those who produced more than average surplus had to pay a higher percentage for the extra portion.[46]

These regulations summarized and confirmed the principles laid out in previous documents issued by the CCP Central Committee, the Seventh Red Army, the Right River Soviet, and other Communist institutions. As Deng Xiaoping held a higher position than Lei Jingtian, Wei Baqun, and Chen Hongtao within the party and was also more familiar than the others with Mao Zedong's land policies in Jinggangshan as well as the party's official policies about land revolution, it can be argued that he contributed more to creating the regulations than the others (Fig. 6.2). Deng later confirmed that he had

FIGURE 6.2 Wei Baqun and Deng Xiaoping. Photograph by the author.

learned about the land revolution in Jinggangshan when he was in Shanghai and tried to apply the Jinggangshan experience to the Right River region in 1930.[47]

There are several important similarities between the regulations of the Right River Soviet and the agrarian law Mao Zedong created in Jinggangshan in 1928. One is the stipulation banning land transactions, and the other is the law that made the Soviet government the sole landowner. Both of these policies were later abandoned by the CCP because they were not popular among the peasants. A key difference between the two documents is that whereas Mao's Agrarian Law of Jinggangshan held that all the land properties, including those of the rich, middle, and poor peasants, should be confiscated, the regulations of the Right River Soviet specified that only the land properties of the landlords, despotic gentry, and counter-revolutionaries should be confiscated. Mao quickly realized the negative effects of the policy of "confiscating all land," and replaced it with the policy of selective confiscation in the Xingguo Agrarian Law promulgated in 1929.

In practice, the Right River Soviet offered the peasants three choices. The first was to confiscate all the land properties of all landowners and then equally redistribute them among all the peasants; the second was to confiscate all the land properties of all landowners and then collectively farm them; and the last was to confiscate the land properties of the landlords, despotic gentry, and counter-revolutionaries and redistribute them among the poor peasants and rural laborers.[48] Obviously, the first choice was the same as the radical practice stipulated in the Agrarian Law of Jinggangshan, and the provisional regulations of the Right River Soviet only defined the third choice. Among the six districts of Donglan, only Dongyuan and Simeng adopted the first option, and the rest all followed the last choice.[49]

However, the Communists preferred collective farming, or the second option. Two weeks after the promulgation of the Provisional Regulations of the Agrarian Law, the Right River Soviet issued a set of regulations about collective farming. If the peasants chose this option, then all the land, forest, ponds and cemeteries became collective properties, and wherever possible former boundaries or signs of private ownership would be destroyed. Tools and animals would be collectively managed by the village. The Soviet government would assess the amount and productivity of the land and land transactions would be prohibited. All adults between ages sixteen and sixty had to perform farm labor. Teenagers would be organized into groups and would receive education while helping to herd buffaloes. The village Soviet would divide all adult peasants into teams of ten and decide the assignments and schedule of work for all teams. Peasants would have meals in their own homes, but when possible the village Soviet could also erect a common cafeteria for all villagers. The annual yield of the village would be equally distributed among all villagers, with every villager aged one year or more receiving an equal share.[50]

Probably to the disappointment of the Communist leaders, most peasants did not like collective farming. Dongli was the only village in Donglan that opted for collective farming, and obviously Wei Baqun played an important part in promoting that option. The Dongli Collective Farm was created on March 29, 1930, before Deng Xiaoping's arrival and the promulgation of the regulations regarding collective farming. At that time there were about 570 people and 120 households living in Dongli and together they owned nearly one thousand mu of land. All residents of Dongli became members of the collective farm and some Yao people from the Western Mountains also joined. The households were divided into seven production teams, and each team was responsible for the cultivation of one major plot of land. The villagers elected the leaders of the farm and teams. Wei Baqun burned all the land deeds of his family. As a result, his family ceased to be the largest landowner in the village and became an equal of all other households. For that act Deng Xiaoping praised Wei Baqun for setting up a good example for other Communists.[51] It was fortunate for Wei Baqun that both his grandfather and father were no longer alive. Otherwise a serious family conflict would have been inevitable.

The collective farm had a great harvest during its first year of operation. The yield was thirty percent higher than that of 1929. Each villager over the age of thirteen received 400 kilograms of grain, and those younger were granted 100 to 250 kilograms each. After that, the collective farm still had 5000 kilograms of surplus that they sent to the Red Army. Both Wei Baqun and Deng Xiaoping wanted to make Dongli a model for other villages to follow, and they offered strong support to Dongli. When they heard that Dongli did not have enough draft animals, they immediately gave twelve buffaloes to the village. In addition to increasing agricultural production, the farm also helped improve the discipline and education of its members. All adult villagers were required to participate in physical exercise in the morning and attend classes in the evening.[52]

Although most Communist writers describe the Dongli Collective Farm as a great success, Lei Jingtian argued that it was a failure partly because some villagers did not support it. A defected Communist also described the experiment as a failure and listed laziness as the primary cause.[53] Later, a few other collective farms were created in the counties of Fengshan, Fengyi and Silin, and they were all located in the home villages of important Communist leaders. In many ways these collective farms were predecessors of the communes that were to be created in rural China in the late 1950s. In 1958, when a commune was created in Wuzhuan, one of Wei Baqun's surviving followers told the villagers that the commune was a revival of the Dongli Collective Farm of 1930 and that the commune system conformed to Wei Baqun's vision of Communism.[54]

The land revolution, in addition to reducing class differences, also contributed to promoting gender and ethnic equality. Women received shares of land equal to those of men. The political program issued by the Donglan

Revolutionary Committee in late 1929, in addition to laying out the regulations of land revolution, also announced several policies regarding the liberation of women, including the elimination of prostitution, polygamy, serfdom, and child brides, and the promotion of equal educational, political, and economic opportunities for women as well as freedom of marriage. During the third revolt, increasing numbers of women joined the CCP, the Red Army, and the Soviet governments. In Donglan, more than three hundred women joined the Red Guard units. From 1929 to 1932, forty-two women from Donglan and about twenty from Fengshan and Baise joined the CCP. Some women became officials and officers. One of them, Li Shunmei, became the commander of a Red Guard unit and died a heroic death at the hands of the anti-Communist militias. The Communist propaganda and policies about the liberation of women even led some women to put forward such slogans as "let women rule men," and "let the husband marry into the wife's family."[55]

The same political program also called for equal treatments for minority groups. The Yao people, who had been forced to live in the mountains, now could move down to the plains to participate in land redistribution. Some received both land and houses.[56] The justification was that because many Yao had been working as hired laborers for the landlord families in the lowland and had been exploited by these families, they should be compensated.

In the Right River region, the various policies that constituted the land revolution were first adopted in Donglan, where land revolution was already underway in March 1930, almost two months before the promulgation of the official policies. By the end of June 1930, land revolution had been completed in the three counties of Donglan, Fengshan, and Lingyun. In these counties, every person received on average one to two mu (one-sixth to one-third acre) of land. The land revolution helped greatly in winning popular support for the Red Army and the CCP. In his report about the political affairs of Guangxi, Deng Gang, who had toured the Right River region as a delegate of the Southern Bureau of the CCP, testified that Donglan and Fengshan were the two counties where land revolution had been thoroughly enforced and where popular support for the CCP was the strongest. He asserted that by August 1930, as many as six thousand people from the two counties had joined the Red Army.[57] After the Seventh Red Army reclaimed Baise and the other counties along the Right River in June 1930, the Communists promoted land revolution in these counties. However, in most of these counties the Communists only had enough time to complete land survey, but not to confiscate and redistribute the land.[58] Although some Communist leaders later accused their comrades from rich peasant families of not showing enough enthusiasm about land revolution or of some corrupt behavior, and cited these as reasons for the slow progress of land revolution in the Right River region, the real reason for their failure in completing land revolution in this area was the lack of time.

Revolution and Modernization

Modernity arrived in Donglan in a slow and fragmentary form after the beginning of the twentieth century, and the first achievement of Donglan's modernization was the creation of Western-style elementary schools. By 1924, the modernization of the educational system had not gone very far. There were only six elementary schools and two advanced elementary schools in the county in that year, and most students in the villages were still attending the traditional Confucian academies.[59] The established local leaders, including Wei Baqun's arch enemy Du Ba, played an important part in the early modernization of Donglan. In the eyes of Wei Baqun and his followers, however, old elites such as Du Ba were primarily barriers to modernization because they had vested interest in maintaining the status quo. In the revolutionary discourses these elites were described as local tyrants and evil gentry as well as supporters of feudalism and imperialism, the two most dangerous enemies of true modernization in China.

Wei Baqun and his supporters saw themselves as the harbingers of modernization. They believed that by introducing the most updated revolutionary ideologies to Donglan and by destroying the existing power holders they were reducing the gap between Donglan and the more advanced regions of China and paving the way for the rise of a new society. Like many other radical intellectuals of their time, they considered revolution a shortcut to modernization. Although older and more moderate elites believed that the best approach to modernization was education and gradual reform of the existing system, young radicals such as Wei Baqun saw an overhaul of the social structure as a precondition for modernization.

To an orthodox Marxist, if it is difficult to justify having a Communist revolution in China due to the lack of an advanced capitalist economy, then it is inconceivable to rationalize a Communist revolution in Donglan, which did not have even a single modern factory in the 1920s. The real proletariat, the people who were supposed to dig the tomb for capitalism, was completely absent in Donglan. So were capitalists and capitalism, the targets of the Communist revolution. Although the CCP would consider counting the rural laborers as rural proletariat, who in backward China were sometimes made to perform the role of urban proletariat, these people formed only a small percentage of the local population, were poorly educated and organized, and were not qualified to lead the revolution. Wei Baqun's enemy, Liao Lei, argued that Communism was not applicable to China and Donglan because there were no factory workers or capitalists in Donglan.[60] Liao and the other leaders of the New Guangxi Clique saw Wei Baqun and the Communists as obstacles to and destroyers of modernization. The New Guangxi Clique had its own blueprint for modernizing Guangxi, which emphasized militarism, order, road construction, and the expansion of education and industry.

What Wei Baqun and his enemies would agree on was that production and construction were important aspects of modernization. Their difference was that whereas the leaders of the New Guangxi Clique believed that progress in production and construction could be achieved within the existing system, Wei Baqun and his followers held that the creation of a new social political system was the only way to promote production and construction. The political program the revolutionaries released at the beginning of the third revolt actually contained some items that might have been acceptable to the New Guangxi Clique. These included road construction, the advancement of agriculture, and the expansion of education, particularly the promotion of education for the Yao, the women, and the youth.[61] However, the program failed to mention anything about the development of industry. Additionally, Wei Baqun and his comrades were too occupied with revolution to implement the projects they laid out in the program.

Although constant fighting made it difficult for either side to concentrate on production and construction, some aspects of economic and technological modernization did proceed during the revolts. For instance, it was during the third revolt that the Communists brought the first modern factory into Donglan—a munitions factory formerly based in Nanning. Wei Baqun had already set up a small arsenal during the first revolt to produce grenades, land mines, and primitive guns,[62] but that one was much smaller in scale and more backward in technology than the munitions factory in Nanning. The Communists took the machines, technicians, and workers of the factory with them when they left Nanning for the Right River region, and decided to relocate the factory in Donglan because they always saw the county as a safe rear base. The factory began to operate in a village near Wuzhuan in late 1929, and it employed more than sixty workers, including forty skilled workers from Nanning and some locals. It had fourteen rooms totaling three hundred square meters, as well as many machines and tools, including thirteen lathes. The workers were divided into three teams working on repairing weapons, making guns, and producing bullets, bombs, hand grenades, and land mines, respectively. From late 1929 to late 1931 the factory turned out 200,000 cartridges and more than sixty guns, and repaired a large number of weapons. The raw materials came from different sources. The workers from Nanning had brought some explosives from their factory, and they also made explosives using the traditional method. Soldiers would collect used cartridge cases from the battlefield and sent them to the factory for reuse; The Soviet government confiscated some metals from the counties along the Right River and had them delivered to the factory. Finally, a local militarist who was a friend of Wei Baqun's offered up as a gift one hundred ingots of tin for making bullet heads. Both Deng Xiaoping and Zhang Yunyi visited the factory in spring 1930. In order to make the technicians and workers from Nanning feel at home, Wei

Baqun encouraged local women to marry these outsiders and villagers to provide meat and other daily necessities for the workers. The factory did not exist for long. In April 1931, it was split into two sections, one of which was moved to the Western Mountains, and the other to the Eastern Mountains. In late 1931, the factory stopped operating completely. The able-bodied workers all joined the Red Guard units, whereas those who were not strong or healthy enough to fight were sent home, and the machines were hidden.[63]

During the third revolt, Wei Baqun created several training programs to modernize his army. He began with two military training programs in Wuzhuan for his Third Column, which opened in early 1930. The first program, which admitted at least sixty students, was an officer school. The teachers were all experienced commanders who had come from Nanning and they taught both politics and fighting skills. Students learned to operate the new weapons they had recently acquired, including mountain guns, mortars, and machine guns. The second program was created to teach his soldiers how to make land mines. The program trained more than one hundred land mine makers, and the land mines they produced would cause significant damage to the anti-Communist troops and militias in subsequent years. In May 1930, Wei Baqun initiated another training program in Fengshan for the officers of his Third Column as part of his effort at transforming his peasant army into a regular army, and more than one hundred officers attended the program.[64]

Wei Baqun was very likely the first to introduce mimeograph to Donglan. As mentioned earlier, he brought back two mimeographs in early 1925 and used them to reproduce textbooks for the first class of Donglan Peasant Movement Institute. In 1931, the Donglan revolutionary government returned to the traditional stone plate method of printing, indicating that for some reason the two mimeographs were out of use. The telegraph was first introduced in Guangxi in 1883, but it had not reached Donglan in the 1920s. The outside Communists were possibly the first to bring the telegraph to Donglan. The Seventh Red Army provided two books of telegraph codes for Wei Baqun's followers, who would use these to compose secret messages for communications during the third revolt, although they never used an actual telegraph.[65]

The Seventh Red Army also brought a modern hospital to Donglan in early 1930, which was the first in the county. The hospital had both modern and traditional doctors, but primarily used herbs as medicine. Doctors could perform simple surgeries. The head doctor, Wu Qingpei, was a native of Fujian and a graduate of Xiamen Medical College. He was one of the more than forty Communists the CCP dispatched to Nanning in 1929. The hospital left Donglan in 1930 with the main force of the Seventh Red Army.[66]

Road construction formed an important part of Wei Baqun's modernization program. In 1927, he called for peasant associations to help construct local roads, and he personally directed the renovation and expansion of four roads in Wuzhuan, totaling forty-five kilometers. These roads were good for horse carts, but not for automobiles. Even his enemy Liao Lei praised Wei Baqun for reconstructing these roads.[67]

The Nationalists also contributed to the introduction of modern technology to Donglan. During the three extermination campaigns in 1931 and 1932, Liao Lei's Seventh Army established two telephone exchange stations in Dongyuan and Wuzhuan, respectively. They brought in six telephones, and there were telephone lines connecting Donglan with Hechi, Tianzhou and Fengshan.[68] This was the earliest telephone service in Donglan. In 1932, the Nationalists established a modern clinic in Dongyuan and two years later a second clinic was set up in Wuzhuan.[69]

This wave of modernization was primarily a product of the wars, and understandably it was focused on the introduction of military or military related knowledge and equipment, and it would end when the war was over. A new wave of modernization would begin after the collapse of the Communist movement, and its major achievement was the construction of the first major automobile road between Hechi and Tianzhou, which was completed in the late 1930s and it passed through Donglan. This new wave was soon interrupted by the Japanese invasion and the last civil war between the Communists and Nationalists. The creation of the first modern factories in Donglan had to wait till after the Communist takeover in 1949.

Integration

The arrival of the outside Communists in the Right River region led to the complete integration of Wei Baqun's Donglan peasant revolution into the larger Communist movement of China. Wei Baqun entered the Communist movement during the second revolt, but a total integration was not achieved then. He had conflicts with some Communists who were critical of his practices and ideologies, his full membership in the CCP was not approved, and after the collapse of the United Front he lost contact with the CCP for a long time.

Wei Baqun's third revolt began with his arrival in Nanning in August 1929 to attend the First Peasant Congress of Guangxi and to be formally verified as a member of the CCP. After that he and his movement were gradually incorporated into the national Communist revolution to the extent that there was no longer a boundary between his peasant revolution and the Communist movement, and that for Wei Baqun and others there was no longer any doubt that he was indeed a Communist and that Donglan was a Communist territory. During the second revolt, the Communists created a cell in Donglan, but failed to preserve it. The third revolt saw a rapid expansion of the CCP in Donglan. After Wei Baqun became a CCP member in 1929, he brought many of his followers into the party. By mid-1930 there were more than four hundred CCP members in Donglan, and by the end of that year the number had further increased to at least one thousand. At that time there were only about two thousand CCP members in the entire Right River region. By late 1931, due to the departure of the main force of the Seventh Red Army, the total number of CCP members in the Right River region was reduced to about seven hundred, of which more than four hundred were in Donglan and Fengshan. Although the quality of these new CCP members raised the concerns of some Communist leaders, and the CCP members of Donglan were particularly criticized for worshipping Wei Baqun, the large number of CCP members nevertheless shows a strong presence of the party in the county. The Donglan County Committee of the CCP came into being in October 1929, and Wei Baqun presided over its founding congress, which was attended by thirteen delegates. Yan Min was the head of the committee, whereas Wei Baqun was in charge of its military affairs. Every township in Donglan set up a CCP branch after that.[70]

By early 1930, Donglan had become one of more than twenty counties that made up the Left River and Right River Revolutionary Base Area. Wei Baqun's peasant army had become part of the Communist Seventh Red Army, and Wei Baqun had been appointed as a formal Red Army officer. Among the seven people who formed the front committee of the Seventh Red Army, which was the highest Communist military organ in the area, Wei Baqun was the only native of the Right River region. By becoming an integral part of the Left River and Right River Revolutionary Base Area, Wei Baqun upgraded himself from a local leader to a national one. Economically, Donglan also became part of the Right River Communist system. The Communists confiscated a lot of cash and opium from the wealthy towns along the Right River, which allowed them to offer much needed financial support to the Donglan Soviet.[71]

For Wei Baqun the third revolt was also his third journey in the sense that it provided great opportunities for him to learn new ideas and methods and make new connections. During the first two journeys and revolts, Wei Baqun was the active and determined initiator, but in the third revolt he was more like a passive receiver. The first two revolts were both designed and launched by Wei Baqun and his local supporters, but the third was primarily planned and executed by the outsiders. During his first two journeys Wei Baqun made strenuous trips to the provincial and national centers to meet the provincial and national leaders and be a guest there. During the third revolt, he made a trip to Nanning and then the leaders came to the Right River region and Donglan. He became a host to these outsiders.

The third revolt brought Wei Baqun into close contact with some old and new patrons and comrades. He strengthened his relations with Yu Zuobai, a strong supporter since the second revolt. Yu was Wei Baqun's last patron among the leading left-wing Nationalists. After the collapse of the Yu-Li regime in October 1929 and Yu's ensuing departure from Guangxi, Wei Baqun's connections with the left-wing Nationalists came to an end. Among Wei Baqun's new Communist patrons, the three most important were Zhang Yunyi, Lei Jingtian and Deng Xiaoping, who were Wei Baqun's superiors in the Seventh Red Army, the Soviet government, and the CCP, respectively. Wei Baqun fought many battles under Zhang Yunyi and spent months with Deng Xiaoping and Lei Jingtian working on governmental affairs. All three were already powerful leaders of the national Communist movement and were to become even more powerful in the future. For Wei Baqun these were connections that had great potential significance.

The outsiders greatly enhanced the power of the revolutionary forces in the Right River region. The Red Armies they created were much better equipped and trained than the local peasant armies. They were more modern than Wei Baqun's peasant army since they had all the components required for a regular army, which enabled them to challenge regular enemy troops. With an efficient war machine, the outsiders were able to temporarily occupy some important towns and cities as well as a large number of counties. Because of the support of the outsiders, Wei Baqun and his followers were able to move out of the Western Mountains to reconquer first Wuzhuan and then the county seat, and eliminate their enemies in Donglan, Fengshan, and other places. The outsiders brought the Communist movement in the Left River and Right River region as well as in Guangxi to a climax, and Wei Baqun obviously welcomed such a development. Like Chen Mianshu during Wei Baqun's second revolt, the outsiders who came in late 1929 acted as protectors of Wei Baqun and his movement, but as protectors they were much more powerful than Chen Mianshu, since Chen did not have a military force to back him.

In addition to a powerful military force, the outsiders also came with new ideas and methods. One of the new ideas they brought to Wei Baqun held that the party should command the army, not vice versa. In the Seventh Red Army, every company had a CCP branch, every column had a political department and the army was jointly captained by a commander-in-chief and a political commissar. This system was somewhat new to Wei Baqun. In previous years, Wei Baqun sometimes would choose one of his followers to serve as the head of the peasant government or peasant association, but he would always hold on to the position of top commander of the peasant army, which may imply that he believed the army should command the government or any other organization, not the other way around. The system of the Soviet government was also something new to Wei Baqun. It was similar to the revolutionary committee and the peasant associations that Wei Baqun had set up, but it was more formal. Many of the policies and procedures of land revolution were new to Wei Baqun. He had been fighting the landlords, confiscating their properties, and helping the poor, but he had not standardized or legalized his policies. Part of the reason was that he had never been able to seize and hold a sizable and permanent base for very long, and hence did not have the conditions to carry out a formal land revolution. Another important reason was that he was not well informed of the new policies of the CCP and the practices of the other revolutionary base areas. For instance, the CCP had adopted the policy of land revolution at the Wuhan meeting of August 7, 1927, but Wei Baqun did not learn about the policy change until 1929.

The integration brought great benefits to Wei Baqun's movement, but it also came at a price. In the new system created by the outsiders, Wei Baqun was recognized as one of the leaders, but no longer the supreme leader of the movement. He lost his independence. It appears that Wei Baqun was more than willing to give away his independence in exchange for the victories of the Communist movement in the region. Unlike the outside Communists coming to Donglan during the second revolt, who left vague accounts about possible conflicts with Wei Baqun, the outside Communists who worked with Wei Baqun during the third revolt reported no clashes. The three most powerful outsiders, Deng Xiaoping, Zhang Yunyi, and Lei Jingtian, all thought highly of Wei Baqun and developed very close relations with him.

In many other revolutionary base areas, the integration of the local Communist revolution into the larger national Communist movement caused serious conflicts between the locals and outsiders. For instance, in the Jinggangshan Revolutionary Base Area, the arrival of the outside Communist force led by Mao Zedong and Zhu De resulted in the incorporation of the small native bandit group headed by Wang Zuo and Yuan Wencai, and the process was completed with the execution of both Wang and Yuan by the party leaders. Later the development of the Central Revolutionary Base Area in southwestern Jiangxi caused clashes between outside Communists led by Mao and local Communists headed by Li Wenlin and the confrontation was resolved by a bloody purge of Li Wenlin and many of his supporters as members of the so-called Anti-Bolshevik Corps. In the Hubei-Henan-Anhui Revolutionary Base Area, Zhang Guotao, the delegate of the CCP Central Committee who arrived there in 1931, established his authority over his comrades by killing many of the native revolutionaries who had created the base area. In the Shaan-Gan-Ning Revolutionary Base Area, conflicts between the delegates of the CCP Central Committee and local Communist leaders led to the arrest of many prominent local Communists in 1935. Many of these local Communists would have been killed by their own comrades if Mao and the other Long Marchers had not arrived in time to save their lives.[72] Bloody purges of local Communist leaders also occurred in the Western Hunan and Hubei Revolutionary base area and other places in the 1930s. Purges of local Communist leaders continued to occur in the PRC era in the name of anti-localism in Guangdong (including

Hainan), Fujian, Zhejiang and other places and it caused the fall of quite a few prominent Communists, including Sha Wenhan of Zhejiang and Fang Fang, Gu Dacun, and Feng Baiju of Guangdong.[73] In most of these cases, the integration of local revolutions into the national movement occurred at the expense of the local leaders. Many lost their positions, and some even lost their lives.

In the Right River region, the incorporation of the Donglan peasant revolution into the Right River Communist movement caused no serious conflicts between the natives and the outsiders. One reason is that in 1929, in the Right River region, Wei Baqun and his local supporters viewed the outside Communists not as conquerors who were only interested in taking over the local movement, but as saviors who came to help strengthen and preserve the local revolution. The outsiders came at a time when the local movement was at low ebb and when native leaders like Wei Baqun were desperately searching for external support. The outsiders performed the roles of providers and protectors by offering weapons, political, and military training, as well as new ideas and policies, and by helping defeat or at least weaken their common enemies. The local leaders were therefore grateful rather than resentful toward the outsiders. On the other hand, the outsiders felt equally grateful to Wei Baqun for providing them with reliable soldiers and officers as well as a dependable base area. They knew how popular Wei Baqun was among his followers and they found it convenient to use him as a rallying point. In this aspect they probably had learned some lessons from the conflicts between Wei Baqun and the other group of Communists during the second revolt.

Another important factor that helped to prevent conflicts between locals and outsiders in the Right River region was that from the very beginning the outsiders showed no interest in permanently staying in the region. Prominent leaders of the party and the leaders of the Seventh Red Army did not find the Right River region suitable for building a permanent base. Four days after the birth of the Seventh Red Army, the Guangdong Provincial Committee of the CCP instructed the army to move toward Hunan and Guangdong in order to get close to the Communist base areas there. One month later the Southern Bureau and the Guangdong Provincial Committee of the CCP ordered the Seventh Red Army to eventually merge with the Red Army led by Mao Zedong and Zhu De.[74] These instructions might serve to encourage leaders of the Seventh Red Army to plan the attack on Nanning in early 1930. In March 1930, the Central Committee of the CCP again asked the Seventh Red Army to move toward the borders of Hunan and Guangdong to join the forces of Mao Zedong and Zhu De. It also instructed the commanders of the army that when they left Guangxi they should take most of the local peasant soldiers with them because these soldiers could become core forces of the Red Army.

After reclaiming some counties along the Right River in June 1930, the leaders of the Seventh Red Army decided that they would stay in the region for three more months to rebuild the army, conduct land revolution and protect the autumn harvest, and then they would move toward Hunan and Guangdong.[75] Lei Jingtian was demoted for being protective of the rich peasants and for opposing the decision to move the Seventh Red Army away. Chen Hongtao was appointed as his successor as the leader of the Soviet government and the head of the Right River Special Committee of the CCP. Wei Baqun was made a member of both the party and government committees. In the perceptions of local peasants, Wei Baqun was a more popular and powerful leader than Chen Hongtao, and in the perceptions of the anti-Communist leaders, Wei Baqun was a more dangerous enemy than Chen Hongtao, but the Communist leaders seemed to have more confidence in Chen than in Wei Baqun. Maybe they had not completely forgotten about Wei Baqun's past contacts and other shortcomings. However, it is also possible that Chen Hongtao was appointed to these top positions based on Wei Baqun's recommendation. Wei Baqun may have been content to retain the position of military commander.

Periphery as a Revolutionary Center

The events in Donglan demonstrate clearly that native revolutionaries like Wei Baqun played a crucial role in making a revolution in this frontier community. They were the ones who determined the directions and features of the movement, and the peasants were primarily their followers. Communist Chen Mianshu argued that oppression and exploitation made the peasant movement in Donglan inevitable, and that even without Wei Baqun there would still have been a peasant movement in Donglan, yet he agreed that without Wei Baqun the timing and form of the Donglan peasant movement would have been different.[76] Gong Chu commented that although peasants were resentful about the exploitation they suffered, they were not able to launch a revolutionary movement without stimulators.[77] Gong himself was a stimulator. So were Wei Baqun and his comrades in Donglan and the Communist revolutionaries in other parts of China. Wei Baqun knew clearly how important the instigators were to the success of his revolution and throughout the three revolts he made strong efforts to recruit and nurture revolutionary intellectuals and entrusted them with the task of mobilizing and organizing the peasants.

The leaders of the New Guangxi Clique were also aware that instigators like Wei Baqun and his comrades were the true makers of the peasant movement in Donglan and the Right River region, and therefore attached great importance to the capturing and killing of these men. Bai Chongxi and Liao Lei even claimed that Wei Baqun was the sole culprit who had single-handedly started the revolution in Donglan and the Right River region. During their campaign against Wei Baqun, the leaders of the New Guangxi Clique announced that they would allow most of Wei Baqun's rank-and-file followers to live if they chose to surrender, and their justification was that these ordinary followers had been deceived or coerced into joining the revolution by the revolutionaries. This lenient policy was not applicable to Wei Baqun, Chen Hongtao, or other leading revolutionaries because the leaders of the New Guangxi Clique believed that these instigators had to be exterminated in order to prevent a future revolution.

By starting their revolution in Donglan, Wei Baqun and the other local revolutionaries turned the county into a hub of political importance. The peasant revolution in Donglan became so influential that for more than a decade this frontier county, which had been little known to outsiders before, remained one of the most prominent centers of revolution in China. As a man from the periphery, Wei Baqun traveled to the metropolis and then returned to his frontier community to launch a revolution based on the ideas and methods he had brought back. Once he and his movement became famous, his frontier community began to exert influence on neighboring areas and other parts of the county and to perform the functions of a center. During the first revolt, Wei Baqun's four attacks on the county seat attracted the attention and support of revolutionaries from neighboring counties and rattled the entire Right River region and Guangxi Province. However, people outside Guangxi still knew little about his movement and thus when he traveled to Guangzhou in late 1924 and early 1925, few Nationalist or Communist leaders thought that Wei Baqun was comparable to Peng Pai. Its remote location made it more difficult for Donglan to attract the national attention that a coastal region like Haifeng could.

But only one year after Wei Baqun returned from Guangzhou, his second revolt made Donglan a focus of national attention. An official Communist document issued in 1926 compared Wei Baqun with Peng Pai for the first time,[78] and Donglan and Hailufeng began to be recognized as the two centers of radical peasant activism in China. During the third revolt, Donglan and the Right River region became one of about a dozen Communist revolutionary base areas, and therefore a center of Communist China.

If the gathering of a group of revolutionaries was the precondition for the outbreak of the revolution in Donglan, then the dispersal of these revolutionaries contributed to spreading the Donglan revolution to other areas. Travel played a very important part in both the rise of the Donglan revolution and the expansion of its influence. Revolutionaries from neighboring counties would travel to Donglan to observe, study, and participate in the movement there and then return to their native places to organize their own revolutions. At the same time, revolutionaries from Donglan also traveled to other counties to help organize peasant associations and peasant armies. Through travels back and forth between Donglan and other places, a revolutionary network was formed. This network consisted of revolutionaries from Donglan, the Right River region and other places, and as the center of this network, Wei Baqun became the leader of the revolutionary movements not just in Donglan, but also in the larger region.

Wei Baqun's spheres of influences were composed of some concentric circles. The innermost circle was indisputably Donglan, but even within Donglan Wei Baqun's influence was not equal in various parts of the county. Wuzhuan, the county seat, and the plains were the contested areas between Wei Baqun and his enemies. When his power was at its zenith, he would make the county seat the center of his movement. He attacked and took the county seat in 1923 and occupied it for a few months. He took it again in 1926 and held it for more than six months. In late 1929, he retook the town and was able to maintain his control over it for more than a year. The attacks on and occupation of the county seat represent the high points of his three revolts.

When he was not able to hold onto the county seat, Wei Baqun would retreat to Wuzhuan, where his influence was very strong. Many of his early supporters were from the Wuzhuan area or were graduates of the schools in the town. In the three classes of Donglan Peasant Movement Institute, students from Wuzhuan outnumbered those from any of the other five districts of Donglan or any other neighboring county. Of the twenty-three most wanted criminals on the list issued by the provincial government in late 1927, nine were from Wuzhuan.[79]

When Wei Baqun was not able to keep Wuzhuan, he would move into the nearby Western Mountains. He first built his base there in 1926 and the region remained his stronghold until 1932. The Central and Eastern Mountains were also essential base areas for Wei Baqun, and as the outer zones of the Western Mountains they were particularly important when the towns and plains were in enemy hands. Among the six districts of Donglan at that time, Wuzhuan and the Western Mountains figured most prominently in Wei Baqun's revolution. Wuzhuan was much more prosperous than the Western Mountains, and there were many educated intellectuals in the district and some of them became leaders of Wei Baqun's movement. The Western Mountains, on the other hand, provided the most determined rank and file soldiers for the peasant movement. To some extent the alliance of Wuzhuan and the Western Mountains represents the unity of a Zhuang area and a Yao-dominated zone as well as the cooperation of revolutionary intellectuals from the plains and the poor peasants living in the mountains. Wei Baqun, who had grown up on the borderline between Wuzhuan and the Western Mountains, was the ideal link binding the two districts.

During his decade-long revolution, Wei Baqun moved frequently between Wuzhuan, Dongyuan, and the Western Mountains, which formed his three primary bases within Donglan. Wei Baqun's power at a given moment can be measured by where he stayed within the county. When his power overwhelmed that of his enemies he would make the county seat the center of his revolution.

When there was a balance of power between his forces and the enemy forces, he would make Wuzhuan his base, from where he could either advance to the county seat in the east or retreat to the Western Mountains in the west. When he was overpowered by his enemies, he would turn the Western, Central and Eastern Mountains into the center of his revolution. Other subcenters of revolution within Donglan included Sanshi (Taiping), Duyi (Datong), Changjiang, and Nadi. Wei Baqun had some loyal supporters from each of these districts, including Lu Haoren, Bai Hanyun, and Huang Fangri from Sanshi, Wei Hanchao from Duyi, Ya Sumin from Changjiang, and Wei Guoying and Lan Zhiren from Nadi. Among the various districts of Donglan, Wei Baqun's influence was the weakest in the part of Donglan located to the east of the county seat and the Red Water River, largely because the river was the most formidable barrier within the county. This area thus made a safe haven for Wei Baqun's local enemies. When Wei Baqun's forces defeated them in the towns and plains on the western bank, they would often move to the eastern bank where they would feel safe.

Beyond Donglan was the circle of Dong-Feng, which was composed of the two counties of Donglan and Fengshan. Fengshan was located to the northwest of Donglan and there was a traditional bond between these two counties. Before 1730, the two counties formed one administrative unit ruled by the hereditary Wei family, but in that year the Qing court separated Fengshan from Donglan. It made Donglan a regular county administered by appointed officials, but permitted Fengshan to remain under the rule of the Wei family. After the separation, the lords of Fengshan were put under the control of the magistrates of Donglan. In that way, Fengshan remained a special region of Donglan and was perceived to be Donglan's frontier. Fengshan was considered more backward than Donglan politically and economically, and it was also more remote than Donglan. Fengshan did not become an independent and regular county until 1919.

During Wei Baqun's three revolts, Fengshan formed an integral part of his movement. The close alliance between revolutionaries from Donglan and Fengshan was sustained by Wei Baqun's friendship with some leading revolutionaries from Fengshan. Wei Baqun's strongest ally from Fengshan was his sworn brother Liao Yuanfang, who remained his loyal supporter from 1916 to 1931. His second most powerful ally from Fengshan was Huang Songjian, who joined Wei Baqun during the second revolt and emerged as the third most powerful leader of the Communist movement in the Right River region. Next to Liao Yuanfang and Huang Songjian was Huang Wentong, who became a supporter of Wei Baqun while a student at the Number Five Provincial High School in Baise. After studying at the first class of Donglan Peasant Movement Institute, he grew into an important leader of the peasant movement in Fengshan. In late 1927, Wei Baqun sent him to Haifeng to study with Peng Pai, and Huang did not return to Guangxi until mid-1929.[80] The three became leaders of the Fengshan peasant movement largely because of Wei Baqun's support and guidance, and their close relations with Wei Baqun ensured the smooth incorporation of the Fengshan peasant movement into Wei Baqun's revolution. On the one hand, Wei Baqun's supporters from Fengshan participated actively in his movement in Donglan; on the other hand, Wei Baqun and his followers from Donglan also frequently offered assistance to their comrades in Fengshan. For instance, in late 1926, Huang Daquan went to Fengshan to help Liao Yuanfang organize peasant associations and peasant armies. In late 1929, a unit of the Donglan peasant army went to Fengshan to help attack the enemy troops occupying the county seat.[81] Wei Baqun personally directed several battles in Fengshan in the early 1930s.

Wei Baqun's enemies were aware of the special relationship between Donglan and Fengshan. In late 1927, they began their campaign against Donglan with an attack on Fengshan. During the third revolt they saw Donglan and Fengshan as the center of the Communist revolution and frequently referred to the Communist base area as Dong-Feng. They believed that "bandit" Wei Baqun's impact was as destructive in Fengshan as it was in Donglan[82] and later took both Donglan and Fengshan as the primary targets of their numerous extermination campaigns. To eliminate the Communists in the two counties, the New Guangxi Clique created the Dong-Feng Extermination Headquarters to direct battles against Wei Baqun and his supporters. In a way, both the Communists and their enemies continued to treat the two counties as one administrative unit.

The next circle was the area of Dong-Feng-Ling-Se, which included the four counties of Donglan, Fengshan, Lingyun, and Baise. Lingyun and Baise were located to the southwest of Donglan and Fengshan. The border area among the four counties formed a vast inseparable mountainous region that was only under the loose control of the four county governments, and the Western, Central, and Eastern Mountains formed part of this mountainous region. There were close cultural, economic, and political links among the four counties. During Wei Baqun's first revolt, there were revolutionaries from Lingyun and Baise participating in his fourth attack on the county seat of Donglan. In the second revolt, Wei Baqun's allies from Lingyun and Baise organized peasant associations and peasant armies in their counties and continued to work with their comrades in Donglan. In the three classes of Donglan Peasant Movement Institute, there were numerous students from the Lingyun and Baise sections of the mountainous region, and in the third class alone there were at least thirteen students from the Baise part of this region.[83]

In Lingyun, Wei Baqun's strongest ally was Huang Boyao, who was an elementary school teacher when he first met Wei Baqun. In late 1925, Huang became a student at the first class of Donglan Peasant Movement Institute.

After graduating from the institute he returned to Lingyun to organize peasant associations and a peasant army with himself as its commander. In late 1926, he collaborated with Donglan peasant soldiers and attacked some powerful families in Lingyun. When the Lingyun Soviet Government was created in early 1930, Huang became its first chairman. After joining the CCP on Wei Baqun's recommendation, Huang also served as the head of the Lingyun special committee of the CCP. During the third revolt, Huang served as a battalion commander in the Third Column of the Seventh Red Army.[84]

In 1927, the peasant armies from the four counties staged joined actions against the local governments. Later that year, under Wei Baqun's command, peasant armies from Donglan, Lingyun, and Fengshan launched an attack on a battalion of enemy troops stationed in the county seat of Fengshan. In 1929, Wei Baqun's supporters in Lingyun staged another rebellion to support the Baise Uprising, and by that time the border area among the four counties had been turned into a unified guerilla zone. In late 1929, Communists from Donglan helped create the CCP organizations in Fengshan, Lingyun, and Baise, and the CCP branches in these counties were directly controlled by the CCP Committee of Donglan. Some female revolutionaries from Donglan were sent to Fengshan, Lingyun, and Baise to help with propaganda work.[85]

In Baise, there was a clear division between the city of Baise and the surrounding villages. Whereas the villagers, particularly those living in the mountainous areas, were prone to leftist and Communist instigations, the city of Baise was a stronghold of counter-revolutionary forces most of the time. General Liu Rifu, one of Wei Baqun's major enemies, made the city his headquarters from 1921 to 1928. In 1928, Governor Huang Shaohong replaced Liu with Zhu Weizheng, who had directed the attack on Wei Baqun in 1927 and 1928.[86] Within Baise, the Number Five Provincial High School of Guangxi, which was founded in 1906 and remained the highest educational institution in the Right River region in the 1920s and 1930s, was the center of radicalism and a gathering place for Wei Baqun's sympathizers. Some of Wei Baqun's close followers, including Chen Bomin, Chen Hongtao, Huang Songjian, Huang Wentong, and Wei Jing, had studied in the school, and quite a few other prominent peasant movement leaders of the Right River region were also graduates of that school.[87] Wei Baqun's young followers in the school helped spread his influence in the city and mobilized support for his movement, and the bonds they forged in the school was to be of great significance for the peasant movement.

Dong-Feng-Ling-Se in turn formed an integral part of a larger circle, the greater Right River region, which included all the counties between the Right River and the Red Water River, plus several counties to the east of the Red Water River and the south of the Right River. In 1923, revolutionaries from several counties of the Right River region joined Wei Baqun's fourth attack on the county seat of Donglan. The three classes of Donglan Peasant Movement

Institute included students from the entire Right River area. The students in the first class represented as many as twelve counties in the region. Some of these students would become prominent peasant movement leaders in their own counties and would remain strong allies of Wei Baqun.

Wei Baqun not only helped train peasant movement leaders for these counties, but occasionally would also send his experienced comrades from Donglan and Fengshan to those counties to help jumpstart peasant movements there. Wei Baqun himself traveled to several counties in the Right River region during the second and third revolts to help his comrades in those places. In August 1926, Wei Baqun recommended three of his followers, Chen Bomin, Chen Shouhe, and Huang Shuxiang, to the provincial government, and they were appointed as peasant movement agents in Fengyi, Enlong, and Guode, respectively. Whereas Chen Bomin did not take his position, Chen Shouhe and Huang Shuxiang worked hard in Enlong and Guode and became important leaders in the two counties. From Guode, Huang Shuxiang gradually expanded his influence to the nearby Nama County.[88]

In late 1927, in order to divert the attention of enemy forces and to expand the peasant movement, Wei Baqun sent Chen Bomin to Du'an County to organize peasant associations and peasant armies there. Several other experienced leaders from Donglan, including Huang Fangri, Chen Gutao, Chen Mingjiu, and Deng Wuwei, worked in Du'an with Chen Bomin. In 1929 and 1930, Wei Baqun twice sent Liao Yuanfang to Nandan and Nadi to organize peasant associations and peasant armies.[89] Yu Zuobai's appointment of Chen Bomin, Huang Daquan, and Huang Shuxiang as county magistrates in 1929 further expanded Donglan's influence in the Right River region. By 1929, revolutionaries from Donglan had firm control over at least five counties in the Right River region: Huang Shuxiang in Guode and Nama, Chen Gutao in Xiangdu, Huang Daquan in Enlong, and Chen Bomin in Du'an. They all followed the Wei Baqun model, becoming local heroes and strongmen within their own respective counties. A leading Communist from Guangxi confirmed in early 1929 that Wei Baqun had strong influence on the peasant movement leaders in the Right River region.[90]

In 1926 and 1927, a second peasant movement center in the Right River region emerged around Pingma on the eastern bank of the Right River. The man who created this second center was Yu Shaojie, a young army officer in the National Revolutionary Army. Born in Guangzhou in 1907, Yu entered Whampoa Military Academy in 1925 and joined the CCP there. After graduating from Whampoa in early 1926, he became an officer in the army unit stationed in Pingma, where he came into contact with some progressive native intellectuals. He converted some of them to communism and created the first CCP branch in the Right River region. Yu was not the first to work on peasant movement in the area, but he brought unity and great momentum to the existing movement.

He also made sure that the peasant movements in the area would develop along the Communist line. To better communicate with his local followers, Yu Shaojie even learned to speak the Zhuang language.[91] After creating a CCP branch, Yu sent activists to Enlong, Fengyi and other counties to organize peasant associations and peasant armies. By March 1927, the Communists had created peasant associations in more than 130 townships in Enlong and Fengyi, and in total nearly ten thousand villagers from the two counties had joined peasant associations. Yu's movement became so powerful that Governor Huang Shaohong considered Wei Baqun and Yu Shaojie to be the two most dangerous rebels in Guangxi in 1927 and 1928.[92] Yu Shaojie saw Wei Baqun as a strong ally. Although he very likely never met Wei Baqun, he became familiar with Wei Baqun's movement by working intimately with some of Wei Baqun's close friends, including Chen Shouhe, Huang Shuxiang, and three peasant movement leaders of the Fengyi County (Huang Zhifeng, Li Zhengru, and Lu Bingtang).[93]

Although Wei Baqun may have been the first to sow the seeds of peasant armed resistance in the Right River region, Yu Shaojie was the first to try to integrate the peasant armies of the various counties into a united armed force and put it under the direct control of the CCP. In early 1927, when the New Guangxi Clique began to purge the Communists in Guangxi, Yu lost contact with his superiors in the CCP. He left the Nationalist Army and created a guerrilla band in the Right River region. In July 1927, he founded the Guangxi Provisional Military and Political Committee to lead the revolution in Guangxi. The Committee had five members and both Wei Baqun and Huang Shuxiang were among the five. Yu Shaojie then reorganized all the peasant armies in the Right River region into three routes, with Wei Baqun as the commander-in-chief of the first route, which was formed by peasant fighters from Dong-Feng-Ling-Se. Huang Zhifeng became the commander-in-chief of the second route, and Yu himself served as the commander-in-chief of the third route.[94] In that way, the rise of Yu Shaojie and the second center actually helped expand Wei Baqun's influence in the Right River region. By appointing Wei Baqun as a member of the Guangxi Provisional Military and Political Committee and the commander-in-chief of the first route of the Right River Peasant Self-Defense Army, Yu Shaojie, who represented the CCP in Guangxi at that time, formally recognized Wei Baqun as a leader of the Communist movement in the greater Right River region. The young and energetic Yu Shaojie had the potential of becoming the second pillar of the peasant movement in the Right River region. Because he enjoyed the full support of the CCP and had won the trust of many local intellectuals, he even had the potential of overshadowing Wei Baqun in the Right River region. Unfortunately, he was killed by the New Guangxi Clique in 1928 at the age of twenty-one.

Realizing that it was impossible for the peasant movement or Communist revolution to succeed in one county, the CCP leaders repeatedly warned against isolationism, and encouraged the expansion of the Donglan peasant movement.[95] Overall, the CCP helped expand Wei Baqun's influence during his second and third revolts in several ways. First, the CCP encouraged Communists and Communist sympathizers in other counties of the Right River region to offer support to Wei Baqun and build or tighten connections with him. Moreover, Communists helped place some of Wei Baqun's followers from Donglan in other counties of the Right River region. Finally, the CCP offered Wei Baqun, Chen Hongtao, and others powerful positions that allowed them to oversee the peasant and Communist movements of the entire Right River region. A Nationalist observer remarked pointedly in 1932 that, without the support of the CCP, Wei Baqun would still have been able to kindle revolution in Donglan and Fengshan, but would not have been able to extend his influence to the entire Right River region.[96]

In 1929, the Greater Right River region became part of a larger Communist sphere of influence that included the areas along both the Right River and Left River, although in reality the areas along the two rivers were not well integrated. Wei Baqun's direct influence in the Left River region was much weaker than that in the Right River region during his three revolts. After his defeat in 1931 and 1932, some of Wei Baqun's followers would move to the Left River region to organize revolution. Because of them Wei Baqun's influence in the Left River area was stronger after his death than during his lifetime.

Wei Baqun's influence also reached Nanning and other parts of Guangxi. He was well known throughout the province, either as a great revolutionary or a notorious bandit. Although the leaders of the New Guangxi Clique saw Wei Baqun as one of their most dangerous enemies inside Guangxi, Wei Baqun's leftist and Communist friends described him and his followers as "pioneers of peasant liberation in Guangxi," and they saw his movement as an important part of the mass movement in Guangxi and China. At the first class of Guangxi Peasant Movement Institute held in 1926, the Communists used the case of Donglan to educate their activists and encouraged the students to follow Wei Baqun's example.[97] Wei Baqun's immediate enemies were the "local tyrants and evil gentry," but standing behind his local enemies was the New Guangxi Clique. Every conflict between Wei Baqun and his local enemies would eventually escalate into a confrontation between Wei Baqun and the New Guangxi Clique or a conflict between all the Communists and all the anti-Communists in Guangxi.

Ultimately, Wei Baqun's revolutions were crushed by the New Guangxi Clique rather than by his local enemies. The fact that the leaders of the New Guangxi Clique decided to display Wei Baqun's head not only in Donglan but also in all other major cities in Guangxi indicates that in their eyes Wei Baqun was not just a local bandit from Donglan, but also an enemy who had influence in the entire province. From 1921 to 1932, within Guangxi Province, if Nanning was the center of counter-revolutionary forces, then Donglan was the stronghold of revolutionary forces. Relations between Nanning and Donglan were comparable to the relations between Nanjing and Ruijin or between Chongqing and Yan'an. In some sense, relations between Nanning and Donglan were also comparable to those between Nanjing and Nanning during the Nanjing Decade. Just as the New Guangxi Clique wanted to keep Guangxi autonomous of Nanjing, Wei Baqun and his followers were determined to keep Donglan and the surrounding areas autonomous of Nanning. The leaders of the New Guangxi Clique feared and hated Donglan so much that they spoke wistfully of their desire to expel the whole county from Guangxi.[98] Revolution turned Donglan and quite a few other poor, backward, and peripheral regions of Republican China into centers of national politics.

Beyond Guangxi, Wei Baqun had strong influence throughout southern China, but particularly in the three provinces of Guangdong, Guizhou, and Yunnan. Among all the major cities in China, Guangzhou had the closest links with Wei Baqun's movement. Wei Baqun made at least three visits to the city during his lifetime and each one had a transformative effect on him. After returning home he would try to apply the ideas and methods he brought back from Guangzhou to change Donglan, and once his experiment became well known it was sometimes used to confirm the radical policies promoted by the political leaders based in Guangzhou. The leftists in Guangzhou considered Wei Baqun's movement in Donglan an integral part of the broader peasant movement of southern China that they were nurturing, and so offered him support and promoted his model. During the third revolt, Wei Baqun received direct instructions from the Guangdong Provincial Committee and the Guangdong and Guangxi Provincial Committee of the CCP, and his movement became an important part of the Communist movement in Guangdong, Guangxi and other parts of southern China. As discussed in the next chapter, Wei Baqun's influence did not reach Guizhou and Yunnan until the last few months of his life, and it grew steadily after his death.

Wei Baqun's influence during the first revolt was confined to Guangxi, during the second it did not extend beyond southern China; however, during the third revolt his movement became an important part of the conflict between the Communists and Nationalists at the national level. The integration of his movement into the Communist revolution made him a revolutionary of national stature, which was symbolically confirmed when he was elected a member of the executive committee of the Chinese Soviet Republic in 1931. The committee had sixty-two members, including Mao Zedong, Zhou Enlai, Zhu De, Fang Zhimin, Ruan Xiaoxian, and Zhang Yunyi. Zhang Yunyi and Wei Baqun were the only two members representing the Right River Soviet and the Seventh Red Army, and Wei Baqun was the only native of Guangxi on the committee.[99] Wei Baqun's role as a leader of national stature was confirmed again in 1934 when at the second congress of the Chinese Soviet Republic, Mao Zedong proposed that all delegates observe three minutes of silence to mourn the death of fifteen leading Communist revolutionaries. Wei Baqun was one of the fifteen, and the others in the group included such famous Communists as Yun Daiying, Deng Zhongxia, Huang Gonglue, and Zhao Bosheng.

Outside China, Wei Baqun's influence reached Vietnam. French Vietnam was the only foreign country he had ever visited. His brief visits left no impact on the colony. However, after his death some of his followers would move to the area along the Sino-Vietnamese border. In the late 1930s, as the Vietnamese Communists began to turn the border area into their revolutionary base area, the Chinese Communists there managed to forge a bond with their Vietnamese comrades and sometimes they would have joint operations. Tan Tongnan, a native of Donglan who joined Wei Baqun's movement in 1923, was dispatched to the border area in 1931 and became one of the most important leaders of the Communist forces there. He remained there until his death in 1947.[100]

When Wei Baqun first launched his movement, one of his slogans was "Save Donglan, Save Guangxi, and Save China." Although he focused his attention on Donglan, he knew clearly that to change and save Donglan, he needed support from other parts of Guangxi and China. He was also aware that it would be impossible for him to save and change Donglan if Guangxi and China remained unchanged. He had strong motivations to win support from and to exert influence on other regions. Although his revolution was a local movement, it was meant to be part of a larger movement that would cover the entire province or the country, or was at least the first stage of a larger provincial or national movement. It was designed to be an open rather than isolated local movement.

It is ironic that the repeated attacks on Wei Baqun's movement launched by his enemies, although eventually causing the collapse of the movement in Donglan, helped spread its influence to other regions. It was pressure from his enemies that motivated Wei Baqun to seek support from outsiders and to send his followers to organize peasant movements in other counties and regions. Both victories and defeats furthered the spread of Wei Baqun's influence.

Overall, the status of Donglan in the 1920s was quite similar to that of Yan'an during the war against Japan. Although they were poor and backward economically and technologically, they were important and influential politically. Students and activists from neighboring counties would travel to Donglan to meet with Wei Baqun, to attend the Donglan Peasant Movement Institute, to observe and participate in the peasant movement in Donglan, just like students and other people from other parts of China would travel to Yan'an to join Mao Zedong and other Communist leaders, to study at the Anti-Japanese Military and Political School of China and other schools, and to participate in the war against Japan. Wei Baqun sent his followers to neighboring counties and provinces to work and fight for the revolution just as Mao sent his subordinates to various parts of the country to build anti-Japanese base areas. Of course, Donglan's influence in the 1920s was in no way comparable to that of Yan'an in the 1930s and 1940s. Whereas Yan'an was the supreme center of Communist revolution in China from 1935 to 1947, Donglan was one of the centers of the peasant movement and Communist revolution from 1921 to 1932. Communist China emerged in the early 1920s as an urban movement, with Beijing, Shanghai, and Guangzhou as major centers of influence. In the late 1920s, a cluster of rural revolutionary base areas emerged in remote parts of the country. From 1927 to 1937, Communist China became a network of a primary center and a number of secondary centers. Whereas Shanghai, Ruijin, and Yan'an served as the primary center of Communist revolution successively, Donglan and the Right River region emerged as one of the most important secondary centers. The biased view held by some outside Communists that the backward and remote Right River region was not an ideal place to build a major revolutionary base area did not prevent the region from actually functioning as a revolutionary center.

Separation

In late September 1930, Deng Gang, the delegate of the CCP Southern Bureau, arrived at Pingma where the headquarters of the Seventh Red Army was based. He had come all the way from Shanghai via Hong Kong, Nanning, and Longzhou, disguising himself as a businessman.[101] Deng Gang came with the most recent directives from the CCP Central Committee, which was under the control of Li Lisan and had adopted the so-called Lisan Line as the official policy of the party. The Lisan Line held that another revolutionary climax was in the making and that it was possible for the Communist revolution to succeed in a few provinces before it would succeed in the entire country. It called on the Red Armies to attack large cities. Based on the Lisan Line, the Southern Bureau ordered the Seventh Red Army to attack Liuzhou and Guilin in northern Guangxi, and then build a base area in northern Guangdong before it would take Guangzhou. The purpose was to turn Guangdong into a Communist province and to prevent the Nationalists in Guangdong from moving their troops to the north so that other Red Army units could defeat the Nationalists in central China and create a base area around Wuhan. The CCP Central Committee issued a letter containing severe criticisms of the leaders of the Seventh Red Army, and the Southern Bureau of the CCP continued to view General Li Mingrui as a warlord and argued that the leaders of the Seventh Red Army had made a grave mistake by not only allowing Li to stay with the army, but also admitting him into the CCP and appointing him as the commander-in-chief of the Seventh and Eighth Red Armies. It urged that

General Li be expelled from both the party and the army, an order the leaders of the Seventh Red Army chose not to heed. The letter also called for a rapid expansion of the Seventh Red Army.[102]

According to most sources, the directives of the CCP Central Committee caused a serious debate among the high-ranking leaders of the Right River Revolutionary Base Area. Deng Xiaoping and Zhang Yunyi thought that the Seventh Red Army was not powerful enough to attack and take major cities, but supported the idea of moving the army out of Guangxi. Lei Jingtian argued that the Seventh Red Army should stay in the Right River region, whereas Deng Gang, Chen Haoren, and Gong Chu fully endorsed the order of the Southern Bureau. Gong Chu, who served as the chief of staff of the Seventh Red Army at that time, recollected that he and Li Mingrui actually proposed to move northward to take Guizhou and turn it into a base area. It appears that Wei Baqun did not participate in the discussions. In the end, it was agreed that the Seventh Red Army would move eastward to enforce the order of the Southern Bureau. The leaders decided to keep their decision a secret, believing that to reveal it immediately would cause anxiety among the soldiers and officers, because most of them were natives of the Right River region and might be reluctant to leave home.[103]

In early October 1930, the Seventh Red Army began to move from the Right River basin toward Hechi in the east. In order to prevent the local soldiers from deserting, the leaders decided that the main force would not pass through Donglan.[104] The two top leaders, Deng Gang and Deng Xiaoping, traveled to Donglan to meet with Wei Baqun and his third column, and they then moved to Hechi together. By early November, all four columns of the Seventh Red Army plus a part of the Eighth Red Army had arrived in Hechi. The Eighth Red Army had been defeated in the Left River area, and its commander Yu Zuoyu escaped to Hong Kong, but was then captured by Nationalist agents in Shenzhen and executed in Guangzhou. In Hechi, the survivors of the Eighth Red Army were incorporated into the Seventh Red Army.

The First CCP Congress of the Seventh Red Army was held in Hechi in early November, and there were approximately five hundred CCP members in the army at that time. The Congress supported the strategy of attacking major cities and elected a new front committee. Deng Xiaoping remained the chairman of the committee, although he had thought about resigning.[105] Wei Baqun was removed from the front committee possibly because it had been decided that he would stay in the Right River region.

The party congress was followed immediately by the reorganization of the Seventh Red Army, and the new Seventh Red Army consisted of three divisions. The former first and third columns formed the Nineteenth Division, and the former second and fourth columns constituted the Twentieth. These two divisions had more than seven thousand soldiers in total and they would march from Guangxi to Guangzhou and would attack some major cities on the way. Wei Baqun was appointed as the commander-in-chief of the Twenty-first Division, which would stay in the Right River region, and Chen Hongtao was made the political commissar of this division. Unfortunately, the Twenty-first Division was seriously undermanned. Wei Baqun's third column was integrated with the Nineteenth Division. He was left with only about eighty old and wounded soldiers. He and Chen Hongtao were ordered to build the Twenty-first Division by reorganizing local peasant armies and recruiting peasant soldiers. The party hoped that the two would gradually expand the Twenty-first Division into an army.[106]

This reorganization was done according to orders from the higher leaders of the CCP. As mentioned earlier, the CCP Central Committee had deliberately and clearly ordered the Seventh Red Army to take most local peasant soldiers along when marching out from Guangxi. The leaders of the Seventh Red Army might think that it was reasonable and legitimate for them to take most troops away because they were expecting fierce battles against very powerful enemies in the major cities. They imagined that Wei Baqun and Chen Hongtao could survive in the mountains even without a large military force, and that it should also be easy for them to rebuild their army as they were so popular among the local peasants.

Lei Jingtian, the dissident among the leading Communists, again preferred to keep the Seventh Red Army in the Right River region. He believed that the border area between Guangxi, Yunnan, and Guizhou was an ideal place for building a base area. If the Seventh Red Army had to leave for Guangdong or Jiangxi, then Lei Jingtian thought that most of the Red Guards and local officials, including Lei himself, should be allowed to stay in the Right River region. Later, in 1945, at a meeting of former Seventh Red Army officers held in Yan'an, Lei argued that if more local troops and officials had been permitted to stay in the Right River region, they would have been able to preserve the revolutionary base area. For his dissident views, Lei Jingtian was deprived of all official positions even before reaching Hechi, and was expelled from the party at the First CCP Congress of the Seventh Red Army. He made the long march to Jiangxi as a soldier. His pregnant wife Yang Jinmei was left with Wei Baqun and was killed not long after the departure of the main force of the Seventh Red Army.[107]

It is not clear what Wei Baqun thought about the strategy of moving the main force of the Seventh Red Army out of the Right River region to attack the major cities and the plan to take most local soldiers with the main force. He would very likely have sided with Lei Jingtian, but it seemed that he never expressed his views, or even if he did his views did not really matter. All important decisions were made by the outsiders and the policy debate was also conducted among the outsiders. Even if Wei Baqun was indeed against the official policy of taking troops away from Guangxi to attack the large cities, as David Goodman argues,[108] Wei did not have a chance to express his views, much less to emerge as the leader of the dissident group. Most decisions had already been made at Pingma by the front committee, very likely in Wei Baqun's absence. It is hard to know whether or not Deng Xiaoping and Deng Gang had already informed Wei Baqun of their decision to take his third column away when they were with Wei Baqun in Donglan. Wei Baqun would have felt betrayed if the two had kept their plan a secret until after their arrival at Hechi. Lei Jingtian thought it very unfair for the top commanders to leave only one company for Wei Baqun, and believed that the native officers and officials who had joined the main force did not get fair treatment. Many of them were offered lower positions than they deserved.[109]

After the decision was made for the main force of the Seventh Red Army to leave the Right River region, Wei Baqun could have argued for one of three options. The first was to stay in the Right River region and keep his third column with him; the second was to join the main force with his third column; and the last was to stay in the Right River region without his third column. All Communist sources held that the outsiders preferred the third option, which was likely the most dangerous one for Wei Baqun, but he did not make any effort to change the decision. Huang Yucheng, a follower of Wei Baqun who later surrendered to the Nationalists, offered a different story, which holds that the outsiders wanted to take Wei Baqun with them, but Wei Baqun feigned illness after arriving at Hechi and asked to be allowed to stay home. Huang explained that Wei Baqun did this because he knew that if he joined the main force he would have to obey the outsiders all the time, but if he stayed home he would be the top leader of the Communist movement in the Right River region.[110] In other words, it was Wei Baqun's desire to be in control that prompted him to stay in the Right River region. Huang was probably right in asserting Wei Baqun's attachment to home and his aspiration for independence, but there are two flaws in his argument. One is that none of those who were with Wei Baqun in Hechi ever mentioned that Wei was sick. On the contrary, they remembered that he was actively involved in meetings and conversations with both top leaders and soldiers. The other is that if the top leaders had decided to take him along, it would have been very unlikely for them to change their minds because of some moderate illness. Mo Wenhua, a middle-ranking officer in the Seventh Red Army in 1930, wrote a brief but very controversial book about the history of the Seventh Red Army in Yan'an in 1944, in which he claimed that Wei Baqun was ordered to leave with the main force of the Seventh Red Army but escaped from Hechi to Donglan with about four hundred followers. A few months later, Mo gave up this claim and confirmed that Wei Baqun was ordered to stay in the Right River region.[111] All other leaders of the Seventh Red Army agreed that it was the party's decision for Wei Baqun to stay.

Some of the soldiers and officers in the third column did not want to leave home, and Wei Baqun had to persuade them to obey the party. He told his soldiers that it was their duty as members of a Communist army to follow the order of the party, and that because their mission was to liberate all mankind they should feel at home wherever they were. He assured them that they would return home once the revolution succeeded. Wei Baqun, the great singer, even composed an impromptu folksong for his former subordinates: "You are going afar for the revolution, and please do not miss home. Follow the Communist Party and strive to become an outstanding Red Army soldier. You are fighting for the people as well as for yourself, and you are fighting for something glorious. When the revolution succeeds, all of us will share happiness."[112]

Not all of the soldiers from Donglan followed Wei Baqun's advice. Qin Yingji, who was a fifteen-year-old soldier from Donglan in 1930, recalled that the soldiers from Guangxi felt that to leave their province was like traveling to a foreign country, and many deserted before leaving Guangxi. Among the more than one hundred soldiers from Qin's village, which was the largest in Donglan, more than half left for home before reaching the border of Guangxi, and among the deserters was a deputy battalion commander.[113] Qin and many other soldiers and officers from Donglan stayed in the main force and were to fight in places far away from home. Some would be able to see home again, but most would never return. The Civil Affairs Department of the Guangxi Zhuang Autonomous Region confirmed in 1982 that at least 550 Donglan natives who left with the Seventh Red Army in 1930 were killed in the various wars fought between the Communists and other forces. Some were killed right after leaving Hechi. Quite a few were killed in Hunan and Guangdong during the journey to Jiangxi. Many died in the Central Revolutionary Base Area in Jiangxi. At least two were killed during the Long March; one was killed in northern China by the Japanese during the war against Japan, and one was killed in 1949 near the Yangtze River in one of the last battles against the Nationalists. Some of these officers and soldiers got lost during the marches or were wounded in battles and then returned to Donglan.[114] Donglan would eventually become known as one of the famous "red counties" in China that dedicated more lives to the Communist revolution than most other counties.

A few of these young peasant soldiers from Donglan who left home in late 1930 survived all the brutal battles and emerged as powerful generals or officials in the People's Liberation Army and the PRC government after 1949. When the People's Liberation Army first created its military rank system in 1955, five Donglan natives received the ranks of general, lieutenant general, and major general, making Donglan one of the few "counties of generals" in China. Several other Donglan fighters took important positions in the government after 1949. The most prominent among this group of Donglan dignitaries was General Wei Guoqing, who would rule Guangxi for a long time and was an influential national leader in the PRC era. He even became an important figure in international politics by serving as the chief Chinese military adviser to Ho Chi-minh during the First Indochina War. All of these leaders were brought into the revolution by or because of Wei Baqun.

Many peasant soldiers from neighboring counties also joined the Seventh Red Army because of Wei Baqun. Some of them also left the Right River region in 1930 and a few became important generals and officials after 1949. For instance, Jiang Maosheng, a poor peasant from Lingyun, joined the peasant movement when he was a teenager. He left for Jiangxi in1930 and became a major general in 1955. More than fifty years after he parted with Wei Baqun in Hechi, Jiang could still recall vividly his last glimpse of Wei Baqun: "He (Wei Baqun) walked to the platform with vigorous strides. He first stood at attention and then saluted the flag [of the Twenty-first division]. After receiving the flag, he walked to the front of the platform, raised the flag, and then bowed to the audience. He received a long and loud round of applause."[115]

Most of those who left with the main force of the Seventh Red Army were young soldiers or low- to mid-ranking officers, and most members of the leading group that Wei Baqun had brought together remained in the Right River region. Those who stayed with Wei Baqun included Liao Yuanfang, Huang Shuxiang, Chen Hongtao, Chen Gutao, Huang Songjian, Huang Daquan, and Lu Haoren. The senior leading group of the local revolution remained virtually intact. Part of the reason was that many of these leaders were working for the local Soviet governments at that time and they were not part of Wei Baqun's third column. They were good political leaders, but not necessarily skillful military commanders. Also, the Seventh Red Army lacked enough positions of rank to offer to Wei Baqun's native leaders. Huang Fangri, who was a battalion commander in the third column, had to be reduced to a company commander after the reorganization because there were not enough battalion-level positions.[116] Among the circle of intellectual revolutionaries that Wei Baqun had created, Huang Fangri was one of the very few who left Donglan permanently with the Seventh Red Army in late 1930, and the only outside leader who stayed with Wei Baqun was Huang Hui, a native of Guilin.[117] Huang was a delegate of the CCP Southern Bureau who had arrived in the Right River region with Deng Gang in September 1930, and he left the Right River region only a few months after the departure of the main force of the Seventh Red Army.

To keep Wei Baqun and the other local leaders in the Right River region conformed to a common Communist practice at that time. Whenever the Communist main force had to retreat from an area, they would always leave some capable leaders behind to "continue the struggle," and most of the time they would leave behind some influential locals to lead the local revolution because these native leaders were familiar with local conditions, spoke the local dialects, and had local connections. The outsiders probably believed that to take only the soldiers but leave the leaders behind would bring about the least damage to the local revolution because these leaders would be able to rebuild an armed force in a very brief period.

Donglan's remoteness made it difficult for it to be impacted by outside events in a timely manner. Sometimes this worked to the favor of the revolutionaries. In 1927, the delay of the anti-Communist purge gave Wei Baqun and his comrades four extra months to strengthen their revolution. Sometimes the time lag was detrimental to the local revolution. The resolutions of the August 7, 1927 CCP Central Committee Meeting were not brought to Donglan until 1929,[118] making it difficult for Wei Baqun to understand and enforce the CCP policies of land revolution. The Lisan Line became the dominant policy of the CCP in June 1930 but was abandoned in September 1930. However, in the Right River region Deng Gang arrived in late September 1930 to enforce the Lisan Line, and when the reorganization of the Seventh Red Army took place in Hechi in October 1930 the leaders of the Seventh Red Army still knew nothing about the change of policy. Had they known that the Lisan Line was no longer the official policy they would very likely have still decided to take the main force out of the Right River region because that decision had been made before Deng Gang's arrival, but maybe they would have left more troops for Wei Baqun. They would have been less focused on expanding the main force if they had known that they did not have to attack the major cities on their way to Jiangxi.

Soon after the reorganization, Wei Baqun and his small cohort parted with the main force and began their journey home. General Zhang Yunyi, commander-in-chief of the Seventh Red Army, accompanied Wei Baqun for the first five kilometers of the journey and had a long conversation with him. While praising Wei Baqun for all his great qualities as a revolutionary leader, Zhang warned him not to rely too much on personal relations because "personal relations are not reliable."[119] Zhang Yunyi probably had the impression that Wei Baqun trusted his relatives and close friends more than he did the outside Communists. In the eyes of orthodox Communists, practices like sworn brotherhood, to which Wei Baqun was committed, were traces of the feudal past, and the most reliable relationship was that based on political comradeship. Two years before Zhang Yunyi made the comment to Wei Baqun, Zhu De had betrayed his sworn brother Fan Shisheng. Fan had offered protection and supplies to Zhu De and his troops when they were in danger, but Zhu De later repaid Fan's generosity by attacking and defeating his troops. Zhu De consoled himself by arguing that "revolution does not allow us to be swayed by personal feelings. We even have to fight against our parents if they belong to the enemy class, not to mention a sworn brother."[120]

It is not certain how Wei Baqun responded to Zhang Yunyi's warnings, but it was probably difficult for Zhang to convince Wei Baqun at that moment that the party was more reliable than his friends and relatives. It is true that the party had created a powerful army, conquered a large piece of territory, and set up a formal government in the Right River region, and had also helped train and equip peasant armies in the area, and as a result had brought about a revolutionary culmination in this frontier territory, but now the party was taking everything away! It would take away not only the revolutionaries from other regions, but also the best soldiers and weapons of the peasant army that Wei Baqun had nurtured for nearly a decade. Wei Baqun had told his friends who were to travel eastward that he would wait for their return to the Right River region in the near future, but deep in his heart he probably knew that it would take quite some time for them to come back, if they could ever return. That meant for Wei Baqun, at least for the foreseeable future, personal relations would remain more reliable than the party.

CHAPTER SEVEN

Defeat

The Ecology and Culture of the Revolution, 1930–1932

By late 1930, the leaders of the New Guangxi Clique had restored and consolidated their rule in Guangxi and were well prepared to deal with the Communist threat. The first two divisions of the Seventh Red Army had to fight fierce battles against the troops of the New Guangxi Clique as soon as they left Hechi. The top leaders of the CCP had ordered the Seventh Red Army to attack Liuzhou and Guilin, and the main force of the Seventh Red Army began to move toward Liuzhou shortly after leaving Hechi. However, they soon discovered that the New Guangxi Clique had built a strong defensive line protecting Liuzhou. The commanders then decided to temporarily abandon the plan to take Liuzhou and moved toward Guilin, with the hope that they would turn back to attack Liuzhou after taking Guilin. At that time, the leaders quarreled constantly about which of the two cities they should attack first.

To reach Guilin, the Communists had to fight two bloody battles and they failed to win either, and the new defeats forced them to move northward and enter Hunan in December 1930. Not ready to give up their dream of taking Guilin, they reentered Guangxi a few days later and seized the town of Quanzhou by surprise. It was here that the leaders of the Seventh Red Army decided to discard the plan to attack major cities, and the two strongest supporters of the plan, Deng Gang, the delegate of the CCP Central Committee, and Chen Haoren, head of the political department of the Seventh Red Army, left for Shanghai to report to the top leaders of the CCP.

At this point, General Bai Chongxi of the New Guangxi Clique came to the rescue of Quanzhou with a whole division of troops. Unwilling to fight the overwhelming enemy force, the Communists then retreated back into Hunan, but only a few days later they moved back to Guangxi and took another county. By this time, the Seventh Red Army had lost half of the more than seven thousand troops it had before its departure from Hechi in November 1930. In January 1931, the main force of the Seventh Red Army finally left Guangxi. In northern Guangdong, the Seventh Red Army fought another bloody battle against six Nationalist regiments, and Li Qian, commander of one of the two divisions of the Seventh Red Army, none other than the younger brother of Li Lisan, was killed. In a way, he was a victim of the Lisan Line, a policy created by his brother. In summer 1931, the Seventh Red Army reached the Communist base area in Jiangxi and joined the forces led by Mao Zedong and Zhu De. By then, the army had passed through four provinces and traveled 3500 kilometers and had only 1,300 troops left.[1] The dangers and losses they encountered during the journey led some Communist leaders to wonder whether or not it would have been a better strategy to keep the Seventh Red Army in the Right River region.[2]

Extermination Campaigns and the Ecology of Revolution

Although the exodus of the main force of the Seventh Red Army drew most of the attention of the New Guangxi Clique in late 1930 and early 1931, the leaders of the clique did not forget about Wei Baqun and his movement in Donglan and the Right River region. It is not certain whether or not the leaders in Nanning knew that Wei Baqun had not left with the main force, but they were obviously aware that there were still Communist forces in the Right River region and that some parts of that region remained beyond their control. By the time the main force of the Seventh Red Army left Hechi in late 1930, the Communists had lost most of the towns and counties along the Right River, and their base area now consisted only of Donglan, Fengshan, Nadi, and parts of Enlong and Baise counties. These were the areas that Wei Baqun and his Twenty-first Division would protect.[3] There were Nationalist troops stationed around this region, but they were not yet ready to launch their attack.

Wei Baqun knew well that the New Guangxi Clique would come to attack sooner or later and began to rebuild his military power as soon as he returned to Donglan from Hechi in November 1930. He had received the designation of the Twenty-first Division of the Seventh Red Army, a flag of the division, and the title of division commander from the leaders of the Seventh Red Army, which would serve as symbols of legitimacy for Wei Baqun. If his first revolt was completely spontaneous in the sense that he received neither approval nor real support from any external power, his second revolt was somewhat spontaneous at beginning but was legitimized by the United Front government after the Donglan Massacre in 1926, then the third revolt was sponsored and supported by the Communists from the beginning to the end. In other words, his third revolt was completely legitimate from the Communist perspective, but absolutely illegal in the eyes of the anti-Communists.

Although Wei Baqun possessed enough symbols of legitimacy, he did not have adequate troops to substantiate his symbolic power. He had taken back with him only about eighty soldiers of his former Third Column from Hechi and had before him the urgent task of recruiting fighters. In building up the Twenty-first Division Wei Baqun's strongest supporter was Chen Hongtao. In late 1930, Chen Hongtao was the head of the Right River Special Committee of the CCP, which was the most powerful CCP organ in the region. Additionally, Chen was also the chairman of the Right River Soviet Government and Political Commissar of the Twenty-first Division. Nominally, Chen was above Wei Baqun in the CCP power structure, but in reality Wei Baqun commanded much more popular power than Chen Hongtao, and Chen was rather obedient to Wei Baqun because the latter enjoyed more local support, was the elder, and had served as Chen Hongtao's patron before Chen became a Communist.

Huang Songjian and Huang Juping were Wei Baqun's two other strong supporters. Like Chen Hongtao, they were well-educated men who were about ten years younger than Wei Baqun, and they had all joined Wei Baqun's movement during the second revolt. Huang Songjian was the head of the Fengshan branch of the CCP and deputy commander of the Twenty-first Division, which made him the third most powerful CCP leader in the Right River region, next only to Chen Hongtao and Wei Baqun. Huang had been ordered to join the main force of the Seventh Red Army, but surprisingly failed to reach Hechi on time.[4] Huang Juping led the Donglan branch of the CCP, but did not hold any important position in the Twenty-first Division.

Wei Baqun and the other leaders decided to build the Twenty-first Division by incorporating the existing Red Guard units of Donglan, Fengshan, and other counties. By early January 1931, they had created four regiments and two independent battalions. Wei Mingzhou, a long-time ally of Wei Baqun, became the commander of one of the four regiments. Wei Baqun's two other close followers, Huang Shuxiang and Liao Yuanfang, commanded two other regiments, respectively, and the fourth regiment was under the control of Teng Guodong, a veteran peasant movement leader from Enlong County. Huang Hui, the outsider, served as chief of staff, but he would leave the Right River region shortly after the creation of the division. After his departure, his position was taken over by Huang Daquan.[5] Obviously, most leading positions were held by Wei Baqun's loyal supporters from Donglan and Fengshan.

Wei Baqun created a training program in Bansheng in the Eastern Mountains to bring up a new generation of officers. Although the outsiders had taken most of the battle-hardened veterans away, they had left behind some powerful weapons for Wei Baqun, which enabled the Twenty-first Division to create a mortar company, a heavy machine gun company, and a light machine gun company. The founding assembly of the division was held in a mountainous town of Enlong in January 1931, which was attended by more than two thousand soldiers from two of the four regiments and about five thusand villagers. In addition to the Twenty-first Division, every county had a Red Guard battalion, and every district or township had a Red Guard team.[6] During the first month after the creation of the Twenty-first Division, Wei Baqun fought several battles against his local enemies in Donglan and neighboring counties, and as usual he won easy victories over these local foes, but as the old cycle of Wei Baqun's revolutions continued to turn, he had to deal with some powerful external enemies who came to the rescue of their local protégés.

Over the next two years, the most powerful external enemy Wei Baqun and his followers had to face was General Liao Lei of the New Guangxi Clique. A native of Guangxi, Liao was a graduate of Baoding Military Academy and joined the New Guangxi Clique in 1928 after serving in the Hunan army for several years. Coincidentally, in early 1931 when he launched his first attack on Donglan, Liao was the commander of the Twenty-first Division of the Seventh Army of the New Guangxi Clique, whereas Wei Baqun was the commander of the Twenty-first Division of the Seventh Red Army.[7] The conflict between the Communists and anti-Communists in the Right River region was therefore a battle between two Twenty-first Divisions and two Seventh Armies.

The New Guangxi Clique began its first extermination campaign against Wei Baqun and his forces shortly after the Spring Festival of 1931. The attacking force came from three directions and consisted of about 10,000 troops, whereas Wei Baqun had only around 2000 soldiers under his direct command. Some of the enemy forces were regular troops and some were local militias. There were even some Guizhou Army units among them. This was the largest enemy force Wei Baqun had ever confronted in Donglan. Knowing that his newly formed division was no match for the enemy force, Wei Baqun and the other leaders decided to give up the towns and plains and to retreat to the Western, Central, and Eastern Mountains in Donglan and Fengshan as well as some other mountainous regions in the neighboring counties. Their strategy was to avoid positional battles and adopt guerrilla tactics.

Liao Lei's troops easily took the county seats of Donglan and Fengshan in late March 1931, killed some Communists and villagers, and defeated some small units of Communist troops, but they were unable to find Wei Baqun and his main force. In all, Liao Lei's soldiers killed and wounded only about one hundred Communist fighters within Donglan during the first extermination campaign. At one point, Wei Baqun was able to play the Guangxi Army against the Guizhou Army, resulting in the death of many enemy troops.[8] In May 1931, Liao Lei had to take his troops out of the Right River region because the New Guangxi Clique had planned another anti-Chiang Kai-shek campaign.

The first extermination campaign thus failed to cause substantial damage to Wei Baqun's movement. To keep pressure on Wei Baqun and his followers, the New Guangxi Clique soon deployed another division into Donglan and the neighboring counties to keep searching for and attacking Wei Baqun's forces. In June 1931, a clash occurred in northern Donglan, and Wei Baqun's sworn brother and long-time supporter Liao Yuanfang was killed. On the western front, Wei Baqun's forces under the command of Huang Shuxiang were able to go on the offensive and seize a county seat.

During the first extermination campaign there was no contact between Wei Baqun and the top leaders of the CCP. Wei Baqun's chief of staff Huang Hui left the Right River region in January 1931 to report to the CCP leaders, but did not send back any message. Wei Baqun made no further effort at reestablishing contact with the outsiders. The Guangdong Provincial Committee of the CCP dispatched a cadre named Chen Fu to serve as the head of the Right River Special Committee of the CCP, but Chen failed to reach Donglan. In May 1931, six months after leaving Hechi with the main force of the Seventh Red Army, Deng Gang returned to the Right River region as the delegate of the newly created Guangdong and Guangxi Provincial Committee of the CCP, which was based in Hong Kong. However, he was not able to find any former contacts or reach Donglan because of the ongoing fighting.[9] In mid-June 1931 he wrote a letter to the leaders of the Twenty-first Division in which he frankly admitted that the Lisan Line, which he had personally brought to the Right River region in September 1930, was a very destructive approach and had caused damage for Communist movements in various areas, including the Right River region. He also informed Wei Baqun and the other local leaders that the CCP Central Committee had decided to change the designation of their armed force from the Twenty-first Division of the Seventh Red Army to the Right River Independent Division of the Chinese Workers' and Peasants' Red Army. Deng urged Wei Baqun to abandon the strategy of passive defense and adopt a more aggressive military tactic. It is interesting to note that although admitting that he knew very little about recent developments in the Right River region, Deng was not hesitant at all about giving very specific orders to the local leaders.[10] The top CCP leaders in Shanghai had done something similar to Mao Zedong, Zhu De, and many other local leaders.

Deng Gang's letter failed to reach Wei Baqun on time. In his report to the CCP Central Committee submitted shortly after the trip, Deng suggested that the Central Committee send a strong political leader and an experienced military commander to the Right River region to serve as Wei Baqun's political commissar and chief of staff. The Central Committee simply ignored Deng's proposal. In late July 1931, shortly after the end of the first extermination campaign, Chen Daosheng, the second delegate of the Guangdong and Guangxi Provincial Committee of the CCP, arrived in the Western Mountains of Donglan. He came all the way from Hong Kong and had to disguise himself as a wandering barber after entering Guangxi.[11] It was from him that Wei Baqun and the other local leaders learned that the Lisan Line had been abandoned as early as September 1930, and that their armed force had been granted the new designation of the Right River Independent Division or the Third Independent Division.

The decision to change the designation was apparently based on the consideration that the long distance between the Right River region and Jiangxi made it difficult for the Twenty-first Division to remain an integral part of the Seventh Red Army, and that the CCP leaders planned to keep the Twenty-first Division in the Right River region rather than moving it to Jiangxi. Besides, a new Twenty-first Division had been created in Jiangxi shortly after the Seventh Red Army arrived there, and in September 1931, the Seventh Red Army was to be reorganized as the Fifth Division of the Third Corps of the Red Army.[12] The change of designation caused no alteration in the commanding system or the structure of the division. The various levels of the local Communist government also went through a name change. "Soviet governments" were replaced by "Revolutionary Committees," and Chen Hongtao was replaced by Huang Juping as the head of the Right River Revolutionary Committee. Chen remained the leader of the Right River Special Committee of the CCP and political commissar of the Right River Independent Division.

In November 1931, Liao Lei's troops returned to the Right River region to launch the second extermination campaign against Wei Baqun, although Liao Lei himself did not accompany his troops. This time the attacking force consisted of four regiments of regulars plus some local militias, totaling more than seven thousand soldiers. By this time, Wei Baqun had only about one thousand soldiers under his immediate command and his base area included the Western, Central, and Eastern Mountains of Donglan and a few spots in eastern Donglan and Fengshan. The mountains in Donglan and Fengshan, particularly the Western Mountains, became the focus of enemy attack. The Nationalist forces easily took the Western Mountains, but they were not able to find Wei Baqun and his troops. Fearing guerrilla attacks, the enemy force soon moved out of the mountains. In eastern Donglan, the attacking troops were able to eliminate some important fortresses held by Communist troops and establish effective control over the region. They also wiped out the Communist forces in Fengshan, leaving the Western, Central, and Eastern Mountains the only remaining Communist strongholds. In late December 1931, some of the attacking forces had to be moved to northern China to fight the invading Japanese troops, and partly because of that the second extermination campaign came to an end. Like the first extermination campaign, the second caused some military defeats and grave economic difficulties for Wei Baqun's forces, but failed to exert fatal damage to the leading group and the main force of the revolution.

However, regular enemy troops and militia forces continued to besiege the Communist base area after the end of the second extermination campaign, making it very difficult for the Communists to acquire grain and other supplies. To alleviate the problem of the shortage of supplies and to lessen the risk for a complete wipe out, Wei Baqun and the other leaders then split the division into ten teams. Each team consisted of three bands, and each band had ten to twelve fighters. In addition to the ten teams, Wei Baqun maintained four independent battalions. The ten teams would operate in the plains and other areas controlled by the enemies, whereas the four battalions would stay in the mountains to protect the base areas. The soldiers who were not in any of the teams or battalions could return home or hide in other places. They were encouraged to join local Red Guard units and to collect intelligence for the leaders. At the same time they were warned not to reveal any information about the reorganization of the Twenty-first Division and not to harm the people. Those living in the mountains were allowed to carry their weapons with them, but those who lived in the plains had to turn in their weapons before leaving. Surplus weapons were hidden in various caches that only Wei Baqun, Chen Hongtao, and Huang Songjian could locate. Some Nationalists held that Wei Baqun even ordered the execution of the soldiers involved in burying the weapons to prevent them from revealing the secret.[13]

By this time, Wei Baqun had begun to rely more and more on the Yao people, who formed the majority of the population in the mountainous areas. Among the four battalions under his command, three were manned primarily by Yao soldiers, and they were based in the Western Mountains, Eastern Mountains, and Duyi on the eastern bank of the Red Water River, respectively. Yao followers also served as Wei Baqun's bodyguards and guides. The encirclement and searches enforced by the enemy had forced Wei Baqun to adopt a nocturnal lifestyle, which made local guides essential for his movements. Wei Baqun's enemies claimed that he was very skillful in exploiting the ethnic conflicts. They argued that Wei Baqun began his movement by mobilizing the Han to kill the Zhuang, he then turned the Zhuang against the Han, and finally he played the Yao against the Zhuang and Han. They believed that Wei Baqun had used slogans like "Keep the Yao and Kill the Zhuang" during the last stage of his revolution. Diana Lary also emphasizes the role of ethnic conflict in the Donglan peasant revolution by arguing that Wei Baqun's movement was motivated more by anti-Han feelings than by a desire for social revolution, and she describes Wei Baqun's peasant movement as an ethnic revolt.[14]

There is no substantial evidence to support such arguments. Wei Baqun had no deep hatred toward all the Han or Zhuang in Donglan. There were Han and Zhuang among both Wei Baqun's followers and enemies throughout the three revolts. The Han community in Donglan was simply not large, wealthy, or powerful enough to warrant an anti-Han revolt. The confrontations in Donglan were primarily political and social in nature. It is true that the Yao people were particularly enthusiastic about the movement and that among Wei Baqun's enemies there were very few Yao. This is mainly because most Yao were at the bottom of the social stratum. Wei Baqun's promotion of Yao rights was consistent throughout all three phases of the movement, and the Yao residents in the mountains remained his strong supporters till the last moment. In early 1930, Wei Baqun's delegates Wei Jing (the elder) and Chen Qing'e reported to the Guangdong Provincial Committee of the CCP that the Miao and Yao were the most loyal supporters of the Soviet and the Red Army.[15] According to one of the folk stories, an old Yao woman brought food to Wei Baqun's cave every day during the last extermination campaign. One day she was captured by the enemy troops, who forced her to guide them to Wei Baqun's hiding place. She agreed and led her captors toward a cliff. She then jumped off the cliff to protect Wei Baqun.

In early 1932, as the situation continued to deteriorate, Wei Baqun and the other leaders held a few meetings and made some important decisions, one of which was to send some of the leaders to other places to build new base areas. In April 1932, a group of about twenty leaders headed by Huang Songjian and Huang Daquan traveled southward to the lower reaches of the Right River to create party, military, and mass organizations there. Shortly after that, Huang Juping took a second group of about fifteen leaders to the border between Guangxi and Guizhou. Their plan was for these two groups to launch or revive the revolution in those two areas in order to divert the attention of the anti-Communist forces. It was agreed that once either of these two new base areas became stable, Wei Baqun and Chen Hongtao would move there. Huang Songjian recalled that before leaving the Western Mountains, he had a brief meeting with Wei Baqun and Chen Hongtao, and at the meeting the three agreed that if any of them were killed, the survivors would automatically take over the leadership.[16]

Another decision made at the meetings was to send delegates to report to the CCP higher authorities in Hong Kong and try to appeal for help. The leaders picked two delegates, and one of them was Wei Baqun's younger brother, Wei Jing, who had served as the party secretary of Fengshan and the commander of one of the four regiments of the Right River Independent Division. The other delegate, Chen Qing'e, was the younger brother of Wei Baqun's wife, Chen Lanfen. He was a staff officer of the Right River Independent Division at that time. The two left the Western Mountains in early 1932 with Chen Daosheng, the delegate of the Guangdong and Guangxi Provincial Committee. The three walked eastward toward the Red Water River and then hid in a cave by the river for two days. On the morning of the third day they took a boat bound for Nanning, and from there they boarded another boat that took them to Hong Kong. They made a report to the Communist leaders there. On their way back to Guangxi, Wei Jing and Chen Qing'e were both captured by the anti-Communist forces and executed. It is not clear if they carried with them any important instructions or promises from Hong Kong.[17]

In June 1932, not knowing that both his brother and brother-in-law had been killed, Wei Baqun sent out another team to report to the CCP leaders in Hong Kong and to find out what had happened to Wei Jing and Chen Qing'e. The team consisted of three members: Wei Baqun's second son, Wei Shuzong, who was only sixteen years old at that time and had just joined the CCP; Bai Hanyun, a long-time follower of Wei Baqun and a member of the CCP Committee of the Right River Independent Division; and Huang Jinyou, commander of the special assignment company. Huang was to serve as the bodyguard for the other two. It is obvious that Wei Baqun only chose his most trusted followers as his delegates to the CCP higher authorities, and the composition of the delegation further indicates that Wei Baqun, rather than Chen Hongtao, was the true leader of the CCP movement in the Right River region.

The second team arrived in Hong Kong, made a report to the CCP leaders there and then returned. It was already October 1932 when they got back to the Right River region, and the anti-Communist forces had launched their third extermination campaign against Wei Baqun. Liao Lei was back in Donglan to direct the third extermination campaign. He toured Wuzhuan and the Western Mountains at the beginning of the campaign, and even Bai Chongxi made a brief visit to Donglan in mid-October 1932.[18] The large number of enemy troops stationed around the Western Mountains made it difficult for the three delegates to return to the base area. Bai Hanyun then decided that he and Wei Shuzong would stay in Bai's ancestral village in Binyang County near Nanning, and Huang Jinyou, the bodyguard, would travel back to Donglan to report to Wei Baqun. By the time Huang reached Donglan, Wei Baqun had already been killed by Wei Ang, and Huang immediately surrendered to the Nationalists. He then led the enemy troops to the hiding place of Bai Hanyun and Wei Shuzong. The two were arrested and taken to Liuzhou, where they were executed. One Nationalist source held that the three never made it to Hong Kong and they moved to Binyang as early as July 1932.[19] They were reluctant to return to Donglan possibly because they had failed to fulfill their mission. Wei Shuzong was Wei Baqun's last surviving son and his death meant the end of Wei Baqun's lineage.

It is hard to determine what kind of support Wei Baqun was expecting from the CCP leaders. Wei Jing and Chen Qing'e reported to the Guangdong Provincial Committee of the CCP that there were many complaints against Chen Hongtao, which probably implies that Wei Baqun was not fully satisfied with Chen Hongtao's performance and that the two perhaps did not get along very well.[20] In the Communist system this report was filed in a very inappropriate way. Since nominally Chen Hongtao was the number one leader of the

Right River branch of the CCP, any report to the higher authorities should be submitted by or through him. For a military commander to file a complaint against his political commissar without the latter's awareness breached a rule. To file a complaint against Chen Hongtao was probably one of the reasons why Wei Baqun had to send his brother, brother-in-law, and son as delegates. That the higher authorities did not consider the complaint an improper act indicates that they recognized Wei Baqun as the actual number one leader of the Communist movement in the Right River region.

Wei Jing and Chen Qing'e also reported that the peasant soldiers were ill-trained and therefore their combat effectiveness was rather low, and that there were not enough weapons and ammunition, partly because there were no skilled workers in the arsenal. They suggested that the provincial and central committees send one or two political-military leaders to help Wei Baqun.[21] Deng Gang had made a similar suggestion in late 1930, but received no response from the top leaders. It is not certain whether or not Wei Jing and Chen Qing'e also asked for money. In fact, according to Wei Baqun's secretary, Wei Jing, and Chen Qing'e hid some gold in their shoes and planned to submit part of the gold to the higher authorities as party membership dues. Bai Hanyun and Wei Shuzong also carried some party membership dues with them,[22] which indicates that they were probably not in desperate need of money.

It was impossible for the CCP leaders to offer substantial assistance to Wei Baqun, because they were too far away from Donglan and they were too busy fighting for their own survival. The CCP leaders in Hong Kong would not have been reluctant to provide instructions, which can be taken as a form of assistance. However, many of their instructions may not have been enforceable. The top leaders would also have been willing to offer political and moral support. A mentioned earlier, in early November 1931, just as Liao Lei was initiating his second extermination campaign, Wei Baqun was elected a member of the central executive committee of the provisional government of the Chinese Soviet Republic, which was headed by Mao Zedong. Due to the collapse of communications between Donglan and the CCP Central Committee, it is very likely Wei Baqun never received any information about the founding of the Chinese Soviet Republic and his prominent role in it. Even if he had received the news, although it would have been meaningful, it would not have helped him much.

For Wei Baqun and his followers, the most urgent issue at that time was survival. The CCP leaders could have offered Wei Baqun some money and weapons, but it would have been impossible to transport these to the mountains in Donglan. The best form of support for Wei Baqun at that time would have been for the CCP leaders to send troops to the Right River region, but that was also an impossible task for them to perform. In 1926, the leftists in Nanning and Guangzhou helped Wei Baqun defeat his local enemies, and in 1929, the

Communists from Nanning helped integrate his movement into a much more powerful revolutionary base area. But in 1931 and 1932, Wei Baqun's outside supporters were unable to offer him any concrete aid.

By early 1932, Wei Baqun and his followers had come to realize that without external support they would not be able to break the encirclement around the base area, and their movement was doomed. The Western, Central, and Eastern Mountains in Donglan offered convenient hiding places, but they could not provide subsistence for a large number of people for long. The encirclement enforced by the enemies made it extremely hazardous for Wei Baqun and his supporters to get supplies from the towns and villages on the plains below the mountains.

Even if they could have ventured out to the plains, they probably would not have found enough grain and other materials. In the early years of the revolution, the revolutionaries could rely on confiscating the property of wealthy families as an important source of supplies, but by 1931 and 1932, the revolution had been going on for a decade and there were not many wealthy families left in the region. The revolution had helped equalize wealth, but had not contributed to its growth. In fact, the constant fighting had caused a lot of destruction in both human lives and property and had made it very difficult for the villagers to engage in normal farming. Survival alone was difficult, not to mention prosperity. Another important source of revenue for the revolutionaries was the taxes they collected from the areas under their control, but the encirclement and extermination campaigns made it impossible for them to collect taxes from the most prosperous areas. Ecologically and economically, the revolution was not sustainable.

The Nationalists were aware of the economic and ecological constraints that the revolutionaries had to deal with and they knew that if they besieged the mountains, the revolutionaries would have only two choices: they would have to either move out of the mountains or die of starvation. The Nationalist strategy adopted in early 1932 called for strengthening the siege of the Western Mountains, cutting off the food supply and water source of the Communists, winning over the Yao people, and forcing the villagers to return the land they had received from the Communists.[23] During their third extermination campaign, which commenced in August 1932, the anti-Communist forces incorporated these measures into a comprehensive approach that combined military, political, and economic measures.

The approach was designed by Bai Chongxi and enforced by Liao Lei, who had about ten thousand troops under his command this time. Militarily, they strengthened the encirclement around the mountains, and then sent many mobile units to "comb" the mountains, hunting for the revolutionaries. Politically, they sent out propagandists to work on winning popular support. Economically, they forced the villagers to move out of the mountains so that they would no longer be able to provide anything for the revolutionaries. The Nationalists even planned to relocate some of the Yao people to the Liuzhou area, and their troops would destroy the property and crops wherever they went and poison the water sources. The Nationalists described their strategy as "pulling the net to catch the fish" or "striping the bamboo shoot." Bai Chongxi confidently predicted in mid-October 1932 when he was in Donglan that "Even if we cannot capture Wei Baqun this time, we will be able to starve him to death."[24] The approach was rather efficient. A number of revolutionaries attempted to leave the mountains. Some succeeded, but others were caught. Many of those who chose to stay in the mountains eventually died of hunger, and these included Wei Baqun's mother, two youngest sons, and his only daughter, as well as two other wives of his father. They were all starved to death in the Western Mountains in 1932.

If Wei Baqun had moved his troops out of the mountains when the Twenty-first Division was still in good shape then he and his followers would probably have had a better chance to survive. In late 1931, Wei Baqun took his troops to eastern Donglan to escape from their pursuers and to acquire supplies. His enemies were quickly able to surround his army on the eastern bank of the Red Water River, and Wei Baqun and his troops were put in a very precarious situation. Although they eventually returned to the mountains safely, the leaders agreed that it was too risky to move troops out of the mountain base, and Wei Baqun would never try to take the entire division out of the mountains again. Although there were enemy troops stationed on every side of their base area, it might just have been possible for the Communists to slip through the Nationalist lines and escape to Guizhou, Yunnan, or Hunan to build a new base area or to join the Communists in other provinces. The Red Water River and the Right River were more formidable barriers than the mountains to the movement of Wei Baqun's troops, and the existence of the two rivers was one of the reasons why the leaders of the Seventh Red Army had not believed that the Right River region was an ideal site for building a revolutionary base area,[25] but there were no major rivers to the north and west of Donglan. Moving northward, they may have had a chance to reach the border between Guangxi and Guizhou, and moving southward would take them to the border between Guangxi and Yunnan.

In the early 1930s, the successful Communist base areas in China such as the Central, the Fujian-Zhejiang-Jiangxi, the Hubei-Henan-Anhui, the Western Hunan and Hubei, and the Shaan-Gan-Ning were all located along borders between provinces, and the Red Army units in these areas all adopted a mobile way of life and warfare in order to take advantage of the conflicts between Chiang Kai-shek and some of the local generals and between military leaders of different provinces as well as the enemies' difficulties in coordinating troops from different provinces. Although Donglan was close to the borders between several provinces, Wei Baqun never tried to move his troops to neighboring provinces to take advantages of Donglan's propitious location. He did send some of his followers to the border between Guizhou and Guangxi in early 1932, but by that stage the group was too small to exert an immediate effect. Before leaving the Right River region in late 1930, the outsiders had instructed Wei Baqun to maintain Donglan and Fengshan as his base area and then try to expand toward Nanning in the southeast to get close to the Communists in southern Guangxi and toward Liuzhou in the east to establish connections with the Central Revolutionary Base Area in Jiangxi.[26] In 1931, an expansion to the east or southeast would be perilous or even suicidal, but a move toward the Guizhou-Guangxi border area in the north was still possible. If the revolutionaries had been mobile and venturous and taken the entire border area rather than just Donglan and Fengshan as a base of operation, they could have acquired more supplies. The top leaders of the CCP had instructed in early 1930 that attack and outward expansion were efficient means of self-preservation and that confining the Communist force to one area would make it vulnerable to the encirclement and pursuit enforced by the enemy.[27] Wei Baqun and his comrades first lost the momentum, and then even the capacity for aggressive mobile warfare. In 1934, the Central Base Area in Jiangxi was to face a military and economic crisis very similar to the one Wei Baqun had to deal with in 1931 and 1932, and the CCP forces in Jiangxi were able to survive only by making the Long March.

In most other revolutionary base areas, the Communists had to fight both local troops and Chiang Kai-shek's Central Army, but in Donglan and the Right River region most of the time Wei Baqun and his followers were fighting against the armies of the New Guangxi Clique (although they sometimes had to deal with troops from Guizhou, Yunnan, and Guangdong). However, this does not mean that Wei Baqun's enemies were easier to subdue than those of the other revolutionary base areas.

The troops of the New Guangxi Clique were among China's most efficient fighters, and the leaders of the New Guangxi Clique were among China's best military commanders at that time. The Guangxi government under the New Guangxi Clique was a military regime that relied on not just its well-equipped and well-trained formal armies, but also a very efficient militia system, which was integrated with the local political and educational systems. At the village level, the same person held the positions of village head, militia chief, and school principal.[28] The leaders of the New Guangxi Clique were very interested in militarizing the entire society. Bai Chongxi created the slogan of "militarizing Guangxi," and for that purpose he even resorted to promoting the lion dance and martial arts.[29] From 1925 to 1927, the New Guangxi Clique was unable to completely suppress the peasant movements in Donglan and the Right River region because at that time it was part of the United Front government that had pledged its support for the peasant movement. From 1927 to 1931, the New Guangxi Clique could not concentrate on cracking down on the Communist movements because it was too busy expanding its power and influence in other provinces, which caused several armed conflicts with Chiang Kai-shek and other local military groups. By 1931, the clique had again decided to cooperate with Chiang Kai-shek and to focus on preserving and developing their base in Guangxi. They wanted to first exterminate their enemies within Guangxi and then transform the province with a reconstruction project. The Baise and Longzhou Uprisings had helped intensify the New Guangxi Clique's fear of Communism and its leaders became more determined than ever before to exterminate the Communist movement in Donglan and the Right River region. The elimination of Communism became an important part of the New Guangxi Clique's grand plan of turning Guangxi into a model province of China. It is interesting to note that while the leaders of the New Guangxi Clique were strong-willed regionalists who used every means at their disposal to maintain their independence from the Nanjing government, they also made every effort to quell any kind of regionalist or subregionalist movement within their domain.

The difficulties that Wei Baqun and his movement encountered in 1931 and 1932 had a devastating effect on the spirit of his followers. To boost morale, Wei Baqun kept reminding his followers that the CCP Central Committee would send instructions soon and that the main force of the Seventh Red Army would eventually return to the Right River region.[30] He stayed in the mountains with his followers and made frequent visits to the various bases to talk with his subordinates. He also resorted to his artistic skills and composed some new folk songs for his followers, one of which goes as follows:

> Folks, we poor people are making a revolution,
> We should reaffirm our determination.
> We are facing difficulties, but we should believe
> That sunlight will arrive to disperse the cloud.
> Thinking of our bright future, we are rejuvenated,
> Even wild grasses taste so delicious.
> Folks, we poor people are making a revolution,
> We should reaffirm our determination.
> When the local tyrants are exterminated,
> We will eat our fill and put on new clothes.
> We are facing difficulties, but we should believe
> That sunlight will arrive to disperse the cloud.[31]

As the poem hinted, food shortage was a serious problem confronting the revolutionaries. Survivors of the revolution later recalled that Wei Baqun and his followers had to collect and eat more than 120 different species of wild grass during that period.[32] Such a claim is contradictory to the Nationalist report that after Liao Lei's troops took the Nongjing area in the Western Mountains in September 1932 they discovered more than 150,000 kilograms of corn.[33] Nongjing was Wei Baqun's headquarters in 1931 and 1932. One of Wei Baqun's followers told that as late as fall 1932 Wei Baqun's family still kept more than one hundred chickens in their temporary home in the Western Mountains,[34] indicating that at least the Wei family still had enough grain. It is possible that the presence of enemy troops made it difficult for the Communists to transport and distribute the grain, and therefore some officers and soldiers did suffer from food shortage, but it is also likely that Wei Baqun and the other leaders wanted to keep reserves for the worst days that they believed had not yet come, and therefore did not allocate enough grain to their followers. The Nationalists also had a motivation to exaggerate the amount of grain they confiscated for propaganda purposes. Some Nationalists held that in order to survive, some Communists even kidnapped village girls for sale and that such activities caused serious frictions between them and some of their Yao supporters.[35]

Wei Baqun became so worried about the erosion of support that he even resorted to killing his wives in order to maintain morale. According to a record left by one of Wei Baqun's local enemies, in September 1931 Wei Baqun received a confidential letter from his brother Wei Jing, who reported that some officers and soldiers feared that the Communist movement was collapsing after learning about an abortion that Wei Baqun's second wife Chen Lanfen had just endured. Lanfen was six months pregnant when Wei Baqun ordered her to abort the pregnancy. Some followers believed that Wei Baqun had given that order because he was pessimistic about the future of his movement. He thought that having a new baby would make it difficult for them to move around and he definitely did not want his wife to be captured again. In order to maintain morale, Wei Baqun had asked Lanfen to keep the abortion a secret, but somehow his followers learned about it. Wei Jing warned that a serious crisis was about to occur if they failed to stop the rumors immediately. Wei Baqun gathered the leaders for a meeting and they decided that the only way to stop the rumors was to have Lanfen executed. Wei Baqun then called Lanfen to his hiding place. The evening after Lanfen arrived he took her out for a walk after dinner. When they reached a creek, Wei Baqun took out his handgun and fired two shots at Lanfen's back, killing her instantly. Wei Baqun then told his followers that he had killed Lanfen because she had aborted the pregnancy without consulting him, which showed her disloyalty to her husband. He therefore had to kill her to prevent further betrayal.[36]

Shortly after he killed Lanfen, Wei Baqun discovered that it was his third wife, Wang Juqiu, who had revealed the secret. Moreover, Wang Juqiu's younger brother had surrendered to the New Guangxi Clique and was actively participating in the second extermination campaign against the revolutionaries.

Wei Baqun therefore became suspicious of Juqiu's loyalty and "in order to prevent Juqiu from betraying him," he ordered her execution in late 1931.[37] The killing of his two wives shows that the tremendous pressure had pushed Wei Baqun to the brink of a mental collapse by that moment. Today, the PRC government recognizes Chen Lanfen as one of the seventeen members of Wei Baqun's family who died for the revolution, but does not grant Wang Juqiu the same honor. Shortly after the brutal death of his two wives, Wei Baqun married a young woman named Huang Xiumei. Xiumei was supposedly the little girl bullied by Du Ba in one of the folk stories about Wei Baqun. Huang Xiumei's two elder brothers were both Wei Baqun's followers, and she joined the revolution when she was only sixteen years old. In 1930, she became a CCP member and the head of the women's association of the Wuzhuan District.[38]

Culture and Revolution

Wei Baqun's revolution in Donglan facilitated the partial amalgamation of two distinct cultures: the imported revolutionary culture and the indigenous culture of the rebels and bandits. One was the higher culture of that time, and the other was the lower culture of ancient origins. What Wei Baqun and his followers tried to do, consciously or unconsciously, was to impose the revolutionary culture onto the native tradition of rebels and bandits, with the ultimate purpose of assimilating the latter into the former. The two cultures have some common traits: one of them was a penchant for violence, and the other was the resentment toward the wealthy and the powerful. The revolutionaries were determined to direct their violence and resentment toward an entire social class, whereas the bandits and rebels often set selected individuals as their targets. These common traits made the revolutionary messages appealing to the local people and these traits were reinforced when the two cultures were brought together.

In Donglan, violent conflicts formed a vicious cycle, and once the cycle was activated, both the Communists and anti-Communists perpetrated excessive and brutal killings. In his study of the tradition of violence in Macheng County of Hubei, William Rowe sees clear links between the violence of the revolutionary era and that of the premodern period in Macheng. He argues that Macheng's violent tradition can be attributed to its strategic location, a strong sense of local pride, class differences, intra-elite feuding, as well as conflicts between city and countryside and between the plains and mountains. Elizabeth Perry emphasizes strategic location and ecological fragility as important factors in the making of a similar violent tradition in Huaibei.[39] Like Macheng and Huaibei, Donglan is also a county with a long violent history, and several factors contributed to the making of that violent tradition, including ethnic conflicts, clashes between natives and new immigrants, and the long period of feudal rule characterized by violent clashes between feudal lords and the central government, between feudal lords and their serfs, among feudal families, and sometimes within a single powerful family. Ecological constraints and class differences were also important factors because they combined to impoverish the peasants, making them prone to rebellious instigations. Finally, the remote location of Donglan and the loose leash of the central government nurtured a localist mentality, which often prompted local strongmen to take matters into their own hands and to use force to achieve their goals.

The Donglan Massacre was not the only mass killing conducted by Wei Baqun's enemies. During the first extermination campaign, Nationalist troops burned down all the houses in Dongli and killed more than three hundred people in Wuzhuan in one day.[40] At about the same time, a Guizhou Army unit entered Lingyun to attack the Red Army there. Unable to find any Red Army soldiers, they rounded up and killed all 380 residents of Haiting village. In all, the Guizhou Army soldiers killed more than two thousand villagers in the area around Haiting. Twenty families were completely wiped out, twenty-four had to move away, and more than forty people were taken to other places for sale. After the massacre, people in that area stopped farming for seven years. In another district of Lingyun, more than two thousand villagers hid in a cave and were protected by a platoon of Red Army soldiers. The Guizhou Army troops were not able to take the cave, but succeeded in besieging it and cutting off its water source. As a result, at least five hundred people died of dehydration.[41] In Fengshan, a group of villagers and Red Army soldiers went to hide in the Hengli Cave near the county seat in early 1931, and immediately some Nationalist troops and militias encircled them. In the next eight months, the Nationalists launched more than one hunderd attacks on the cave, but failed to take it. When the cave fell to the Nationalists eleven months later, all those inside the cave, including small children and a pregnant woman, were killed. After 1949, surviving local people found the remains of 374 people in the cave.[42] In late 1931, after taking a Communist village in southeastern Donglan, Liao Lei's troops found 290 villagers, including women, old people, and children. The regiment commander ordered that all villagers be killed; only four men from the village survived the massacre because they happened to be away from home on that day.[43] During the three extermination campaigns in 1931 and 1932, Huang Daquan's village near Wuzhuan was burned down seven times and forty-six unarmed villagers were killed.[44] Liao Lei's Seventh Army reported that it sentenced about five hundred captured Communists to death by court martial in 1931. In the Western Mountains, the Nationalists killed almost all the Yao people who could read and write and as a result Yao parents no longer dared to send their children to school. It is estimated that during the extermination campaigns in 1931 and 1932, Liao Lei's troops and local militias burned down in excess of ten thousand houses and killed between twenty- and thirty thousand people in Donglan and Fengshan. Another source holds that more than seventy percent of the village houses in Donglan were destroyed during the three extermination campaigns.[45]

When revolutionaries could not be found, the Nationalist soldiers and militias would release their frustration by punishing the relatives of the revolutionaries. Most of Wei Baqun's relatives, including all of his children, were starved to death, killed, or sold by the Nationalists during the third revolt. Chen Bomin's father was killed in 1928.[46] Chen Hongtao's family suffered similar losses. During the third revolt, his mother hid on a mountain that was completely sealed by Nationalist troops. Her enemies tried to persuade her to come out, but she refused and was starved to death. Chen Hongtao's wife, Pan Xiaomei, and their infant son were captured during the third extermination campaign. When Pan refused to reveal Chen Hongtao's hideout, her captors killed their son in front of her immediately. One of Chen Hongtao's sisters jumped into a river and drowned herself when she was about to be captured by a group of pursuers. After Wei Baqun was killed, Chen Hongtao and his father hid somewhere in the Western Mountains. In order to help his son escape, the father drew all enemy attention to himself. He was captured and executed. Shortly after Chen Hongtao's execution in December 1932, his wife Pan Xiaomei also died, and the only survivor of the Chen family was one of Chen Hongtao's younger sisters.[47] Huang Songjian was the only survivor of his family, as his enemies killed all of his relatives.[48] Liang Qinglan, a female Communist from the Western Mountains, served as the head of a district-level women's association during the third revolt. In one of those extermination campaigns, enemy troops rounded up her eight relatives and executed all of them.[49] Wei Hanchao was a follower of Wei Baqun from southeastern Donglan. During the confrontation between Wei Baqun's peasant army and the Nationalists in late 1927, he lost his mother, wife, and all younger siblings. In neighboring Lingyun, the leading Communist Huang Boyao's mother, wife, and daughter were kidnapped and killed by the Nationalists in 1932.[50] In September 1932, Luo Huo, a regiment commander in Liao Lei's army who was also Liao's nephew, surrounded about eighty Communist soldiers led by the famous Communist Lan Zhiren in northern Donglan. Unable to overwhelm the Communists, Luo ordered his soldiers to bring about sixty relatives of the Communists to the battlefront, threatening that if the Communists did not surrender, he would kill their relatives. The Communists refused to yield and Luo ordered the execution of all the relatives of the revolutionaries on the spot. At about the same time, another group of Nationalist troops rounded up more than forty Yao villagers from the Eastern Mountains and forced them to help capture the famous Yao Communist Lan Maocai. The villagers refused to cooperate and were all killed.[51]

The red terror was initially a response to the white terror, but once it was set in motion, it proved no less bloody and violent than the white one. During the first revolt Wei Baqun and his followers attacked the county seat as well as some powerful families, but did not kill many people. It would have been easy for them to capture and kill Du Ba, but they did not. They captured Wei Longfu's son during their fourth attack on the county seat in 1923. Although they saw Wei Longfu as an archenemy, they did not kill his son. In the early phase of the second revolt, they continued to exercise restraint. They had a plan to kill Long Xianyun, but Long was able to escape. Even after Magistrate Huang Shouxian destroyed the peasant movement institute and the houses of several peasant movement leaders, Wei Baqun and his comrades still decided to release Huang Shouxian's brother, Huang Zhiyuan, who was the police chief of the county and had participated in the campaign against the peasant movement. It was during the Donglan Massacre that Wei Baqun and his followers began to assassinate their enemies and the scale of killings escalated gradually as the conflict became more and more intense. In responding to real and imagined atrocities committed by their enemies and possibly also encouraged by radical revolutionaries in other parts of China, Wei Baqun and his followers came to believe that peasant associations had the right to arrest, torture, and kill "local tyrants." At mass meetings, if one person proposed that a certain local tyrant should be killed and others supported the proposal, the local tyrant would meet his death, and often his or her relatives would also be punished. At a CCP training program held in Wuzhuan in early 1930, one student asked about how the Communists should deal with the parents and children of the local tyrants. Should they be killed or spared? And if they were spared, should they be given some land? The answer was that the most thorough method was to kill them all and that those who were spared should be provided for by the Soviet government, but not given any land. One of the slogans issued by the Donglan Soviet in August 1930 called for the execution of all local tyrants and landlords. In late 1930, the anti-rich peasant policy advocated by the CCP Central Committee gave some Communists justification to kill all the rich peasants.[52]

In the name of revolution the revolutionaries brought death to many people. Wei Baqun's murder of his two wives was extremely cruel. Nationalist sources claimed that he also killed his last wife as well as two of his father's wives.[53] In early 1927, a group of Wei Baqun's followers led by Huang Songjian killed thirteen "local tyrants" in Fengshan and confiscated their properties. The victims included the head of the educational bureau of Fengshan and his two sons. In at least one case the attackers cut off the heads of the victims for public display.[54] At about the same time, some of Wei Baqun's other followers attacked a Sun family in Dongyuan and a Wei family in Simeng in western Donglan. The attackers killed all eleven members of the Sun family and all six members of the

Wei family. Wei Baqun's local enemies reported to the provincial government in June 1927 that such killings had caused much anxiety among the people of Donglan and Fengshan. In August 1929, the provincial government claimed that in the past few years Wei Baqun and his supporters in Donglan had burned down more than one thousand homes, killed several hundred people, taken several thousand horses and buffaloes from people, and seized a large amount of grain and other properties.[55] In late 1929, Huang Daquan and others led peasant soldiers to attack some anti-Communist villages in Fengshan. In one district they killed more than five hundred people and burned down at least three hundred homes, and in another they killed more than two hundred and burned down more than three hundred houses.[56] CCP leaders repeatedly warned their comrades in the Right River region not to continue with arbitrary and excessive killings and burnings,[57] but these warnings were not taken seriously. In 1931, before retreating from the county seat and Wuzhuan, Wei Baqun executed the 220 criminals who had been held by the revolutionaries in the county prison and Wuzhaun.[58] Liao Lei reported that the Right River Soviet Government had announced that from May 1931 to February 1932 the Communists killed 15,987 people in the Right River region. Liao commented that Wei Baqun was more prone to killing and burning than the Communists in Hunan and Hubei and more brutal than Li Zicheng, the well-known rebel of the Ming Dynasty. Bai Chongxi estimated that the Communists killed 17,000 people in Donglan in 1930 and 1931.[59]

Kidnapping for ransom was another staple of the bandits that was embraced by both Nationalists and Communists. In a sense, Wei Baqun's second imprisonment was a kidnapping. It was not unusual for the power holders to arrest someone for a trumped-up charge and then release the suspect after taking a ransom. A one-time victim of kidnapping, Wei Baqun would make kidnapping an important source of cash income during the difficult years of his movement. In 1923, Wei Baqun collected more than one thousand silver dollars from his enemy Wei Longfu and then released his son. He then used the money to buy four rifles and five hundred cartridges.[60] In early 1929, after learning that a wealthy man in Wuzhuan named Huang Bangdeng had complained about the revolution. Wei Baqun sent a note to Huang asking to borrow eighty silver dollars. Huang refused to lend any money and vehemently scolded the revolutionaries. Shortly after that a group of people broke into Huang's home and took his thirteen-year-old son. Huang later found that his son had been taken to the Western Mountains and then sent a middleman to negotiate with Wei Baqun, who demanded eight hundred silver dollars for the release of the boy. Huang paid the money and got his son back. During the third revolt, Wei Baqun ordered that all important captives be sent to his headquarters. In spring 1931, some of his followers attacked the new home of Ya Yugui, commander of an anti-Communist militia unit. Ya escaped, but his wife and sister were taken. The two women were soon brought to Wei Baqun's headquarters. Wei Baqun had a note sent to Ya demanding eight hundred silver dollars for the release of the two women, threatening to kill them if Ya failed to pay the amount. Ya yielded and paid the money.[61]

The bandit culture characterized by arbitrary killing, kidnapping, and looting had a particularly strong effect on the Red Guard units and village officials. According to Lei Jingtian, who headed the Right River Soviet in 1929 and 1930, the Seventh Red Army and the higher-level Soviet governments were rather cautious in ordering death penalties, but district and township governments were reckless about killing. One cause of random and excessive killings was that the Communists did not have a standard law about who had the power to mete out the death penalty. In some areas the power resided with the county governments, but in others township governments could order executions. Some local leaders and Red Guards would immediately shoot any local tyrant or landlord they could lay their hands on, and would see all the people who lived beyond the border of the Right River Soviet as enemies who deserved the death penalty. An announcement made by the front committee of the Seventh Red Army accused some local Communists of following the policy of killing and burning all and warned that such practices would serve to force the peasants to side with the local tyrants.[62]

Chen Haoren, head of the political department of the Seventh Red Army, made a similar comment in a report submitted to the CCP Central Committee. According to Chen the peasant soldiers would burn down everything after taking a village held by a local tyrant, and they did not make any distinction between the houses of the landlords and those of the peasants. As a result, the peasants in these villages would always stand by the landlords. Like the bandits, some Red Guards would force people to provide grain and would collect taxes and ransoms from the peasants.[63] A document issued by the Seventh Red Army admitted that many Red Guard units had committed the crimes of oppressing and exploiting the peasants, raping women, and arbitrary burnings and killings and it argued that these crimes happened because most of those units were not controlled by real revolutionaries. Like the bandit leaders, commanders of some Red Guard units would see their armed units as their private armies rather than a part of the Communist revolutionary force.[64] Similar discrepancies between CCP policies and the actions of local leaders regarding the use of violence occurred in other revolutionary base areas, including the Hubei-Henan-Anhui base area, where local peasant leaders tended to ignore CCP policies against random acts of violence and indulge in practices of social banditry.[65]

The killings conducted by the Communists, along with their confiscation of property and kidnappings, gave the Nationalists good reasons to describe the Communists as bandits. Liao Lei told the people of Donglan during the third extermination campaign that Wei Baqun was not a real Communist, but was a bandit.[66] Likewise, the Communists also had persuasive reasons to call the Nationalists bandits. The killings, burnings, lootings, and kidnappings committed by both sides divided the entire population into two opposing groups, and in many cases gave rise to endless feuds between Communist villages and anti-Communist villages. The killings also caused a shortage of labor and had a destructive effect on the local economy. According to Bai Chongxi, in 1925 Donglan and Fengshan had a population of 170,000, but in 1932 there were only about 50,000 people left in the two counties, and most of the survivors were women, the old, and the weak. Bai, of course, blamed the rapid population decrease on the Communists. Bai's claim was confirmed by another Nationalist estimate made in 1932, which showed that the population density of Donglan had decreased from more than 100 people per square kilometer to 16.44 per square kilometer in 1932, making Donglan the fifty-third most densely populated county among the ninety-four counties in Guangxi Province.[67] However, a traveler from Shanghai who visited Donglan in 1933 reported that Donglan had a total population of nearly 93,000, which indicates that Bai Chongxi had exaggerated Donglan's population decrease. Communist authors agree that population shrinkage occurred between 1921 and 1933, but they attribute it to the Nationalist policy of "looting all, killing all, and burning all."[68]

Whereas the predilection for violence shows that there was some congruence between the revolutionary culture and local tradition, there were also many differences between the two. There are reports about how the revolutionary culture succeeded in changing local traditional practices such as discrimination against women, arranged marriage, extravagant weddings, and superstitions, but there is also evidence showing how conflicting elements of the two cultures coexisted with each other without causing serious problems. For instance, the Communists made great efforts to eliminate religion and superstition, and they even called on the boy scouts to help destroy Buddhist temples, yet the peasants continued to make stories about Wei Baqun's mysterious powers to deify him. In social relations, revolutionary comradeship went side by side with sworn brotherhood. On one occasion, an oath taken by some revolutionaries cum sworn brothers began with the revolutionary message about obliterating superstition and ended with the traditional warning that anyone who dared to break the oath would be struck by a lightning bolt.[69]

In late 1929, after Wei Baqun and his followers took the county seat for the third time, they issued a list of political programs that they planned to enforce. One of the programs had to do with the elimination of polygamy, yet Wei Baqun still had two wives at that time.[70] According to an unpublished account provided by one of Wei Baqun's close associates, sometime in 1930, Wei Baqun decided to divorce both of his wives, possibly as an effort to abide by the political programs of his own making. In a letter to his comrades, Wei Baqun complained that he had been fed up with the pains of polygamy, and was upset that his two wives could not get along with each other. He argued that after divorcing his two wives he would be able to concentrate more on the revolution. A group of Wei Baqun's followers then wrote him a joint letter trying to persuade him to keep his second wife Chen Lanfen and divorce his third wife Wang Juqiu. They portrayed Wang Juqiu as the troublemaker and Lanfen as a loyal wife who had won admiration of most people around her. They argued that it is not wise for a man to live without a wife and reminded Wei Baqun of how Lanfen had striven to have him released from prison in 1922 and how she had sent money to Wei Baqun in Hong Kong to enable him to travel to Guangzhou in late 1924.[71] Wei Baqun eventually decided to keep both of his wives and in 1931 both Chen Lanfen and Wang Juqiu were still his wives when they were killed.

At times, differences between the revolutionary culture and the culture of the rebels and bandits could have very destructive effects. A prominent example is the different perceptions of loyalty and surrender held by the revolutionaries and bandits. Both revolutionaries and bandits emphasized loyalty. However, for revolutionaries, at least in theory, it meant loyalty to their ideology, political cause, class, and party. For bandits, on the other hand, loyalty meant obeying one's leader, and the degree of loyalty was often determined by what the leader could offer his followers. If the leader could provide protection, promotion, and subsistence—as Wei Baqun did in the early years of his movement—his followers would remain loyal to him. If the leader ceased to function as a patron, a provider, and a protector, his followers could leave him for another leader, or they could even turn him in for personal gains. By mid-1931, it had become clear to many followers of Wei Baqun that their leader could no longer offer them much and as a result there arose a wave of betrayals. During the late Qing and early Republican era, it became customary in Guangxi and other places for the local governments to offer amnesty and official positions to leading bandits. The purpose was to eliminate banditry by incorporating the bandits into the official system, but it caused unexpected results when some began to take banditry as a shortcut to higher positions. Wei Baqun's followers were all familiar with this practice and quite many of them took advantage of it. Surrender or changing sides were not permissible in the revolutionary culture, but were customary in the local culture of rebels and bandits.

There are other factors in the making of the wave of betrayals. Wei Baqun's strategy of forced dispersal, which kept only a small number of followers in the mountains and sent most others back to their villages, caused some of his followers to believe that their leaders had abandoned them. They felt, then, in light of this perceived betrayal, that it was justifiable for them to leave or turn against their leaders. Once in their villages, they were helpless and were at the mercy of their enemies, who would either persecute or recruit them. Often, the only way to survive was to help the enemies capture or kill their higher-ups.

In explaining why Wei Baqun was able to keep so many followers together, Communists would emphasize Wei Baqun's popularity and how receptive the peasants were to his messages, whereas Wei Baqun's enemies would stress the coercive methods that Wei Baqun supposedly had adopted. For instance, Bai Chongxi believed that Wei Baqun's secret for holding his followers together was the use of force. Bai's informants told him that in the area controlled by Wei Baqun and his comrades, if a person failed to show up for one of Wei Baqun's meetings, he was warned; if he was absent a second time, he was jailed; a third time he was beheaded. It is hard to prove the existence of such a brutal rule, but it is certain that Wei Baqun and his followers did use coercion in organizing the peasants. Bai Chongxi, surprisingly, claimed that Wei Baqun's use of force was justified.[72] Wei Baqun and the other leaders could continue to exert forceful control over their followers when they were together in the mountains, but once the officers and soldiers returned to their villages, Wei Baqun could no longer apply coercion on them and they would also be exposed to a completely different kind of propaganda and coercion, making it hard for them to remain loyal to the revolutionary cause.

Another fundamental reason for the appearance of so many defectors during and after 1931 was that most people had realized by then that Wei Baqun and his comrades had failed to deliver the promises they had made at the beginning of the revolution. Looking back, many felt that their living conditions had deteriorated rather than improved during the revolutionary decade. Many had lost loved ones, homes, land, and other properties. People could hardly do any farming in 1931 and 1932 because of the fighting. Tian Shulan, a traveler from Shanghai who made a brief stay in Donglan in 1933, was told that before 1924 Donglan had a self-sufficient economy based on the cultivation of food crops such as rice, maize, wheat, sweet potatoes, taro, and soy beans, and cash crops like tung tree, tea-oil camellia, star anise, tobacco, indigo, sugarcane, and cotton, as well as different varieties of fruit. By 1933, however, Donglan was no longer able to produce enough food for its population. The decade-long conflict had caused a decrease not only in agriculture, but also animal husbandry, handicraft industry, and trade.[73]

The fighting and economic destruction brought about severe suffering for the people. It was reported in June 1932 that every day twenty to thirty people were starved to death in Donglan and some had to sell their children to survive. Many more became homeless, and in 1932 there were 13,000 to 14,000 refugees in Fengshan. In order to revive the economy, the government had to offer a three-year tax exemption to the residents of Donglan and also annulled all tax payments in arrears.[74] If, at the beginning of his revolution Wei Baqun was seen as a destroyer only by his enemies, but a patron and protector by the weak and poor, by the early 1930s increasing numbers of people, including some of the poor and weak, began to view him largely as a destroyer. The burning enthusiasm that characterized the movement when it was successful and robust had been lost, and defeat had nurtured lethargy. More people began to feel that they were experiencing a disaster. They believed that Wei Baqun and his close followers were the cause of that disaster, and therefore they turned their leaders in with the hope of ending the calamity and returning to normal life as soon as possible.

The killing of Wei Baqun's two wives failed to maintain the morale of his followers and prevent many of them from abandoning the revolutionary cause and betraying their leaders. Although there were many people who became followers of Wei Baqun because they truly identified with him and his movement, many others joined his movement for safety or other personal gain. Whereas many of his followers were willing to die for the movement, many others would change sides when they realized that Wei Baqun's movement was destined to fail. Gong Chu, who joined Zhu De in southern Hunan in 1928 and later worked for Mao in Jinggangshan, commented that many poor peasants joined Zhu De's army unit when it was stationed in southern Hunan because at that time Zhu was able to provide each soldier with a monthly stipend of twelve silver dollars. Besides, the soldiers could share the pigs, chicken, and ducks they took from the wealthy families. After the army unit moved to Jinggangshan, the monthly stipend was reduced to three silver dollars, and since the wealthy people had all fled, the soldiers did not even have enough to eat. As a result, some soldiers and officers became resentful and decided to run away.[75] Wei Baqun's followers in Donglan and the Right River region also experienced the transition from the good days of the early years to the bad time of 1931 and 1932. In the early years, they could easily confiscate the properties of wealthy families, and when the Seventh Red Army was first created, each soldier and officer received a monthly stipend of twenty silver dollars. Although the stipend was offered only for the first month, in 1929 and 1930 soldiers had enough to eat and received cash stipends from time to time.[76] In the difficult years of 1931 and 1932, however, many of Wei Baqun's followers could barely fill their stomaches. Many defected because they felt that the revolution had failed to meet their expectations.

It was not long after the departure of the main force of the Seventh Red Army that Wei Baqun composed a short poem that read, "Unity is strength, and division means death. I am afraid that defeat will cause our comrades to betray."[77] It did not take long for Wei Baqun's fear to come true. As mentioned earlier, during the second revolt, Chen Yuzao, Liang Shishu, and Chen Shouhe, all founding members of the Association for Reforming Donglan, were executed for betraying Wei Baqun. There were two other prominent traitors during the second revolt. One was Huang Haiju, a graduate of the first class of Donglan Peasant Movement Institute and the nephew of a powerful landlord. In early 1926, he helped the Gong Regiment during the Donglan Massacre, and later that year Wei Baqun had him shot.[78] The other traitor was Long Jinbiao, a retired army officer who served as the military instructor for the third class of Donglan Peasant Movement Institute. He turned against Wei Baqun in September 1927 and killed Wei Baqun's younger brother Wei Jing (the younger). He soon met his death at the hands of another revolutionary. It is apparent that treachery was not yet a serious problem during the second revolt and Wei Baqun was able to enforce severe punishments for people considered to be traitors.

In 1931 and 1932, when it became obvious that Wei Baqun would not be able to rise again, an increasing number of his supporters began to see him as a burden rather than a symbol of hope. Defectors appeared one after another and Wei Baqun was no longer able to punish all of them. In June 1931, Wei Baqun's follower Deng Peng changed sides and schemed to have Liao Yuanfang killed. Although Wei Ang was the one who killed Wei Baqun, it was another defector, Huang Jiakang, who sent Wei Baqun to Wei Ang's hiding place. Huang had served under Wei Baqun as a battalion commander, and he knew most of Wei Baqun's hiding places in the Western Mountains. He defected in mid-October 1932 and then led the enemy troops to search Wei Baqun's hideouts, forcing Wei to move out of the Western Mountains.[79]

Two other battalion commanders had surrendered before Huang Jiakang did. One of them was Wei Chaoqun. An intellectual who joined Wei Baqun during the second revolt, Wei Chaoqun became one of his most capable commanders. According to one source, he was injured in battle in October 1930 and did not get enough money from Wei Baqun for curing the wound. He became resentful and surrendered to the New Guangxi Clique in late 1931.[80] Another source holds that Wei Chaoqun surrendered for a different reason. During an attack on a landlord he took an accidental glimpse of the beautiful daughter of another landlord and immediately fell in love with her. He then killed her husband and took her as his wife. To win the trust of his father-in-law, Wei Chaoqun presented the landlord a handgun as a gift. For this he was severely scolded by Wei Baqun and when the revolution took a downturn he decided to surrender to the Nationalists. In order to negotiate a deal, he took a painstaking journey to southern Guangxi to meet with Governor Huang Xuchu's father. His strategy worked and the provincial government appointed him as the commander of an anti-Communist militia unit. He immediately gathered his former subordinates in the Right River Independent Division and collected the weapons they had hidden. Together they became a powerful enemy of Wei Baqun and his loyal supporters.[81]

Huang Shaoxian was the other battalion commander who surrendered and he also became an officer in the anti-Communist militia system. In May and June 1932, he took a group of militias to search Wei Baqun's hideouts in the mountains. The militias killed quite a few Communists and discovered many weapons. Huang even won an award from the provincial government for his contribution to the defeat of the Communists. Wei Baqun was able to have Huang assassinated, but soon after killing Huang the assassin himself changed sides.[82]

When it became difficult for the revolutionaries to get basic necessities, and when killings became rampant, the amnesty and monetary rewards offered by the enemies became attractive to many of Wei Baqun's followers. The government began to offer monetary rewards for capturing and killing Wei Baqun and the other leaders in late 1927. At that time, the reward for capturing or killing Wei Baqun was five thousand silver dollars, and Chen Hongtao was not even on the list of the most wanted criminals. By May 1931 the bounty on Wei Baqun had increased to ten thousand silver dollars and that on Chen Hongtao was five thousand silver dollars.[83] It is not clear why by early 1932 the reward on Wei Baqun was reduced to seven thousand silver dollars. It was at that point that Wei Baqun decided to make fun of Liao Lei. He asked one of his soldiers to put a poster at an intersection and on the poster he wrote: "One penny is offered for Liao Lei's head."[84]

In April 1932, Wei Baqun decided to claim the bounty on his own head so that he could buy some grain and other supplies. He sent two of his close followers to Wuzhuan to negotiate with the militia leaders. The two claimed that they had tied Wei Baqun up and hidden him in a cave, and that they would be happy to hand Wei Baqun to the government if the government would pay them the reward money. Liang Xuqiu, the militia leader, then sent his two younger brothers, a former follower of Wei Baqun named Chen Shouxian, and some other people to verify the claim. They went with the two followers of Wei Baqun to a hideout in the mountains where they saw a seemingly severely injured Wei Baqun who was tied tightly and being beaten up and scolded by a few girls. His face, chest, and back were all covered with blood. Wei Baqun was groaning with his eyes closed. He begged the girls not to beat him anymore and asked them to kill him immediately and then present his head to the militias so that he would not suffer more torture at the hands of his enemies. One of the messengers for the militia forces then went back to report about Wei Baqun's misfortune, whereas the two Liang brothers and Chen Shouxian were persuaded to stay in the hideout to help "guard Wei Baqun." Assured that he could buy Wei Baqun or at least his head with a few thousand silver dollars, Liang Xuqiu persuaded a wealthy friend to lend him two thousand silver dollars which he had delivered to the cave where Wei Baqun was kept, promising he would deliver five thousand more silver dollars once Wei Baqun was transferred to the militia headquarters. The kidnappers took the silver dollars, but the militias who went to take Wei Baqun were ambushed. When the militias finally took the hideout, they discovered that Wei Baqun had disappeared and the two Liang brothers and Chen Shouxian had all been killed. Chen had been a revolutionary before surrendering to the militias in late 1931. The major newspaper in Nanning carried at least two false reports about the capture of Wei Baqun and one of the reports even predicted that Wei would be taken to Baise for execution. The magistrate of Donglan lost his position because of this embarrassing episode.[85]

All participants in the plot received a share of the reward money, but to Wei Baqun's disappointment, some of them immediately gambled away their money.[86] Wei Ang played a very important part in this plot—he was one of the two who went to report about their kidnapping of Wei Baqun and to negotiate with the militias. Wei Ang's role in the plot helped strengthen Wei Baqun's trust in him. It probably had never occurred to Wei Baqun that in only six months Wei Ang was to play that plot again, only this time Wei Baqun would be the real rather than fake victim. By that time the bounty for Wei Baqun had skyrocketed to 14,000 silver dollars.

Although Wei Ang was the one who actually killed Wei Baqun, another follower of Wei Baqun's had considered murdering him a few months before. In early 1932, while Wei Baqun was hiding in the Eastern Mountains, a local Communist leader named Qin Shouchun attempted to assassinate him. The commander of the local anti-Communist militias had promised Qin that he would be permitted to live if he could kill Wei Baqun. Qin also received from the militia commander twenty cartridges and twenty silver dollars to prepare for the killing. Knowing that Wei Baqun liked to eat dog meat, Qin killed a dog and invited Wei Baqun for dinner, planning to slay him while he ate the dog meat. Qin was surprised to discover that Wei Baqun came with twenty-four bodyguards. While six of the guards patrolled outside Qin's house, the remaining eighteen formed two circles around Wei Baqun inside the house, making it difficult for Qin to carry out his scheme. Urged by his father, Qin Shouchun abandoned his plan. Wei Baqun later learned about Qin's trick, and Qin was so scared that he fled his village. He murdered the man who divulged his secret and tried to regain Wei Baqun's trust by killing the nephew of the militia commander who had masterminded the plot, but Wei Baqun would never trust him again. Four months later, Qin Shouchun and his seventy-year-old father were both shot to death in their hiding place.[87]

The fact that Wei Baqun had to take twenty-four bodyguards with him to a dog meat dinner shows that he did not have much trust in Qin Shouchun even before he learned about Qin's intrigue. The appearance of a large number of defectors made Wei Baqun suspicious of many around him during the last months of his life. He killed his third wife Wang Juqiu since he believed that because her brother had joined the enemy forces she would very likely betray the revolution. He did not fully trust his nephew Wei Ang either. The day before he moved to the Fragrant Tea Cave, Wei Baqun sent Chen Hongtao to test Wei Ang. Chen appeared in the cave and suggested to Wei Ang that as the situation had become so desperate and the reward for capturing or killing Wei Baqun was so high, the two of them should tie Wei Baqun up and send him to the enemy forces or kill him and turn in his head to end the crisis and also to get rich. Wei Ang shook his head, saying that Uncle Baqun was the pillar of the party and therefore should be protected rather than harmed. He told Chen Hongtao that although the situation was quite hopeless at the moment, the enemy forces would leave Donglan sooner or later and after that the Communist movement would be revived. Wei Ang passed the test and Chen Hongtao returned to report to Wei Baqun that Wei Ang was reliable.[88] It is obvious that Wei Baqun trusted Chen Hongtao much more than he did most other people. It is hard to know whether Wei Ang passed the test because he knew that Chen Hongtao was testing him or because he did not want to share the reward money with Chen. In order to prevent his followers from betraying the movement, Wei Baqun and the other leaders issued regulations about how to punish traitors and also organized small, armed units to eliminate the traitors. However, these measures failed to prevent further betrayals.

A group of officials and scholars who visited Wuzhuan in the early 1950s on behalf of the PRC government came away with the impression that there was an ethnic difference regarding betrayal. They argued that during Wei Baqun's revolution many Zhuang and Han would change sides when the revolution did not go well, but very few Yao betrayed the revolution, and they cite this as one of the reasons why Wei Baqun had so much trust in his Yao followers. Some Yao revolutionaries in the Western Mountains told the group that the Zhuang would force the Yao to be at the forefront in battles, would be quick to claim credit for any victory and put blame on the Yao for any defeat, and would often surrender after being defeated. Sometimes the Zhuang would even kill their fellow Yao revolutionaries before surrendering in order to show their sincerity to their enemies.[89]

The troops of the New Guangxi Clique under Liao Lei were an external enemy too formidable for Wei Baqun and his followers to deal with. The three extermination campaigns that the New Guangxi Clique staged in 1931 and 1932 actually formed a single anti-Communist war because even during the intervals between the three campaigns there were still a large number of external troops stationed around the base area. The encirclement was never removed after it was first enforced in early 1931. After the first extermination campaign it was no longer possible for Wei Baqun to hold his division together, although most of the leaders and soldiers survived; after the second extermination campaign, Wei Baqun's armed force lost most of its fighting power; and when the third extermination campaign began in August 1932, survival became the most urgent issue for Wei Baqun and his supporters and it seemed that a total collapse was imminent. In September 1932, Wei Baqun's loyal supporters, Lan Zhiren and Wei Hanchao, were both defeated. Both Lan and Wei had been battalion commanders. Lan had been the leader of a base area in northern Donglan and Wei had controlled another base area in southeastern Donglan. Like many of his followers, Wei Baqun had sensed the danger before he died. In mid-October 1932, Bai Chongxi arrived in Donglan to urge his troops to finish their work. A few days later, Wei Baqun felt that the Western Mountains were no longer safe, and he managed to sneak through three checkpoints to arrive at the Fragrant Tea Cave, which was located on the fringe of the Western Mountains, adjacent to his native village Dongli (Fig. 7.1).

On October 18, 1932, Wei Baqun sent for Chen Hongtao, who was hiding in another cave nearby, and the two had a brief meeting at the cave on that evening. At the meeting they decided that they both would try to escape the encirclement and move to Guizhou the next morning. It seemed that their final destination would be the Central Revolutionary Base Area in Jiangxi, because shortly before his meeting with Chen Hongtao, Wei Baqun had told his sister-in-law that he and Chen Hongtao would soon leave to find the CCP Central Committee and would stay out of Donglan for a long time. Some even believed that Wei Baqun had planned to travel to the Soviet Union to study. Still not knowing that his younger brother had been killed, Wei Baqun told his sister-in-law that his younger brother, Wei Jing, would serve as the leader of the local revolution during his absence.[90]

Wei Baqun and Chen Hongtao agreed on that fateful evening that they would move separately. After their meeting, Chen Hongtao returned to his own cave. Before leaving, he warned Wei Baqun not to wear his red leather hat the

FIGURE 7.1 Entrance to the Fragrant Tea Cave. Photograph by the author.

next day: "Many people know that you always wear that hat. Wearing it would make it easy for the enemies to recognize you."

There are at least three different accounts about what kind of meal Wei Baqun had for his last dinner. According to the first account, on the morning of October 18, Luo Rikuai and Wei Ang went out of the cave to meet someone who was supposed to come with some rice, but that person never showed up. Therefore, that evening the only food they had was some corn Chen Hongtao had prepared. The second account insists that Wei Baqun asked Wei Ang to prepare some porridge and Luo Rikuai to cook some beans for dinner. He was too sick to eat other food. The last account holds that Wei Ang killed a chicken and prepared a nice meal for Wei Baqun, Chen Hongtao, and Luo Rikuai. Although it is doubtful that Wei Ang could get his hands on a chicken under such grave circumstances, there were good reasons for him to prepare a delicious meal for Wei Baqun because he knew that it would be his uncle's last dinner.

During his years as a revolutionary leader, Wei Baqun had taught his followers that true revolutionaries should show no hesitation in sacrificing their own lives, the lives of their relatives and friends, and their family property for the revolution.[91] By the time of his death, Wei Baqun had already dedicated to his movement the entire family fortune that his grandfather and father had bequeathed him as well as the lives of many relatives and friends. His death further confirms that he was a true revolutionary by his own standards.

Many of Wei Baqun's followers failed to heed his teachings. Increasingly, more of them abandoned or betrayed the revolutionary cause after Wei Baqun was killed. Chen Hongtao's bodyguard Wei Hua surrendered to the government immediately after Wei Baqun's death. He was the one who had accompanied Wei Ang to negotiate with the militias in their earlier scheme to claim the bounty for Wei Baqun. Now he and Wei Ang became partners again and they guided the militias to the Western Mountains to search for Chen Hongtao. Luo Guifa, the commander of the Western Mountains Yao Independent Battalion, also surrendered. This contradicts a claim made by some Yao revolutionaries that during the more than twenty years of revolution not a single Yao had ever surrendered to the enemy. Wei Hua, Luo Guifa, and more than twenty other revolutionaries were summarily executed by the Nationalists after their surrender for failing to defect before Wei Baqun's death. During the ten days after Wei Baqun's death, his followers in Wuzhuan submitted more than four hundred guns to the government, and only a month after Wei Baqun's death, Huang Jinyou turned in Bai Hanyun and Wei Shuzong, to the enemy troops.[92]

Chen Hongtao was deeply shocked when he learned that Wei Ang had murdered Wei Baqun. He wrote a moving eulogy in which he described Wei Baqun as "a comrade," "a friend," and "a mentor." He promised that he would kill the traitor and present his head as sacrifice to Wei Baqun. Unfortunately, he would not get the chance to make good on that promise. By December 1932,

Chen had moved out of Donglan and traveled to a village near the Right River. He tried to contact Wang Tingye, a former subordinate and sworn brother. But Wang, in order to save his own life and to collect the five thousand silver dollar reward, guided Chen into a trap set by enemy troops. In late December 1932, Chen was executed in Baise.[93] Liao Lei had predicted shortly after Wei Baqun's death that Chen Hongtao's days were numbered. Liao also made it clear that he considered Chen Hongtao the number two criminal next only to Wei Baqun and that he would not spare Chen's life even if Chen surrendered.[94] Chen Hongtao never begged for his life after his arrest. He suffered severe torture and died a heroic death. On several occasions leading revolutionaries were arrested or killed when they tried to approach their former followers who had been dispersed to their native villages, not knowing that these former comrades had agreed to cooperate with the enemies. About the same time that Chen Hongtao was captured and executed, Qin Daoping, chairman of the Right River Revolutionary Committee, was also turned in by a former follower. The Nationalist troops discovered him in a cave in the Western Mountains and took him to Wuzhuan where he was shot.[95] By late 1932, the CCP system in Donglan had collapsed. Before the commencement of the three anti-Communist campaigns in early 1931, there were thirty-seven CCP branches and more than four hundred CCP members in Donglan. Now only seven branches and barely twenty CCP members were still operative.[96]

Only six months after Chen Hongtao's execution, Huang Daquan, Wei Baqun's chief of staff and the fourth or fifth most important leader of the Right River Communist movement, was captured in Tianbao County located to the south of Baise. Although in the Communist system Huang's position was lower than that of Chen Hongtao, the Nationalists believed that he "had caused more calamities than Chen Hongtao" partly because Huang had been with Wei Baqun for a longer period, was more influential than Chen Hongtao among the Communists in Donglan and Fengshan, and was also a more experienced military commander than Chen. Huang and his wife were betrayed by some former followers in the peasant army. Three months later, Huang Daquan was executed under a kapok tree.[97]

More than three years after Wei Baqun and Chen Hongtao were killed, Lu Haoren, who held a position equal to or slightly above that of Huang Daquan, also met his death at the hands of a former follower. By that time, three of five members of the Right River Special Committee of the CCP had lost their lives because of betrayals. Among the four men who were appointed as regimental commanders of the Right River Independent Division in early 1931, three were killed because of betrayals and the last became a traitor himself. Among the three who were killed, the first to die was Liao Yuanfang. The second was Huang Shuxiang, who was killed in May 1933 after one of his followers revealed his hiding place to the enemy. The third to die was Teng Guodong and he was killed in 1936 along with Lu Haoren.[98] Wei Mingzhou was the last of the four regimental commanders. He was demoted only shortly after being appointed a regimental commander in 1931 for failing to carry out an important order. After Wei Baqun's death, Wei Mingzhou and a group of his followers surrendered to their pursuers. The anti-Communist forces initially offered them amnesty, but did not keep the promise. After they were disarmed, Wei Mingzhou and his followers were all executed.

Whereas most former rank-and-file soldiers in the revolutionary movement chose to submit to the government after Wei Baqun's death so that they could live normal lives, there were a few loyalist villagers who refused to abandon the revolutionary cause. A Yao man named Wei Ting'an lived the life of a lonely revolutionary for seventeen years after Wei Baqun's death. He was from the Western Mountains and very likely had been an ordinary follower of Wei Baqun rather than a CCP member or an officer. In other words, the Nationalists would most likely not make much trouble for him if he surrendered and the surviving underground Communists would not consider him a comrade if he did not. Yet he refused to capitulate even after the defeat of 1932. Some of his friends would ask him: "Why don't you just come out and surrender? It is impossible to revive the revolution, and Wei Baqun will never come back. What can you do with that broken gun of yours?" During the seventeen years his house was burned down nineteen times by the Nationalists and most of the time he had to adopt a nomadic lifestyle. Wei Ting'an later complained that some Zhuang did not have firm belief, which caused them to surrender, but he conceded that even the Yao of his own village would call him "a red bandit" and did not permit him to stay in the village. After the Communist takeover in 1949, when the peasant associations were being restored, the local leaders decided to appoint someone who had never surrendered as the chairman of the peasant association of Wei Ting'an's village. The villagers unanimously agreed that Wei Ting'an was the only choice for that position![99]

It is hard to determine whether or not Wei Baqun would have had a better chance to survive if he had left the Right River region with the main force of the Seventh Red Army in November 1930. He could easily have been killed during the journey to Jiangxi, considering the fact that only 1,300 of more than 7,000 officers and soldiers of the Seventh Red Army arrived in Jiangxi safely. Those killed during the journey included some high-ranking officers. Even if Wei Baqun had survived the journey, he could still have been killed at the hands of either his enemies or comrades. Li Mingrui, the commander-in-chief of the Seventh Red Army, was killed in October 1931 by his own comrades. According to Gong Chu, Li Mingrui became upset when he was persecuted for his past contact with Wang Jingwei's Reorganization Faction and decided to escape from the Communist base area. As soon as he revealed his plan to a small group of close followers, one of them, who was a secret agent for the

Communist security bureau, shot him dead. Several other high-ranking officers of the Seventh Red Army were also executed by their comrades for the false charge that they were agents for the Reorganization Faction.[100]

Gong Chu was not with Li Mingrui when Li was killed. Qin Yingji, who saw Li Mingrui a few hours before his death, provided a different and more reliable version of the story. Qin was a low-ranking officer in the Seventh Red Army at that time. He saw Li Mingrui and a few other officers arrive at his company on an afternoon in October 1931. That evening, the captain of his company called all the Cantonese speakers together and sent them to a nearby family temple. They were not allowed to move out of the temple because there had been rumors that Li Mingrui had planned to escape and wanted to take the Cantonese with him. At about 11 PM, Qin heard gunshots and noise from Li Mingrui's room and was then told that Li had died in an accident. They then bought a fancy coffin and had Li buried.[101]

Whereas Gong Chu believed that Mao Zedong had masterminded the purge because some officers in the Seventh Red Army had resisted Mao's attempt at reorganizing the army, most others point their fingers at the members of the Wang Ming Clique, which was the dominant faction in the Central Revolutionary Base Area at that time. Lei Jingtian was also slated for execution, but Mao saved his life. This suggests that even if it was not Mao's decision to kill Li Mingrui, Mao was powerful enough to save Li's life but chose not to. Mao had not lost his control over the army at that time. Deng Xiaoping was very bitter about Li's death, and in the 1970s he told Mao several times that "it was wrong to kill Li Mingrui." Deng was the head of the CCP branch of a county at that time and was probably not powerful enough to save Li. Li and the other victims of the purge were all rehabilitated posthumously in 1945 at the Seventh Congress of the CCP. Although it is not certain whether or not Mao played any role in their deaths, it is pretty clear that he played a very important part in clearing their names. Mao also offered an apology for his bad attitude toward the Seventh Red Army and his mistakes in handling personnel issues regarding the Seventh Red Army, but did not admit his role in Li Mingrui's death. During the Cultural Revolution the Red Guards would once again attack Li as a traitor, but after Deng Xiaoping came back to power in the late 1970s, Li was again rehabilitated.[102]

If Wei Baqun had arrived in Jiangxi, his close contact with Yu Zuobai and other left-wing Nationalists and his supposed connections with the anarchists could have caused him serious trouble. If he had been lucky enough to survive the various waves of purges, he could still have died in the 1930s and 1940s at the hands of the Nationalists or the Japanese. Of the 1,300 soldiers and officers of the Seventh Red Army who arrived in Jiangxi in 1931, only a few dozen were still alive in 1949.[103] If he had survived the wars in Jiangxi and had been permitted to join the Long March after the Communists were defeated in Jiangxi in 1934, then as a high-ranking officer he would have had a better chance to survive. If he had been chosen to stay in Jiangxi to "continue the struggle," he would have more likely been killed. Most of the high-ranking Communist officials and officers left in Jiangxi in 1934 were slain shortly after the departure of the Long Marchers. Another possibility was for the CCP Central Committee to send Wei Baqun from Jiangxi back to the Right River region to revive the revolution. If that had happened, then he could have been captured and executed by the Nationalists at any of the many checkpoints. Only weeks after Wei Baqun was killed, the Nationalists executed his friend and supporter, Huang Zhifeng. Huang was a graduate of the first class of Donglan Peasant Movement Institute and a veteran peasant movement leader from Fengyi County by the Right River. He made the journey from Hechi to Jiangxi as the deputy commander of one of the two divisions of the Seventh Red Army. In late 1932, the CCP leaders decided to send Huang Zhifeng and Huang Wentong back to the Right River region to lead the local revolution. The two were captured by the Nationalists near the border between Hunan and Guangxi and were immediately shot to death.[104] Most likely the decision to keep Wei Baqun in Donglan and the Right River region was made by the outsiders. If that had been the case, there were no reasons for Wei Baqun to regret because he did not have any choice in the first place. Even if it had been Wei Baqun's own decision to stay in Donglan, there were still not many reasons for him to regret because not all of those who stayed were killed and not all of those who left with the main force of the Seventh Red Army survived. Revolution was a dangerous business and Wei Baqun knew that very well.

Aftermath

Even before Wei Baqun's death, the New Guangxi Clique had begun to organize the Dong-Feng Reconstruction Committee for dealing with the aftermath of the Communist revolution in the two counties. The committee began to operate on November 1, 1932. It was initially headed by Liao Lei and, after Liao's departure, by his nephew, Luo Huo.[105] The committee intensified the effort at "normalizing" the local society with the purpose of forestalling any new revolution. The residents of the mountainous areas who had been forced to move out of their villages were now allowed to return home. All residents were ordered to submit their guns to the government. Many participants in the revolution were killed or jailed.

Relatives of the revolutionary leaders were severely punished. Their family property was confiscated, and female members of their families were often taken to other parts of Guangxi and sold to the peasants. For instance, Wei Baqun's younger sister Wei Dizhuang was taken to Liuzhou and sold there in late 1932.

She was never seen again.[106] Wei Baqun's last wife, Huang Xiumei, parted with him in the Western Mountains just before Wei Baqun made his deadly trip to the Fragrant Tea Cave and was captured by the Nationalists shortly after Wei Baqun was killed. She was taken to Liuzhou, imprisoned there for several months, and then sold to a man from Beiliu County in southeastern Guangxi. After 1949 she joined the local Communist government, but died of illness in 1952. Wei Baqun's follower Xie Fumin claims that Huang Xiumei was killed in April 1932 for protecting Wei Baqun, one Nationalist source holds that Wei Baqun killed her, but a more reliable Nationalist source confirmed that she was captured shortly after Wei Baqun's death.[107] There are also those who contend that she was sold after Wei Baqun's death and was never heard of again. Wei Baqun's sister-in-law and Huang Shuxiang's sister, Huang Meilun, was arrested in October 1932 and sold to a villager in Luchuan County in southeastern Guangxi, where she joined the underground Communist movement in the late 1940s. She returned to Donglan in 1953 and became an official in the Communist government, but was not permitted to rejoin the CCP until 1980. She died in Donglan in 2004 at the age of 104.[108] Wei Baqun's two adopted daughters, Shuangfeng and Feilai, were also kidnapped and sold. In 1922, Wei Baqun and his soldiers found three abandoned little girls by a road. Wei Baqun adopted two of them and Huang Daquan took the third one to his home. By 1932, both daughters had grown up, and Wei Ang helped the Nationalists find them. They were both taken to Hechi where they disappeared without a trace.[109] Huang Zhengxiu, former chairwoman of the Donglan Women's Association and wife of Bai Hanyun, was also sold, but in the end survived.

On the other hand, in order to put an end to the vicious cycle of arbitrary burning and killing, the reconstruction committee ordered the victims of the revolutions not to seek revenge. At the mass assembly held at Wuzhuan to celebrate Wei Baqun's death, Liao Lei told the audience that the days of the Chinese nation would have been numbered if all the people in China had been as brutal and vengeful as the residents of Donglan and Fengshan.[110] To win the trust of the peasants, the government announced that it would punish the local tyrants and evil gentry, and the reconstruction committee actually put one local tyrant from Fengshan to death.[111] Most of the powerful and wealthy families that had been destroyed by Wei Baqun and the revolutionaries failed to fully restore their power and wealth, partly because many members of those families had perished. A survey conducted by Communist scholars shows that just before the land reform in the early 1950s, among the 3,665 households in the Wuzhuan District, only 98 had a limited amount of surplus land to rent out. In the Western Mountains all the landlords and rich peasants were killed and by the 1950s there was not a single landlord.[112]

Once peace was restored, the government was able to conduct a census, which showed that many families had been entirely wiped out, and that

Donglan had a population of refugees and orphans. An orphanage was built in the county seat to take in the orphans found in Donglan.[113] A psychological reconstruction project was adopted, and separate programs were created for the educated and the common people, respectively. Villagers were then organized into the Baojia system, which was based on the principle of collective responsibility. Another measure the government adopted was to strengthen the anti-Communist militia system, and Liao Lei initiated a program to train militia leaders only eleven days after Wei Baqun's death.[114] The government also had plans to rebuild houses for the villagers and to build roads in the two counties. The provincial government allocated some money to assist the poor residents and refugees in Donglan and Fengshan, but the county magistrate of Donglan gave only a small portion of the funds to the villagers and kept the rest in his own pockets.[115] With Wei Baqun and most of the other leading revolutionaries captured or dead, the local power holders became arrogant and corrupt again, believing that there was nobody who dared to challenge them.

Shortly before the villagers of Dongli were able to build the Red God Temple, Wei Baqun's enemies had constructed two symbolic monuments in the county seat to honor their victory. One was the Sun Yat-sen Park, which was supposed to serve to remind the local people that Donglan followed the Three Principles of the People rather than communism. Located near the foot of the Saddle-shaped Mountain on the eastern side of the town, the park had a pavilion and many trees and flowers. It was later destroyed during the Sino-Japanese War. The government also rebuilt three main roads in the county seat and named them Sun Yat-sen Road, Five Rights Road and People's Livelihood Road, respectively.[116] The other symbolic monument was the Memorial to the Extermination of the Communists in Donglan and Fengshan, which cost eight hundred silver dollars. Every household in the two counties was made to contribute ten cents. The construction of the memorial lasted eight months, and the heart of the memorial was a stone pillar inscribed with an article written by Bai Chongxi, in which Bai compared Wei Baqun to such famous or notorious rebels as Zhang Jiao of the Han Dynasty, Huang Chao of the Tang Dynasty, and Li Zicheng of the Ming Dynasty. He argued that Wei Baqun's death showed the power of heaven, and predicted that it would take twenty years for Donglan and Fengshan to recover from the destruction perpetrated by the Communists.[117]

In 1934, in order to keep a close eye on the troublesome mountainous border region between Donglan, Fengshan, and other counties, the provincial government carved out a new county in the frontier regions of Fengshan, Baise, and Enlong. The new county was named Wangang, meaning ten thousand hills. This invention, however, failed to root out revolution in the region. Wei Baqun's followers continued to conduct underground work in the area and in the late 1940s Wangang instead of Donglan became the center of the last round of local Communist revolts against the Nationalist government. To eliminate Wei Baqun's hometown Wuzhuan as a source of unrest, the government divided it into three separate townships. Two years before Wei Baqun's death, the name Wuzhuan, which contains the character Wu, meaning martial or militant, was changed to Zhonghe, meaning harmony. The symbol of Wuzhuan, the Tower of the Literary Star, was remodeled following some fengshui principles. Its pointed top was cut off and replaced with a flat ceiling, and the entire tower was painted white, demonstrating that the white or bai, which represented Bai Chongxi or white terror, would subdue the red, which stood for communism and Wei Baqun.[118]

After the defeat of Wei Baqun's first two revolts, Wei Baqun and most of his closest allies remained together and they later easily revived their revolution when the conditions became opportune. During and after the third revolt, partly because of the many defectors, Wei Baqun and most other important leaders were killed, and it therefore became very difficult to revitalize the revolution. Besides, starting in the early 1930s, the New Guangxi Clique established stable and energetic rule over the province and gradually turned Guangxi into a model province of Nationalist China. It therefore became difficult for the Communists to operate there. In late 1934, the main force of the Communist Red Army entered Guangxi during their Long March, but they did not stay there long. In Donglan and the Right River region, Huang Songjian, Huang Juping, and others tried to revive Communist organizations, but the Communists would have to wait till the late 1940s to launch another revolution.

Just as Wei Baqun's victories were not his victories alone, because they could not have been won without strong external support, Wei Baqun's defeat in 1932 was not entirely his own defeat in the sense that he was defeated largely because his patrons had failed to offer much needed support in time. Although his setback in 1932 was inevitable, his death in that year was not. If he had not stayed with Wei Ang in the Fragrant Tea Cave on that cool October evening, or if Wei Ang had behaved like a filial nephew or a loyal revolutionary on that evening, Wei Baqun could have survived by moving to Guizhou or some other place. If Wei Baqun could have lived for five more years, then the New Guangxi Clique would have become his fighting ally during the war against Japan. If he could have lived for fourteen more years, he would have been able to witness the defeat of Japan and the outbreak of another civil war between the Communists and Nationalists. If he could have lived for seventeen more years, he would have been able to experience the Communist victory in 1949. Suppose that during all those years he had traveled the normal path of a Communist leader and never made any serious mistake, then in 1949 he would have been a very powerful figure in the Communist system to the extent that he could even have stood on the Gate of the Heavenly Peace on October 1, 1949 to hear Mao Zedong declare the founding of the People's Republic of China.

CHAPTER EIGHT

Red God as a Mediating and Unifying Agent

Wei Baqun's role as a bridge between the periphery and the center and between his frontier community and the Chinese nation did not end with his death. In his lifetime he performed two seemingly conflicting roles. On the one hand, he was a transmitter who brought ideas and culture from the center to the periphery, helping to strengthen the link and diminish the gap between the frontier and the more advanced regions of China. On the other hand, he was the leader of a powerful frontier revolution against the center, which had the potential effect of tearing his community away from the nation. The conflict between Wei Baqun's two roles would disappear if we locate him in the era of Republican China, when there were always opposing centers in the country. Wei Baqun always identified with some centers and fought against others. In the early years of his life, he allied himself with Sun Yat-sen and fought against the local and national warlords. After the mid-1920s, as the conflict between the Nationalists and the warlords began to be overshadowed by the confrontation between the Nationalists and Communists, Wei Baqun became a supporter of the Communist center and a rebel against the Nationalist center and its local representatives. To the Nationalists, Wei Baqun was a rebel or a bandit, and a brutal destroyer who had to be eliminated, but the Communists saw him as a great revolutionary and a founder of the new order represented by the forthcoming Communist state. If the Nationalists saw him as a destructive agent who worked to break the connections between his community and the Nationalist state, the Communists perceived him as a constructive mediator and unifier who helped link his frontier community to the emerging Communist system.

In death Wei Baqun was transformed into the Red God by the local villagers, a perfect Communist by his comrades and followers, and a Zhuang who is not a Han by the PRC government. The Communist takeover of China was a decisive factor in the evolution of the Wei Baqun cult. If the Communist movement had failed, Wei Baqun might still have been worshipped by some local peasants, but would definitely have been condemned as a rebel or bandit by the Nationalist government. The Communist victory guaranteed Wei Baqun a spot in the state hall of honor. In the PRC, Wei Baqun represents the rebellious and revolutionary spirit of the people and performs the role of a mediating and unifying agent between his community and the Communist state. For various reasons, villagers, local officials, and central leaders have been involved in mythologizing Wei Baqun. Although the images of Wei Baqun created by the various groups are not exactly the same, they all display the same desire to treat him in larger-than-life terms and make the dead hero serve the living.

Becoming the Red God

Just as the peasants in Hailufeng had already begun to worship Peng Pai as a deity while he was still alive, the villagers in Donglan began to tell stories about Wei Baqun's godly features long before his death. In a way, the deification of Wei Baqun began shortly after his birth when his date and year of birth, his weight, and his facial features were taken as omens of greatness. After he became a popular peasant leader, the local people, including both his supporters and enemies, began to tell stories about his mysterious powers. According to one story, one day in 1927, when a group of enemy soldiers heard that Wei Baqun was staying in a village in the Western Mountains, they rushed to the village and searched every house, but found no trace of Wei Baqun. They then concluded that "Wei Baqun is not an ordinary person. He has changed himself into someone else and escaped." The truth was that Wei Baqun had quickly left the village before the arrival of his enemies.[1] On another occasion, a group of soldiers pursued Wei Baqun into Dongli. They saw him run to the shore of a pond, but when the soldiers reached the pond Wei Baqun had completely disappeared. The pursuers then came to the conclusion that Wei Baqun was an expert in witchcraft and therefore it was impossible to capture him. What the pursuers did not know was that there was a deep cave linked to the pond and a fisherman had sailed Wei Baqun into the cave using a small fishing boat.[2] On another day, another group of Wei Baqun's pursuers came away with the belief that Wei Baqun had the power of turning himself into a tiger. They saw Wei Baqun on a mountain and then besieged it. Believing that there was no way for Wei Baqun to escape, they decided to burn all the trees and grasses of that mountain. The fire started at the foot of the mountain and then gradually reached the top. Suddenly a tiger jumped out of the fire and ran away in an instant. The pursuers agreed that the tiger had to be Wei Baqun, and this confirmed the villagers' belief that Wei Baqun was the reincarnation of the spirit of the White Tiger.[3]

Many other stories relate Wei Baqun to snakes or dragons rather than tigers. One story tells that one day, Wei Baqun, masquerading as a guard for a mountainside Buddhist temple, warned some enemy officers and soldiers stationed there about the fearful power of Wei Baqun. Presently, a local landlord arrived at the temple and immediately saw through Wei Baqun's disguise—but before he could raise the call to arms, Wei Baqun disappeared. Although the soldiers scoured the mountainside, they only managed to turn up Wei Baqun's straw hat. Once they lifted it off the ground, they saw a long, fat snake curling on the grass, and believed Wei Baqun had transformed himself into a snake.

The local Yao people viewed the incident as confirmation that Wei Baqun was a reincarnation of a dragon, and therefore could easily ascend to the sky or descend to the underground world. A similar story holds that one day, when Wei Baqun was besieged by his pursuers in a mountain, he managed to escape through a cave. When the pursuers reached the entrance of the cave, they found his straw hat and a wounded snake. After a thorough but fruitless search, they took the snake and presented it to their commander Liao Lei, showing the hat as proof that the snake was Wei Baqun. Liao Lei rewarded them with a severe scolding.[4]

Locals considered stories that linked Wei Baqun to snakes and dragons plausible due to the popular belief that January 1 of the lunar year—Wei Baqun's birthday—was also the birthday of the dragon. An old villager claimed that he had personally witnessed Wei Baqun turning himself into a dragon. He told how one day he and some other poor villagers watched anxiously as Wei Baqun was cornered by a large group of enemy militias. Suddenly, there appeared a flash of light and Wei Baqun became a blue dragon and flew away into the cloud. A group of children also recounted the day when Wei Baqun, surrounded by enemies, climbed into the upper canopy of a huge camphor tree and then flew away as a blue dragon, leaving his pursuers land-bound and bewildered. On another occasion, Wei Baqun and his bodyguard were trapped by a group of enemy soldiers in the Western Mountains. The soldiers searched the area many times and finally set fire to the grass and trees. The fire blazed for more than a day. After everything was burned down the soldiers searched the bald mountain again and all they could find was one of their own whom Wei Baqun had killed. The soldiers concluded that Wei Baqun was a deity who could change himself into a snake that was immune to fire.[5]

There were many other stories about Wei Baqun's supernatural powers and unusual deeds. Some people believed that he had a magic talisman that could help him foresee enemy activities and therefore his enemies could never find him. Some claimed that he could go anywhere he wanted and could easily turn himself into a peasant, a merchant, a student, a teacher, or a celestial being. Some held that he could see through walls and could see clearly over a span of many kilometers. Some thought that he was a man with red hair and red beard, or a martial arts master with a red face and red eyes who was determined to help the poor to fight the powerful.[6] Some of Wei Baqun's enemies believed that he had the power to descend into the earth and was immune to bomb shells, that he could fly, or was a reincarnation of some rebellious demon that could only be subdued by a more powerful heavenly deity, or that he was a son of heaven and thus invincible.[7] What emerges from these folk stories is a very powerful man who is a great friend of the weak and poor and immune to enemy attacks. Many of Wei Baqun's younger followers became his admirers after hearing some of these stories.

Wei Baqun played an active role in his deification. His many talents led his peasant followers to believe that he possessed some supernatural power. He was a great composer and singer of folksongs, and was good at martial arts as well as several other sports. He was a charismatic orator and could speak quite a few languages and dialects.[8] Finally, he was a great political and military schemer who was very efficient in mobilizing mass support and manipulating his enemies.

Wei Baqun sometimes would try to awe the villagers with devices he had brought back from other places to convince them of his immense power. Once he gathered a huge crowd of people at the foot of a mountain. He then took something from his pocket and threw it away, and in a moment it exploded, leaving a crater in the earth with soil and pebbles raining down. Wei Baqun told his frightened audience that this was a "Russian bomb" he and an ironsmith had made. The onlookers were shocked, and agreed that the bomb was much more powerful than a rifle and that it should make the local tyrants tremble. One of them remarked that "Elder Brother Ba has visited every corner of the world, has seen everything and knows everything."[9]

Another device Wei Baqun brought back from the cities was a flashlight. He showed it to the Yao people and easily won their devotion.[10]According to one tale, even the more informed town dwellers were daunted by the flashlight. The legend holds that once Wei Baqun and his enemy Du Ba entered a contest to show the people which of the two had the power to order the Lord of Heaven to open his eyes. Du Ba went first and gave his order, but nothing happened. Then Wei Baqun took his turn. As soon as he gave his order, lightning arose from the horizon and it was followed by peals of thunder. Du Ba was overwhelmed and the audience claimed, "Elder Brother Ba is a celestial being!" The lightning came from a long flashlight that Chen Bomin was operating from a distance. Chen also exploded some hand grenades to make the "thunder."[11]

To win the admiration and support of the villagers by using and manipulating their ignorance and backwardness was a common practice among revolutionaries in early twentieth-century China. Peng Pai liked to perform magic for the villagers of Haifeng when he first began his movement, and quite a few leading Communists warned their comrades who worked among the peasants not to show disrespect to the deities of the villagers. If Wei Baqun's purpose in demonstrating these devices was to win the admiration and support of the villagers, then he overshot his goal. Some villagers saw him not just as their leader, but also as their deity.

After Wei Baqun was killed, some local peasants believed that he was not dead, or that he had become a deity. They claimed that he had risen after the murder, that he had evolved into a red fire ball and then ascended to heaven, that he had become a white horse to chase the demons in every corner of the world, that he had turned himself into a blue dragon and then flown to join the Communists in Jiangxi, or that he had become a red divine dog and flown to join some other deity in heaven. The peasants in Dongli believed that after Wei Baqun's body was burned, his followers were able to discover from the ashes "a fresh red heart as big as a bowl."[12] The villagers of Dongli admitted that Wei Baqun was dead and wanted to do whatever it took to preserve his remains and to show due respect to their Red God. Once the Red God Temple was erected, the villagers planted two persimmon trees by the temple because persimmon was Wei Baqun's favorite fruit. Villagers would regularly bring sacrifices to the temple (Fig. 8.1).

FIGURE 8.1 The Red God Temple. Photograph by the author.

As if to show his power as a deity, most of Wei Baqun's direct enemies were hunted down by his comrades and received severe punishments after his death. Wei Ang spent several comfortable years in Liuzhou with his second wife, Chen Dibo, following Wei Baqun's death. After squandering all the money they received from the provincial government, the two moved to a village in Hechi in the late 1930s and made their living by collecting and selling firewood. Not long after they moved to Hechi, Wei Ang was mysteriously murdered. It is believed that the Communists killed him, and some hold that Huang Juping, head of the Donglan Branch of the CCP, was personally involved in ordering the killing. However, there is at least one source claiming that he was actually killed by the Nationalists.[13]

Chen Dibo disappeared after Wei Ang's death, but Wei Baqun's supporters did not forget about her. In 1960, a former follower of Wei Baqun wrote a letter to the head of the provincial public security bureau, urging him to identify and arrest all those involved in the murder of Wei Baqun. The bureau then dispatched two experienced police chiefs to Donglan to investigate the case. The two soon found a valuable informant, Xu Jiayu, who had been an officer in Liao Lei's Seventh Army as well as the magistrate of Donglan from April 1932 to April 1933. He knew all the secrets about the plot against Wei Baqun. The Communists captured Xu in 1950 and he was sentenced to fifteen years in prison. He was still in prison in 1960. Xu told the two police chiefs that Liu Zhi, a captain from the Baise Militia Headquarters and Chen Dibo, were directly involved in Wei Baqun's death. In 1932, during the third extermination campaign, Liu Zhi was dispatched to Donglan to help find Wei Baqun. One of Liu's superiors at the Baise Militia Headquarters was none other than Huang Qi, the commander who put Wei Baqun in prison in Nanning in late 1922 for inciting a group of soldiers to desert.[14] General Huang probably regretted that he had released Wei Baqun ten years earlier, but at the same time he might have felt relieved because he had another opportunity to capture Wei Baqun. Captain Liu discovered Chen Dibo's hiding place and had her arrested. Unable to bear the torture or resist the temptation of the large sum of reward money, Chen agreed to cooperate and helped Captain Liu capture her husband. Liu and Chen then tried to persuade Wei Ang to help kill Wei Baqun. After showing some hesitancy, Wei Ang agreed.

In 1960, the police chiefs discovered a new clue, which led them to Captain Liu's birthplace, a village not far from Baise. In the village, they found Liu's wife, who told them that she had not seen her husband since 1949. She had heard that the captain had become a live-in son-in-law in a mountainous village in the Right River region. The police then sent investigators to all the communes in that area and they were soon able to identify an old porridge seller as the former captain and had him detained.[15]

Chen Dibo was found and arrested shortly after. After Wei Ang was killed, she moved to a village in Rongshui County near Liuzhou and in 1944 married a Miao man. He died four years later, and she remarried in the same village. In the 1950s, she and her new husband moved to the county seat of Rongshui, where they lived by "a stinky creek." Once she was tracked down she confessed to the police that she was in the Fragrant Tea Cave on the early morning of October 19, 1932. She confirmed that Wei Ang was hesitant about killing his uncle, but she pushed him to do it. Both Captain Liu and Chen Dibo were sentenced to death, but before their sentences were approved by higher authorities both died in the Donglan prison.[16]

Although Wei Ang was killed long before the Communist victory in 1949, the Communists had to wait until after 1949 to punish the more powerful traitors. Wei Chaoqun, the battalion commander under Wei Baqun who changed sides in 1931, caused significant damage to the Communist movement in Donglan, and was rewarded with military and political positions by the New Guangxi Clique. In summer 1949, he became the last Nationalist magistrate of Donglan. After the Communists took Donglan he was captured and became one of the fifty-three counter-revolutionaries publicly executed in December 1950.[17]

One of Wei Chaoqun's predecessors as the magistrate of Donglan was Chen Shusen, who had a tortuous relationship with Wei Baqun. Chen followed his sworn brother Wei Baqun into the Guizhou Army in 1916 and spent many years in the armies of Guizhou militarists, the Old Guangxi Clique, the New Guangxi Clique, and Chiang Kai-shek's Nanjing government. In 1922, he played a role in bringing Wei Baqun out of his second imprisonment. In early 1931, while on his way back to Donglan as a battalion commander in Liao Lei's Twenty-first Division, he was ordered to go back to Nanning after Liao Lei discovered his early relations with Wei Baqun. Soon thereafter, Wei Baqun's soldiers accidentally killed Chen's father, which helped Chen to win Liao Lei's trust. The following year, Chen returned to Donglan as a battalion commander and played a significant part in destroying Wei Baqun's movement.[18] In November 1944, Chen became the magistrate of Donglan, and in January 1946 he left Donglan to serve as the deputy commander-in-chief of the militia system of the Baise District. In 1949, only a few days before the Communists took over Donglan, he poisoned himself in a village on the eastern bank of the Red Water River. Chen's three sons all joined the Communist government.[19]

The leaders of local anti-Communist militias, who were Wei Baqun's permanent enemies from 1921 to 1932, received their punishments one after another. Chen Rujin was magistrate of Donglan for five months in 1930 and the commander of the anti-Communist militias in Donglan from 1924 to 1934. He was a ferocious enemy of Wei Baqun during the second and third revolts.

On New Year's Eve in 1934, a group of Wei Baqun's followers found him at his home on the eastern bank of the Red Water River and shot him dead.

His brother, Chen Ruzhen, was one of Wei Baqun's earliest sworn brothers. When Wei Baqun was in the Guizhou Army, Chen was a teacher at Donglan Advanced Elementary School, and Wei sent the radical magazine *New Youth* to Chen at least three times.[20] However, *New Youth* failed to turn Chen into a revolutionary. In 1922, he served as the magistrate of Donglan for two months. After that he worked briefly as the chairman of the county assembly and became a longtime militia leader, which pitted him against Wei Baqun. Although Chen claimed that in 1926 he tried to prevent the Gong Regiment from attacking the peasants and protected Wei Baqun's wife Chen Lanfen and their son (partly because Lanfen was a relative),[21] Wei Baqun felt no gratitude toward him, believing that Chen was involved in the making of the Donglan Massacre. The Communists imprisoned Chen after 1949.

Chen Shusen and Chen Ruzhen were not the only sworn brothers of Wei Baqun who were punished after 1949 for their actions against Wei Baqun. Qin Caiwu, Chen Ruzhen, Huang Hongju, Qin Ruiwu, and Wei Baqun became sworn bothers when they were in elementary school and Wei Baqun was the youngest.[22] Like Chen Ruzhen, Qin Caiwu and Huang Hongju also participated later in the anti-Communist movement. During the extermination campaigns of 1931 and 1932, Qin became the leader of an anti-Communist militia and later wrote a very detailed account of Wei Baqun's revolutions and their suppression. Qin was captured and executed in 1952,[23] and Huang Hongju was also punished after 1949.

Among the fifty-three counter-revolutionaries executed in December 1950 were two other long-time rivals of Wei Baqun from Wuzhuan. One was Liang Xuqiu, the militia leader of Wuzhuan in the early 1930s, who lost two brothers in Wei Baqun's plot to claim the bounty in 1932, and the other was Du Ba's son, Du Bohao.[24]

Two outside enemies of Wei Baqun, Gong Shouyi and Huang Mingyuan, officers in Liu Rifu's army who were involved in directing the Donglan Massacre in 1926, both died brutal death at the hands of the Communists. Huang Mingyuan later became a close follower of Governor Huang Shaohong. In 1934, when Huang Shaohong became the governor of Zhejiang Province, Huang Mingyuan also went to Zhejiang, where he became an official and was later killed by the Communists. Gong Shouyi was later promoted to the position of brigade commander in the army of the New Guangxi Clique. He returned to his home village in Luchuan County in southeastern Guangxi after retiring from the army. In 1953, during the land reform, he was put on trial and then executed by dismemberment.[25]

Huang Shaohong, who was governor of Guangxi from 1925 to 1929 and supported the repression of Wei Baqun's movement during those years, would change sides two or three times. In 1929, he left the New Guangxi Clique and joined Chiang Kai-shek's government. Chiang offered him powerful positions, including the minister of internal affairs and governor of Zhejiang and Hubei Provinces. In 1948, when Chiang Kai-shek and Li Zongren entered another round of political contention, Huang abandoned Chiang and sided with his old boss, Li Zongren. At the same time, Huang became a strong supporter for peace negotiation with the Communists. In 1949, when General Li Zongren became the interim president of the Republic of China, he sent Huang as one of his delegates to negotiate with the Communists for peace. The negotiation failed, but the Communists succeeded in persuading Huang Shaohong to join them, and for that Huang was expelled from the KMT. After the founding of the PRC, Huang was treated as an ally from 1949 to 1957 as if the Communists had completely forgiven him for his entire anti-Communist career. But in 1957, Huang was branded a rightist for criticizing some Communist policies and after that he began to be persecuted for his "historic problems," including his participation in Chiang Kai-shek's purge of the Communists after 1927 and his suppression of Wei Baqun's movement. He killed himself during the Cultural Revolution.

Huang Shouxian, the magistrate of Donglan in 1925 and 1926 who masterminded the Donglan Massacre in early 1926, also managed to turn himself into a Communist ally after 1949. He changed his name to Huang Shaozu and was made a delegate to the Guangxi Political Consultative Conference. At the 1954 Political Consultative Conference, he was allocated to the same discussion group as two former followers of Wei Baqun from Donglan, Qin Liankui and Huang Meilun. Qin had been jailed by Huang in the 1920s and was able to recognize him immediately. He then reported his discovery to Huang Juping, Huang Songjian, Qin Yingji, and Wei Guoqing, who were all Wei Baqun's followers in the 1920s and 1930s and were holding important positions in the government in the 1950s. They confirmed that Delegate Huang Shaozu was indeed Magistrate Huang Shouxian. In 1959, Huang Shaozu was arrested by the police and taken back to Donglan where he was put on trial and sentenced to death.[26] For Wei Guoqing, the top leader of Guangxi at that time, this was also a personal revenge. Huang had killed Wei's father and uncle in early 1926.[27] It is not clear why the victors waited five years before they arrested Huang Shaozu. Maybe it was because Huang Shaozu was indeed Huang Shaohong's relative. Before 1957, Huang Shaohong was treated as a dignitary and it would have been difficult for the Donglan Communists to bring a charge against his uncle. After Huang Shaohong's downfall in 1957 it became safe and easy to deal with Huang Shaozu.

Liao Lei, the commander-in-chief of the New Guangxi Clique troops that enforced the extermination campaigns in the Right River region in 1931 and 1932, was one of the very few enemies of Wei Baqun who escaped punishment. In 1934, Liao Lei fought the Communists again in northern Guangxi, when the

Communists were passing through Guangxi during their Long March. After the outbreak of the war against Japan in 1937, Liao and his troops were dispatched to Anhui Province to fight the Japanese, and in 1938 he became the governor of Anhui. In that position he developed a close working relationship with the Communist leaders of the New Fourth Army, one of whom was Zhang Yunyi, the former commander in chief of the Seventh Red Army. Zhang was Liao's teacher at Baoding Military Academy and in the late 1930s was the chief of staff of the Communist New Fourth Army. Liao Lei even invited Zhang to teach the officers of his Guangxi army about guerrilla warfare. Within the New Guangxi Clique, Liao was a strong supporter of the Second United Front, and he even allowed some Communists to work in his government and army. Anhui under Liao Lei was described as "the anti-Japanese model province." When he died in Anhui in 1939, Communist dignitaries such as Zhou Enlai, Ye Jianying, Peng Dehuai, Ye Ting, and others all presented beautiful eulogies.[28] It is not certain whether Liao Lei ever regretted his brutal extermination of Wei Baqun and other Communists in Donglan, and whether or not his experience in Donglan had anything to do with the change of his attitude toward the Communists during the war against Japan.

Liao Lei's superior, Bai Chongxi, also escaped punishment. In 1949, after the troops of the New Guangxi Clique were demolished by the Communists in Guangxi and southern China, Bai Chongxi fled to Taiwan with Chiang Kai-shek. After 1949, about 90,000 followers of Bai Chongxi remained in the mountains of Guangxi fighting the Communists.[29] They were now branded bandits by the Communists, and by 1952 they had all been killed or captured. Bai Chongxi later dictated a memoir in which he did not even mention Wei Baqun. Bai died of illness in Taiwan in 1966.

Like Bai Chongxi, the other two top leaders of the New Guangxi Clique, Li Zongren and Huang Xuchu, suffered no serious retributions after 1949 for their hostility toward Wei Baqun and his movement. Li refused to join Chiang Kai-shek in Taiwan, but exiled himself to the United States in 1949. In 1965, he returned to Mainland China. For that act he was treated as a great patriot by his former enemies and spent four comfortable years in Beijing before cancer took his life in 1969. Huang Xuchu fled to Hong Kong in 1949 and refused to move to either Taiwan or Mainland China. He died in Hong Kong in 1975. It is not certain whether or not he was in close contact with Wei Baqun's other erstwhile enemy, Huang Qi. In 1945, Huang Qi was the magistrate of a county in western Guangxi when he encouraged the local peasants to grow opium. When his opium smuggling business was later exposed, Governor Huang Xuchu pretended that he would punish Huang Qi, but secretly advised him to escape. Huang Qi fled to Hong Kong that year and died there in 1970.[30]

Just as many deities are imageless, Wei Baqun left no photos of himself, which contributed to his mysterious aura. Wei Baqun visited many cities in his lifetime and should have taken some photos, but none survived. Possibly he deliberately destroyed them to protect himself after becoming a revolutionary, but it is also likely that his enemies had unintentionally destroyed his photos by burning down his house at least twice. Ya Guohua, a follower of Wei Baqun, recalled that shortly before his death Wei Bequn gave Ya a photo to keep. It was a photo of Wei Baqun's torso, and it is obvious that Wei Baqun did not mean to leave that photo for Ya, but wanted Ya to keep it and then hand it to his other comrades. After 1949, a museum in Nanning acquired the photo, but shortly thereafter lost it.[31]

Since then, the PRC government has made great efforts to search for photos of Wei Baqun, and so far two possible photos have been discovered, but neither has been verified. The first was found in 1984 by the Archives of Yongning County near Nanning. The photo was taken in Longzhou in 1929, and it shows two men. One of the two was Huang Xiaopeng, a native of Yongning who served as the magistrate of Longzhou County from July to October 1929. The other man was taller than Huang Xiaopeng and was believed to be Wei Baqun. Wei and Huang were good friends and fellow revolutionaries, and frequently visited each other at that time. Huang was not a Communist, but was a close associate of Yu Zuobai and a strong supporter of the peasant movement. He was killed in November 1929 by some local enemies.[32] The photo was shown to more than thirty people who were familiar with Wei Baqun. Among these people, thirteen confirmed that the tall man in the photo was Wei Baqun. When Wei Baqun's two sisters saw the photo, they both burst into tears and pronounced that it was, without a doubt, Wei Baqun. So did Wei Baqun's bodyguard. Fourteen people thought the man looked somewhat like Wei Baqun, but could not confirm. Five people, including Wei Baqun's former secretary, were certain that the tall man was not Wei Baqun. The photo was then taken to Beijing and presented to Deng Xiaoping, and Deng's response was that the man looked somewhat like Wei Baqun, but he could not confirm. He added that Wei Baqun did not travel to Longzhou in 1929. Although most of those who had been close to Wei Baqun thought that the man in the photo looked similar to Wei Baqun, the government has not accepted the photo as Wei Baqun's official image.[33]

In 2009, a local historian in Guangxi discovered another photo at the former residence of Liang Lieya in Nanning's suburb. It is a group photo showing more than one hundred people and it was taken on November 26, 1921 during Sun Yat-sen's visit to Nanning. The caption says that among the large group shown in the photo are dignitaries like Sun Yat-sen, Ma Junwu, Hu Hanmin, Chen Jiongming, and Wei Baqun. Liang was an active member of the Association for Reforming Guangxi and was serving as the magistrate of Yongning County at that time. He was also Wei Baqun's close friend.[34] Although some local people were certain that a bearded man in the photo was

Wei Baqun, it has yet to be verified by the government. The problem is that there were too many people in the photo and it is not easy to see clearly the facial features of each person. Besides, by 2009 almost all of those close to Wei Baqun had died, and therefore no one could confirm whether or not the bearded man was indeed Wei Baqun.

In verifying both photos, the only physical evidence available to researchers was Wei Baqun's skull. The search for Wei Baqun's skull was much more successful than that for his photo. An account written in the 1930s by Qin Caiwu, Wei Baqun's former sworn brother who later became his enemy, held that Wei Baqun's skull was buried in Beishan Park in Wuzhou City. A local newspaper also carried a report about when and where the skull was buried. It took the PRC government more than ten years to verify the validity of the accounts and to identify the exact location of the skull. The excavation began on December 12, 1961, and the next morning the excavators discovered a fish tank with a skull inside. Surgeons and forensic experts in Nanning concluded that the skull showed a square face, and it belonged to a man in his thirties. They also discovered a golden tooth and two bullet holes, confirming that it was indeed Wei Baqun's skull.[35] The skull was later sent to Beijing, a place Wei Baqun never visited.

Becoming a Perfect Communist

Some of Wei Baqun's Communist comrades saw him as a problematic party member when he was alive, citing his supposed past connections with the anarchists, his Robin Hood-style revolt and revolution, his tolerance and promotion of excessive violence, his deity-like status among the peasants, and his reliance on personal relationships. After his death, his comrades stopped talking about his flaws. Instead, they unanimously portrayed him as a perfect Communist. Although Wei Baqun was not the first Communist in the Right River region, and in his lifetime he never served as the number one leader of the Right River branch of the CCP, in death he was transformed into the most prestigious Communist of the entire Right River region.

Three groups of people have played the most important part in creating the eulogistic image of Wei Baqun. The first group consisted of the Communists from the outside, including top Communist leaders such as Mao Zedong and Zhou Enlai, who never met Wei Baqun but were familiar with his deeds. Although Mao Zedong never mentioned Wei Baqun in his formal writings, he liked to talk about Wei Baqun whenever he came across a native of Guangxi, whether a bodyguard from Du'an, an artist from eastern Guangxi, or high-ranking officials like Wei Guoqing, Qin Yingji, Xie Fumin, and Huang Juping. Zhou Enlai also made comments about Wei Baqun on various occasions, and he was one of the first to compare Wei Baqun to Fang Zhimin of Jiangxi and Peng Pai of Guangdong. In 1981, on the occasion of celebrating the sixtieth anniversary of the CCP, Hu Yaobang, then general secretary of the CCP, compared Wei Baqun to Fang Zhimin, Liu Zhidan, Huang Gonglue, and Xu Jishen, and described them as early commanders of the Communist army who dedicated their lives to the party and the nation, and who should be forever remembered.[36]

Those outsiders who worked with Wei Baqun played a more concrete role in promoting him as a perfect Communist. Some of them perhaps felt grateful to Wei Baqun for his hospitality, and guilty for not leaving more troops and weapons for Wei Baqun, for not taking him along in late 1930, or for not returning to the Right River region sooner to help rescue him and his movement. After writing his first eulogy for Wei Baqun in 1962, Deng Xiaoping wrote a second one in 1981 to mourn the deaths of Li Mingrui, Wei Baqun, and others. During a visit to Guilin in 1953, Zhang Yunyi, the former commander-in-chief of the Seventh Red Army, bitterly commented that "if Comrade Wei Baqun were still alive, he could definitely make greater contributions to the party and the people." In 1957, he handwrote the name of the Donglan Cemetery of Revolutionary Martyrs, which was the new home to Wei Baqun's remains. In an article about the Baise Uprising written in the late 1950s, Zhang describes Wei Baqun as an outstanding people's leader of the Right River region who made contributions of historical significance. In 1959, Zhang wrote a preface for a biography of Wei Baqun, in which he offered more praise. On the Qingming Festival of 1961, Zhang made a long journey from Beijing to Donglan to pay tribute to Wei Baqun's tomb. He told the local officials that Wei Baqun was a national hero, the pride of Guangxi, and an outstanding son of the party who should never be forgotten. The following year he wrote a long eulogy for Wei Baqun, which was as extolling as that of Deng Xiaoping. In it Zhang described Wei Baqun as a model for all Communists, revolutionary soldiers and all other people, and praised him for his utmost loyalty to the party, his deep love for the people, as well as his bravery, persistence, and other qualities.[37]

Mo Wenhua and Ye Jizhuang, two mid-ranking officers in the Seventh Red Army, also wrote articles and books to exalt Wei Baqun. Mo recalled that when he first learned about Wei Baqun's death and the collapse of the Right River Communist movement from some Guangxi soldiers captured by the Red Army in Jiangxi, he regretted that he had not been able to fight alongside Wei Baqun and protect him. Mo later became the first mayor of Nanning after 1949. He remembered that when he reentered Nanning from its northern gate as a People's Liberation Army (PLA) commander in late 1949, it immediately occurred to him that it was on that same gate that Wei Baqun's severed head was hung on display in late 1932, and he imagined that Elder Brother Ba was now smiling while watching his comrades taking the city.[38] Ye praised Wei Baqun for his determination and his close relations with the people, as well as his contributions to the expansion of the Seventh Red Army and the founding of the Right River Revolutionary Base Area.[39]

Native supporters of Wei Baqun from Donglan and the Right River region formed the second group that have contributed greatly to promoting Wei Baqun as a model Communist. Some of these native supporters left the Right River region in 1930 with the main force of the Seventh Red Army, and others stayed with Wei Baqun and continued to work in the area after his death. Understandably, many of them were more familiar with Wei Baqun's activities than the outsiders, and together they provided important information about Wei Baqun's revolutionary career and also played their part to secure Wei Baqun's eventual legacy. Xie Fumin, a peasant movement activist from Fengyi who left home with the main force of the Seventh Red Army in 1930, was the author of one of the first biographies of Wei Baqun, which collected many of the popular stories about Wei Baqun and was published in Beijing in 1958. In 1978, a publishing house in Shanghai brought out a two-volume, illustrated book based on Xie's biography and as many as 500,000 copies were printed and sold.[40] Joining Xie in lauding Wei Baqun were Wei Jie, Qin Yingji, Wei Guoqing, and Lu Xiuxuan. All were natives of Donglan who joined Wei Baqun's revolution in the 1920s and left with the Seventh Red Army in 1930 when they were still teenagers. They all became important leaders after 1949 and all wrote articles to commemorate their Elder Brother Ba. Huang Songjian and Huang Juping, the two top leaders of the Communist movement in the Right River region after Wei Baqun's death, also held important positions after 1949 and were both prolific writers about Wei Baqun's greatness. No matter how powerful they became, these native followers of Wei Baqun would never forget the man who brought them into the revolution.

On the occasion of the thirtieth anniversary of Wei Baqun's death, his former comrades put together a collection of articles about his revolutionary activities and achievements. For some reason, these articles were not published until 1979. On the fiftieth anniversary of Wei Baqun's death, the Donglan county government held a memorial service in front of his tomb. Some of his former followers, his two sisters, and a sister-in-law attended the service, and Wei Guoqing, Qin Yingji, Huang Songjian, and several other Donglan revolutionaries wrote articles for leading journals and newspapers to honor him.[41] Wei Guoqing was a distant relative of Wei Baqun's, and in 1982 he was the director of the political department of the PLA, and Qin Yingji was the governor of Guangxi at that time.

On February 6, 1994, which was Wei Baqun's one hundreth birthday, *the Guangxi Daily* published a long article to honor him. The author was Huang Rong, a graduate of the third class of Donglan Peasant Movement Institute who became an official in the provincial government after 1949. The local and nonlocal leaders were unanimous in praising Wei Baqun for allowing his best troops to be incorporated into the main force of the Seventh Red Army in late 1930, and for sacrificing his entire family for the revolution. Although most sources show that in late 1930 it was the outside Communists who ordered that most of the officers and soldiers of Wei Baqun's Third Column be reorganized into the main force of the Seventh Red Army, some of Wei Baqun's local followers later argued that it was Wei Baqun who voluntarily offered his troops.[42]

During the Cultural Revolution, when Wei Baqun's former comrades Peng Pai, Deng Xiaoping, and many other living and dead revolutionaries became targets of the Red Guards, there was some doubt about Wei Baqun's legacy. In Donglan, nearly 250 former Red Army soldiers and underground Communists were branded traitors, and these even included Wei Baqun's close friend Huang Daquan, whose name was removed from the list of revolutionary martyrs. Wei Baqun's sister-in-law Huang Meilun was demoted in 1967 and was not rehabilitated until 1979.[43] Wei Baqun's tomb was closed to the public for several years, but Wei Baqun was never openly attacked. Part of the reason might be that Wei Baqun's follower, Wei Guoqing, managed to maintain his tight control over Guangxi during that chaotic decade.

In addition to senior revolutionaries who have provided official appraisals and eyewitness accounts of Wei Baqun's greatness, local historians have formed the third group that has participated actively in creating an image of Wei Baqun as a perfect Communist. Particularly vigorous are the historians affiliated with the various levels of the offices of CCP history in Guangxi. Numerous biographies of Wei Baqun have been published, and even more numerous articles have appeared in local and national journals. Most recently, on the occasion of Wei Baqun's 115th birthday, a symposium on the spirit of Wei Baqun was held in Donglan. Officials and scholars believe that the most striking features of Wei Baqun's spirit are his loyalty to the party, the people, and the truth, his perseverance and selflessness, and his belief that the interests of the nation should be put above local interests.[44] In addition to the "Baqun spirit," some Guangxi scholars and officials have recently advocated the study of the Baqun thought and the Baqun personality.[45] To help promote Wei Baqun as a great Communist revolutionary, some local historians have been reluctant to admit that Wei Baqun was from a landlord family or that Wei Baqun was not an officially recognized Communist prior to his third revolt.

To make up for a real photo of Wei Baqun, artists in China have created quite a few portraits based on descriptions of his physical features provided by his relatives, comrades, and friends. The first official portrait of Wei Baqun was created by a group of artists in 1958, and displayed at the assembly celebrating the founding of the Guangxi Zhuang Autonomous Region. However, Wei Baqun's relatives and comrades thought that the portrait was not "real" enough. It was later revised several times, but was still not satisfactory. In 1978 and 1979, the Beijing Film Studio produced a feature film about Wei Baqun. In 1981 and 1983, two illustrated books about Wei Baqun were published in Shanghai and Nanning, respectively. In the 1990s, a TV series about Wei Baqun was produced, and most recently a second TV series about the Seventh Red Army was released in 2010. These provided new images of Wei Baqun, but of course none of these can be more real than the 1958 portrait. In 2002, China's state post bureau issued five stamps featuring five early revolutionaries, including Wei Baqun. The portrait of Wei Baqun on the stamp differs markedly from the 1958 portrait. The new portrait was based on the old portrait and the photo of Wei Baqun's severed head, but to the public it is still not a satisfactory one (Fig. 8.2).[46]

In addition to books, articles, films, TV programs, stamps, and paintings honoring Wei Baqun, the government has built numerous memorials and erected many statues of Wei Baqun in places where Wei Baqun had worked and lived. As manifestations of what Paul Cohen has described as "local boosterism,"[47] these memorials and monuments serve to confirm Wei Baqun's role as a perfect Communist, and, more importantly, as a local Zhuang Communist who made great contributions to the national revolutionary movement. The number of these memorials is testament to the importance of Wei Baqun's legacy as a revolutionary who helped unify the Zhuang and the Han and integrate frontier Donglan with the nation.

FIGURE 8.2 Left: The 1958 Portrait of Wei Baqun. Photograph from *People's Daily*, July 21, 2009. Middle: Statue of Wei Baqun. Memorial Hall of the Baise Uprising. Photograph by the author. Right: Wei Baqun Memorial Stamp. Photograph from State Post Bureau of the PRC, 2002.

Wei Baqun's family residence in Dongli was burned down by his enemies in 1926, and the new house he built on another location was destroyed in 1931. After 1949, the Donglan county government rebuilt the second house, which stands next to the Red God Temple. It was used by Baqun Elementary School as classrooms and offices for nearly forty years. In 1987, the school relocated and the residence was turned into a memorial open to the public. In front of the memorial was a long line of tombs for Wei Baqun's seventeen relatives. In addition to Baqun Elementary School, several other local landmarks and institutes were named after him. These included a reservoir in Wuzhuan and a normal school at the county seat.[48]

The Fragrant Tea Cave, which was part of Donglan in 1932, belongs to the Bama Yao Autonomous County today. The county government of Bama has built many layers of stone steps leading to the cave from the nearest paved road and by the steps are numerous stone tablets carved with Wei Baqun's teachings. In front of the cave stands a screen-like wall inscribed with Chen Hongtao's eulogy for Wei Baqun. Above the eulogy are a few characters affirming that "Wei Baqun's Spirit Will Shine Forever!" Behind the wall, and by the entrance to the cave, sits a white statue of Wei Baqun, and there are now thirty-eight steps leading from the entrance to the bottom of the cave, with each step symbolizing one year of Wei Baqun's life.

The Beidi Cave, where Wei Baqun held the first class of Donglan Peasant Movement Institute in 1925, was renamed the Lenin Cave in 1930 by Zhang Yunyi. It was designated a provincial key cultural site in 1963 and turned into a memorial in 1987.

At the town of Wuzhuan, the Tower of the Literary Star, which had served as the headquarters of the peasant association of Wuzhuan, the Seventh Red Army, as well as the residence of Wei Baqun, Deng Xiaoping, and other leaders, was also designated a provincial key cultural site in 1963. It was renovated in 1974 and open to the public in 1978. In 1995, it became an official site for patriotic education. The tower once also served as the headquarters of the anti-Communist troops and militias, and it was above the entrance to the tower that Wei Baqun's head was first hung for public display on the morning of October 19, 1932.

In 1950, the provincial government led by Zhang Yunyi ordered that Wei Baqun's tomb be rebuilt with government funds. As a result, Wei Baqun's charred remains were moved to the county seat and reburied on the campus of Donglan High School. The Red God Temple remained a shrine after the remains were moved out. In 1956, at a meeting of the People's Congress of Guangxi, the two delegates from Donglan, including Wei Baqun's sister-in-law Huang Meilun, proposed that the government build a cemetery for Wei Baqun. The provincial government accepted the proposal and decided to construct the Donglan Cemetery of Revolutionary Martyrs on a hill in the eastern part of the county seat. Wei Baqun's remains were moved again from Donglan High School to the cemetery. A stele inscribed with a brief biography of Wei Baqun was erected on the right side of his new tomb, and it lists the important positions Wei Baqun had held during his lifetime and concludes by saying that "he died a glorious death at the hands of a traitor on October 19, 1932."

Not far from Wei Baqun's new tomb in the cemetery is a memorial hall dedicated to all the revolutionary martyrs of Donglan and a monument honoring the more than thirty PLA soldiers killed in 1949 in the last battle between the Communists and Nationalists in Donglan. These soldiers were from places as far away as Hunan, Sichuan, Jiangxi, Henan, Shanxi, and Gansu.[49] In a way, they died fighting for Wei Baqun's cause and were paying back their debt to revolutionaries from Donglan who had fought and died in other parts of China as well as to the Donglan fighters left behind by the main force of the Seventh Red Army in late 1930. Wei Baqun was thus moved from frontier Dongli to the political center of Donglan and was moved away from his relatives and put among fellow revolutionaries.

The cemetery cum park occupies about two thousand mu of land and also consists of an arch, a pavilion, and other structures. It was first opened to the public during the Spring Festival of 1958 and was designated a key cultural preservation unit of the province in 1963. It has been considered one of the three most important revolutionary memorials in Guangxi (Fig. 8.3).[50]

Figure 8.3 Wei Baqun's Tomb in the Donglan Cemetery for Revolutionary Martyrs. Photograph by the author.

In 2009, on the occasion of Wei Baqun's 115th birthday, a new memorial hall (Fig. 8.4) was built to the northern side of his tomb to honor him. It is a huge multi-story structure that houses seven large rooms. Each room is devoted to exhibitions about one particular period or aspect of Wei Baqun's life. In front of the memorial hall is the large Baqun Square. On the western side of the square stand seventeen bronze statues, including Wei Baqun's own statue and those of his comrades and followers such as Zhang Yunyi, Chen Hongtao, Wei Guoqing, and Huang Songjian. The entire structure is much more magnificent than the Red God Temple, showing the huge gap between the grandeur of state worship and the modesty of folk worship. Another important site in the county seat is the campus of Donglan Workers Elementary School, which was the cradle of young revolutionaries when the county seat was under the control of Wei Baqun in 1929 and 1930.[51] The headquarters of the Third Column of the Seventh Red Army was also based there. The school is still there today and is still called the Workers Elementary School (Fig. 8.5).

Further from home, in Baise, the office of the former Guangdong Chamber of Commerce, which consists of a cluster of traditional style two-story wooden houses, is now a memorial honoring the Baise Uprising. Wei Baqun lived there briefly during the uprising. In 1961, a memorial hall dedicated to the Baise Uprising was built in the eastern suburb of Baise, and was replaced by a fancier and much larger memorial hall constructed recently. The new

FIGURE 8.4 The Memorial Hall of Wei Baqun. Photograph by the author.

FIGURE 8.5 The County Seat of Donglan Today. Photograph by the author.

structure sits on the bank of the Right River and contains a special exhibition about the Donglan peasant movement. It has been designated a national key site for patriotic education.

In the town of Jinchengjiang, which is the capital of Hechi Prefecture, is a statue of Wei Baqun in a park near the downtown area; The park occupies the highest point in the city. In the old town of Hechi near Jinchengjiang is a modest yellow building where the headquarters of the Seventh Red Army was based in October and November 1930. It was here that the leaders decided that Wei Baqun and Chen Hongtao would stay in the Right River region while most of their soldiers would leave with the main force. It was near that building that Wei Baqun said goodbye to his comrades who were to embark on their long journey to Jiangxi. After 1949, the owner of the building accidentally discovered, when renovating the house, dozens of slogans left on the walls by the Seventh Red Army; These slogans remain there today.

In 1984, to commemorate the fifty-fifth anniversary of the Baise Uprising, a memorial honoring Li Mingrui and Wei Baqun was constructed near the beautiful Southern Lake in downtown Nanning, the capital of the Guangxi Zhuang Autonomous Region. The memorial consists of an exhibition hall and a pillar with statues of the two men. The pillar carries the inscriptions of Deng Xiaoping's handwritten eulogy, which reads "To the Memory of Li Mingrui, Wei Baqun and Other Comrades! Long Live the Revolutionary Martyrs!" (Fig. 8.6). The memorial is a provincial key site for patriotic education as well as one of twenty-seven national bases for education about ethnic solidarity. The political message is strong and clear: Li Mingrui was a Han from southern

FIGURE 8.6 A Statue at the Donglan Cemetery of Revolutionary Martyrs. Photograph by the author.

Guangxi, and Wei Baqun a Zhuang from northern Guangxi. They were united by Communism and both played significant roles in the Baise Uprising and the Communist revolution in Guangxi and China. They thus set good examples for their Han and Zhuang offspring to follow. It is understandable that Deng Xiaoping and the other leaders of the Baise Uprising should feel deeply grateful to Li Mingrui and Wei Baqun, because most of the officers and soldiers who formed the Seventh Red Army were former subordinates of either Li Mingrui or Wei Baqun. It would have been nearly impossible to stage the Baise Uprising without the support of these two Guangxi natives.

Also in 1984, another memorial for Wei Baqun was erected at Zhongshan (Sun Yat-sen) Park in the city of Wuzhou. It is a two-story building that houses exhibitions about Wei Baqun's activities and it is near the site where Wei Baqun's skull was excavated in the early 1960s. In his afterlife, Wei Baqun has continued to be closely affiliated with Sun Yat-sen.

These memorials, along with all the media coverage, political and scholarly writings, as well as art and literary works, helped keep Wei Baqun on the minds of many people as a great revolutionary and national hero. In 2009, as part of the celebration for the sixtieth birthday of the PRC, eleven central government agencies in Beijing jointly called for the election of one hundred heroes who had made great contributions to the founding of the PRC, and Wei Baqun was elected as one of them. He was the only one from Guangxi, the only Zhuang and one of about ten non-Han heroes on the list. Li Mingrui, Wei Baqun's superior in the Seventh Red Army, was also a candidate, but failed to get elected. When Wei Baqun was a student at Donglan Advanced Elementary School, he often told his friends, "if I cannot leave a good name for a hundred generations, I'll try to go down in history as a byword of infamy."[52] He obviously achieved his goal. Both his enemies and comrades would agree that Wei Baqun was no ordinary person.

Becoming a Zhuang Who Was Not a Han

In Wei Baqun's time, most Zhuang people in Donglan considered themselves both Zhuang and Han. The local people referred to the Zhuang as early Han, and the other Han as later Han.[53] Many outsiders agreed that the Zhuang and the Han were the same. Bai Chongxi claimed that there were no differences between the Zhuang and Han and was very critical of the PRC government for "creating" the minority group Zhuang. Former governor Huang Shaohong openly opposed the creation of the Guangxi Zhuang Autonomous Region in the 1950s and suffered severe persecution partly because of that. In the Republican era, most Nationalists saw the Zhuang as a subgroup of the Han. A high school geography teacher from Shanghai who visited Donglan in 1933 reported that Han and Yao were the only two ethnic groups he found in Donglan and that the Han could be divided into two groups: Turen, or descendants of immigrants from northern China who arrived in Donglan during the Song; and Keren, offspring of immigrants from neighboring provinces who moved into Donglan during the Qing. He estimated that among Donglan's total population of about 93,000 in 1933, there were several thousand Yao, about 10, 000 Keren, and the rest were Turen. Some Western scholars also concur that the Zhuang were indistinguishable from the Han and some of them agree with Bai Chongxi that the Zhuang minority was an artificial construct of the PRC government.[54]

Wei Baqun and his followers did not have a strong Zhuang minority identity. They did not feel that they were very different from the Han residents of Donglan, or that they were a minority group as opposed to the majority Han. A group of scholars and officials visiting the Western Mountains in the early 1950s on behalf of the PRC government reported that the Zhuang in that area all considered themselves Han.[55] To Wei Baqun and his supporters, the true minority group in Donglan was the Yao, and they adopted many measures to promote the rights of the Yao and improve their educational levels and living conditions.

Communist accounts written during the Republican era also listed the Yao and the Han as the only two major ethnic groups in the Right River region. The writers all considered the Zhuang and the Han as one group. For example, Lei Jingtian reported in 1945 that in the Right River region the Yao and the Han lived together, but did not mention the Zhuang. He further commented that whereas in the past the local Han people all used derogatory terms to refer to the Yao, Wei Baqun called them "Yao friends," and thus won them over.[56] Lei Jingtian was a Han from suburban Nanning and he obviously believed that Wei Baqun was also a Han.

Official documents issued by various levels of Communist authorities frequently raised the ethnic issue in the Right River region, but they all focused on the Yao and none of them ever listed the Zhuang as a minority group. To both the local and outside Communists, in the Right River region, ethnic equality meant equality between the Han and the Yao, and Zhuang were considered part of the Han. One of the documents called for the Communists to encourage the Yao to revolt against the Han ruling class.[57] In much of the Right River region, there was no such a thing as a Han ruling class if the Zhuang were not considered Han.

The founding of the PRC in 1949 caused the revival of the Zhuang identity. If the prejudice and discrimination against non-Han groups had prompted many Zhuang to hide or to deliberately forget about their minority identities and to claim Han identity, the new policy of ethnic equality motivated many of those who had described themselves as "Han who speak the local dialect (Zhuang)" to reclaim their Zhuang identity. When the Communists first called on the people to report their ethnic identity, only several hundred thousand residents of Guangxi declared that they were Zhuang. In 1952, the number of people who identified themselves as Zhuang reached five to six million. When the first official census was taken in June 1953, as many as 6.6 million people registered themselves as Zhuang, nearly all living in Guangxi.[58] In 1952, three years after they took over Guangxi, the Communists created the Western Guangxi Zhuang Autonomous Region, a prefectural-level government that covered the areas along the Left River, the Right River and the Red Water River. Donglan became part of this autonomous region, and Qin Yingji, a former follower of Wei Baqun's from Donglan, became the head of its government. The official ethnic identification began in 1953 and most Zhuang speakers were identified as Zhuang, and these included most residents in Donglan and the Right River region.

More than twenty years after his death, Wei Baqun was formally identified as a Zhuang who was not a Han, as opposed to a Zhuang who was also a Han. Naturally, he was also immediately recognized as the most prominent Zhuang revolutionary. In the PRC era it became beneficial and convenient for both the central government and the local people to promote Wei Baqun as a symbol of the Zhuang people. For the central government, Wei Baqun's movement shows that many Zhuang joined the Communist movement as early as the 1920s, and the unity between the Han and the Zhuang, which has been sustained by Communism, is firm and strong. Wei Baqun is thus an icon who links the Zhuang to Communism, the Han revolutionaries, and the PRC. For the local people, Wei Baqun's career demonstrates clearly what an illustrious contribution the Zhuang people have made to the founding of the new state. They can legitimately claim that Wei Baqun is the solid proof that as the largest minority group in China the Zhuang have made greater contributions to the Communist victory than most if not all other minority groups.

The revival of the Zhuang identity led some local scholars to emphasize Wei Baqun's connections with the Zhuang culture and community. For instance, Huang Xianfan, one of the most well-known Zhuang historians from Guangxi, argues that Wei Baqun was not just a Communist, but also a successor to a long list of Zhuang rebels and revolutionaries in the past, including Nong Zhigao and the Taiping leader, Shi Dakai. He believes that Wei Baqun had a strong Zhuang identity and that the Zhuang culture and tradition was an important factor in the making of Wei Baqun the Communist revolutionary. Specifically, he holds that Wei Baqun's guerrilla strategy and other military tactics, his policies toward the Yao, his methods of organization and mobilization, his way of treating soldiers, his lifestyle, as well as his wisdom and bravery were all developed under the strong influence of Zhuang culture and tradition.[59]

After 1949, many of the preferential policies Wei Baqun had created for the Yao became applicable to the Zhuang as well. In 1958, Guangxi Province was turned into the Guangxi Zhuang Autonomous Region, and the leaders chose December 11, a date loaded with political importance for Guangxi, as the official birthday of the autonomous region. It was on December 11, 1929 that the Baise Uprising broke out and the Seventh Red Army came into being. Exactly twenty years later, on December 11, 1949, the PLA troops marched to the Sino-Vietnamese border and stormed the Zhennan Fortress, marking their takeover of the entire Guangxi Province. In the government of the autonomous region, former followers of Wei Baqun from Donglan and the Right River region began to play important roles.

Zhuang leaders such as Cen Yuying, Cen Chunxuan and Lu Rongting had held powerful provincial and national positions during the late Qing and early Republican era, but from 1925 to 1955 the Han dominated the governments of Guangxi. The New Guangxi Clique that ruled the province from 1925 to 1949 was formed by two groups of Han Chinese. One consisted of Cantonese speakers from southeast Guangxi, particularly Rong County, and their leader was Huang Shaohong before 1929 and Huang Xuchu after 1929; the other was a group of Mandarin speakers from northeastern Guangxi, and their leaders were Li Zongren and Bai Chongxi. Bai Chongxi, although a Hui, preferred to describe himself as a Han who followed Islam.

After 1949, the Han Communists of the former Seventh Red Army initially ruled Guangxi. Zhang Yunyi became both the secretary of the Guangxi branch of the CCP and the governor of Guangxi in 1949. Lei Jingtian returned to Guangxi in late 1949 to take the position of vice governor.[60] Zhang's former subordinates in the Seventh Red Army, Chen Manyuan and Mo Wenhua, also became his important assistants. Lei, Chen, and Mo were all natives of Guangxi, but they were all Han from the more advanced regions of Guangxi. Qin Yingji, a Donglan native and a young follower of Wei Baqun who left home with Zhang Yunyi in 1930, was transferred from Hebei to Guangxi in late 1949 and appointed police chief of the province, becoming the highest-ranking Zhuang official in Guangxi at that time.

By mid-1955, however, the four Han officials (Zhang Yunyi, Lei Jingtian, Chen Manyuan, and Mo Wenhua), had lost their control over Guangxi. Part of the reason was that they failed to eliminate banditry in Guangxi as early as Mao Zedong had demanded. It is interesting to note that these Nationalist bandits now adopted many of the tactics that Wei Baqun had used. For instance, they formed small groups of guerrilla fighters and made efficient use of the mountains and caves. On the other hand, in fighting the Nationalist bandits the Communist government adopted tactics very similar to those used by the New Guangxi Clique in its extermination campaigns against Wei Baqun. The Communist government offered amnesty to the soldiers who chose to surrender, but was much less lenient toward the top commanders. Communist troops would sometimes besiege the stone mountains, making it difficult for the Nationalists to acquire supplies, and many of them were starved to death in the caves.[61]

The Zhuang revolutionary elites began to dominate the provincial government in the mid-1950s. In 1952, Qin Yingji was promoted to the position of vice governor. In 1955, General Wei Guoqing became the governor of Guangxi and he remained the actual ruler of the province during the next twenty years. In the same year, he became the highest-ranking officer in the PLA among all the soldiers and officers from Donglan who joined the Red Army in 1929 and 1930. He played an important role in the creation of the Guangxi Zhuang Autonomous Region in 1958.[62] Serving under Wei Guoqing in the government and party apparatus of Guangxi were several other former followers of Wei Baqun from Donglan and the Right River region. After Wei Guoqing was transferred to Guangzhou in 1975 and Beijing a few years later, Qin Yingji served as governor from 1979 to 1984. These two natives of Donglan ruled Guangxi for about thirty years. Largely thanks to Wei Baqun, the Zhuang revolutionary elite from the periphery emerged as a powerful group in the Guangxi Zhuang Autonomous Region during the PRC era, and their power and influence did not begin to decline until the 1980s.

Within Donglan, Wei Baqun's long time follower Huang Juping became the leader of the county government immediately after the 1949 takeover. In 1955, veteran revolutionary Wei Jingyi returned to Donglan to serve successively as deputy magistrate, magistrate, and deputy party secretary of the county. He joined the Donglan Peasant Self Defense Army in 1929, left for Jiangxi in late 1930, and did not return to Donglan until 1950. Wei remained an important leader of the county until his death in 1960,[63] and some other followers of Wei Baqun, including his sister-in-law Huang Meilun, would continue to serve in the county government until the 1980s.

The same policy of ethnic equality, while granting the Zhuang minority equal status and special treatment, led to the rearrangement of Donglan's borders. In 1953, the provincial government eliminated Wangang County, possibly because it was created by the Nationalists with an anti-Communist purpose. The four districts of Wangang adjacent to Donglan were incorporated into Donglan. Only three years later, in order to show political equality between the Yao, the Han, and the Zhuang, the provincial government created the Bama Yao Autonomous County, which ruled roughly the same territory of former Wangang County. A large part of the Western Mountains, situated so close to Dongli and Wuzhuan and had played such an important role in Wei Baqun's revolution, became part of the new autonomous county for the obvious reason that the Yao formed the majority of the population in that region. In the south, Donglan lost some territory to Du'an and Dahua Yao Autonomous Counties.

In his lifetime, Wei Baqun often played a confusing, conflicting, and controversial role between his frontier community and the various centers of the Chinese nation. Part of the reason was that he lived in a chaotic era and had to deal with many conflicting forces. His real and imagined contacts with anarchists, left-wing Nationalists and Communists, as well as the flaws that were supposed to have plagued his style and methods of revolutionary work, gave rise to confusion and controversy among his comrades, and his image and practices as a radical revolutionary inevitably caused the Nationalists and Communists to have completely divergent views of Wei Baqun and his role as an agent between his community and the state.

The PRC eventually evolved into a much more orderly state than the Republic of China known to Wei Baqun, and in death, Wei Baqun was assigned a fixed role in the new order and made to perform some important functions for the new society. In this new order, the confusion, conflict, and controversy about Wei Baqun all disappeared, and he came to possess a clear and definite image as the Red God, a perfect Communist, and a Zhuang hero. In this revised image, Wei Baqun began to perform his role as a mediating and unifying agent who would contribute to the unity between the peasants and Communists, and between the Zhuang and the Han, as well as to the further integration of frontier Donglan and the Right River region into the Chinese nation.

Conclusion

During the first half of the twentieth century, China was dominated by three major groups of militarists. The first consisted of Yuan Shikai and his subordinates who maintained military rule over the country before the late 1920s. The second was formed by the Nationalist militarists who claimed to be disciples of Sun Yat-sen and were closely related to Chiang Kai-shek. And the third included the Communist militarists who emerged after the collapse of the KMT-CCP United Front in 1927. Some of Yuan Shikai's disciples were Sun Yat-sen's allies at one point or another, but eventually they convinced Sun of the necessity of creating an armed force of his own with their betrayals. The Nationalists and Communists were also allies at the beginning, but Chiang Kai-shek's purge in 1927 compelled the Communists to build their own army. If the delivery room of the Yuan Shikai group was the imperial New Army created by the Manchu court, and the cradle of the Nationalist generals was Whampoa Military Academy, then the nursery for the Communist militarists was the villages. Although the first Communist uprisings took place in cities and many early officers in the Communist army were graduates of urban schools, all Communist strongmen went through a long phase of rural revolution.

Wei Baqun was one of the many militarists who emerged in China in the early twentieth century. He began his political career in the warlord era, but he had little in common with a typical warlord other than his abiding faith in military power. Wei Baqun's political outlook was much more progressive and radical than most militarists of the Yuan Shikai group, and his first political act was to organize a small peasant army to fight against Yuan Shikai. As a long-time loyal supporter of Sun Yat-sen and a member of the KMT, Wei Baqun had close connections with some Nationalist leaders. However, his political views differed markedly from those of the right-wing Nationalists, and he never allied himself with the Nationalist government created by Chiang Kai-shek. In fact, the right-wing generals in Guangxi, notably the leaders of the New Guangxi Clique, were Wei Baqun's deadliest enemies. The radical policies Wei Baqun adopted in Donglan conformed to those advocated by the left-wing Nationalists and Communists. Therefore, his enemies treated him as a Communist long before he actually became a full member of the CCP, and eventually he did become a determined Communist revolutionary. Compared with the other two groups of militarists, the Communist generals were more ideological and better disciplined. They were also more self-reliant in the sense that many of them, including Wei Baqun, had to build their armies with their bare hands. Most of them first emerged as local guerrilla fighters in the late 1920s, and their casualty rate was very high. Wei Baqun was one of many Communist militarists who failed to survive the first civil war between the Communists and the Nationalists. Another unique feature of the Communist militarists is that most of them were not just military commanders, but also influential leaders of the people and the community. As a military commander, Wei Baqun never had more than several thousand soldiers under his direct command and was thus much less powerful than many other militarists of his time, but as a social-political leader, Wei Baqun could mobilize an entire local community and had influence not only in his own region but also in other parts of the province and the nation, and therefore was much more influential than many non-Communist militarists.

Wei Baqun was a convert to some foreign ideologies, but at the same time, he never ceased to be a product and retainer of the local tradition of a remote frontier region. Partly as a result of that, Wei Baqun's movement carried both global and local features. Global ideologies such as Republicanism and anarchism had some impact on Wei Baqun, but eventually he converted to communism. During his second revolt, he hung Lenin's portrait in front of the classroom at Donglan Peasant Movement Institute, which also offered classes about the Russian Revolution and Leninist theories. After 1926, his movement was gradually integrated into the Communist revolution in China and became part of the global Communist movement directed by the Comintern in Moscow. Wei Baqun thus became a link in the global Communist network. The leading Communists in China's metropolises, who created and controlled the CCP, served as intermediaries between the Communist leaders of the Soviet Union and local Communists like Wei Baqun. Some of the orders that the CCP sent to Wei Baqun, such as those about the land revolution, came ultimately from the Comintern. The class war that characterized Wei Baqun's movement was a common feature of Communist revolutions in every part of the world, whereas active peasant participation in the revolution was a striking feature of Communist revolutions in the Third World. Wei Baqun was aware that whereas the CCP represented the Communist center in China, Moscow was the global center of Communism. In order to impress his local followers, Wei Baqun or his comrades may have spread the rumor that Wei Baqun had studied in the Soviet Union during one of his journeys. Shortly before his death, Wei Baqun told some close friends that he would leave the Right River region to study in the Soviet Union. His personality and working style also carried the traits of a universal Communist culture at that time.

Local cultures, connections, and concerns also featured prominently in Wei Baqun's revolution. He was extremely adept at using local culture and nature to promote his movement. Most local peasants were illiterate, but very fond of singing and dancing. Wei Baqun thus composed many folksongs to spread revolutionary ideas. Local people attached great importance to sworn brotherhood, and Wei Baqun turned many of his friends into sworn brothers before transforming them into revolutionary comrades. When the nonlocal Communists criticized Wei Baqun for relying too much on personal relations, they were actually attacking the local culture. In order to draw as many supporters as possible in a multiethnic region, Wei Baqun became one of the first Chinese revolutionaries to enforce policies promoting ethnic solidarity and equality. His military strategies, which were characterized by a strong reliance on the mountains and caves and hit and run tactics, as well as his methods of communication, were all similar to those favored by local rebels throughout history.

However, local cultures, connections and concerns did not always work to the favor of Wei Baqun and his movement. His strong attachment to Donglan and the surrounding areas prevented him from adopting a more mobile and aggressive military strategy, making him a victim of the Nationalist sieges. The excessive killing, looting, burning, and kidnapping conducted by Wei Baqun and his followers served as reminders of traditional feuds and the practices of local rebel and bandit groups. These brutal acts helped to annihilate enemies, but also had the effect of generating fear among the people, disrupting agricultural production, depleting resources, and alienating increasing numbers of local people. In the long run, they had destructive effect on his revolution. Furthermore, the bandit sensibility that required leaders to provide subsistence and protection in exchange for loyalties, and that also did not condemn a shift of loyalty to win amnesty, monetary rewards, or official positions, had devastating consequences for Wei Baqun's movement. The betrayal of his old comrades when he needed them the most undermined his final resistance against the Nationalist armies, and his assassination at the hands of his own nephew stemmed directly from this small-time bandit pragmatism.

Although Wei Baqun's movement shared similarities with revolutions in other parts of China and the world, and were part of a national or even global movement, and his movement had influence on the entire Guangxi Province and many other pats of the country, Wei Baqun's actual power rarely went beyond the small area of Donglan or Dong-Feng. In that sense, his was primarily a local movement. Within that local area, Wei Baqun could easily defeat his local enemies, but his local enemies had many outside supporters, who always posed a serious threat to Wei Baqun. Wei Baqun also had external supporters, but they were not able to provide him with consistent assistance. He was defeated in 1932 because at that moment in Guangxi the anti-Communist forces were much more powerful than the Communist forces. It is arguable that one of the most important causes of Wei Baqun's defeat was that he was not able to keep his movement completely local. The fate of any local movement was determined by the balance of external powers in that particular region.

In the late 1920s and early 1930s, the Chinese Communist movement consisted of many local revolutions such as the one led by Wei Baqun. Some of these movements were defeated or eliminated, whereas others survived and eventually expanded, and the defeat of some movements contributed to the survival and expansion of others. For example, the defeat of the Communists in southern China caused the Long March, resulting in the survival of the Communist base area in northern Shaanxi and the expansion of Communist influence in northern China. The collapse of Wei Baqun's movement in the Right River region partly resulted from the departure of the main force of the Seventh Red Army, which contributed to strengthening the Red Army of the Central Base Area in Jiangxi. In that sense, none of the many local Communist movements was truly local and none of the local movements was ever completely defeated because each of them played a role in the Communist victory in 1949, which was a victory for all the local Communist movements, successful or unsuccessful in their respective local areas.

Before the late 1940s, the Communists were never able to establish permanent dominance over any province. Even the Communist base areas in southern Jiangxi and later northern Shaanxi, although considered "centers" by the Communists and their supporters, were rather local. When these surviving and expanded local movements were eventually linked up with one another, they became a powerful and eventually victorious national Communist movement. Although Wei Baqun was defeated, his movement was not completely crushed. Some of his followers survived the repeated extermination campaigns and were able to maintain a local movement that was reincorporated into the national Communist system in the late 1940s. Although Wei Baqun was dead, his many followers continued to fight for the Communist cause in both the central Communist army and the local Communist force in the Right River region.

As a local leader, Wei Baqun played two contrasting roles in the relations between his peripheral community and the national centers during his lifetime. He played a disruptive role in the relations between his local area and the incumbent Nationalist center, but served as a mediator and unifier between his community and the emerging Communist center. Within Guangxi, the New Guangxi Clique was part of the Nationalist system, while Wei Baqun stood for the Communist path. To his comrades and followers, Wei Baqun's defeat meant that he was an admirable fallen hero, not a pitiful loser. They have been unanimous in recognizing his great contribution to the Communist victory over the Nationalists in China—in fact, they were much more generous in offering praises after his death than during his lifetime, and the Communist victory in 1949 determined Wei Baqun's prominent posthumous status in his local community as well as in the nation.

In the PRC era, because Wei Baqun was officially identified as a Zhuang and the Zhuang were officially recognized as a minority group, Wei Baqun's revolution has served to prove that the Communist revolution was not just a revolution of the Han, but was also a movement for, of and by all the ethnic groups of China. If in his lifetime Wei Baqun was primarily a rebel, revolutionary, and disruptor, in his afterlife he has been mainly made to perform the role of a unifier and mediator. After 1949, people began to measure his contribution not just by the actual change he brought about in his lifetime, but also by the sacrifices he and his followers made and his spiritual and symbolic influence.

Poverty was one of the factors driving many Donglan natives to join Wei Baqun's revolution in the 1920s and 1930s. Donglan today is much better off economically than it was nearly a century ago, but it is still a poor and backward county compared with the more advanced and prosperous regions of China. In 2010, the per capita gross domestic product (GDP) of Donglan stood at 6,785 yuan, which was the second lowest among the seventy-five counties and cities in Guangxi, whereas the per capita GDP for the Guangxi Zhuang Autonomous Region was 20,645 yuan, and that for China reached 29,970 yuan in the same year. Donglan is officially recognized as one of the twenty-eight poor counties in Guangxi. Politically, however, largely thanks to Wei Baqun, Donglan is now in the mainstream. In Wei Baqun's time, the provincial and central governments had only loose control over the county and saw it as a remote and poor place without much value, or a troubled area deserved to be destroyed or discarded. Today, Donglan is one of the red counties that feature notably in the official media and political map of China. The political prominence of Donglan brings with it some economic benefits. Donglan earned special treatment from the provincial and central governments because it not only is a minority area, a frontier region, and a poor county, but also is a former revolutionary base area. The central government has provided economic aid and preferential tax policies for all former revolutionary base areas, and the central and provincial governments have helped build infrastructure and provide subsidies for the poor families in Donglan.

The development of the so-called red tourism in China in recent years has turned Donglan into a popular tourist destination and provided another means of transforming Donglan's political capital into economic capital. The county government has decided to make tourism the priority industry of the county and has spent a large sum of money in recent years to renovate memorials and monuments dedicated to Wei Baqun and his revolution, with the hope that such investment would earn great returns. To make it easy for tourists to visit the remote sites in the mountains, the county government has constructed the Baqun Road that connects Dongli Village, the Fragrant Tea Cave, and the former headquarters of the Twenty-first Division of the Seventh Red Army. The official flyers describe Donglan as the land of bronze drums, chestnuts, black-bone chickens, medicinal herbs, green environment, and above all revolutionary generals. Donglan is also portrayed as "the birthplace of the Seventh Red Army, the heartland of the Right River Revolutionary Base Area, the cradle of the Baise Uprising, the place where senior revolutionaries such as Deng Xiaoping, Zhang Yunyi and Wei Baqun had lived and fought, and the home to 2,241 officially recognized revolutionary martyrs." No other county in Guangxi has more revolutionary martyrs than Donglan, and among the 2,241 martyrs, nearly 2,100 were killed as participants of Wei Baqun's revolution.[1]

Today, next to Wei Baqun's tomb and memorial in the western fringe of the county seat, stands the most luxurious hotel in the county, and a businessman from Singapore has built a resort village by a tranquil lake in Donglan. Businessmen from Tianjin, Jiangsu, and other provinces have also made investments in Donglan. The many karst mountains in Donglan, which once offered protection to Wei Baqun and his followers, are now valued principally for their natural beauty and for the fresh and clean air they provide. Donglan's neighbor, the Bama Yao Autonomous County, which now rules the Western Mountains, has become known as the "land of longevity" for the large number of centenarians in the county, and many attribute their longevity to Bama's green environment, which Donglan also shares. The many caves in the mountains, which Wei Baqun and his followers took as shelters, are now points of interests for adventurers, and the discovery of each new cave arouses great excitement.[2] In the first nine months of 2010, nearly 120,000 people visited the various revolutionary memorials in Donglan, and altogether they spent nearly ten million dollars in the county.[3] In that way, Wei Baqun and his movement have become not only a political asset, but also a profitable economic asset for Donglan. Domestic and foreign capitalists are happy making money by exploiting this asset, resulting in further promoting Wei Baqun's influence. Few still remember that Wei Baqun was an enemy of capitalism and that wealthy business people and landlords had suffered miserably at his hands in the 1920s and early 1930s. Obviously, capitalists are now confident that Wei Baqun's Communist successors are not interested in inheriting this very important part of Wei Baqun's legacy.[4]

Just as Wei Baqun and his followers learned after a long decade of struggles that it would be nearly impossible for them to win their revolution in one county without consistent external support, today both locals and nonlocals have come to agree that it would be very difficult for Donglan to catch up with the more developed regions of the country without outside help. As part of the commemorative program honoring Wei Baqun's 115th birthday, a group of retired PLA generals held a meeting in Beijing's Diaoyutai State House to call for support for Donglan's economic development. In Nanning there is an association for supporting the development of Donglan consisting of officials, scholars, business people, and others. The government has created a grand plan for developing infrastructure of the three counties of Donglan, Bama and Fengshan with the purpose of bringing prosperity to the region. In the revolutionary period, the three counties joined together in revolution, and in the era of economic development, they are again brought into a unified zone. If the provincial and central governments need any rationale for providing special aid for Donglan, then Wei Baqun would serve as the best justification. Wei Baqun and his followers had promised the people of Donglan more than eighty years ago that revolution would bring happiness to Donglan. He was killed before he could deliver that promise, and his revolutionary successors naturally have the duty of fulfilling that promise for him.

Notes

Introduction

1. Fang Daheng and Zou Wensheng, "Zuoyoujiang geming genjudi de sufan baowei gongzuo." In *ZYJGMGJD,* 1155. Beijing: Zhonggong dangshi ziliao chubanshe, 1989.

2. Luo Rikuai, "Huiyi Weishizhang xisheng qianhou." *WCSLZJ* (Wei Baqun Chen Hongtao shiliao zhuanji), 462. Nanning: 2006.

3. Ibid., 462.

4. Qin Caiwu, *Donglan tongshi.* 1934–1935. *ZYJGMSLHB*, Vol. 3, 259.

5. *Nanning minguo ribao*, "Baifuzongzuo ling jiang gaifei shouji jiesong laiyong xuan zhongshang gouji gongfei Huang Daquan dengwen." October 25, 1932.

6. *Wuzhou minguo ribao*, "Weifei shouji shizhong hou yanmai." November 20, 1932.

7. Huang Xianfan, Gan Wenjie, and Gan Wenhao, *Wei Baqun pingzhuan*, 518. Guilin: Guangxi shifan daxue, 2008,

8. Lan Huaichang and Li Dehan, *Renmin qunzhong de lingxiu Wei Baqun*, dedication. Beijing: Zhongguo qingnian, 2009.

9. Angus W. McDonald, *Urban Origins of Rural Revolution: Elites and the Masses in Hunan* Province, China, 1911–1927. University of California Press, 1978.

10. Huang Xianfan, Gan Wenjie, and Gan Wenhao, *Wei Baqun pingzhuan*, 518.

11. Diana Lary, "Communism and Ethnic Revolt: Some Notes on the Chuang Peasant Movement in Kwangsi 1921–31." *The China Quarterly*, 49, 126–135.

12. Gregor Benton, *Mountain Fires: The Red Army's Three-Year War in South China, 1934–1938*. xx–xxiii. University of California Press, 1992.

13. Joseph Esherick, "Ten Theses on the Chinese Revolution," 50. In Jeffrey N. Wasserstrom, ed., *Twentieth-Centuy China: New Approaches*, 37–65. Routledge, 2003.

14. For discussions about the debate on the relative importance of the two factors, see Frederick Wakeman Jr., "Rebellion and Revolution: The Study of Popular Movements in Chinese History." *The Journal of Asian Studies*, Vol. 36, No. 2 (1977), 222–224; Kathleen Hartford and Steven M. Goldstein, eds., *Single Sparks: China's Rural Revolutions*, 4–9, 13–20. M. E. Sharpe, Inc. 1989. For representative studies, see Chalmers Johnson, *Peasant Nationalism and Communist Power: The Emergence of Revolutionary China, 1937–1945*. Stanford University Press, 1962; Mark Selden, *The Yenan Way in Revolutionary*

China. Harvard University Press, 1971; Lucien Bianco, *Origins of the Chinese Revolution, 1915–1949*. Stanford University Press, 1971.

15. For selected English works on the other peasant movement leaders, see Benjamin Schwartz, *Chinese Communism and the Rise of Mao*. Harvard University Press, 1951; Stuart Shram, *Mao Tse-tung*. Penguin, 1966; Roy Hofheinz Jr., *The Broken Wave: the Chinese Communist Peasant Movement, 1922–1928*. Harvard University Press, 1977; Li Jui, *The Early Revolutionary Activities of Comrade Mao Tse-tung*. M. E. Sharpe, 1977; Guy Alitto, *The Last Confucian: Liang Shu-ming and the Chinese Dilemma of Modernity*. University of California Press, 1979; Robert Marks, *Rural Revolution in South China: Peasants and the Making of History in Haifeng County, 1570–1930*. University of Wisconsin Press, 1984; Fernando Galbiati, *Peng Pai and the Hai-Lu-Feng Soviet*. Stanford University Press, 1985; Kamal Sheel, *Peasant Society and Marxist Intellectuals in China: Fang Zhimin and the Origin of a Revolutionary Movement in the Xinjiang Region*. Princeton University Press, 1989; Charles Hayford, *To the People: James Yen and Village China*. Columbia University Press, 1990; Keith Shoppa, *Blood Road: The Mystery of Shen Dingyi in Revolutionary China*. University of California Press, 1995; Ross Terrill, *Mao: A Biography*. Stanford University Press, 1999; Philip Short, *Mao: A Life*. Henry Holt, 2000; Jonathan Spence, Mao *Zedong*. Lipper/Viking, 2006; Maurice Meisner, *Mao Zedong: A Political and Intellectual Portrait*. Polity, 2007.

16. Ma Yin, ed., *Zhongguo shaoshu minzu,* 504. Beijing: Renmin, 1984.

Chapter One

1. Diana Lary, "A Zone of Nebulous Menace: The Guangxi/Indochina Border in the Republican Period." In Diana Lary, ed., *The Chinese State at the Borders*, 183–190. University of British Columbia Press, 2007.

2. For a collection of folksongs from Donglan, see Wei Wenjun and Ma Yongquan, eds., *Donglan geyao ji*. Donglan: Donglanxian minjianwenxue jichengxiaozu, 1987; for the legend about Third Sister Liu, see Liu Xifan, *Lingbiao jiman*, 166–167. Shanghai: Shangwu, 1934; for recent studies of Third Sister Liu, see Pan Qixu, "Gexian Liu Sanjie de chansheng shi gexu xingcheng de biaozhi." In Tang Zhengzhu, ed., *Hongshuihe wenhua yanjiu*, 529–552. Nanning: Guangxi renmin, 2001; Eddy U, "Third Sister Liu and the Making of the Intellectual in Socialist China." *The Journal of Asian Studies*, 69, 57–83.

3. Liu Xifan, *Lingbiao jiman*, 39–40; Huang Xianfan, Huang Zengqing, and Zhang Yimin, *Zhuangzu tongshi*, 658–659 Nanning: Guangxi minzu, 1988.

4. Qin Jianping, "Kenhuang zhimian." In Tang Nonglin, ed. *Guihai yizhu*, 148–149. Shanghai: Shanghai shudian, 1994.

5. Huang Xianfan, Huang Zengqing, and Zhang Yimin, *Zhuangzu tongshi*, 20–21.

6. Ibid., 706–715.

7. Qin Jianping, "Tonggu zhi xiang." In Tang Nonglin, ed. *Guihai yizhu*, 171.

8. *Donglan xianzhi*, 564. Nanning: Guangxi renmin, 1994.

9. Zhongyang fangwentuan diyi fentuan lianluozu, *Guangxi Donglanxian diwuqu (Zhonghequ) minzu gaikuang* 1951 (A), 5–6; Zhongyang fangwentuan diyi fentuan

lianluozu, *Guangxi Donglanxian Xishanqu minzu gaikuang,*1951 (B), 6–7; Wei Hanchen, "Jianguoqian Donglan fazhan shaoshuminzu jiaoyu gaikuang." *Donglan wenshi* 4 (2001), 183.

10. Wei Shukui, "Meng Bumen qiren qishi." *Donglan wenshi* 4 (2001), 196–205; *ZYJGMSLHB*, Vol. 1, 5–6; *Donglan xianzhi*, 1994, 56; *Donglan xianzhi*, 1960, section on society, 2; 6.

11. *ZYJGMSLHB*, Vol. 1, 5; *Donglan xianzhi*, 1960, section on society, 7.

12. Bai Yaotian, *Nong Zhigao: Lishi de xingyun'er yu qi'er*, 36. Beijing: Minzu, 2006.

13. Today the Zhuang still form the majority of the local population. It is estimated that in 2004, the population of the county was 280,000 and of it, eighty-five percent was Zhuang.

14. Li Guozhou and Yan Yongtong, *Wei Baqun zhuan, 3.* Guilin: Guangxi shifan daxue, 1989.

15. Zhongyang fangwentuan diyi fentuan lianluozu, *Guangxi Donglanxian diwuqu (Zhonghequ) minzu gaikuang*, 2–3; 5–6.

16. Ibid., 6.

17. Jiang Huang, *Donglan xianzheng jiyao*, 16. Guilin: Guangxi shengli Guilin zhiyexuexiao yinshuachang, 1947; Lu Xiuxiang, "1929 nian Donglan renkou kaozheng." In Lu Xiuxiang, ed., *Donglan geming genjudi*, 402–403. Donglan: Zhonggong Donglan xianwei dangshi bangongshi, 1990.

18. Tang Ling, "Qingchao tongguang shiqi Guangxi renkou wenti chutan," 300. In Zhong Wendian, ed., *Jindai Guangxi shehui yanjiu.* Nanning: Guangxi renmin, 1990.

19. Gu Zuyu, *Dushi fangyu jiyao*, Section 109, 6763. Beijing: Zhonghua shuju, 2005.

20. Chen Mianshu, "Guangxi Donglan nongmin yundong zhi shiji zhuangkuang," *Nongmin yundong* (Wuhan), 22 & 23. In *WCSLZJ*, 50.

21. *Donglan xianzhi*, 1994, 45.

22. Guangxisheng minzhengting, *Guangxi gexian gaikuang.* Nanning: Dacheng yinshuguan, 1934.

23. Wei Ruilin, "Lu Rongting," 51. In Guangxi xinhai gemingshi yanjiuhui, ed., *Minguo Guangxi renwu zhuan*, Vol. 1. Nanning: Guangxi renmin, 1983.

24. He Weidian. ed., *Donglanxian diming zhi*, 4. Donglan: Donglanxian diming bangongshi, 1988; *Donglan xianzhi*, 1960, 2; Huang Bingli, "Jisheng xiangche Donglan cheng," 45. In Hechi ribaoshe, ed., *Zhuixun Hongqijun zuji.* Nanning: Guangxi renmin, 1990; Qin Yingji, *Xiaoyan suiyue*, 1–2. Beijing: Zhonggong dangshi, 1991; Lu Xianling, "Huiyi cantong liangjianshi," 32. *Donglan wenshi ziliao*, 2.

25. For discussions on the two concepts, see William Skinner, "Introduction: Urban Development in Imperial China." In Skinner, G. William, ed., *The City in Late Imperial China*, 18. Stanford University Press, 1977.

26. Chen Mianshu, "Guangxi Donglan nongmin yundong zhi shiji zhuangkuang," 50.

27. Li Zongren and Tang Degang, *Li Zongren huiyilu*, 113, 187. Nanning: Guangxi shifan daxue, 2005; Huang Shaohong, *Huang Shaohong huiyilu*, 161. Nanning: Guangxi renmin, 1991; Diana Lary, *Region and Nation: The Kwangsi Clique in Chinese Politics, 1925–1937,* 110. Cambridge University Press, 1974; Fan Honggui and Gu

Youshi, et al., *Zhuangzu lishi yu wenhua*, 187–188. Nanning: Guangxi minzu, 1997; Guangxisheng minzhengting, *Guangxi gexian gaikuang*.

28. *Donglan xianzhi*, 1994, 380.

29. Chen Rukai, "Donglan shiyan zhuanmai gongdian gaikuang." *Donglan wenshi ziliao*, 2, 18.

30. *Donglan xianzhi*, 1994, 414.

31. Ibid., 380; 414; Chen Rukai, "Donglan shiyan zhuanmai gongdian kaikuang," 18; Qin Yingji, *Xiaoyan suiyue*, 1; *Donglan xianzhi*, 1960, 4.

32. *Zhongguo qingnian bao*, "Donglanxian guanfang huiying tiaoshui laoren guiqiu zhengfu xiulu shijian," 2010, 3, 28.

33. Zhong Wendian, ed., *Ershi shiji sanshi niandai de Guangxi*, 208. Guilin: Guangxi shifandaxue, 1992.

34. Fan Honggui and Gu Youshi et al., *Zhuangzu lishi yu wenhua*, 178.

35. Chen Xiewu, "Chenbuzhang yanshuogao." In Lu Xiuxiang, ed., *Donglan nongmin yundong, 1921–1927*, 74. Nanning: Guangxi minzu, 1986.

36. Huang Xianfan, Huang Zengqing, and Zhang Yimin, *Zhuangzu tongshi*, 279–287, 312–313, 746–749.

37. Wei Tianfu, "Donglan Weishi tusi de xingshuai." *Donglan wenshi*, 4, 116–117.

38. Zhu Wanli, "Zhuangzu Weixing qiyuan sanshuo." *Wenshi chunqiu*, 10 (1995, No. 3), 50–51; Su Guanchang, *Guangxi tuguan zhidu yanjiu*, 185–211. Nanning: Guangxi minzu, 2000. Su argues that most hereditary lords in Guangxi, including the Weis in Donglan, were of Zhuang origins.

39. *Donglan xianzhi*, 1994, 152.

40. Yang Xiangchao, "Lingyunxian Sicheng Zhuangzu yehun xisu." In Tang Nonglin, ed., *Guihai yizhu*, 146–147.

41. Liang Tingwang, *Zhuangzu wenhua gailun*, 317–331. Nanning: Guangxi jiaoyu, 2000.

42. Jeffrey Barlow, "The Zhuang Minority Peoples of the Sino-Vietnamese Frontier in the Song Period." *Journal of Southeast Asian Studies*, 18(2), 264; Jeffrey Barlow, "The Zhuang Minority in the Ming Era." *Ming Studies*, 28, 25–26, 31–32.

43. Qin Jianping, "Wei Zhengbao san dai kangwo jianqigong." *Wenshi chunqiu*, 36 (1995, No. 5), 31–32; Huang Feng, "Weishi sandai kang wokiu," *Donglan wenshi*, 4, 112–115; Wei Tianfu, "Donglan Weishi tusi de xingshuai," 118–122; Wenshizu, "Wei Huchen zhuanlue." *Donglan wenshi*, 4, 132–133.

44. Wei Tianfu, "Donglan Weishi tusi de xingshuai," 118–122; *Donglan xianzhi*, 1994, 721; David Faure, "The Yao Wars in the Mid-Ming and Their Impact on Yao Ethnicity," 175–178; 184–187. In Pamela Kyle Crossley, Helen F. Siu, and Donald S. Sutton, eds., *Empire at the Margins: Culture, Ethnicity, and Frontier in Early Modern China*. University of California Press, 2006; Jeffrey Barlow, "The Zhuang Minority in the Ming Era," 30–31.

45. William Rowe, *Saving the World: Chen Hongmou and Elite Consciousness in Eighteenth-Century China, 22*. Stanford University Press, 2001; Li Zongren and Tang Degang, *Li Zongren huiyilu*, 8.

46. Ping-ti Ho, *The Ladder of Success in Imperial China: Aspects of Social Mobility, 1368–1911*, 229. John Wiley & Sons, 1964; Huang Hanzhong, "Qingchao keju zhidu zai Donglan." *Donglan wenshi ziliao*, 1, 1–7.

47. Willaim Skinner, "Introduction: Urban and Rural in Chinese Society." In Skinner, G. William, ed., *The City in Late Imperial China*, 263. Stanford University Press, 1977.

48. *Donglan xianzhi*, 1960.

49. William Rowe, *Saving the World: Chen Hongmou and Elite Consciousness in Eighteenth-Century China*, 24.

50. Yeh Wen-hsin, *Provincial Passages: Culture, Space, and the Origins of Chinese Communism*, 6–7. University of California Press, 1996.

51. *Donglan xianzhi*, 1994, 2–3; 81.

52. Li Guoxiang and Yang Chang, eds., *Mingshilu leizuan: Guangxi shiliao juan*, 26–59. Guilin: Guangxi shifan daxue, 1990; Diana Lary, *Region and Nation: The Kwangsi Clique in Chinese Politics, 1925–1937,* 23; Fan Honggui and Gu Youshi, et al., *Zhuangzu lishi yu wenhua*, 135–136.

53. Wei Ruilin, "Lu Rongting," 49. In Guangxi Xinhai gemingshi yanjiuhui, ed. *Minguo Guangxi renwu zhuan*, Vol. 1; Wei Ruilin, "Mo Rongxin," 72. In Guangxi xinhai gemingshi yanjiuhui, ed. *Minguo Guangxi renwu zhuan*, Vol. 1.

54. Li Zongren and Tang Degang, *Li Zongren huiyilu*, 49.

55. Phil Billingsley, *Bandits in Republican China*, 38. Stanford University Press, 1988; Li Zongren and Tang Degang, *Li Zongren huiyilu*, 451.

56. *Donglan xianzhi*, 1994, 2–3.

57. BSD, 083-002-062-002, "Yaozu renmin qiyi."

58. *ZYJGMSLHB*, Vol. 1, 8; Zhu Hongyuan, *Cong bianluan dao junsheng: Guangxi de chuqi xiandaihua, 1860–1937*, 136–138; 141. Taipei: Zhongyang yanjiuyuan jindaishi yanjiusuo zhuankan, 76 (1995). For arms smuggling in Guangdong, see Qiu Jie and He Wenping, "Minguo chunian Guangdong de minjian wuqi." *Zhongguo shehui kexue*, 2005 (1), 178–190.

59. Zhongyang fangwentuan diyi fentuan lianluozu, *Guangxi Donglanxian Xishanqu minzu gaikuang*, 17.

60. For the rise of Baise, See Yang Yexing & Huang Xiongying, eds., *Youjiang liuyu Zhuangzu jingji shigao*, 144–167. Nanning: Guangxi renmin, 1995.

61. Li Changshou, "Baise qiyi he Hongjun zai Baise." *Baise shizhi*, No. 1, 4; Fan Honggui and Gu Youshi, et al., *Zhuangzu lishi yu wenhua*, 186; Cen Jianying, "Guangxi Baise de yanbang." *GXWSZLXJ*, 3 (1963), 155–160; Bai Chongxi, *Bai Chongxi huiyilu*, 11. Beijing: Jiefangjun, 1987.

62. Guangxi tewei, "Guangxi dang zhengzhi renwu jueyi'an." September 13, 1929. *ZYJGMGJD*, Vol. 1, 54; Zhonggong zhongyang, "Zhonggong zhongyang gei Guangdong shengwei zhuan qijun qianwei de zhishi." 1930, 3, 2. *ZYJGMGJD*, Vol. 1, 232.

63. *Junshi tongxun*, "Dui Guangxi Hongjun gongzuo buzhi de taolun." *ZYJGMGJD*, Vol. 1, 178.

64. For a dramatic account of Liu Yongfu's Black Flags, see Henry McAleavy, *Black Flags in Vietnam: The Story of a Chinese Intervention*. Allen & Unwin, 1968.

65. Yang Yexing & Huang Xiongying, eds., *Youjiang liuyu Zhuangzu jingji shigao*, 213.

66. *Donglan xianzhi*, 1960, 4.

67. Chen Xiewu,"Guangxi Donglan nongmin zhi can'an." *Nongmin yundong* (Guangzhou), No. 6 & 7. September 7 & 14, 1926. *WCSLZJ*, 45; Chen Mianshu, "Guangxi Donglan nongmin yundong zhi shiji zhuangkuang," 50.

68. *Donglan xianzhi*, 1994, 612.

69. Xie Fumin, *Wei Baqun,* 2. Beijing: Gongren, 1958.

70. Lan Leibin, "Wei Baqun xiangpian zhi mi." *Guangxi wenshi*, 2009(3), 77–80.

71. Lan Handong and Lan Qixuan, *Wei Baqun*, 1. Beijing: Zhongguo qingnian, 1986; Zeng Qiqiang, ed., *Zhongguo zaoqi nongmin yundong lingxiu Wei Baqun*, 2nd edition, 1. Donglan: Zhonggong Donglan xianwei dangshi yanjiushi, 2010; Huang Xianfan, Gan Wenjie and Gan Wenhao, *Wei Baqun pingzhuan*, 4.

72. Huang Xianfan, Gan Wenjie and Gan Wenhao, *Wei Baqun pingzhuan*, 5.

73. Li Guozhou, *Lun Wei Baqun*, 128–129. Nanning: Guangxi renmin, 1989; Li Guozhou and Yan Yongtong, *Wei Baqun zhuan*, 7; Huang Xianfan, Gan Wenjie and Gan Wenhao, *Wei Baqun pingzhuan*, 6; BSD, 083-002-0017-004, "Baqun de qizi he ernu."

74. Lan Handong and Lan Qixuan, *Wei Baqun*, 3; Li Guozhou and Yan Yongtong, *Wei Baqun zhuan*, 7.

75. Xie Fumin, *Wei Baqun*, 2–3; Zeng Qiqiang, ed., *Zhongguo zaoqi nongmin yundong lingxiu Wei Baqun*, 3; Chen Xinde, "Wei Baqun." In Hu Hua, ed., *Zhonggong dangshi renwu zhuan*, Vol. 12, 183–216. Xi'an: Shanxi renmin, 1983.

76. *ZYJGMSLHB*, Vol. 1, 10; Zeng Qiqiang, ed., *Zhongguo zaoqi nongmin yundong lingxiu Wei Baqun*, 8.

77. Li Guozhou and Yan Yongtong, *Wei Baqun zhuan*, 8–9.

78. Zong Ying, et al., *Wei Baqun lieshi de gushi*, 1–2. Beijing: Zuojia, 1959; Zhu Zhongyu, *Wei Baqun*, 5–7. Beijing: Zhonghua shuju, 1959.

79. Lan Handong and Lan Qixuan, *Wei Baqun*, 16–17.

80. Ibid., 3; Huang Xianfan, Gan Wenjie, & Gan Wenhao, *Wei Baqun pingzhuan*, 9.

81. Zong Ying, *Wei Baqun lieshi de gushi*, 2–6; Li Guozhou and Yan Yongtong, *Wei Baqun zhuan*, 9–11.

82. Lan Handong and Lan Qixuan, *Wei Baqun*, 11–14.

83. Xie Fumin, *Wei Baqun*, 6–7; Li Guozhou and Yan Yongtong, *Wei Baqun zhuan*, 13–14; Lan Handong and Lan Qixuan, *Wei Baqun*, 3–5.

84. Huang Hanzhong and Chen Baxian, "Yucai gaodeng xiaoxue yange gaikuang." *Donglan wenshi*, 4 (2001), 171.

85. Chen Mianshu, "Guangxi Donglan nongmin yundong zhi shiji zhuangkuang," 55.

86. Jeffrey G. Barlow, "The Zhuang Minority Peoples of the Sino-Vietnamese Frontier in the Song Period"; Bai Yaotian, *Nong Zhigao: Lishi de xingyun'er yu qi'er*, 52; James Anderson, *The Rebel Den of Nung Tri Cao: Loyalty and Identity along the Sino-Vietnamese Frontier*. University of Washington Press, 2007.

87. He Weidian. ed., *Donglanxian diming zhi*, 117.

88. Ma Yin, ed., *Zhongguo shaoshu minzu*, 502; Fan Honggui and Gu Youshi, et al., *Zhuangzu lishi yu wenhua,* 200; Jonathan Spence, *God's Chinese Son: The Taiping Heavenly Kingdom of Hong Xiuquan*, 79–95; 114. W. W. Norton & Company, 1996.

89. Lan Handong and Lan Qixuan, *Wei Baqun*, 7–9; 18–20.

90. Yang Shiheng and Qin Jiancai, "Cenxunwang." In Nong Guanpin and Cao Tingwei, eds., *Zhuangzu minjian gushi xuan*, Vol. 1, 20–22. Nanning: Guangxi renmin, 1982; Li Guozhou and Yan Yongtong, *Wei Baqun zhuan*, 4–5.

91. Li Guozhou and Yan Yongtong, *Wei Baqun zhuan*, 5–6.

92. He Weidian. ed. *Donglanxian diming zhi*, 239.

93. Huang Hanzhong, "Yinhaizhou gaikuang." *Donglan wenshi ziliao*, 1 (1985), 77–81.

94. Li Guozhou and Yan Yongtong, *Wei Baqun zhuan*, 4.

95. Huang Xianfan, Gan Wenjie and Gan Wenhao, *Wei Baqun pingzhuan*, 7.

96. Xie Fumin, *Wei Baqun*, 3.

97. Li Guozhou and Yan Yongtong, *Wei Baqun zhuan*, 12–13.

98. Zhu Hongyuan, *Cong bianluan dao junsheng: Guangxi de chuqi xiandaihua, 1860–1937*, 461.

99. Huang Xianfan, Gan Wenjie and Gan Wenhao, *Wei Baqun pingzhuan*, 7.

100. Guangxi shaoshuminzu lishidiaocha zu, *Guangxi Zhuangzu zizhiqu Donglanxian Zhonghe renmingongshe Donglitun shehuilishi diaocha baogao*, 19. Nanning: Zhongguo shehui kexueyuan minzu yanjiusuo Guangxi shaoshuminzu shehui lishi diaochazu, 1964.

101. Zhu Hongyuan, *Cong bianluan dao junsheng: Guangxi de chuqi xiandaihua, 1860–1937*, 461.

102. Jiang Huang, *Donglan xianzheng jiyao*, 7. The same author reported that after 1921, the postman would arrive in Donglan once every three days.

103. Chen Xinde, "Wei Baqun" (1983), 184; Huang Xianfan, Gan Wenjie & Gan Wenhao, *Wei Baqun pingzhuan*, 9.

104. Zhu Hongyuan, *Cong bianluan dao junsheng: Guangxi de chuqi xiandaihua, 1860–1937*, 461–462.

105. Xie Fumin, *Wei Baqun*, 6–8; Li Guozhou and Yan Yongtong, *Wei Baqun zhuan*, 16–18.

106. For Hong's attack on Confucianism, see Jonathan Spence, *God's Chinese Son: The Taiping Heavenly Kingdom of Hong Xiuquan*, 97–98.

107. Xie Fumin, *Wei Baqun*, 8–9; Li Guozhou and Yan Yongtong, *Wei Baqun zhuan*, 18–19.

Chapter Two

1. Lan Handong and Lan Qixuan, *Wei Baqun*, 25; Xie Fumin, *Wei Baqun*, 9.

2. Li Guozhou and Yan Yongtong, *Wei Baqun zhuan*, 20; Huang Xianfan, Gan Wenjie and Gan Wenhao, *Wei Baqun pingzhuan*, 20–22.

3. Zeng Qiqiang, ed., *Zhongguo zaoqi nongmin yundong lingxiu Wei Baqun*, 25; Lan Handong and Lan Qixuan, *Wei Baqun*, 25.

4. Jiang Maosheng, *Qianli lailong*, 40. Fuzhou: Fujian renmin, 1985.

5. BSD, 083-002-0013, "Baqun waichu youli."

6. Chen Mianshu, "Guangxi Donglan nongmin yundong zhi shiji zhuangkuang."

7. Li Guozhou and Yan Yongtong, *Wei Baqun zhuan*, 20–21; Huang Xianfan, Gan Wenjie and Gan Wenhao, *Wei Baqun pingzhuan*, 23–24.

8. Zeng Qiqiang, ed., *Zhongguo zaoqi nongmin yundong lingxiu Wei Baqun*, 25–30.

9. BSD, 083-002-0013, "Baqun waichu youli."

10. Zeng Qiqiang, ed., *Zhongguo zaoqi nongmin yundong lingxiu Wei Baqun*, 27.

11. Li Zongren and Tang Degang, *Li Zongren huiyilu*, 61; 72.

12. Huang Shaohong, *Huang Shaohong huiyilu*, 22; Zhu Hongyuan, *Cong bianluan dao junsheng: Guangxi de chuqi xiandaihua, 1860–1937*, 417–423.

13. Qin Yingji, *Xiaoyan suiyue*, 14; Mo Wenhua, *Huiyi Hongqijun*, 54, 73. Nanning: Guangxi renmin, 1962; Yan Heng, "Yan Heng tongzhi guanyu diqijun de baogao." *ZYJGMGJD*, Vol. 1, 383; Deng Xiaoping, "Qijun gongzuo baogao." *ZYJGMGJD*, Vol. 1, 400; Jiang Maosheng, *Qianli lailong*, 70.

14. Zeng Qiqiang, ed., *Zhongguo zaoqi nongmin yundong lingxiu Wei Baqun*, 29.

15. Huang Hanzhong and Chen Rukai, "Chen Shusen qiren qishi." *Donglan wenshi ziliao*, 2 (1987), 46; Ning Xianbiao, "Hongshuihegu de gushi." Nandan zhengxie wang, October 31, 2006.

16. Zeng Qiqiang, ed., *Zhongguo zaoqi nongmin yundong lingxiu Wei Baqun*, 31–32.

17. For further discussions, see Xiaorong Han, *Chinese Discourses on the Peasant, 1900–1949*, 19–24. State University of New York Press, 2005.

18. Lan Qixuan, "Huang Bangwei." In *ZGGXDSRWZ*, Vol. 4, 1–7; Huang Guangwei, "Huang Bangwei lieshi mu beiwen." In Lu Xiuxiang, ed. *Donglan nongmin yundong, 1921–1927*, 69.

19. Huang Yingjun, "Huang Daquan." In Lu Xiuxiang, Huang Jianping and Huang Yingjun, eds. *Zhonggong Donglan dangshi renwu zhuan*, 111–123. Donglan: Zhonggong Donglan xianwei dangshi bangongshi, 1988.

20. Ban Feng and Luo Zhaowen, "Liao Yuanfang." In *ZGGXDSRWZ*. Vol. 1, 202–211.

21. *Donglan xianzhi*, 1994, 723; Huang Hanzhong and Chen Rukai, "Chen Shusen qiren qishi"; Han Jianmeng, "Ya Sumin." *ZGGXDSRWZ*. Vol. 4, 347.

22. Huang Xuchu, "Wei Baqun luan Donglan huo Guangxi shimo." *Chunqiu*, 187 (1965).

23. Edward Friedman, *Backward toward Revolution: The Chinese Revolutionary Party*, 117–164. University of California Press, 1974.

24. Xie Fumin, *Wei Baqun*, 10–11.

25. *ZYJGMSLHB*, Vol. 1, 11.

26. Zeng Qiqiang, ed., *Zhongguo zaoqi nongmin yundong lingxiu Wei Baqun*, 318–320.

27. Mo Wenhua, *Huiyi hongqijun*, 25.

28. Peng Yuanzhong, "Wei Baqun budang xianzhang," 9. In Tang Nonglin, ed., *Guihai yizhu*; Zeng Qiqiang, ed., *Zhongguo zaoqi nongmin yundong lingxiu Wei Baqun*, 39.

29. Zeng Qiqiang, ed., *Zhongguo zaoqi nongmin yundong lingxiu Wei Baqun*, 39.

30. For brief biographies of Lu Tao, see Qin Huaru, "Lu Tao zhuanlue." In *GXWSZL*. 21 (1984), 1–17; Wei Zhihua, "Lu Tao." In *ZGGXDSRWZ*. Vol. 3, 258–264.

31. Xie Fumin, *Wei Baqun*, 9; Huang Xuchu, "Wei Baqun luan Donglan huo Guangxi shimo."

32. Wei Qirong and Huang Jianping, "Chen Bomin," 139–140. In *ZGGXDSRWZ*, Vol. 1, 139–147; *WCYZJHXJ*, 78–79.

33. Wei Qirong & Huang Jianping, "Chen Bomin," 140; Huang Naiwen, "Chen Bomin zhuanlue." *Donglan wenshi*, 4 (2001), 58.

34. *Donglan xianzhi*, 1960, section on history, 2; Li Guozhou and Yan Yongtong, *Wei Baqun zhuan*, 29; Lan Handong and Lan Qixuan, *Wei Baqun*, 45; Zeng Qiqiang, ed., *Zhongguo zaoqi nongmin yundong lingxiu Wei Baqun*, 40.

35. Chen Xinde, "Wei Baqun" (1983), 186.

36. Hua Cheng, "Ma Junwu," 26. In Guangxi xinhai gemingshi yanjiuhui, ed., *Minguo Guangxi renwu zhuan*, Vol. 1.

37. Liang Lieya, "Gaizao Guangxi tongzhihui de chengli jiqi douzheng," 154–157. *GXWSZLXJ*. Vol. 6 (1963).

38. Ibid., 166.

39. Ibid., 168–169.

40. Ibid., 163–164.

41. Ou Zhengren, *Ma Junwu zhuan*, 120.

42. Li Zongren and Tang Degang, *Li Zongren huiyilu*, 113; 125.

43. Liang Lieya, "Gaizao Guangxi tongzhihui de chengli jiqi douzheng," 167–169; Huang Xuchu, "Wei Baqun luan Donglan huo Guangxi shimo;" Xie Fumin, *Wei Baqun*, 12; Lan Leibin, "Wei Baqun xiangpian zhi mi," 77–80.

44. Hua Cheng, "Ma Junwu," 28; Ou Zhengren, *Ma Junwu zhuan*, 23–25, 29–30, 86. Nanning: Zhengxie Guangxi Zhuangzu zizhiqu weiyuanhui wenshiziliao yanjiushi, 1982.

45. Huang Yucheng, "Gongchandang xingzhengzuzhi neimu qingkuang," 1005–1006. In *ZYJGMGJD*, Vol. 2; Huang Chao, "Dui Hongqijun jianli yishu de jidian yijian," 229. In Qin Wenliang, ed., *Donglanxian geming yingming lu. Donglan wenshi ziliao*, 3 (1988); Zhu Xi'ang, "Zhu Xi'ang gei zhongyang xunshiyuan he Guangdong shengwei de baogao." January 27, 1929. In Lan Yingbo and Deng Lineng, eds., *Guangxi geming lishi wenjian huiji*. 1982.

46. Arif Derlik, *The Origins of Chinese Communism*, 75. Oxford University Press, 1989; Peter Zarrow, *China in War and Revolution, 1895–1945*, 140. Routledge, 2005. For their researches on Chinese anarchism, see Arif Derlik, *Anarchism in Chinese Revolution*. University of California Press, 1993; and Peter Zarrow, *Anarchism and Chinese Political Culture*. Columbia University Press, 1990.

47. Li Zongren and Tang Degang, *Li Zongren huiyilu*, 736.

48. Chen Hanming, "Lun jindai zhongguo wuzhengfu zhuyi sichao." Xueshuo lianxian, http://www.xslx.com/Html/sxgc/200408/6950.html

49. Sheng Ming, "Wuzhengfu zhuyi zai Sichuan de liuchuan." *Sichuan dangshi*, 1995(3), 46.

50. Arif Derlik, *The Origins of Chinese Communism*, 77–78.

51. Peter Zarrow, *China in War and Revolution, 1895–1945*, 50; 142; Xiaorong Han, *Chinese Discourses on the Peasant, 1900–1949*, 27–28.

52. Tang Songqiu, "Yan Min." *ZGGXDSRWZ*, Vol. 1 (1992), 135.

53. Arif Derlik, *Anarchism in Chinese Revolution*, 2; Peter Zarrow, *China in War and Revolution, 1895–1945*, 140–141; Maurice Meisner, *Li Ta-chao and the Origins of Chinese Marxism*, 13–14. Harvard University Press, 1967; Maurice Meisner, *Mao Zedong: A Political and Intellectual Portrait*, 14–16; 22–23.

54. Chen Hanming, "Lun jindai zhongguo wuzhengfu zhuyi sichao;" Peter Zarrow, *China in War and Revolution, 1895–1945*, 140; Yeh Wen-hsin, *Provincial Passages: Culture, Space, and the Origins of Chinese Communism*, 216.

55. Zhu Xi'ang, "Zhu Xi'ang gei Zhongyang xunshiyuan he Guangdong shengwei de baogao."

56. Peter Zarrow, *China in War and Revolution, 1895–1945*, 142; Arif Derlik, *The Origins of Chinese Communism*, 75.

57. Zeng Qiqiang, ed., *Zhongguo zaoqi nongmin yundong lingxiu Wei Baqun*, 40.

Chapter Three

1. James DeFronzo, *Revolutions and Revolutionary Movements*, 15–17. Westview Press, 2011.

2. Wei Qirong and Huang Jianping, "Chen Bomin," 141.

3. Philip A. Kuhn, *Origins of the Modern Chinese State*, 101. Stanford University Press, 2002.

4. *ZYJGMSLHB*, Vol. 1, 7; *Donglan nongmin yundong*, 20.

5. Huang Shaohong, *Huang Shaohong huiyilu*, 89.

6. There is a problem with the dating of this event. Some sources claim that Liu Rifu took Baise after June 1922 rather than in later 1921, which means it was impossible for the general to meet with Wei Baqun and Chen Bomin in Baise in early 1922. One other source holds that the meeting did not take place until winter 1924. This is very unlikely because Wei Baqun was not even in the Right River region at that time. Huang Shaohong, *Huang Shaohong huiyilu*, 659; Li Changshou, "Echeng zhanshi shihua." *Baise shizhi*, 4 (1988), 38–40; Wu Zhongcai, Huang Yuanzheng and Chen Xinde, *Baise qiyi shigao*, 8. Guilin: Guangxi shifan daxue, 2004; *Donglan xianzhi*, 1960, section on history, 13–14.

7. Huang Xianfan, Gan Wenjie, and Gan Wenhao, *Wei Baqun pingzhuan*, 40.

8. Huang Hanzhong and Chen Baxian, "Yucai gaodeng xiaoxue yange gaikuang," 171.

9. Ibid., 170.

10. Wu Delin and Huang Hanzhong, "Kuixinglou gaikuang." *Donglan wenshi ziliao*, 1 (1985), 71–76; Fan Honggui and Gu Youshi, et al., *Zhuangzu lishi yu wenhua*, 293; For Chen Hongmou's life, see William Rowe, *Saving the World: Chen Hongmou and Elite Consciousness in Eighteenth-Century China*.

11. Zeng Qiqiang, ed. *Zhongguo gongchandang Donglan lishi*, 11. Beijing: Zhonggong dangshi, 2007; Zeng Qiqiang, ed., *Zhongguo zaoqi nongmin yundong lingxiu Wei Baqun*, 57.

12. Huang Hanzhong and Chen Baxian, "Yucai gaodeng xiaoxue yange gaikuang," 172.

13. *ZYJGMSLHB*, Vol. 1, 13; Ban Feng and Luo Zhaowen, "Liao Yuanfang," 203; Huang Yingjun, "Huang Daquan." *ZGGXDSRWZ*, Vol. 1, 316; Lan Qixuan, "Huang Bangwei," 3.

14. Qin Yingwu, "Chen Hongtao xiaozhuan." *Donglan wenshi*, 4 (2001), 45.

15. Lucien Bianco, *Wretched Rebels: Rural Disturbances on the Eve of the Chinese Revolution*. Harvard East Asian Monographs, 2009, xii; 3; 85–86; 122; 213.

16. Jean Chesneaux, *Peasant Revolts in China, 1840–1949*, 56. W. W. Norton & Company, Inc., 1973; Lucien Bianco, *Wretched Rebels: Rural Disturbances on the Eve of the Chinese Revolution*, 130–143.

17. Huang Hanzhong and Chen Baxian, "Yucai gaodeng xiaoxue yange gaikuang," 171.

18. Zeng Qiqiang, ed., *Zhongguo gongchandang Donglan lishi*, 12.

19. Mo Shujie, "Lin Junting." In Guangxi xinhai gemingshi yanjiuhui, ed. *Minguo Guangxi renwu zhuan*, Vol. 1, 109–113; Li Jiaxian, "Zizhijun zhanling Nanning hou Guangxi de jumian." In *GXWSZLXJ*, Vol. 3 (1963), 135–142.

20. Xie Fumin, *Wei Baqun*, 15; Huang Xuchu, "Wei Baqun luan Donglan huo Guangxi shimo."

21. *ZYJGMSLHB*, Vol. 1, 14.

22. Huang Xuchu, "Wei Baqun luan Donglan huo Guangxi shimo."

23. *ZYJGMSLHB*, Vol. 1, 14.

24. Zeng Qiqiang, ed., *Zhongguo zaoqi nongmin yundong lingxiu Wei Baqun*, 57.

25. Huang Jiashi, "Yi qingsuan Wei Longfu he sanda Donglancheng." Lu Xiuxiang, ed., *Donglan nongmin yundong, 1921–1927*, 165; Huang Yulu, ed., *Zhongguo gongchandang Guangxi Zhuangzu zizhiqu Donglanxian zuzhishi ziliao, 1926–1987*, 4. Nanning: Guangxi renmin, 1994.

26. Xie Fumin, *Wei Baqun*, 15.

27. Ya Meiyuan and Chen Shidu, "Wei Baqun jianli geming wuzhuang de huiyi." *Donglan wenshi ziliao*, 1 (1985), 54–55.

28. Chen Xinde, "Wei Baqun" (1983), 188.

29. Ya Meiyuan and Chen Shidu, "Wei Baqun jianli geming wuzhuang de huiyi," 55–56.

30. Chen Xinde, "Wei Baqun" (1983), 188.

31. Zeng Qiqiang, ed., *Zhongguo zaoqi nongmin yundong lingxiu Wei Baqun*, 59.

32. *Donglan xianzhi*, 1960, section on society, 8.

33. Wenshizu, "Sanda Donglan cheng." *Donglan wenshi ziliao*, 1 (1985), 26; *Donglan xianzhi*, 1994, 230.

34. *ZYJGMSLHB*, Vol. 1, 13–14; Lan Qixuan, "Huang Bangwei," 2.

35. Guangxi shaoshuminzu lishidiaocha zu, ed., *Guangxi Zhuangzu zizhiqu Donglanxian Zhonghe renmingongshe Donglitun shehuilishi diaocha baogao*, 30.

36. Lu Xiuxuan, "Dadao Wei Longfu, Ganzou Meng Yuanliang." *Huiyi Wei Baqun*, 62–64. Nanning: Guangxi renmin, 1979; Wenshizu, "Sanda Donglan cheng," 28–29.

37. *ZYJGMSLHB*, Vol. 1, 16.

38. Huang Jiashi, "Yi qingsuan Wei Longfu he sanda Donglancheng," 167.

39. Qin Shaokuan, "Jiuping he zhadan." In Guangxi minjian wenxue yanjiuhui, ed., *Dadan youmaqi: Zuoyoujiang geming lingdaoren gushi chuanshuo*, 144–146. *Guangxi minjian wenxue congkan*, No. 11. Nanning, 1984.

40. Chen Xinde, "Wei Baqun" (1983), 189; Zeng Qiqiang, ed., *Zhongguo zaoqi nongmin yundong lingxiu Wei Baqun.*

41. Huang Jiashi, "Yi qingsuan Wei Longfu he sanda Donglancheng," 168.

42. Chen Xinde, "Wei Baqun" (1983), 189.

43. *ZYJGMSLHB*, Vol. 1, 17; Ban Feng and Luo Zhaowen, "Liao Yuanfang," 203–204.

44. Marcus J. Kurtz, "Understanding Peasant Revolution: From Concept to Theory and Case." *Theory and Society*, No. 29 (2000), 108.

45. Clifton B. Kroeber, "Theory and History of Revolution." *Journal of World History*, Vol. 7, No. 1 (1996), 22, 26; Theda Skocpol, *States and Social Revolutions: A Comparative Analysis of France, Russia, and China.* Cambridge University Press, 1979.

46. Diana Lary, *Region and Nation: The Kwangsi Clique in Chinese Politics, 1925–1937*, 43.

47. Lucien Bianco, *Peasants Without the Party: Grassroots Movements in Twentieth-Century China*. M. E. Sharpe, 2001.

48. Chen Xinde, "Wei Baqun" (1983), 190.

49. Wenshizu, "Sanda Donglan cheng," 31.

50. Zeng Qiqiang, ed., *Zhongguo zaoqi nongmin yundong lingxiu Wei Baqun*, 67–68; Chen Xinde, "Wei Baqun" (1983), 190; Chen Xinde, "Wei Baqun." *ZGGXDSRWZ*, Vol. 1 (1992), 247.

51. *Donglan xianzhi*, 1994, 722.

Chapter Four

1. Huang Xianfan, Gan Wenjie, and Gan Wenhao, *Wei Baqun pingzhuan*, 91.

2. Li Guozhou and Yan Yongtong, *Wei Baqun zhuan*, 50–52; Huang Xianfan, Gan Wenjie, and Gan Wenhao, *Wei Baqun pingzhuan*, 91–92.

3. Liu Lidao, "Zhang Qihuang," 106. In Guangxi xinhai gemingshi yanjiuhui, ed. *Minguo Guangxi renwu zhuan*, Vol. 1.

4. James E. Sheridan, *China in Disintegration: The Republican Era in Chinese History, 1912–1949*, 61–77. The Free Press, 1975.

5. Diana Lary, *Region and Nation: The Kwangsi Clique in Chinese Politics, 1925–1937*, 15–17.

6. Huang Runsheng, "Qu Guangzhou diliujie nongjiangsuo xuexi qianhou de huiyi." 1974. In Lu Xiuxiang, ed., *Donglan nongmin yundong, 1921–1927*, 232–233. Nanning: Guangxi minzu, 1986.

7. Ibid., 233.

8. Li Guozhou and Yan Yongtong, *Wei Baqun zhuan*, 52.

9. Ibid., 52.

10. Ibid., 53.

11. Peng Pai, "Haifeng nongmin yundong." *Peng Pai wenji*, 111–113. Beijing: Renmin, 1981.

12. Wei Baqun, "Anwei qinren ge." In *WCSLZJ*, 221.

13. Wang Luyong, "Guangzhou nongmin yundong jiangxisuo de chuangban jiqi lishigongji." *Fujian dangshi yuekan*, 2005(2), 39–41; Huang Xianfan, Gan Wenjie, and Gan Wenhao, *Wei Baqun pingzhuan*, 95.

14. Wang Luyong, "Guangzhou nongmin yundong jiangxisuo de chuangban jiqi lishigongji."

15. Chen Xinde, "Wei Baqun" (1983), 191.

16. Huang Xianfan, Gan Wenjie, and Gan Wenhao, *Wei Baqun pingzhuan*, 94.

17. Ibid., 94–95.

18. Wang Luyong, "Guangzhou nongmin yundong jiangxisuo de chuangban jiqi lishigongji"; Lin Jinwen, ed., *Guangzhou nongmin yundong jiangxisuo ziliao xuanbian*. Beijing: Renmin, 1987.

19. Huang Xianfan, Gan Wenjie, and Gan Wenhao, *Wei Baqun pingzhuan*, 95–96.

20. Ibid., 93.

21. Ibid., 96; Chen Xinde, "Wei Baqun" (1983), 191.

22. Ruan Xiaoxian, "Quanguo nongmin yundong de xingshi jiqi zai guomingeming zhong de diwei." August 19, 1926. *Ruan Xiaoxian wenji*, 282. Guangzhou: Guangdong renmin, 1984.

23. Ya Meiyuan, "Huiyi dageming he tudigeming shiqi Donglan shehui zhi'an gaikuang." *Donglan wenshi ziliao*, 1 (1985), 44.

24. Li Zongren and Tang Degang, *Li Zongren huiyilu*, 113–114; 122–123.

25. Huang Shaohong, *Huang Shaohong huiyilu*, 55; 661.

26. Huang Runsheng, "Qu Guangzhou diliujie nongjiangsuo xuexi qianhou de huiyi," 233.

27. Ibid., 233.

28. Mo Shujie, "Lin Junting," 113.

29. Li Zongren and Tang Degang, *Li Zongren huiyilu*, 179.

30. Guangxisheng zhengfu, "Guangxisheng zhengfu dui Donglan nong'an zhi jingguo." *Zhongguo guomindang guomin gemingjun diqijun tebiedangbu banyuekan*, No. 11. December 15, 1926. In *ZYJGMSLHB*, Vol. 3, 2–4.

31. Lan Handong and Lan Qixuan, *Wei Baqun*, 88; Huang Xianfan, Gan Wenjie, and Gan Wenhao, *Wei Baqun pingzhuan*, 96; Chen Xinde, "Wei Baqun" (1983), 191–192; Qin Yingji, Huang Songjian and Huang Rong, "Zhuoyue de gongchanzhuyi zhanshi Wei Baqun." *Guangxi ribao*. October 19, 1982. In *ZYJGMGJD*, Vol. 2, 655–664.

32. Huang Xianfan, Gan Wenjie and Gan Wenhao, *Wei Baqun pingzhuan*, 93.

33. Xu Shu, "Zhu De rudang de yibosanzhe." *Dang de wenxian*, No. 135 (2010, No. 3), 118–119.

34. Ruan Xiaoxian, "Quanguo nongmin yundong de xingshi jiqi zai guomingeming zhong de diwei," 288.

Chapter Five

1. Huang Shaohong, *Huang Shaohong huiyilu*, 49–50; Qin Yingwu, "Chen Hongtao xiaozhuan," 44.

2. Huang Yingjun, "Huang Daquan" (1992), 317.

3. Wei Qiang, "Huang Bangcheng." Lu Xiuxiang, Huang Jianping and Huang Yingjun, eds., *Zhonggong Donglan dangshi renwu zhuan*, 64–75; *Donglan xianzhi*, 1994, 618–619; Huang Xianfan, Gan Wenjie and Gan Wenhao, *Wei Baqun pingzhuan*, 98.

4. Huang Dakun, "Li Zhengru." *ZGGXDSRWZ*, Vol. 4, 443–446.

5. Zhonggong Donglan xianwei dangshi bangongshi, "Guanyu jinggao tongbaoshu fabiao shijian de kanfa." In Lu Xiuxiang, ed., *Donglan nongmin yundong, 1921–1927*; Wei Baqun et al., "Jinggao tongbaoshu." In *WCSLZJ*, 26–27.

6. *Donglan nongmin yundong*, 21.

7. *ZYJGMSLHB*, Vol. 1, 21; Ya Yuanbo, "Wei Baqun deng jinggao tongbao chengwen fabu shijian kao." *Hechi shizhuan xuebao*, 21 (3), 30–32. 2001. See also Li Xiang, "1897–1927 nian 'guomingeming' gainian yanbian kaoshi" (*Yunnan shehui kexue*, 2008 (2), 140–144) for discussions about the evolution of the concept of National Revolution.

8. Wang Luyong, "Guangzhou nongmin yundong jiangxisuo de chuangban jiqi lishigongji."

9. *Donglan xianzhi*, 1994, 624–625; Huang Yingjun, "Huang Daquan" (1992), 315–323.

10. Huang Runsheng, "Qu Guangzhou diliujie nongjiangsuo xuexi qianhou de huiyi," 232–233; Huang Zhiping, ed., *Hongtu zhi hun: Donglan yingxiong pu*, 64. Nanning: Guangxi Zhonggong dangshi xuehui, 2003; Liang Yaodong, "Chen Gutao." In *ZGGXDSRWZ*, Vol. 4 (2004), 531–535.

11. Ya Meiyuan and Qin Yingwu, "Yi Chen Hongtao tongzhi." *Donglan wenshi*, 4 (2001), 40–43; Qin Yingwu, "Chen Hongtao xiaozhuan"; Lan Tian, "Chen Hongtao." In *ZGGXDSRWZ*, Vol. 1, 273–285; Wang Lintao, Cheng Zongshan and Lin Weicai, "Chen Hongtao," 206–208. In Hu Hua, ed., *Zhonggong dangshi renwu zhuan*, Vol. 7. Xi'an: Shanxi renmin chubanshe, 1983.

12. Wei Xinyin and Huang Yongsheng, "Huang Songjian zhuanlue." Wei Xinyin, ed., *Qingsong gaojie: Huang Songjian shiliao zhuanji*, 399–427. Nanning: Guangxi renmin, 1999.

13. Huang Yingjun, "Bai Hanyun." In Lu Xiuxiang, Huang Jianping and Huang Yingjun, eds., *Zhonggong Donglan dangshi renwu zhuan*, 76–91; Wei Qirong, "Huang Fangri." In Bai Xianjing, ed., *Hongqijun Hongbajun yinglie zhuan*, 585–591. Beijing: Jiefangjun, 1991; Lu Xiuxiang, "Lu Haoren." In Lu Xiuxiang, Huang Jianping and Huang Yingjun, eds. *Zhonggong Donglan dangshi renwu zhuan*, 138–160; Luo Xiulong, "Huang Wentong," 536–539. In *ZGGXDSRWZ*, Vol. 4, 536–539.

14. Wei Jie, "Sanci jian Bage." *Huiyi Wei Baqun*, 41–44.

15. *ZYJGMSLHB*, Vol. 1, 25; Huang Runsheng, "Qu Guangzhou diliujie nongjiangsuo xuexi qianhou de huiyi," 233; Wang Lintao, Cheng Zongshan and Lin Weicai, "Chen Hongtao," 207.

16. *ZYJGMSLHB*, Vol. 1, 25; Lu Xiuxiang, ed., *Donglan nongmin yundong, 1921–1927*, 12.

17. Zeng Qiqiang, ed., *Zhongguo zaoqi nongmin yundong lingxiu Wei Baqun*, 80–81.

18. Chen Mianshu, "Guangxi Donglan nongmin yundong zhi shiji zhuangkuang," 53; Guangxisheng nongminbu, "Guangxisheng nongminbu gongzuo baogao." *ZYJGMSLHB*, Vol. 2, 56–57.

19. *ZYJGMSLHB*, Vol. 2, 4; Huang Zhengxiu, "Zai xian nongmin xiehui gongzuo de huiyi." *WCSLZJ*, 353.

20. Huang Juping, "Lieningyan." *Huiyi Wei Baqun,* 70–71.

21. Ibid.," 71; Huang Yushan, "Huiyi Donglan nongmin yundong jiangxisuo." In Lu Xiuxiang, ed., *Donglan nongmin yundong, 1921–1927*, 170–171; Chen Xinde, "Wei Baqun" (1983), 193; *ZYJGMSLHB*, Vol. 1, 27; Xie Fumin, *Wei Baqun*, 24–25.

22. *ZYJGMSLHB*, Vol. 1, 26.

23. Lu Xiuxiang, ed., *Donglan nongmin yundong, 1921–1927*, 40–46; Huang Yushan, "Huiyi Donglan nongmin yundong jiangxisuo," 171–172; *ZYJGMSLHB*, Vol. 1, 26.

24. Lu Xiuxiang, ed., *Donglan nongmin yundong, 1921–1927*, 9–10.

25. Huang Juping, "Lieningyan," 71–72; Huang Yushan, "Huiyi Donglan nongmin yundong jiangxisuo," 171–172; 175–177.

26. BSD, 083-02-100-002, "Maliezhuyi chuanru Donglan he yingxiang."

27. Chen Mianshu, "Guangxi Donglan nongmin yundong zhi shiji zhuangkuang," 54.

28. Huang Juping, "Lieningyan," 73–74.

29. Qin Yingji, *Xiaoyan suiyue*, 5.

30. Chen Mianshu, "Guangxi Donglan nongmin yundong zhi shiji zhuangkuang," 53.

31. Mao Zedong, "Report on the Peasant Movement in Hunan." In Staurt Shram, ed., *Mao's Road to Power*. Vol. 2, 429–464. M. E. Sharpe, 1994; Harold R. Isaacs, *The Tragedy of the Chinese Revolution*, 223–224. Stanford University Press, 1961.

32. Huang Yushan, "Huiyi Donglan nongmin yundong jiangxisuo," 173; Chen Mianshu, "Guangxi Donglan nongmin yundong zhi shiji zhuangkuang," 51; *Donglan xianzhi*, 1994, 723; Han Jianmeng, "Ya Sumin," 345.

33. Xie Fumin, *Wei Baqun*, 25.

34. *ZYJGMSLHB*, Vol. 1, 28–29; Lu Xiuxiang, *Donglan nongmin yundong, 1921–1927*, 18; Xie Fumin, *Wei Baqun*, 25.

35. Huang Naiwen, "Chen Bomin zhuanlue," 61; Huang Yushan, "Huiyi Donglan nongmin yundong jiangxisuo," 177.

36. Lan Qixuan and Su Xing, "Wei Baqun tongzhi rudang shijian kaozheng," *Geming renwu*, 1987 (1), 30.

37. Chen Shidu, "Fanji Huang Shouxian dui nongsuo de pohuai." In Lu Xiuxiang, ed., *Donglan nongmin yundong, 1921–1927*, 179; *ZYJGMSLHB*, Vol. 1, 29.

38. *Chen Shidu, "Fanji Huang Shouxian dui nongsuo de pohuai,"* 179–182; Huang Juping, "Lieningyan," 79–80; *ZYJGMSLHB*, Vol. 1, 29.

39. Chen Xiewu, "Guangxi Donglan nongmin zhi can'an."

40. Huang Shaohong, "Siyi'er shibian qianhou wo qinshen jingli de huiyi." *Guangxi wenshi ziliao*, 7 (1978), 9.

41. Chen Mianshu, "Guangxi Donglan nongmin yundong zhi shiji zhuangkuang," 51.

42. Huang Xuchu, "Wei Baqun luan Donglan huo Guangxi shimo"; Huang Shaohong, *Huang Shaohong huiyilu*, 189; Li Zongren and Tang Degang, *Li Zongren huiyilu*, 227; 305; 319–321.

43. Zhao Bingzhuang, "Lu Jizhang." In *ZGGXDSRWZ*, Vol. 1, 8–9; Chen Xinde, "Wei Baqun" (1983), 193–194.

44. One source holds that Meng appointed Du Ba's elder brother Du Qi as the new county magistrate. Chen Mianshu, "Guangxi Donglan nongmin yundong zhi shiji zhuangkuang," 51.

45. Chen Mianshu, "Guangxi Donglan nongmin yundong zhi shiji zhuangkuang," 51.

46. Chen Xiewu, "Guangxi Donglan nongmin zhi can'an," 39; Lu Xiuxiang, ed., *Donglan nongmin yundong, 1921–1927*, 19; *ZYJGMSLHB*, Vol. 1, 43.

47. Chen Xiewu, "Guangxi Donglan nongmin zhi can'an," 43; Donglanxian nongmin xiehui, "Kuaiyou daidian." May 1926. In *WCSLZJ*, 30; *Donglan xianzhi*, 1994, 88.

48. Chen Mianshu, "Guangxi Donglan nongmin yundong zhi shiji zhuangkuang," 51–52.

49. Ibid., 52.

50. Peng Pai, "Haifeng nongmin yundong"; Peng Pai, "Huaxian tuanfei cansha nongmin de jingguo." September 1926. *Peng Pai wenji*, 207–257; Peng Pai, "Wei Wuhua nongyou ku yisheng." October 1926. *Peng Pai wenji*, 263–270; Mao Zedong, "Report on the Peasant Movement in Hunan"; Harold R. Issacs, *The Tragedy of the Chinese Revolution*, 225–227; William Rowe, *Crimson Rain: Seven Centuries of Violence in a Chinese County*, 262–268. Stanford University Press, 2007.

51. Chen Xiewu, "Guangxi Donglan nongmin zhi can'an," 44–45; Chen Mianshu, "Guangxi Donglan nongmin yundong zhi shiji zhuangkuang," 52–53.

52. Donglanxian nongmin xiehui, "Kuaiyou daidian," 30–31.

53. Huang Shaohong, "Siyi'er shibian qianhou wo qinshen jingli de huiyi," 3–4, 18.

54. Huang Chengshou, "He Jiannan." *ZGGXDSRWZ*, Vol. 1, 124; Long'anxian zhengxie wenshiwei, "Liang Di." *ZGGXDSRWZ*, Vol. 4, 50; Li Fuhua, "Lei Peitao." *ZGGXDSRWZ*, Vol. 1, 14–16; Yu Xinshun, "Liang Liudu." *ZGGXDSRWZ*, Vol. 4, 53–62; Wei Xianzhi, "Chen Liya." *ZGGXDSRWZ*, Vol. 4, 63–68; Chen Xinde, "Lei Tianzhuang." *ZGGXDSRWZ*, Vol. 4, 74–78.

55. Wei Ruilin, "Lu Rongting," 53; Liang Lieya, "Gaizao Guangxi tongzhihui de chengli jiqi douzheng," 289; Huang Chaoying and Guan Lixiong, "Chen Xiewu." *ZGGXDSRWZ*, Vol. 2, 156–157; Chen Mianshu, "Guangxi Donglan nongmin yundong zhi shiji zhuangkuang," 47.

56. Wang Jinxia and Chen Youming, "Chen Mianshu." *ZGGXDSRWZ*, Vol. 1, 376–388.

57. Chen Mianshu, "Guangxi Donglan nongmin yundong zhi shiji zhuangkuang," 47.

58. Lu Xiuxiang, ed., *Donglan nongmin yundong, 1921–1927*, 12.

59. Zeng Qiqiang, ed., *Zhongguo zaoqi nongmin yundong lingxiu Wei Baqun*, 318–319.

60. Lu Xiuxiang, ed., *Donglan nongmin yundong, 1921–1927*, 20.

61. Huang Chaoying and Guan Lixiong, "Chen Xiewu," 158; Lu Xiuxiang, ed., *Donglan nongmin yundong, 1921–1927*, 20.

62. Ya Meiyuan, "Diyici gemingzhanzheng shiqi guonei ge renmintuanti ji gejierenshi zhiyuan Donglan nongminyundong de huiyi." *Donglan wenshi ziliao*, 1 (1985), 20.

63. Huang Shaohong, "Siyi'er shibian guanyu Guangxi fangmian cailiao de buchong." *Guangxi wenshi ziliao*, 7 (1978), 47.

64. Chen Xiewu, "Guangxi Donglan nongmin zhi can'an," 39–46; Huang Chaoying and Guan Lixiong, "Chen Xiewu," 158.

65. Wang Jinxia and Chen Youming, "Chen Mianshu," 381–382; Huang Chaoying and Guan Lixiong, "Chen Xiewu," 158.

66. Hu Bingqiong, "Yuanzhu Donglan de nongyou." June 6, 1926. *WCSLZJ*, 34.

67. Hu Bingqiong, "Yuanzhu Donglan de nongyou," 34–35.

68. Liao Mengqiao, "Gei Donglan xianzhang Huang Shouxian yifeng gongkai de xin." June 8, 1926. In *WCSLZJ*, 36–37; Huang Longxing and Gao Wanzhang, "Liao Mengqiao." *ZGGXDSRWZ*, Vol. 1, 47–49.

69. Ruan Xiaoxian, "Quanguo nongmin yundong de xingshi jiqi zai guomingeming zhong de diwei," 288.

70. Chang Kuo-tao, *The Rise of the Chinese Communist Party: the Autobiography of Chang Kuo-tao*, Vol. 1, 604. University Press of Kansas, 1971.

71. Xie Shenghua, "Duiyu Guangxi Donglan nongmin beinan de wogan." *WCSLZJ*, 60–63; Shuang Cai, "Zhide zhuyi de Donglan nongmin yundong." *WCSLZJ*, 32–33.

72. Chen Xiewu, "Guangxi Donglan nongmin zhi can'an," 46; Li Guozhou and Yan Yongtong, *Wei Baqun zhuan*, 106.

73. Zeng Qiqiang, ed., *Zhongguo zaoqi nongmin yundong lingxiu Wei Baqun*, 315; Li Guozhou and Yan Yongtong, *Wei Baqun zhuan*, 106.

74. Chen Mianshu, "Guangxi Donglan nongmin yundong zhi shiji zhuangkuang," 53; Lu Xiuxiang, ed., *Donglan nongmin yundong, 1921–1927*, 21.

75. Bai Chongxi, *Bai Chongxi huiyilu*, 24.

76. Lu Xiuxiang, ed., *Donglan nongmin yundong, 1921–1927*, 21.

77. Li Qishi, et al., "Guanyu Guangxi de zuzhiqingkuang, gongnong geming yundong ji dui jinhou gongzuo yijian." February 7, 1928. *WCSLZJ*, 83–84.

78. For a study of the Communist promotion of peasant movement in southern China during the Northern Expedition, see Hans J. Van De Ven, *From Friends to Comrades: The Founding of the Chinese Communist Party, 1920–1927*, 181–198. University of California Press, 1991.

79. Zhonggong zhongyang, "Muqian nongyun jihua." November 15, 1926. *WCSLZJ*, 67.

80. Shi Hua, "Guangxi gongchandang de guoqu ji xianzai." *Xiandai shiliao*, 1(11). *WCSLZJ*, 622.

81. Chen Mianshu, "Guangxi Donglan nongmin yundong zhi shiji zhuangkuang," 48.

82. Zhonggong Donglan xianwei dangshi bangongshi, "Guanyu jinggao tongbaoshu fabiao shijian de kanfa," 282–283; Wu Delin, "Dui Donglan nongyun de jidian huiyi." In Lu Xiuxiang, ed., *Donglan nongmin yundong, 1921–1927*, 241.

83. Guangxisheng zhengfu, "Guangxisheng zhengfu dui Donglan nong'an zhi jingguo," 2–3; Wang Jinxia and Chen Youming, "Chen Mianshu," 382–383.

84. *ZYJGMSLHB*, Vol. 1, 49; Li Guozhou and Yan Yongtong, *Wei Baqun zhuan*, 108; Wang Jinxia and Chen Youming, "Chen Mianshu," 382; Chen Xinde, "Wei Baqun" (1983), 197.

85. Chen Bomin, Ya Sumin and Qin Kongxian, "Donglanxian dangwu Baogao." *Zhongguo guomindang Guangxisheng di'erci daibiaodahui rikan*. March 13, 1927. *WCSLZJ*, 76.

86. Lu Xiuxiang, ed., *Donglan nongmin yundong, 1921–1927*, 10, 46–48; Huang Jinqiu, "Huiyi dierjie nongjiangsuo funuban." 199–202; Huang Meilun, "Bage yinwo zoushang geminglu," 183–185.

87. Wang Lintao, Cheng Zongshan and Lin Weicai, "Chen Hongtao," 208; Lu Xiuxiang, ed., *Donglan nongmin yundong, 1921–1927*, 40–41.

88. Huang Jinqiu, "Huiyi dierjie nongjiangsuo funuban," 199–202; Huang Meilun, "Bage yinwo zoushang geminglu," 183–185.

89. *Donglan xianzhi*, 1994, 104; Huang Zhengxiu, "Zai xian nongmin xiehui gongzuo de huiyi," 352.

90. Yang Shaojuan, "Zuoyoujiang geming genjudi de funu yundong." *ZYJGMGJD*, Vol. 2, 1111–1112.

91. Chen Mianshu, "Guangxi Donglan nongmin yundong zhi shiji zhuangkuang," 53; Wenshizu, "Donglan nongyun zhong de fuyun gaikuang." *Donglan wenshi*, 4 (2001),

94–96; Chen Bomin, Ya Sumin and Qin Kongxian, "Donglanxian dangwu baogao," 76; Ya Meiyuan, "Geming xianzhang Chen Mianshu." *Donglan wenshi*, 4 (2001), 75.

92. Chen Mianshu, "Guangxi Donglan nongmin yundong zhi shiji zhuangkuang," 53.

93. Huang Yumei, "Chongpo laolong gangeming." *Guangxi geming douzheng huiyilu*, Vol. 2 (1984), 100–103; Huang Zhengxiu, "Zai xian nongmin xiehui gongzuo de huiyi," 353.

94. Huang Meilun, "Donglan geming chuqi de funu yundong pianduan." *Guangxi geming douzheng huiyilu*, Vol. 2 (1984), 94–99; Huang Yumei, "Chongpo laolong gangeming," 100–105; William Rowe, *Crimson Rain: Seven Centuries of Violence in a Chinese County*, 255–256; Wei Baqun, "Shige shishou;" "Shange shiwushou." *WCYZJHXJ*, 70–87; Peng Pai, "Shige shiyishou." *Peng Pai wenji*, 330–337; Lu Xiuxiang, ed., *Donglan geming genjudi*, 405. Donglan: Zhonggong Donglan xianwei dangshi bangongshi, 1990.

95. Tan Qingrong, "Wo dang nongjun jiaotong de huiyi." In Lu Xiuxiang, ed., *Donglan nongmin yundong, 1921–1927*, 212–215; Huang Yumei, "Chongpo laolong gangeming," 105–108.

96. Chen Mianshu, "Guangxi Donglan nongmin yundong zhi shiji zhuangkuang," 53; Wang Jinxia and Chen Youming, "Chen Mianshu," 383.

97. Ya Meiyuan, "Diyici gemingzhanzheng shiqi guonei ge renmintuanti ji gejierenshi zhiyuan Donglan nongminyundong de huiyi," 21–22; Wang Jinxia and Chen Youming, "Chen Mianshu," 383; Gao Yaoguang, "Chen Mianshu ersanshi." In Lu Xiuxiang, ed., *Donglan nongmin yundong, 1921–1927*, 190–195.

98. *ZYJGMSLHB*, Vol. 1, 51.

99. Guangxisheng zhengfu, "Guangxisheng zhengfu xunling di 37 hao,"14–15. *Guangxisheng zhengfu gongbao*, No. 59. January 21, 1928. *ZYJGMSLHB*, Vol. 3, 14–15.

100. Ya Meiyuan and Qin Yingwu, "Yi Chen Hongtao tongzhi," 40–41; Qin Yingwu, "Chen Hongtao xiaozhuan," 44–46; Lan Tian, "Chen Hongtao," 273–275; Liang Yaodong, "Chen Gutao," 531–532; Wang Jinxia and Chen Youming, "Chen Mianshu," 383; Tang Songqiu, "Yan Min," 130–135.

101. Huang Hongyi (?), *Weishizhang Baqun lingdao Donglan geming*, Vol. 2, Section 66. Unpublished manuscript.

102. Lan Handong and Lan Qixuan, *Wei Baqun*, 120.

103. As late as early 1929, a leading Communist from Guangxi still described Wei Baqun as "a leftist Nationalist." Zhu Xi'ang, "Zhu Xi'ang gei zhongyang xunshiyuan he Guangdong shengwei de baogao." For more discussions about the issue, see Huang Maotian, "Wei Baqun rudang shijian de kaozheng." *WCSLZJ*, 483–486; Ya Yuanbo, "Wei Baqun tongzhi rudang shijian zai kaozheng," 76–78; Lan Qixuan and Su Xing, "Wei Baqun tongzhi rudang shijian kaozheng," 30–34; Chen Xinde, "Wei Baqun" (1983), 200; *ZYJGMSLHB*, Vol. 1, 89–90; Mo Wenhua, *Huiyi Hongqijun*, 4; Gao Yaoguang, "Chen Mianshu ersanshi," 190.

104. Ya Yuanbo, "Wei Baqun tongzhi rudang shijian zai kaozheng," 77; Lan Qixuan and Su Xing, "Wei Baqun tongzhi rudang shijian kaozheng," 32.

105. Zhonggong Guangxi tewei, "Zhonggong Guangxi tewei gei Guangdong shengwei de xin." October 20, 1929. In *WCSLZJ*, 94.

106. Yun Daiying, "Gei Zhonggong zhongyang de baogao." October 24, 1927. *WCSLZJ*, 82.

107. Chen Mianshu, "Guangxi Donglan nongmin yundong zhi shiji zhuangkuang," 57.

108. Ya Meiyuan, "Diyici gemingzhanzheng shiqi guonei ge renmintuanti ji gejierenshi zhiyuan Donglan nongminyundong de huiyi," 21–22.

109. BSD, 084, "Wei Baqun mishu Wei Libo zhi Liu Pinqing." 1927.

110. Chen Haoren. "Qijun qianwei baogao." January 1930. *ZYJGMGJD*, Vol. 1, 164.

111. Tang Songqiu, "Yan Min," 135–136.

112. Lan Qixuan and Lan Baoshi, "Huang Zhifeng," 270–271.

113. Zhonggong Guangxi tewei, "Zhonggong Guangxi tewei gei Guangdong shengwei de xin," 95.

114. Lan Qixuan and Su Xing, "Wei Baqun tongzhi rudang shijian kaozheng," 32.

115. *ZYJGMSLHB*, Vol. 1, 52; Zhonggong Guangxi tewei "Zhonggong Guangxi tewei gei Guangdong shengwei de xin," 94.

116. BSD, 084, "Wei Baqun mishu Wei Libo zhi Liu Pinqing." 1927.

117. Tang Songqiu, "Yan Min," 135–136.

118. BSD, 084, "Wei Baqun mishu Wei Libo zhi Liu Pinqing." 1927.

119. Gao Yaoguang, "Chen Mianshu ersanshi," 194–195.

120. Lei Jingtian, "Yan Min zai Guangxi geming douzheng shilue." 1959. *ZYJGMGJD*, Vol. 2, 826.

121. Chen Mianshu, "Guangxi Donglan nongmin yundong zhi shiji zhuangkuang," 47–57.

122. Li Guozhou and Yan Yongtong, *Wei Baqun zhuan*, 108–109.

123. Diana Lary, *Region and Nation: The Kwangsi Clique in Chinese Politics, 1925–1937*, 76; Huang Xianfan, Gan Wenjie, and Gan Wenhao, *Wei Baqun pingzhuan*, 230.

124. Bai Chongxi, *Bai Chongxi huiyilu*, 46.

125. Huang Shaohong, "Siyi'er shibian qianhou wo qinshen jingli de huiyi," 5–10; 13.

126. Huang Shaohong, "Siyi'er shibian qianhou wo qinshen jingli de huiyi," 26; Li Zongren and Tang Degang, *Li Zongren huiyilu*, 324; Lei Rongjia, Chen Yeqiang and Jin Kaishan, "Lei Peihong." Guangxi xinhai gemingshi yanjiuhui, ed. *Minguo Guangxi renwu zhuan*, Vol. 1, 35.

127. Huang Shaohong, "Siyi'er shibian qianhou wo qinshen jingli de huiyi," 9; Huang Xuchu, "Guangxi Li Bai Huang yu qingdang zhiyi." *Chunqiu*, No. 108 (1962).

128. Guangxisheng zhengfu, "Guangxisheng zhengfu xunling minzheng sifa liangting jiang Huang Shouxian qian zai Donglanxian zhishi rennei yin lan'an suoshou zhi chufen chexiao wen." *Guangxisheng zhengfu gongbao*, No. 49. October 11, 1927. *ZYJGMSLHB*, Vol. 3, 8–9; Guangxisheng zhengfu, "Guangxisheng zhengfu xunling di 37 hao,"14–15; Guangxisheng zhengfu, "Guangxisheng zhengfu zhiling di 439 hao." *Guangxisheng zhengfu gongbao*, No. 66. April 1, 1928. *ZYJGMSLHB*, Vol. 3, 20–22; *Guangxi minzheng yuekan*, "Donglanxian diyici quanshu tuanwu huiyilu." January 1928. *ZYJGMSLHB*, Vol. 3, 15–17; Guangxisheng zhengfu, "Guangxisheng zhengfu xunling ge xianzhang ge jingtingju an ju Tiannan qingxiang zongban Liu Rifu cheng yiding

shangge gouji shouyao feidang Wei Baqun deng yangji yiti xieji wuhuo gui'an xunban wen [fu shangge]." December 12, 1927. *ZYJGMSLHB*, Vol. 3, 12–13; Guangxisheng zhengfu, "Guangxisheng zhengfu yudian." *Guangxisheng zhengfu gongbao*, No. 66. April 1, 1928. *ZYJGMSLHB*, Vol. 3, 22–23.

129. Huang Shaohong, *Huang Shaohong huiyilu*, 665; Li Guozhou and Yan Yongtong, *Wei Baqun zhuan*, 124.

130. Huang Huanmin, "Disanjie nongjiangsuo shenghuo pianduan." *WCSLZJ*, 359–363; Lu Xiuxiang, ed., *Donglan nongmin yundong, 1921–1927*, 10–11, 48–50.

131. *Donglan xianzhi*, 1960, section on history, 20.

132. Huang Xianfan, Gan Wenjie and Gan Wenhao, *Wei Baqun pingzhuan*, 204–205; Lu Xiuxiang, ed., *Donglan nongmin yundong, 1921–1927*, 10–11, 40–41.

133. Bi Mengping, "Wo zai Donglan disanjie jiangxisuo renjiao qianhou." *WCSLZJ*, 364–365; Huang Yingjun, "Wei Jing." *ZGGXDSRWZ*, Vol. 4, 515–516.

134. *ZYJGMSLHB*, Vol. 1, 54; Zeng Qiqiang, ed. *Zhongguo zaoqi nongmin yundong lingxiu Wei Baqun*, 12; Xie Fumin, *Wei Baqun*, 40–41; Li Guozhou and Yan Yongtong, *Wei Baqun zhuan*, 123; Lu Xiuxiang, ed., *Donglan nongmin yundong, 1921–1927*, 14; Huang Xianfan, Gan Wenjie and Gan Wenhao, *Wei Baqun pingzhuan*, 187–188.

135. *Donglan xianzhi*, 1994, 722.

136. Ban Feng and Luo Zhaowen, "Liao Yuanfang," 205–206; Li Guozhou and Yan Yongtong, *Wei Baqun zhuan*, 124–126.

137. Zeng Qiqiang, ed., *Zhongguo zaoqi nongmin yundong lingxiu Wei Baqun*, 317; Li Guozhou and Yan Yongtong, *Wei Baqun zhuan*, 127.

138. Li Guozhou and Yan Yongtong, *Wei Baqun zhuan*, 128.

139. Guangxisheng zhengfu, "Guangxisheng zhengfu xunling ge xianzhang ge jingtingju an ju Tiannan qingxiang zongban Liu Rifu cheng yiding shangge gouji shouyao feidang Wei Baqun deng yangji yiti xieji wuhuo gui'an xunban wen [fu shangge]."

140. Qin Wenliang, ed., *Donglanxian geming yingming lu*, 25–26; Wei Tianfu, ed., *Donglanxian minzheng zhi*, 190. Donglan: Donglanxian renmin zhengfu minzhengju and Donglanxian difangzhi bangongshi, 2001.

141. Zeng Qiqiang, ed., *Zhongguo zaoqi nongmin yundong lingxiu Wei Baqun*, 320.

142. Huang Songjian, "Guanyu Hongqijun junji wenti de huiyi." In Wei Xinyin, ed., *Qingsong gaojie: Huang Songjian shiliao zhuanji*, 144–146.

143. Yu Xinshun, "Zuoyoujiang diqu de nongmin wuzhuang douzheng." *ZYJGMGJD*, Vol. 2, 1060–1061; Wei Zhihong, Wu Zhongcai and Gao Xiong, ed., *Baise qiyi renwuzhi*, 50. Nanning: Guangxi renmin, 1999; *Donglan xianzhi*, 1994, 89; Huang Chao, "Gensui Bage naogeming." 1981. *WCSLZJ*, 348.

144. Chang Kuo-tao, *The Rise of the Chinese Communist Party: the Autobiography of Chang Kuo-tao*, Vol. 1, 607.

145. BSD, 083-002-099-002, "Youguan Donglan geming de cankao ziliao;" BSD, 083-02-100-002, "Maliezhuyi chuanru Donglan he yingxiang."

Chapter Six

1. Wu Zhongcai, Huang Yuanzheng and Chen Xinde, *Baise qiyi shigao*, 29–30.

2. Yu Xinshun, "Yu Zuoyu." Bai Xianjing, ed., *Hongqijun Hongbajun yinglie zhuan*, 158.

3. Wei Qirong and Huang Jianping, "Chen Bomin," 143.

4. For Deng's early life, see Marilyn Levine, *The Found Generation: Chinese Communists in Europe during the Twenties*, 4–6, 85–86, 206–209. The University of Washington Press, 1993; David Goodman, *Deng Xiaoping and the Chinese Revolution: A Political Biography*, 22–29. Routeledge, 1994; Benjamin Yang, "The Making of a Pragmatic Communist: The Early Life of Deng Xiaoping, 1904–1949," 444–448; *China Quarterly*, 135 (1993); Mao Mao, *Wode fuqin Deng Xiaoping*, Vol. 1, 55–195. Beijing: Zhongyang wenxian, 1993; Ezra Vogel, *Deng Xiaoping and the Transformation of China*, 15–28. Belknap Press of Harvard University Press, 2011.

5. Wei Zhihong, Wu Zhongcai and Gao Xiong, ed., *Baise qiyi renwuzhi*, 22–23; 58–59.

6. Gong Chu, *Wo yu hongjun*, 167–169. Hong Kong: South Wind Publishing Co., 1954.

7. Wei Zhihong, Wu Zhongcai and Gao Xiong, ed., *Baise qiyi renwuzhi*, 71–72.

8. Chen Xinde, "Zongshu," 7. In *ZYJGMGJD*, Vol. 1.

9. Nong Qizhen, "Zuojiang geming yundong pianduan huiyi," 890. In *ZYJGMGJD*, Vol. 2, 889–892; Huang Chaoying and Guan Lixiong, "Chen Xiewu," 160; Wei Qinglan and Huang Chaoyin, "Chen Mengwu." In *ZGGXDSRWZ*, Vol. 4, 169–172.

10. Huang Rong and Huang Yuyang, "Deng Xiaoping yu Wei Baqun." In Ya Zukun and Wei Jiabo, eds., *Deng Xiaoping yu Donglan*, 1–8. Nanning: Donglanxian geming laoqu jianshe cujinhui, 2005; Yuan Renyuan, "Cong Baise dao Xianggan." *ZYJGMGJD*, Vol. 2, 624; Mao Mao, *Wode fuqin Deng Xiaoping*, Vol. 1, 209; Zhang Yunyi, "Baise qiyi yu hongqijun de jianli." *Xinghuo Liaoyuan*, Vol. 1, 415–416; Chen Xinde, "Huang Fangri." *ZGGXDSRWZ*, Vol. 1, 327; Wu Zhongcai, Huang Yuanzheng and Chen Xinde, *Baise qiyi shigao*, 4; Wei Zhihong, Wu Zhongcai and Gao Xiong, ed., *Baise qiyi renwuzhi*, 50.

11. Wei Zhihong, Wu Zhongcai and Gao Xiong, ed., *Baise qiyi renwuzhi*, 71–72; Wu Zhongcai, Huang Yuanzheng and Chen Xinde, *Baise qiyi shigao*, 44–45; *Gongpingbao*, "Guiren shu Yu Zuobai shidazui." October 8, 1929. *ZYJGMSLHB*, Vol. 3, 34–35; *Zhongyang ribao*, "Gui shengwei shengtao Yuni Zuobai jiefa Yuni huo Gui zuizhuang." October 15, 1929. *ZYJGMSLHB*, Vol. 3, 40–42.

12. Wu Zhongcai, Huang Yuanzheng and Chen Xinde, *Baise qiyi shigao*, 41–42.

13. Zhonggong Guangxi tewei, "Zhonggong Guangxi tewei gei Guangdong shengwei de xin," 76.

14. Chen Xinde, "Zongshu," 9; Huang Rong and Huang Yuyang, "Deng Xiaoping yu Wei Baqun"; Huang Juping, "Donglan geming genjudi de jianli." In Lu Xiuxiang, ed., *Donglan geming genjudi*, 138; Huang Juping & Xie Fumin, "Yi Donglan baodong." In Ou Jiwen, ed., *Guangxi Hongjun*, 135–136. Nanning: Guangxi xinsijun lishi yanjiuhui, 2007.

15. He Jiarong, "Huiyi Hongbajun." In *ZYJGMGJD*, Vol. 2, 869; Gong Chu, *Wo yu hongjun*, 204–205; Mo Wenhua, *Huiyi hongqijun*, 14–15; *ZYJGMSLHB*, Vol. 1, 129.

16. Deng Xiaoping, "Wo de zishu." 1968. http://hetai2.blog.hexun.com/40777325_d.html

17. Ye Jizhuang, "Dui Wei Baqun tongzhi de jidian huiyi." *Huiyi Wei Baqun*, 3.

18. Zhang Yunyi, "Baise qiyi yu hongqijun de jianli," 419; Li Tianyou, "Huiyi Baise qiyi." *ZYJGMGJD*, Vol. 2, 599; Lei Jingtian, "Guangxi de Suwei'ai yundong." *ZYJGMGJD*, Vol. 2, 607.

19. Qin Yingji, *Xiaoyan suiyue*, 8; Chen Xinde, "Zongshu," 14–15; Wu Delin, "Huiyi Weishizhang yu hongjun Youjiang dulishi." Lu Xiuxiang, ed., *Donglan geming genjudi*, 202.

20. Wu Zhongcai, Huang Yuanzheng and Chen Xinde, *Baise qiyi shigao*, 84–89; *Donglan xianzhi*, 1994, 101; Lu Xiuxiang, ed., *Donglan nongmin yundong, 1921–1927*, 14; Chen Zhenwei, "Xishanxing." Hechi ribaoshe, ed., *Zhuixun hongqijun zuji*, 43. Nanning: Guangxi renmin, 1990; Xie Fumin, *Wei Baqun*, 54; Huang Hanzhong, "Tingsi zhanyi hou de shangyuan jiuhu." *Donglan wenshi*, 4 (2001), 104–105.

21. Wu Zhongcai, Huang Yuanzheng and Chen Xinde, *Baise qiyi shigao*, 92.

22. Zhang Yunyi, "Baise qiyi yu hongqijun de jianli," 419; Mo Wenhua, *Huiyi hongqijun*, 10; Wu Delin, "Huiyi Weishizhang yu hongjun Youjiang dulishi," 201; Chen Xinde, "Zongshu," 16.

23. Chen Xinde, "Zongshu," 1; Lei Jingtian, "Guangxi de Suwei'ai yundong," 612.

24. Guangdong shengwei, "Yuesheng dui qijun qianwei de zhishixin." December 25, 1929. *ZYJGMGJD*, Vol. 1, 142.

25. Chen Xinde, "Zongshu," 14; 17.

26. Mo Wenhua, *Mo Wenhua huiyilu*, 60. Beijing: Jiefangjun, 1996.

27. Lei Jingtian, "Guangxi de Suwei'ai yundong," 613.

28. Huang Mingzheng, "Dengzhengwei guanxin shangbingyuan." In Ya Zukun and Wei Jiabo, eds., *Deng Xiaoping yu Donglan*, 11–13.

29. Wei Tianfu, "Yu Zuobai yu Donglan geming ersanshi." *Donglan wenshi*, 4 (2001), 70–71; Wei Qirong and Huang Jianping, "Chen Bomin," 146–147.

30. Qin Yingji, Huang Songjian and Huang Rong, "Zhuoyue de gongchanzhuyi zhanshi Wei Baqun," 664; Han Jianmeng, "Ya Sumin," 343–350.

31. Chen Haoren, "Qijun gongzuo zongbaogao." March 9, 1931. *ZYJGMGJD*, Vol. 1, 372.

32. For eyewitness accounts of how the Nationalist politicians and army officers changed their views of the Communists and the United Front because of the rise of radical peasant movements, see Gong Chu, *Wo yu hongjun*, 47; Zheng Chaolin, *An Oppositionist for Life, Memoirs of the Chinese Revolutionary Zheng Chaolin*, 130–131, 185. Gregor Benton, trans. Humanities Press, 1997; Aleksei Vasilevich Blagodatov, *Zhongguo geming zhaji: 1925–1927*, 177. Zhang Kai, trans. Beijing: Xinhua, 1985; Zhou Enlai, "Guanyu yijiuersi zhi yijiuerliu nian dang dui guomindang de guanxi." *Zhou Enlai xuanji*, Vol. 1, 117. Beijing: Renmin, 1980; Hua Gang, *Zhongguo dageming shi*, 276. 1931. Reprinted by Beijing: Wenshi ziliao, 1982; Chen Gongbo, *Kuxiaolu: Chen gongbo huiyi, 1925–1936*, Vol. 1, 122–123. 1939. Hong Kong: University of Hong Kong Centre of Asian Studies Occasional Papers and Monographs, No. 36, 1979; For academic discussions of the issue, see Jiang Yongjing, *Baoluoting yu Wuhan zhengquan*, 311. Taipei: Zhongguo xueshu zhuzuo jiangzhu weiyuanwei, 1963; Lei Xiaocen, *Sanshinian dongluaan Zhongguo*, 76. Hong Kong: Yazhou, 1955; Wu Tien-wei, "A Review of the Wuhan Debacle," 132. *Journal of Asian Studies*, 29(1), 1969; Harold Isaacs, *The Tragedy of the Chinese Revolution*, 214; Robert North and Xenia Eudin, *M. N. Roy's Mission to China*, 97–98, 118. University of California Press, 1963.

33. Zhonggong zhongyang, "Zuijin nongmin douzheng de jueyi'an." In Zhongyang dang'anguan, ed., *Zhonggong zhongyang wenjian xuanji*, Vol. 4, 294–297. Beijing: Zhonggong zhongyang dangxiao, 1989; Zhonggong zhongyang, "Nongmin

yundong jueyi'an." In Zhongyang dang'anguan, ed., *Zhonggong zhongyang wenjian xuanji*, Vol. 4, 357; Zhonggong zhongyang, "Zhonggong zhongyang gei Guangdong shengwei zhuan qijun qianwei de zhishi." *ZYJGMGJD*, Vol. 1, 228.

34. Guangxi tewei, "Guangxi dang zhengzhi renwu jueyi'an." *ZYJGMGJD*, Vol. 1, 58, 61–62.

35. Lei Jingtian, "Guangxi de Suwei'ai yundong," 605.

36. Zhonggong Guangxi tewei, "Zhonggong Guangxi tewei gei Guangdong shengwei de xin," 83.

37. Zhen, "Muqian zhuyao de renwu." *ZYJGMGJD*, Vol. 1, 121; Hongqijun, "Tudi geming." *ZYJGMGJD*, Vol. 1, 129–135.

38. Youjiang Suwei'ai zhengfu, "Youjiang Suwei'ai zhengfu kouhao." *ZYJGMGJD*, Vol. 1, 146.

39. Hongqijun, "Hongqijun zai Baise xie de biaoyu." *ZYJGMSLHB*, Vol. 2, 91; Hongqijun, "Hongqijun zai Hechi xie de biaoyu." *ZYJGMSLHB*, Vol. 2, 172–175; Youjiang Suwei'ai zhengfu, "Gongnongbing shizi keben." *ZYJGMSLHB*, Vol. 2,136–150.

40. Deng Xiaoping, "Fazhan zhongri guanxi yao kande yuanxie." *Deng Xiaoping wenxuan*, Vol. 3, 31–32. Beijing: Renmin, 1993.

41. Benjamin Yang, "The Making of a Pragmatic Communist: The Early Life of Deng Xiaoping, 1904–1949," 449.

42. Deng Xiaoping, "Wo de zishu."

43. Gong Chu, *Wo yu hongjun*, 177, 200; Chenshi zongqin luntan, "Jinian Baise qiyi diyihao lingdaoren Chen Haoren tongzhi danchen yibai zhounian." http://bbs.chens.org.cn/showtopic.asp?TOPIC_ID=14953&Forum_ID=37

44. Chen Zuncheng, "Dengzhengwei zai Enlong." *Tiandong wenshi ziliao*, Vol. 1 (1987), 22–31; Huang Meilun, "Dengzhengwei laidao Wuzhuan." In *ZYJGMGJD*, Vol. 2, 682–686.

45. Wei Shiba, "Husong Dengzhengwei ji wo beishang de huiyi." In Lu Xiuxiang, ed., *Donglan geming genjudi*, 249–251.

46. Youjiang Suwei'ai zhengfu, "Tudifa zanxing tiaoli." *ZYJGMGJD*, Vol. 1, 265–269.

47. Mao Mao, *Wode fuqin Deng Xiaoping*, Vol. 1, 238; for discussion on the evolution of the agrarian policy in Mao Zedong's base area in Jiangxi, see John E. Rue, *Mao Tse-tung in Opposition, 1927–1935*, 196–203. Stanford University Press, 1966.

48. Deng Xiaoping, "Qijun gongzuo baogao." *ZYJGMGJD*, Vol. 1, 405; Wu Zhongcai, Huang Yuanzheng and Chen Xinde, *Baise qiyi shigao*, 154–155; Lu Xiuxiang, "Deng Xiaoping zai Donglan." Ya Zukun and Wei Jiabo, eds., *Deng Xiaoping yu Donglan*, 33–34.

49. *Donglan xianzhi*, 1960, section on history, 4.

50. Youjiang Suwei'ai zhengfu, "Gonggen tiaoli." In *ZYJGMGJD*, Vol. 1, 271–274.

51. *ZYJGMSLHB*, Vol. 1, 188–189; Huang Meilun, "Dengzhengwei laidao Wuzhuan," 685.

52. Wu Zhongcai, Huang Yuanzheng and Chen Xinde, *Baise qiyi shigao*, 154–155; Lu Xiuxiang, "Deng Xiaoping zai Donglan," 33–34; Yang Dongquan, "Deng Xiaoping he Wei Baqun." In Ya Zukun and Wei Jiabo, eds., *Deng Xiaoping yu Donglan*, 17–19; Chen Xinde, "Wei Baqun" (1983), 206; *Donglan xianzhi*, 1960, section on history, 7.

53. Lei Jingtian, "Guangxi de Suwei'ai yundong," 605; Huang Yucheng, "Gongchandang xingzhengzuzhi neimu qingkuang." *ZYJGMGJD*, Vol. 2, 1017.

54. Guangxi shaoshuminzu lishidiaocha zu, ed., *Guangxi Zhuangzu zizhiqu Donglanxian Zhonghe renmingongshe Donglitun shehuilishi diaocha baogao*, 17, 73–75.

55. Yang Shaojuan, "Zuoyoujiang geming genjudi de funu yundong," 1115; 1117; *Donglan xianzhi*, 1994, 105; Lei Jingtian, "Guangxi de Suwei'ai yundong," 610–612.

56. Donglanxian geming weiyuanhui, "Guangxi Donglanxian geming weiyuanhui zuidi zhenggang cao'an." In *ZYJGMGJD*, Vol. 1, 93–94; Huang Yiping, "Hongqijun chuchuang shiqi de ruogan zhengce." *ZYJGMGJD*, Vol. 2, 690.

57. Deng Baqi, "Muqian Guangxi de zhengzhi xingshi." *ZYJGMGJD*, Vol. 1, 424; Qin Liankui, "Donglan dangzuzhi jianshe he fanweijiao douzheng." Lu Xiuxiang, ed., *Donglan nongmin yundong, 1921–1927*, 201; Lu Xiuxiang, ed., *Donglan nongmin yundong, 1921–1927*, 9, 10.

58. Chen Xinde, "Zongshu," 20–21; Wu Zhongcai, Huang Yuanzheng and Chen Xinde, *Baise qiyi shigao*, 164–165.

59. *Donglan xianzhi*, 1994, 491.

60. Liao Lei, "Chedi suqing gongfei Wei Baqun banfa." In *WCSLZJ*, 597–598.

61. Donglanxian geming weiyuanhui, "Guangxi Donglanxian geming weiyuanhui zuidi zhenggang cao'an," 93–94.

62. Ya Meiyuan and Chen Shidu, "Wei Baqun jianli geming wuzhuang de huiyi," 55–56.

63. Huang Mingzheng, "Dengzhengwei guanxin shangbingyuan"; Huang Meilun, "Dengzhengwei laidao Wuzhuan"; *ZYJGMSLHB*, Vol. 1, 111; 196; Li Zhuoren, Ye Xueming and Lu Yuan, "Zuoyoujiang geming genjudi de caizheng jingji jianshe." *ZYJGMGJD*, Vol. 2, 1096; Lu Xiuxiang, ed., *Donglan nongmin yundong, 1921–1927*, 13; *Donglan xianzhi*, 1994, 362–363; Chen Shidu, "Huiyi Mian'e binggongchang." *Donglan wenshi ziliao*, 1 (1985), 24–25.

64. Huang Yushan, "Hongqijun shenghuo huiyi." *ZYJGMGJD*, Vol. 2, 744–745; Qin Jian, "Fu Pingma lingqiang qianhou." In Lu Xiuxiang, ed., *Donglan geming genjudi*, 172; Wu Delin, "Huiyi Weishizhang yu hongjun Youjiang dulishi," 204; Lu Xiuxiang, ed., *Donglan nongmin yundong, 1921–1927*, 12; Mo Li, "Yici nanwang de baogaohui." *Huiyi Wei Baqun*, 102–106; Li Yanfu, Wei Wei and Huang Qihui, "Zuoyoujiang geming genjudi de jiaoyu shiye." *ZYJGMGJD*, Vol. 2, 1150.

65. Zhong Wendian, ed. *Ershi shiji sanshi niandai de Guangxi*, 440; *Donglan xianzhi*, 1994, 373; 398.

66. Tang Shishu and Shen Gengzhi, "Hongqijun de yiyao weisheng gongzuo." *ZYJGMGJD*, Vol. 2, 1158; Yu Xinshun, ed., *Zuoyoujiang geming genjudi renwuzhi*, 228. Nanning: Guangxi renmin, 1998; *Donglan xianzhi*, 1994, 534; Li Huaqing, "Yi hongqijun junyi chuzhang Wu Qingpei tongzhi." Ou Jiwen, ed., *Guangxi Hongjun*, 260–263.

67. *Donglan xianzhi*, 1994, 380; Liao Lei, "Jinhou Dongfeng shanhou banfa ji minzhong ying nuli yaodian." In *WCSLZJ*, 602.

68. *Donglan xianzhi*, 1994, 396.

69. Jiang Huang, *Donglan xianzheng jiyao*, 28.

70. Deng Baqi, "Baqi guanyu Guangxi gongzuo baogao." In *ZYJGMGJD*, Vol. 1, 430; Wang Yushu, "Wang Yushu guanyu qibajun qingxing baogao." *ZYJGMGJD*, Vol. 1, 330; Zhonggong Dongfeng xianwei, "Zhonggong Dongfeng xianwei tonggao."

ZYJGMGJD, Vol. 1, 351; *ZYJGMSLHB*, Vol. 1, 180; Chen Xinde, "Zongshu," 23; *Donglan nongmin yundong*, 31.

71. Zhonggong zhongyang, "Zhonggong zhongyang gei Guangdong shengwei zhuan qijun qianwei de zhishi," 248; Ya Meiyuan, "Donglanxian sufu caijing gaikuang." Lu Xiuxiang, ed., *Donglan geming genjudi*, 228.

72. Stephen Averill, *Revolution in the Highlands: China's Jinggangshan Base Area*, 379–388. Rowman & Littlefield Publishers, 2006; Dai Xiangqing, "Lun ABtuan he Futian shibian." *Zhonggong dangshi yanjiu*, 1989(1), 24–29; Chen Yung-fa, "The Futian Incident and the Anti-Bolshevik League: The 'Terror' and CCP Rovolution." *Republican China*, Vol. XIX, No. 2 (April 1994), 1–51; Gao Hua, "Su ABtuan shijian de lishi kaocha." *Ershiyi shiji*, 54 (1999), 60–71; Ross Terrill, *Mao: A Biography*, 139–140; Maurice Meisner, *Mao Zedong: A Political and Intellectual Portrait*, 63–69; Chen Yung-fa, "Zhengzhi kongzhi he qunzhong dongyuan: Eyuwan sufan." *Dalu zazhi*, 86(1), 20–38; 86(2), 19–30; 86(3), 24–33. 1993; William Rowe, *Crimson Rain: Seven Centuries of Violence in a Chinese County*, 309–316; Chang Kuo-tao, *The Rise of the Chinese Communist Party: the Autobiography of Chang Kuo-tao*, Vol. 2, 257–276. University Press of Kansas, 1972; Zhang Xiushan, *Wode bashiwu nian*, 83–88. Beijing: Zhonggong dangshi, 2007; Guo Hongtao, *Guo Hongtao huiyilu*, 72–90. Beijing: Zhonggong dangshi, 2004.

73. Keith Forster, "Localism, Central Policy, and the Provincial Purges of 1957–1958: The Case of Zhejiang." In Timothy Cheek and Tony Saich, eds., *New Perspectives on State Socialism in China*. M. E. Sharpe, 1997; Xiaorong Han, "Localism in Chinese Communist Politics Before and After 1949—The Case of Feng Baiju." *Chinese Historical Review*, 11(1), 23–56. 2004.

74. Guangdong shengwei, "Yuesheng dui qijun qianwei de zhishixin," 142; *Junshi tongxun*, "Dui Guangxi Hongjun gongzuo buzhi de taolun," 198.

75. Wu Zhongcai, Huang Yuanzheng and Chen Xinde, *Baise qiyi shigao*, 227–228.

76. Chen Mianshu, "Guangxi Donglan nongmin yundong zhi shiji zhuangkuang," 50.

77. Gong Chu, *Wo yu hongjun*, 27.

78. Zhonggong zhongyang, "Zhongyangju baogao." *WCSLZJ*, 69.

79. Lu Xiuxiang, ed., *Donglan nongmin yundong, 1921–1927*, 42–50; Guangxisheng zhengfu, "Guangxisheng zhengfu xunling ge xianzhang ge jingtingju an ju Tiannan qingxiang zongban Liu Rifu cheng yiding shangge gouji shouyao feidang Wei Baqun deng yangji yiti xieji wuhuo gui'an xunban wen [fu shangge]."

80. Luo Xiulong, "Huang Wentong," 536–539.

81. Ibid., 537.

82. *Wuzhou minguo ribao*, "Fengshan chihuo diaocha." *ZYJGMSLHB*, Vol. 3, 156.

83. Lu Xiuxiang, ed., *Donglan nongmin yundong, 1921–1927*, 42–50.

84. Huang Zhizhen, "Huang Boyao." *ZGGXDSRWZ*, Vol. 2, 144–148.

85. Huang Songjian, "Sanlu nongjun weigong Fengshan xiancheng." In Wei Xinyin, ed., *Qingsong gaojie: Huang Songjian shiliao zhuanji*, 136–139; Luo Xiulong, "Huang Wentong," 537; Liang Hanming, He Guang and Huang Wencai, "Li Zhihua." *ZGGXDSRWZ*, Vol. 1, 117; *Lingyun wenshi ziliao*, "Lingyun renmin fandui tongzhizhe de douzheng." *Lingyun wenshi ziliao*, 4 (1989): 4–5; Yu Xinshun, "Zuoyoujiang geming genjudi de dangzuzhi." *ZYJGMGJD*, Vol. 2, 1169–1170; *Donglan xianzhi*, 1994, 105.

86. *ZYJGMSLHB*, Vol. 1, 88.

87. Lu Jinlun, "Baise zhongxue lieshi zhiduoshao." *Baise shizhi*, Vol. 3 (1988), 19–22.

88. *ZYJGMSLHB*, Vol. 1, 41, 56, 60; Wei Chengzhu, Li Dingzhong and Qin Maocai, "Huang Shuxiang zai Nama geming huodong pianduan." *Mashan wenshi ziliao*, 1(1986), 21–26; Huang Zenong, "Huiyi Guode nongmin xiehui de douzheng lichen." Yu Xinshun, ed., *Dang de chuangjian he dageming shiqi de Guangxi nongmin yundong*, 566–570. Nanning: Guangxi renmin, 2003; Li Xiulang, ed., *Huang Shuxiang geming shengya*. Nanning: Guangxi minzu, 2009.

89. Wei Qirong and Huang Jianping, "Chen Bomin," 144; Wei Shilin, "Du'an nongmin yundong de xingqi." In Yu Xinshun, ed., *Dang de chuangjian he dageming shiqi de Guangxi nongmin yundong*, 560–561; Qin Guohan, "Honghe jilang." Yu Xinshun, ed., *Dang de chuangjian he dageming shiqi de Guangxi nongmin yundong*, 562–565; Ban Feng and Luo Zhaowen, "Liao Yuanfang," 207, 209.

90. Zhu Xi'ang, "Zhu Xi'ang gei zhongyang xunshiyuan he Guangdong shengwei de baogao."

91. Huang Xianfan, Huang Zengqing, and Zhang Yimin, *Zhuangzu tongshi*, 828.

92. (Huang) Shaohong, "Quansheng zhengzhi gaikuang." *Xin Guangxi*, 3(10). February 21, 1929. In *ZYJGMSLHB*, Vol. 3, 29–30.

93. Zhao Bingzhuang, "Diyige lai Enlongxian jianli gongchandang zuzhi de Yu Shaojie." *Tiandong wenshi ziliao*, Vol. 1 (1987), 36; *ZYJGMSLHB*, Vol. 1, 56, 60; Huang Guoguang, "Huang Zhifeng." *ZGGXDSRWZ*, Vol. 1, 286–289; Huang Dakun, "Diexue liuqiangu: Li Zhengru lieshi zhuanlue." *Baise diqu dangshi ziliao: renwu*, Vol. 2 (1992), 26–27; Zhao Bingzhuang, "Lu Jizhang," 8–9.

94. Lu Julie, "Yu Shaojie." *ZGGXDSRWZ*, Vol. 1, 82–88.

95. Guangxisheng nonghui choubeichu, "Nongmin yundong de celue." In *WCSLZJ*, 86–87; Zhonggong Guangdong shengwei, "Zhonggong Guangdong shengwei gei Guangxi tewei zhishixin." In *WCSLZJ*, 102.

96. *Wuzhou minguo ribao*, "Fengshan chihuo diaocha," 157.

97. Shuang Cai, "Zhide zhuyi de Donglan nongmin yundong," 32; Hu Bingqiong, "Yuanzhu Donglan de nongyou," 34–35; Chen Mianshu, "Guangxi Donglan nongmin yundong zhi shiji zhuangkuang," 56; He Bingfen, "Ning Peiying." *ZGGXDSRWZ*, Vol. 1, 77–78.

98. Huang Guoguang, "Huang Zhifeng," 292.

99. Zhonghua Suwei'ai gongheguo, "Zhonghua Suwei'ai gongheguo linshi zhongyang zhengfu bugao." In *WCSLZJ*, 205.

100. Huang Hanji and Huang Yulu, "Tan Tongnan." In *ZGGXDSRWZ*, Vol. 3, 42–47.

101. Wu Xi, "Quzhe de lichen." In *ZYJGMGJD*, Vol. 2, 839–841.

102. Wei Zhihong, Wu Zhongcai and Gao Xiong, ed., *Baise qiyi renwuzhi*, 83; Zhonggong zhongyang, "Zhonggong zhongyang gei junwei nanfang banshichu bingzhuan qijun qianwei zhishixin." In *ZYJGMGJD*, Vol. 1, 315–317; Chen Haoren, "Qijun gongzuo zongbaogao," 377.

103. Gong Chu, *Wo yu hongjun*, 197–198; Chen Xinde, "Zongshu," 33; Wei Zhihong, Wu Zhongcai and Gao Xiong, ed., *Baise qiyi renwuzhi*, 65; *ZYJGMSLHB*, Vol. 1, 198.

104. Deng Xiaoping, "Qijun gongzuo baogao," 398.

105. Mao Mao, *Wode fuqin Deng Xiaoping*, Vol. 1, 258.

106. Deng Xiaoping, "Qijun gongzuo baogao," 398.

107. Lei Jingtian, "Guangxi de Suwei'ai yundong," 608–614; Wang Lintao, "Lei Jingtian." In Hu Hua, ed., *Zhonggong dangshi renwu zhuan*, Vol. 20, 350–352. Xi'an: Shanxi renmin, 1984; Chen Zuncheng, "Yang Jinmei." *ZGGXDSRWZ*, Vol. 4, 455–457. Yang Jinmei was one of the young educated women who joined the Communist movement during the Baise Uprising. A small number of women from the Right River region left with the main force of the Seventh Red Army for Jiangxi. One of them was Wei Rong from Silin County, who served as a nurse in the military hospital. She arrived in Jiangxi in 1931 and was killed there by her comrades in 1934. One source claims that at least one of these women participated in the Long March, but most records about female participants in the Long March from the Central Red Army do not include any women from the Right River region. Yu Xinshun, ed., *Zuoyoujiang geming genjudi renwuzhi*, 132; Wei Xiukang, "Wei Rong." In Bai Xianjing, ed., *Hongqijun Hongbajun yinglie zhuan*, 659–667; Lu Jinlun, "Guan Chonghe." *ZGGXDSRWZ*, Vol. 4, 383.

108. David Goodman, *Deng Xiaoping and the Chinese Revolution: A Political Biography*, 32.

109. Lei Jingtian, "Guangxi de Suwei'ai yundong," 610–611.

110. Huang Yucheng, "Gongchandang xingzhengzuzhi neimu qingkuang," 1006–1007.

111. Huang Chao, "Dui Hongqijun jianli yishu de jidian yijian," 228; Yuan Renyuan and Mo Wenhua, "Guanyu Guangxi suwei'ai yundong yu hongjun diqijun zongjie de yijianshu." Ou Jiwen, ed., *Guangxi Hongjun*, 77–79; Mo Wenhua, *Huiyi hongqijun*, 47.

112. Xie Fumin, "Baqun tongzhi zhandou de yisheng." *Huiyi Wei Baqun*, 26–27; Wei Guoqing, "Yingfan yongcun." *Minzu tuanjie*, 1982(10). *ZYJGMGJD*, Vol. 2, 652; Qin Yingji, Huang Songjian and Huang Rong, "Zhuoyue de gongchanzhuyi zhanshi Wei Baqun," 661; Zeng Qiqiang, ed., *Zhongguo zaoqi nongmin yundong lingxiu Wei Baqun*, 314.

113. Qin Yingji, *Xiaoyan suiyue*, 13.

114. Li Dehan, "Huang Shixin." *ZGGXDSRWZ*, Vol. 2, 95–100; Wei Dingxin and Lu Xiuxiang, "Beishang Jiangxi hou de qinshen jingli." Lu Xiuxiang, ed., *Donglan geming genjudi*, 324–331; Li Xianxian and Lu Xiuxiang, "Beishang Jiangxi hou de pianduan huiyi." Lu Xiuxiang, ed., *Donglan geming genjudi*, 332–335; Chen Guopei and Lu Xiuxiang, "Beishang Jiangxi he canjia fanweijiao douzheng de huiyi." Lu Xiuxiang, ed., *Donglan geming genjudi*, 336–338.

115. Jiang Maosheng, *Qianli lailong*, 51.

116. Wei Qirong, "Huang Fangri," 589.

117. Huang Yucheng, "Gongchandang xingzhengzuzhi neimu qingkuang," 1007.

118. Lan Qixuan and Su Xing, "Wei Baqun tongzhi rudang shijian kaozheng," 34.

119. Xie Fumin, *Wei Baqun*, 57.

120. Gong Chu, *Wo yu hongjun*, 150.

Chapter Seven

1. Yuan Renyuan, "Cong Baise dao Xianggan," 631–632; Jiang Yuli and Chen Shichang, "Dashiji." *ZYJGMGJD*, Vol. 2, 1273–1274; Cao Yuwen and Lu Jiaxiang,

Xinguixi yu Zhongguo gongchandang, 47–52. Nanning: Guihai luncong zazhishe, 1994; Chen Xinde, "Li Qian." *ZGGXDSRWZ*, Vol. 4, 447–454; Mo Wenhua, *Huiyi hongqijun*, 111.

2. Yan Heng, "Yan Heng tongzhi guanyu diqijun de baogao," 391.

3. Lan Tian and Huang Zhizhen, eds., *Zhongguo gongnong hongjun Youjiang dulishi*, 24. Nanning: Guangxi renmin, 1992.

4. Huang Songjian, "Hongqijun zhuli beishang yihou." *ZYJGMGJD*, Vol. 2, 898.

5. *ZYJGMSLHB*, Vol. 1, 222; Lan Tian and Huang Zhizhen, eds., *Zhongguo gongnong hongjun Youjiang dulishi*, 22–23.

6. Huang Hongyi(?), *Weishizhang Baqun lingdao donglan geming*, Vol. 2, Section 66; Ya Meiyuan and Chen Shidu, "Wei Baqun jianli geming wuzhuang de huiyi," 60–61; Huang Songjian, "Hongqijun zhuli beishang yihou"; Lan Tian, "Youjiang geming genjudi de fanweijiao douzheng." 1992. In *WCSLZJ*, 496.

7. Mo Fengxin, "Liao Lei." Guangxi xinhai gemingshi yanjiuhui, ed., *Minguo Guangxi renwu zhuan*, Vol. 1, 114–119.

8. Lu Xiuxiang, ed., *Donglan geming genjudi*, 21–22; Huang Zhizhen, "Huang Boyao," 147.

9. Deng Baqi, "Baqi guanyu Guangxi gongzuo baogao," 430–431; Yu Xinshun, "Deng Baqi." *ZGGXDSRWZ*, Vol. 1, 238.

10. Deng Baqi, "Deng Baqi gei Zhonggong Youjiang tewei ji ershiyishi shiwei xin." In *ZYJGMGJD*, Vol. 1, 415–420.

11. Deng Baqi, "Baqi guanyu Guangxi gongzuo baogao," 435; *ZYJGMSLHB*, Vol. 1, 239.

12. Huang Songjian, "Hong 21shi gaibianwei dulishi hou de douzheng." In Wei Xinyin, ed., *Qingsong gaojie: Huang Songjian shiliao zhuanji*, 163; *ZYJGMSLHB*, Vol. 1, 216.

13. Huang Songjian, "Hong 21shi gaibianwei dulishi hou de douzheng." In Wei Xinyin, ed., *Qingsong gaojie: Huang Songjian shiliao zhuanji*, 170; Wang Lintao, Cheng Zongshan & Lin Weicai, "Chen Hongtao," 216; *ZYJGMSLHB*, Vol. 1, 248; Bai Chongxi, "Zuoyoujiang zhengzhi shicha baogao." In *ZYJGMSLHB*, Vol. 3, 142; Qin Caiwu, *Donglan tongshi*, 249.

14. Bai Chongxi, "Zuoyoujiang zhengzhi shicha baogao," 141–142; Jiang Huang, *Donglan xianzheng jiyao*; Diana Lary, "Communism and Ethnic Revolt: Some Notes on the Chuang Peasant Movement in Kwangsi 1921–31." *The China Quarterly*, No. 49 (1972), 126–128, 130–131; Diana Lary, *Region and Nation: The Kwangsi Clique in Chinese Politics, 1925–1937*, 103.

15. Hong Bo, "Hong Bo gei Zhonggong zhongyang de baogao [diyihao]." *ZYJGMGJD*, Vol. 1, 436.

16. Huang Songjian, "Hong 21shi gaibianwei dulishi hou de douzheng." In Wei Xinyin, ed., *Qingsong gaojie: Huang Songjian shiliao zhuanji*, 171–174.

17. Huang Yingjun, "Wei Jing," 520.

18. *Wuzhou minguo ribao*. "Baifuzuo you Baise zhuanfu Donglan." October 10, 1932.

19. *Nanning minguo ribao*, "Dongfeng jiaofei ji shanhou jinkuang." In *ZYJGMSLHB*, Vol. 3, 176–177.

20. Hong Bo, "Hong Bo gei Zhonggong zhongyang de baogao [diyihao]," 436–437.

21. Ibid.

22. Wu Delin, "Huiyi Weishizhang yu hongjun Youjiang dulishi," 215; Huang Meilun, "Huiyi Wei Jing fu Xianggang huibao." In Lu Xiuxiang, ed., *Donglan geming genjudi*, 274–275.

23. Huang Songjian, "Wo zai Youjiang xiayou de huodong ji liangci fu Shanghai huibao gongzuo de qingkuang." In Wei Xinyin, ed., *Qingsong gaojie: Huang Songjian shiliao zhuanji*, 179.

24. *Wuzhou minguo ribao*, "Liaojunzhang dushi jiao Dongfeng gongfei." September 20, 1932; Bai Chongxi, "Guangxi jinhou de zhengzhifangzhen he women dui guojia de zeren." In *WCSLZJ*, 575–576.

25. Lei Jingtian, "Guangxi de Suwei'ai yundong," 614.

26. Deng Baqi, "Deng Baqi gei Zhonggong Youjiang tewei ji ershiyishi shiwei xin," 420.

27. Zhonggong zhongyang, "Zhonggong zhongyang gei Guangdong shengwei zhuan qijun qianwei de zhishi," 240–241.

28. James E. Sheridan, *China in Disintegration: The Republican Era in Chinese History, 1912–1949*, 196. For the militia organizations under the New Guangxi Clique, see Zhong Wendian, ed., *Ershi shiji sanshi niandai de Guangxi*, 551–583.

29. Rao Kai, "Bai Chongxi chongshang guoshu." In Guangxi wenshi yanjiuguan, ed., *Bagui xiangxielu*, 12–14. Shanghai: Shanghai shudian, 1992.

30. Lu Xiuxuan and Huang Juping, *Youjiang xinghuo*, 52–53. 1956.

31. Wei Baqun, "Geming daodi." *Benteng de Zuoyoujiang*, 22.

32. Chen Xinde, "Wei Baqun" (1983), 214.

33. *Junshi yuekan*, "Canmouchu gongzuo gaikuang." *ZYJGMSLHB*, Vol. 3, 114.

34. Ya Guohua, "Jidian de huiyi." Lu Xiuxiang, ed., *Donglan geming genjudi*, 308.

35. Qin Caiwu, *Donglan tongshi*, 247.

36. Ibid., 236–237.

37. Zeng Qiqiang, ed., *Zhongguo zaoqi nongmin yundong lingxiu Wei Baqun*, 319.

38. BSD, 083-002-0017-004, "Baqun de qizi he ernu;" BSD, 083-002-0017-005, "Hongse nuyoujiduiyuan: Weilieshi de airen Huang Xiumei tongzhi."

39. William Rowe, *Crimson Rain: Seven Centuries of Violence in a Chinese County*, 322–324; Elizabeth Perry, *Rebels and Revolutionaries in North China, 1845–1945*. Stanford University Press, 1980.

40. *Donglan nongmin yundong*, 48.

41. Tian Shulan, *Guangxi luxingji*, 170–173. Shanghai: Zhonghua shuju, 1935; Li Tianxin, "Sanshiliupo douzheng jishi." *ZYJGMGJD*, Vol. 2, 921, 924.

42. Yu Xinshun and Ban Feng, "Hengli Hongjunyan lieshi." *ZGGXDSRWZ*, Vol. 4, 562–569; Wei Tingzhang, ed., *Fengshan xianzhi*, 578–580. Nanning: Guangxi renmin, 2008.

43. Qin Caiwu, *Donglan tongshi*, 240–241.

44. He Weidian, ed., *Donglanxian diming zhi*, 242.

45. *Diqijun yuandan tekan*, "Junfachu yinianlai gongzuo zhi gaikuang." *ZYJGMGJD*, Vol. 2, 948; Zhongyang fangwentuan diyi fentuan lianluozu, *Guangxi*

Donglanxian Xishanqu minzu gaikuang, 10; Wang Lintao, Cheng Zongshan and Lin Weicai, "Chen Hongtao," 218; *Donglan xianzhi*, 1994, 111, 556.

46. Huang Naiwen, "Chen Bomin zhuanlue," 58.

47. Wang Lintao, Cheng Zongshan and Lin Weicai, "Chen Hongtao," 218, 221; Wei Chun, "Fengbei, yili zai renmin xinzhong." Hechi ribaoshe, ed., *Zhuixun Hongqijun zuji*, 51.

48. Shaosheng et al., "Cifu, yanshi: Yi fuqin Huang Songjian." In Wei Xinyin, ed., *Qingsong gaojie: Huang Songjian shiliao zhuanji*, 370.

49. Yang Shaojuan, "Zuoyoujiang geming genjudi de funu yundong," 1122.

50. Wei Ronggang, "Wei Hanchao." *ZGGXDSRWZ*, Vol. 2, 15; Huang Zhizhen, "Huang Boyao," 148.

51. Lan Tian and Huang Zhizhen, eds., *Zhongguo gongnong hongjun Youjiang dulishi*, 41; Lan Guixiang and Huang Shiping, "Lan Maocai." *ZGGXDSRWZ*, Vol. 2, 126–127.

52. *ZYJGMSLHB*, Vol. 2, 184; Donglanxian Suwei'ai, "Muqian xuanchuan biaoyu." *ZYJGMGJD*, Vol. 1, 320; Hongqijun, "Qianwei tonggao diqihao." *ZYJGMGJD*, Vol. 1, 347.

53. Qin Caiwu, *Donglan tongshi*, 265.

54. Guangxisheng zhengfu, "Guangxisheng zhengfu ruidian ju renmin chengkong Donglan gequ nonghui bufa xingwei bing chi gaixian nongminxiehui su zunzhao danggang qieshi zhengli wen." *ZYJGMSLHB*, Vol. 3, 5–6.

55. GXZZD, L4/1/11-1, "Guangxisheng zhengfu kuaiyou daidian"; GXZZD, L4/1/11-4, "Guangxisheng zhengfu youguan Wei Baqun he Huang Daquan dangan."

56. *Wuzhou minguo ribao*, "Fengshan chihuo diaocha," 156–157.

57. *Junshi tongxun*, "Dui Guangxi hongjun gongzuo buzhi de taolun," 176; Zhonggong zhongyang, "Zhonggong zhongyang gei Guangdong shengwei zhuan qijun qianwei de zhishi," 229.

58. Qin Caiwu, *Donglan tongshi*, 222–223.

59. *ZYJGMSLHB*, Vol. 3, 199; Bai Chongxi, "Zuoyoujiang zhengzhi shicha baogao," 143.

60. Qin Jiancai, "Wei Longfu shuhunji." Guangxi minjian wenxue yanjiuhui, ed., *Dadan youmaqi: Zuoyoujiang geming lingdaoren gushi chuanshuo*, 191.

61. Huang Jinqiu and Lu Xiuxiang, "Huiyi zai Nonglao maimi song Xishan." Lu Xiuxiang, ed., *Donglan geming* genjudi, 311–312; Wei Zhongquan and Lu Xiuxiang, "Huiyi hongjun he chiweidui zai Beihe de huodong." Lu Xiuxiang, ed., *Donglan geming* genjudi, 297–298.

62. Fang Daheng and Zou Wensheng, "Zuoyoujiang geming genjudi de sufan baowei gongzuo," 1126–1127; Lei Jingtian, "Guangxi de Suwei'ai yundong," 606; Hongqijun, "Qianwei tonggao diqihao," 347.

63. Chen Haoren, "Qijun gongzuo zongbaogao," 360, 374.

64. Hongqijun, "Qianwei tonggao diqihao," 345; Deng Xiaoping, "Qijun gongzuo baogao," 407.

65. Odoric, Y. K. Wou, *Mobilizing the Masses: Building Revolution in Henan*, 138–139. Stanford University Press, 1994.

66. Liao Lei, "Chedi suqing gongfei Wei Baqun banfa." *WCSLZJ*, 597–598.

67. Guangxisheng minzhengting, *Guangxi gexian gaikuang*. Today Tonglan has a land area of 2,435 square kilometers. Its current population density is about 115 people per square kilometer, which is many times higher than that of the Republican era.

68. Qin Caiwu, *Donglan tongshi*, 265; Tian Shulan, *Guangxi luxingji*, 193; *Donglan xianzhi*, 1960, section on society, 1.

69. Tian Shulan, *Guangxi luxingji*, 195; Qin Yingji, *Xiaoyan suiyue*, 4; Wei Chengzhu, Li Dingzhong and Qin Maocai, "Huang Shuxiang zai Nama geming huodong pianduan," 23.

70. Donglanxian geming weiyuanhui, "Guangxi Donglanxian geming weiyuanhui zuidi zhenggang cao'an," 78.

71. Huang Hongyi(?), *Weishizhang Baqun lingdao Donglan geming*, Vol. 2, Sections 89–90.

72. Eugene William Levich, *The Kwangsi Way in Kuomintang China, 1931–1939*, 161. M. E. Sharpe, 1997.

73. Tian Shulan, *Guangxi luxingji*, 193–194.

74. *Wuzhou minguo ribao*, "Fengshan chihuo diaocha," 158; *Nanning minguo ribao*, "Donglan zhi zhenzai fenji qingxing." *ZYJGMSLHB*, Vol. 3, 91; *Nanning minguo ribao*, "Shengfu ling cui Dongfeng chouyi shanhou banfa." *ZYJGMSLHB*, Vol. 3, 97–98.

75. Gong Chu, *Wo yu hongjun*, 145–146.

76. Mo Wenhua, *Huiyi hongqijun*, 8; Huang Xianfan, Huang Zengqing, and Zhang Yimin, *Zhuangzu tongshi*, 802.

77. Wei Baqun, "Xiaoshi ershou." In *WCSLZJ*, 222.

78. Li Guozhou and Yan Yongtong, *Wei Baqun zhuan*, 113.

79. Luo Huo, "Diqijun diershisishi diqishiertuan yinianlai gongzuo baogao." *ZYJGMSLHB*, Vol. 3, 273; Qin Caiwu, *Donglan tongshi*, 224–225, 258.

80. Wu Delin, "Huiyi Weishizhang yu hongjun Youjiang dulishi," 214–215.

81. *Donglan xianzhi*, 1994, 726; Ya Meiyuan, "Guixi junfa tongzhi shiqi de Donglan tanguan haoshen." *Donglan wenshi*, 4 (2001), 140–141; Qin Caiwu, *Donglan tongshi*, 251–252.

82. *Nanning minguo ribao*, "Li Ruixiong diancheng jiao Donglan gongfei qingxing." *ZYJGMSLHB*, Vol. 3, 82; *Guangxi minzheng yuekan*, "Minzhengting dianfu Donglan xianzhang jubao gaixian houbeiduizhang Huang Shaoxian souhuo nifei paijipaodan qingxing yang zhuanling jiajiang you." June 1932. *ZYJGMSLHB*, Vol. 3, 97; *ZYJGMSLHB*, Vol. 1, 254–255.

83. *Guangxi Gongbao*, "Shengfu xuanhong gouji Weifei Baqun ji Chen Hongtao deng Bugao." May 21, 1931. *WCSLZJ*, 546.

84. Chen Xinde, "Wei Baqun" (1983), 210–211.

85. *Nanning minguo ribao*, "Shengfu yi yiwanyuan gouji zhi gongfei Wei Baqun beishengqin." *ZYJGMSLHB*, Vol. 3, 85; *Nanning minguo ribao*, "Gongfei Wei Baqun beiqin zhengshi." *ZYJGMSLHB*, Vol. 3, 85; Qin Caiwu, *Donglan tongshi*, 254.

86. Ya Guohua, "Jidian de huiyi," 307; Chen Guoying, "Zai shizhang he zhengwei shenbian gongzuo de rizi." *WCSLZJ*, 450.

87. Qin Caiwu, *Donglan tongshi*, 228–230.

88. Ibid., 258.

89. Zhongyang fangwentuan diyi fentuan lianluozu, *Guangxi Donglanxian diwuqu (Zhonghequ) minzu gaikuang*, 3; Zhongyang fangwentuan diyi fentuan lianluozu, *Guangxi Donglanxian Xishanqu minzu gaikuang*, 7–8.

90. *Nanning minguo ribao*, "Raoluan Donglan zhi gongfei yinmou." *ZYJGMSLHB*, Vol. 3, 91; Liu Lin, "Jiankufendou de Zhuangzu funu Huang Meilun." *Youjiang ribao*, July 9, 11, 13, 15, 1957.

91. Huang Songjian, "Hong21shi gaibianwei dulishi hou de douzheng." In Wei Xinyin, ed., *Qingsong gaojie: Huang Songjian shiliao zhuanji*, 172.

92. *ZYJGMSLHB*, Vol. 1, 261; *Nanning minguo ribao*, "Xiezhihui tan Dongfeng qingkuang." *ZYJGMSLHB*, Vol. 3, 165; Zhongyang fangwentuan diyi fentuan lianluozu, *Guangxi Donglanxian Xishanqu minzu gaikuang*, 7; Qin Caiwu, *Donglan tongshi*, 258.

93. Chen Hongtao, "Dao Baqun tongzhi." *WCSLZJ*, 225; Ya Meiyuan and Qin Yingwu, "Yi Chen Hongtao tongzhi," 42–43; Lan Tian, "Chen Hongtao," 283; *Nanning minguo ribao*, "Gongfei Wei Baqun yunie Chen Hongtao beiqin zongbu ling jie se xunban." *WCSLZJ*, 609–610; *Nanning minguo ribao*, "Weifei Baqun zhi tewu duizhang jiuqin yu Chen Hongtao yibing jie Baise xunban." *WCSLZJ*, 611–612; *Nanning minguo ribao*, "Chenfei Hongtao deng jing zai se qiangjue." *WCSLZJ*, 615; Huang Juping, "Chen Hongtao tongzhi xunnanji." *ZYJGMGJD*, Vol. 2, 906–913.

94. *Wuzhou minguo ribao*, "Chenfei Hongtao bujiu ke jiuqin." November 9, 1932; Liao Lei, "Jinhou Dongfeng shanhou banfa ji minzhong ying nuli yaodian," 603.

95. Su Xing, "Qin Daoping." *ZGGXDSRWZ*, Vol. 1, 300.

96. Huang Yulu, ed., *Zhongguo gongchandang Guangxi Zhuangzu zizhiqu Donglanxian zuzhishi ziliao, 1926–1987*, 4.

97. *Wuzhou minguo ribao*. "Xuanshang ji gongfei shouyao." October 5, 1932; Huang Yingjun, "Huang Daquan" (1992), 320–322.

98. Lu Yongke and Huang Yingjun, "Huang Shuxiang." *ZGGXDSRWZ*, Vol. 1, 313–314; *ZYJGMSLHB*, Vol. 1, 274–275; Chen Zuncheng, "Teng Guodong." In Lan Tian and Huang Zhizhen, eds., *Zhongguo gongnong hongjun Youjiang dulishi*, 385.

99. BSD, 083-002-099-003, Wei Ting'an, "Jianchi geming 30 nian, xingfu meihao zai jintian."

100. Gong Chu, *Wo yu hongjun*, 243–244, 262–263.

101. Qin Yingji, *Xiaoyan suiyue*, 22–23.

102. Mao Mao, *Wode fuqin Deng Xiaoping*, Volume 1, 273; Qin Yingji, et al., "Hongjun de youxiu zhihuiyuan, dangde zhongzhen zhanshi." *ZYJGMGJD*, Vol. 2, 644–645; Mo Wenhua, *Mo Wenhua huiyilu*, 203–205, 413–417; Graham Hutchings, "The Troubled Life and After-Life of a Guangxi Communist: Some Notes on Li Mingrui and the Communist Movement in Guangxi Province before 1949." *China Quarterly*, No. 104 (1985), 700–708.

103. Huang Zheng, "Huiyi Youjiang chiweijun shi'erlian." *ZYJGMGJD*, Vol. 2, 754.

104. Huang Guoguang, "Huang Zhifeng," 295; Luo Xiulong, "Huang Wentong," 539; Huang Zhifeng's follower Xie Fumin believed that Huang left Jiangxi in 1934 and was killed in that year. See Xie Fumin, "Yi Youjiang chiweijun zongzhihui Huang Zhifeng." *ZYJGMGJD*, Vol. 2, 673, 681.

105. *Wuzhou minguo ribao*, "Dongfeng shanhou weiyuanhui chengli." November 3, 1932.

106. Zeng Qiqiang, ed., *Zhongguo zaoqi nongmin yundong lingxiu Wei Baqun*, 318.

107. Luo Rikuai, "Huiyi Weishizhang xisheng qianhou." *WCSLZJ*, 461; BSD, 083-002-0017-005, "Hongse nuyoujiduiyuan: Weilieshi de airen Huang Xiumei tongzhi;" Xie Fumin, *Wei Baqun*, 46; *Wuzhou minguo ribao*, "Chenfei Hongtao bujiu ke jiuqin." November 9, 1932.

108. Liu Lin, "Jiankufendou de Zhuangzu funu Huang Meilun"; Huang Zhiping, ed., *Hongtu zhi hun: Donglan yingxiong pu*, 80; Huang Meilun, "Bage he Sange dai wo zoushang geminglu." *Dangdai Guangxi*, 23 (December 2009), 18.

109. Huang Meilun, "Shuangfeng feilai." *Donglan wenshi ziliao*, 2 (1987), 62–67.

110. Liao Lei, "Jinhou Dongfeng shanhou banfa ji minzhong ying nuli yaodian," 603–604.

111. Huang Hanzhong, "Donglan shanhou weiyuanhui zhenxiang." *Donglan wenshi*, 4 (2001), 144–146.

112. Zhongyang fangwentuan diyi fentuan lianluozu, *Guangxi Donglanxian diwuqu (Zhonghequ) minzu gaikuang*, 2; 4; Zhongyang fangwentuan diyi fentuan lianluozu, *Guangxi Donglanxian Xishanqu minzu gaikuang*, 17.

113. *Nanning minguo ribao*, "Dongfeng shanhou weiyuanhui zuijin gongzuo qingkuang." *ZYJGMSLHB*, Vol. 3, 169–170.

114. *Wuzhou minguo ribao*. "Liaojunzhang zai Dongfeng ban shanhou." October 26, 1932.

115. Qin Caiwu, *Donglan tongshi*, 262–263.

116. *Donglan xianzhi*, 1994, 404, 407.

117. Qin Caiwu, *Donglan tongshi*, 264–265.

118. He Weidian, ed., *Donglanxian diming zhi*, 117, 237.

Chapter Eight

1. Zong Ying, et al., *Wei Baqun lieshi de gushi*, 9.

2. Huang Hanzhong, "Wei Baqun guju Dongli." *Donglan wenshi ziliao*, 1 (1985), 83.

3. Qin Jiancai, "Wei Baqun bian hu le." Guangxi minjian wenxue yanjiuhui, ed., *Dadan youmaqi: Zuoyoujiang geming lingdaoren gushi chuanshuo*, 192–196; BSD, 083-002-0013, "Wei Baqun tongzhi de gushi."

4. Zong Ying, et al., *Wei Baqun lieshi de gushi*, 17–18; Xie Fumin, *Wei Baqun*, 74; Huang Huanying, "Bianlong." Guangxi minjian wenxue yanjiuhui, ed., *Dadan youmaqi: Zuoyoujiang geming lingdaoren gushi chuanshuo,* 242–246.

5. Xie Fumin, *Wei Baqun*, 37; Wei Jie, "Sanci jian Bage," 41; Zhou Jizhong, "Xishan tuwei ji." *Huiyi Wei Baqun*, 119–124.

6. Huang Chao, Huang Huiliang, and Tan Qingrong, "Shaizi tuidi." *Huiyi Wei Baqun,* 51–52; Lu Yongke, "Youjiang geming de bozhongren Wei Baqun." *Huiyi Wei Baqun*, 95; BSD, 083-002-0013, "Wei Baqun bianxian"; Xie Fumin, *Wei Baqun*, 42; Wei Jie, "Sanci jian Bage," 47; Ou Zhifu, "Yi Wei Baqun tongzhi dui Fengyi yidai nongmin yundong de yingxiang." *Huiyi Wei Baqun*, 56.

7. Huang Xiang, "Yexi Nalutun." Guangxi minjian wenxue yanjiuhui, ed., *Dadan youmaqi: Zuoyoujiang geming lingdaoren gushi chuanshuo*, 172; Su Changxian, "Paodan

yepa Wei Baqun." *Dadan youmaqi: Zuoyoujiang geming lingdaoren gushi chuanshuo*, 205–207; Qin Chengqin, "Bage hui fei." *Dadan youmaqi: Zuoyoujiang geming lingdaoren gushi chuanshuo*, 220–221; Lan Handong and Lan Qixuan, *Wei Baqun*, 64; Li Guozhou and Yan Yongtong, "Bage de gushi." *Dadan youmaqi: Zuoyoujiang geming lingdaoren gushi chuanshuo*, 125.

8. Qin Chengqin, "Bage shuo Yaohua." Guangxi minjian wenxue yanjiuhui, ed., *Dadan youmaqi: Zuoyoujiang geming lingdaoren gushi chuanshuo*, 133–135; Huang Xianfan, Huang Zengqing, and Zhang Yimin, *Zhuangzu tongshi*, 828.

9. Huang Qifeng, "Shizha Eguo dan." *Dadan youmaqi: Zuoyoujiang geming lingdaoren gushi chuanshuo*, 131–133; Lu Xiuxuan, "Shuqi yiqi zhengjiu nongmin." *WCSLZJ*, 290.

10. Bai Chongxi, "Guangxi jinhou de zhengzhifangzhen he women dui guojia de zeren," 132.

11. Huang Huanying, "Bage jiao tian kai." *Dadan youmaqi: Zuoyoujiang geming lingdaoren gushi chuanshuo*, 141–144.

12. Zong Ying, et al., *Wei Baqun lieshi de gushi*, 1; Lan Handong and Lan Qixuan, *Wei Baqun*, 219; Huang Xianfan, Gan Wenjie and Gan Wenhao, *Wei Baqun pingzhuan*, 2; BSD, 083-002-0013, "Teyamiao de mimi."

13. Xie Fumin, *Wei Baqun*, 81–82.

14. *Nanning minguo ribao*, "Gedi fugongfenzi ruxi xiecong zhunyu zixin."

15. Xiong Hongming and Yang Zijian, "Wei Baqun lieshi beihai'an zhenpoji." *Nanguo zaobao*, November 13, 2009.

16. Yang Wenke, "Cedong shahai wo hongqijun Wei Baqun shizhang de zuifan Chen Dibo luoru fawang." *Rongshui wenshi ziliao*, 5 (1989), 124–127; Xiong Hongming and Yang Zijian, "Wei Baqun lieshi beihai'an zhenpoji."

17. Huang Yulu, "Donglan jiefang jishi." *Donglan wenshi*, 5 (2004), 1–12; Ya Meiyuan, "Guixi junfa tongzhi shiqi de Donglan tanguan haoshen," 140–141.

18. Wu Delin, "Huiyi Weishizhang yu hongjun Youjiang dulishi," 212.

19. Ya Meiyuan, "Guixi junfa tongzhi shiqi de Donglan tanguan haoshen," 139–140; Huang Hanzhong and Chen Rukai, "Chen Shusen qiren qishi," 46–50.

20. Huang Huanmin, "Pubumie de huoyan." *ZYJGMGJD*, Vol. 2, 914; Ya Meiyuan, "Guixi junfa tongzhi shiqi de Donglan tanguan haoshen," 141–142; *Donglan xianzhi*, 1994, 113, 156, 725–726; Huang Hongyi(?), *Weishizhang Baqun lingdao Donglan geming*, Vol. 2, Sections 84; Wu Delin, "Dui Donglan nongyun de jidian huiyi," 239.

21. Chen Ruzhen, "Chen Ruzhen zizhuan." *WCSLZJ*, 680; Chen Mianshu, "Guangxi Donglan nongmin yundong zhi shiji zhuangkuang," 55.

22. Huang Hongyi(?), *Weishizhang Baqun lingdao donglan geming*, Vol. 2, Sections 91(7).

23. *Donglan xianzhi*, 1994, 726.

24. Ibid., 224.

25. Ya Meiyuan, "Guixi junfa tongzhi shiqi de Donglan tanguan haoshen," 139.

26. Ibid., 137–139.

27. Qin Yingwu, "Huang Shouxian de kechi xiachang." *Donglan wenshi ziliao*, 2 (1987), 12–13.

28. Cheng Siyuan, *Zhenghai mixin*. Beifang wenyi, 1991, 108; Liu Chuanzeng, "Liao Lei he xinsijun lingdao tongzhi." *Luchuan wenshi ziliao*, 4 (1988), 25–31; Lin

Jinghua, "Liao Lei zai kangzhanzhong de yiduan gushi." *Luchuan wenshi ziliao*, 10 (1999), 101–103; *Luchuan wenshi ziliao*, Nos. 8–9; Liao Ruizhen and He Detang, "Wo suo zhidao de Liao Lei." *Luchuan wenshi ziliao*, 1 (1985), 65–71. The authors of the official biography of Zhang Yunyi, however, emphasize Liao Lei's hostility toward the Communists during the war against Japan. Zhang Yunyi zhuan bianxiezu, *Zhang Yunyi Zhuan*, 135, 155. Beijing: Dangdai zhongguo, 2012.

29. Mo Wenhua, *Mo Wenhua huiyilu*, 618–619.

30. Cen Jianying, "Guangxi Baise de yanbang," 159.

31. Ya Guohua, "Jidian de huiyi," 308–309.

32. Huang Ruhai and Fang Sunzhen, "Huang Xiaopeng." In *ZGGXDSRWZ*, Vol. 4, 232–236.

33. Huang Xianfan, Gan Wenjie and Gan Wenhao, *Wei Baqun pingzhuan*, 516–517.

34. *Nanning wanbao*, "Zhezhang heying shang guozhen you Wei Baqun ma." March 30, 2010; Lan Leibin, "Wei Baqun xiangpian zhi mi."

35. Wang Yanyi, "Wei Baqun lieshi yongyuan huozai women xinzhong: Wei Baqun lieshi tougu chutuji." *Wuzhou wenshi ziliao*, No. 11, 19–21.

36. Liang Baowei, "Dui Wei Baqun haopingruchao qianxi." Li Li, ed., *Wei Baqun jingshen lun*, 244–246. Beijing: Jiefangjun, 2009; Title page, Li Li, ed., *Wei Baqun jingshen lun*.

37. Wei Tianfu and Tan Lu, "Wei Baqun yunan qianhou." *Donglan wenshi*, No. 4, 37; Qin Guohan, "Gaobie: Yi zai Hechi zhengbian zhong de Wei Baqun tongzhi." *WCSLZJ*, 413; Wenshizu, "Donglanxian geming lieshi lingyuan." *Donglan wenshi ziliao*, No. 1, 86–92; Zhang Yunyi, "Baise qiyi yu hongqijun de jianli," 416; Xie Fumin, *Wei Baqun*, I-III; Qin Guohan, Huang Chao and Tan Qingrong, "Geming zhandou youyi." *Guangxi geming douzheng huiyilu*, Vol. 2, 164; Liang Baowei, "Dui Wei Baqun haopingruchao qianxi," 247; Zhang Yunyi, "Xuexi Wei Baqun tongzhi." *Huiyi Wei Baqun*, front page.

38. Mo Wenhua, "Huiyi Wei Baqun tongzhi." *Huiyi Wei Baqun*, 11–12.

39. Ye Jizhuang, "Dui Wei Baqun tongzhi de jidian huiyi."

40. Xie Fumin, *Wei Baqun*; Xie Fumin, Yuwen and Qian Shengfa, *Wei Baqun*, 2 vols. Shanghai: Shanghai renmin meishu, 1978.

41. *Donglan xianzhi*, 1994, 19; Wei Guoqing, "Yingfan yongcun"; Qin Yingji, Huang Songjian and Huang Rong, "Zhuoyue de gongchanzhuyi zhanshi Wei Baqun"; Huang Songjian, "Gongxian zhuozhu fengfan yongcun." *Renmin ribao*, October 21, 1982.

42. Lan Handong and Lan Qixuan, "Zhanyou shenqing." *Dadan youmaqi: Zuoyoujiang geming lingdaoren gushi chuanshuo*, 106; Huang Songjian, "Gongxian zhuozhu fengfan yongcun."

43. Wenshiwei, "Wenhua dageming zai Donglan fasheng he fazhan de zhuyao shiji." *Donglan wenshi*, 5 (2004), 180; Huang Yulu, ed., *Zhongguo gongchandang Guangxi Zhuangzu zizhiqu Donglanxian zuzhishi ziliao, 1926–1987*, 180, 382, 392.

44. Lan Tianli, "Hongyang Baqun jingshen, cujin kexue fazhan." Li Li, ed., *Wei Baqun jingshen lun*, 7.

45. Huang Xianfan, Gan Wenjie and Gan Wenhao, *Wei Baqun pingzhuan*, 9.

46. Huang Yingjun, "Wei Baqun lieshi huaxiang zhimi." *Dangshi bolan*, 2003(3), 50–51.

47. Paul Cohen, *History in Three Keys: The Boxers as Event, Experience, and Myth*, 219. Columbia University Press, 1997.

48. Guangxi shaoshuminzu lishidiaocha zu, *Guangxi Zhuangzu zizhiqu Donglanxian Zhonghe renmingongshe Donglitun shehuilishi diaocha baogao*, 4, 55–58, 60–62.

49. Wei Tianfu, ed., *Donglanxian minzheng zhi*, 299–302.

50. Ibid., 157–161.

51. Qin Shimian, "Yi Donglan geming laodong xiaoxue." *ZYJGMGJD*, Vol. 2, 778.

52. Lu Xiuxiang, "Wei Baqun." Lu Xiuxiang, Huang Jianping and Huang Yingjun, eds., *Zhonggong Donglan dangshi renwu zhuan*, 3.

53. Zhongyang fangwentuan diyi fentuan lianluozu, *Guangxi Donglanxian diwuqu (Zhonghequ) minzu gaikuang*, 5.

54. Tian Shulan, *Guangxi luxingji*, 193; Katherine Kaup, *Creating the Zhuang: Ethnic Politics in China*, 3, 11. Lynne Rienner, 2000.

55. Zhongyang fangwentuan diyi fentuan lianluozu, *Guangxi Donglanxian Xishanqu minzu gaikuang*, 2.

56. Lei Jingtian, "Guangxi de Suwei'ai yundong," 600, 609.

57. *Junshi tongxun*, "Dui Guangxi hongjun gongzuo buzhi de taolun," 179, 195; Zhonggong zhongyang, "Zhonggong zhongyang gei Guangdong shengwei zhuan qijun qianwei de zhishi," 239; Deng Baqi, "Deng Baqi gei Zhonggong Youjiang tewei ji ershiyishi shiwei xin," 417.

58. Fan Honggui and Gu Youshi, et al., *Zhuangzu lishi yu wenhua*, 256.

59. Huang Xianfan, Gan Wenjie and Gan Wenhao, *Wei Baqun pingzhuan*, 37–39, 46, 135–138, 244, 276, 307–308, 323–324, 417–420, 422–429, 467–468, 507.

60. Wang Lintao, "Lei Jingtian," 357.

61. See Zhonggong Guangxi Zhuangzu zizhiqu wenyuanhui dangshi yanjiushi, ed., *Guangxi jiaofei shi*. Beijing: Zhonggong dangshi, 2008; Huang Jishu, *Baibing chengfei: 1949 nian dao 1952 nian de jiaofei wangshi*. Beijing: Wenhua yishu, 2011.

62. Xiaolin Guo, *State and Ethnicity in China's Southwest*, 45. Brill, 2008.

63. *Donglan xianzhi*, 1994, 630.

Conclusion

1. Liu Yanzhi, "Donglan dali wajue hongyang hongse ziyuan." Donglan dangjianwang, October 12, 2007; *Donglan xianzhi*, 1994, 117.

2. Huang Bin,"Donglan faxian yi shenqi rongdong, luyou kaifa qianjing kanhao." Guangxi daxuesheng cunguanwang, May 7, 2010.

3. Liu Yanzhi, "Donglan dali wajue hongyang hongse ziyuan."

Glossary of Chinese Names and Terms

Bage	拔哥
Bai Chongxi	白崇禧
Bai Hanyun	白汉云
Baiyue	百越
Baise	百色
Bansheng	板升
Baojia	保甲
Beidi	北帝
Beihai	北海
Beiliu	北流
Bi Xueping	闭雪平
Binyang	宾阳
Bohao	波豪
Cai E	蔡锷
Cangjie	仓颉
Cen Chunxuan	岑椿萱
Cen Yuying	岑毓英
Cenxun	岑逊
Changjiang	长江
Chen Bomin	陈伯民
Chen Daosheng	陈道生
Chen Dibo	陈的伯
Chen Enshen	陈恩深
Chen Fu	陈福
Chen Gutao	陈鼓涛
Chen Haoren	陈豪人
Chen Henglong	陈衡龙
Chen Hongmou	陈宏谋
Chen Hongtao	陈洪涛
Chen Jiongming	陈炯明
Chen Lanfen	陈兰芬

Chen Manyuan	陈漫远
Chen Mengwu	陈孟武
Chen Mianshu	陈勉恕
Chen Mingjiu	陈铭玖
Chen Qinglian	陈庆连
Chen Qing'e	陈庆锷
Chen Rujin	陈儒瑾
Chen Ruzhen	陈儒珍
Chen Shouhe	陈守和
Chen Shouxian	陈守先
Chen Shusen	陈树森
Chen Xiewu	陈协五
Chen Yannian	陈延年
Chen Yuzao	陈毓藻
Daodi	到底
Daxian	达县
Deng Gang (Baqi)	邓岗（拔奇）
Deng Bin (Xiaoping)	邓斌 (小平)
Deng Bucai	邓卜才
Deng Peng	邓鹏
Deng Wuwei	邓无畏
Di Qing	狄青
Dong	峒
Dong-Feng	东凤
Donglan	东兰
Dongli	东里
Dongping River	东平河
Dongshan	东山
Dongyuan	东院
Longjiang	龙江
Du Ba	杜八
Du Bohao	杜伯豪
Du Qi	杜七
Duyi	都彝
Enlong	恩隆
Fan Shisheng	范石生
Fan Yao	番瑶
Fang Fang	方方
Fang Zhimin	方志敏
Fenbuping	忿不平
Feng Baiju	冯白驹
Fengshan	凤山

Fengyi	奉议
Gao Yaoguang	高瑶光
Gong Chu (Hecun)	龚楚 (鹤村)
Gong Shouyi	龚寿仪
Gu Dacun	古大存
Guo Moruo	郭沫若
Haifeng	海丰
Hailufeng	海陆丰
Haiting	海亭
He Yingqin	何应钦
Hechi	河池
Hengli	恒里
Hongshenmiao	红神庙
Hong Xiuquan	洪秀全
Hongshuihe	红水河
Hu Hanmin	胡汉民
Huaibei	淮北
Huaiyuan	怀远
Huang Bangcheng	黄榜呈
Huang Bangdeng	黄榜登
Huang Bangwei	黄榜巍
Huang Boyao	黄伯尧
Huang Chao	黄巢
Huang Daquan	黄大权
Huang Daye	黄大业
Huang Fangri	黄昉日
Huang Fengtao	黄凤桃
Huang Gonglue	黄公略
Huang Haiju	黄海驹
Huang Hongfu	黄鸿富
Huang Hongju	黄鸿举
Huang Hongyi	黄鸿翼
Huang Huabiao	黄华表
Huang Hui	黄晖
Huang Jiakang	黄家康
Huang Jinyou	黄金尤
Huang Juping	黄举平
Huang Meilun	黄美伦
Huang Qi	黄琪
Huang Qiongyao	黄琼瑶
Huang Ruoshan	黄若珊
Huang Shaohong	黄绍竑

Huang Shaoxian	黄绍先
Huang Shouxian (Shaozu)	黄守先 (绍祖)
Huang Shulin	黄树林
Huang Shuxiang	黄书祥
Huang Songjian	黄松坚
Huang Xianfan	黄现璠
Huang Xiaopeng	黄肖鹏
Huang Xiumei	黄秀梅
Huang Xuchu	黄旭初
Huang Yucheng	黄羽成
Huang Yumei	黄玉美
Huang Yun	黄云
Huang Zhengxiu	黄正秀
Huang Zhifeng	黄治峰
Huang Zhiyuan	黄智渊
Huang Zuyu	黄祖谕
Jianchi	坚持
Jiang Maosheng	姜茂生
Jiangping	江平
Jinchengjiang	金城江
Jinggangshan	井冈山
Jiujiang	九江
Jiuqu River (Jiuqu he)	九曲河
Kuixinglou	魁星楼
Lajia	拉甲
Lan Maocai	兰茂才
Lan Zhiren	蓝志仁
Lang	俍
Lansi	兰泗
Lei Jingtian	雷经天
Lengshuitan	冷水滩
Li Dingguo	李定国
Li Dingjian	黎鼎鉴
Li Jishen	李济深
Li Lisan	李立三
Li Mingrui	李明瑞
Li Pu	李朴
Li Qian	李谦
Li Shunmei	李顺妹
Li Wenlin	李文林
Li Zhengru	李正儒
Li Zicheng	李自成

Li Zongren 李宗仁
Liang Fuzhen 梁福臻
Liang Lieya 梁烈亚
Liang Shi'e 梁士谔
Liang Shishu 梁士书
Liang Shixun 梁士训
Liang Shuming 梁漱溟
Liang Xuqiu 梁旭秋
Liao Lei 廖磊
Liao Yuanfang 廖源芳
Liao Zhongkai 廖仲恺
Liliao 俚僚
Lin Huating 林华亭
Lin Junting 林俊廷
Lingui 临桂
Lingyun 凌云
Liu Rifu 刘日福
Liu Sanjie 刘三姐
Liu Shipei 刘师培
Liu Yongfu 刘永福
Liu Zhenhuan 刘震寰
Liu Zhi 刘治
Liu Zhidan 刘志丹
Liuzhou 柳州
Long Jinbiao 龙锦标
Long Xianyun 龙显云
Long Yun 龙云
Longzhou 龙州
Lu Haoren 陆皓仁
Lu Rongting 陆荣廷
Lu Tao 卢涛
Lu Xiuxuan 陆秀轩
Lu Yongfen 陆永芬
Lunxu 仑圩
Luo Buduo 罗卜多
Luo Guifa 罗贵发
Luo Huo 罗活
Luo Rikuai 罗日块
Luo Yiyuan 罗猗园
Luo Wenjian 罗文鉴
Luoyue 骆越
Macheng 麻城

Ma Junwu	马君武
Meng Renqian	蒙仁潜
Meng Yuanliang	蒙元良
Mo Rongxin	莫荣新
Mo Wenhua	莫文骅
Nadi	那地
Nandan	南丹
Nanning	南宁
Nong Yousan	农友三
Nong Zhigao	侬智高
Nongjing	弄京
Oertai	鄂尔泰
Pan Xiaomei	潘小梅
Peng Pai	彭湃
Panyang	盘阳
Pingma	平马
Qin Daoping	覃道平
Qin Kongxian	覃孔贤
Qin Liankui	覃联魁
Qin Ruiwu	覃瑞五
Qin Shouchun	覃寿春
Qin Yingji	覃应机
Qingyuan	庆远
Quanzhou	全州
Rong County	容县
Ruan Xiaoxian	阮啸仙
Sanshi	三石
Sha Wenhan	沙文汉
Shaan-Gan-Ning	陕甘宁
Shen Dingyi	沈定一
Shi Dakai	石达开
Simeng	泗孟
Tang Jiyao	唐继尧
Tao Qigan	陶其淦
Teng Guodong	滕国栋
Tianbao	天保
Tian'e	天峨
Tianzhou	田州
Tu Yao	土瑶
Turen	土人
Tusi	土司
Wang Juqiu	王菊秋

Wang Tingye	王廷业
Wang Zuo	王佐
Wei Ang	韦昂
Wei Baqun (Cui)	韦拔群 (萃)
Wei Bingji (Bingqian)	韦秉吉 (秉乾)
Wei Chaoqun	韦超群
Wei Erzhang	韦尔章
Wei Guoqing	韦国清
Wei Guoying	韦国英
Wei Hanchao	韦汉超
Wei Hongqing	韦鸿卿
Wei Hua	韦华
Wei Huchen	韦虎臣
Wei Jie	韦杰
Wei Jing	韦茎
Wei Jing	韦菁
Wei Jingdai	韦景岱
Wei Jingyi	韦经益
Wei Libo	韦礼伯
Wei Longfu	韦龙甫
Wei Mingzhou	韦命周
Wei Naien	韦奶恩
Wei Qianbao	韦钱宝
Wei Qiyun	韦起云
Wei Shuzong	韦述宗
Wei Shuzu	韦述祖
Wei Ting'an	韦廷安
Wei Zhengbao	韦正宝
Wu Jiashu	吴家书
Wu Peifu	吴佩孚
Wu Qingpei	吴清培
Wuhu	乌浒
Wuhua	五华
Wuyi	武夷
Wuzhou	梧州
Wuzhuan	武篆
Xiangchadong	香茶洞
Xie Fumin	谢扶民
Xiong Kecheng	熊克诚
Xishan	西山
Xiou	西瓯
Xu Jiayu	徐家豫

Xu Jishen 许继慎
Ya Guohua 牙国华
Ya Sumin 牙苏民
Ya Yufan 牙玉璠
Ya Yugui 牙玉贵
Yan Min 严敏
Yan Yangchu (James Yen) 晏阳初
Yang Jinmei 杨金梅
Yang Ximin 杨希闵
Yao 瑶
Ye Jizhuang 叶季壮
Ye Yimao 叶一矛
Yi Zhenxing 易振兴
Yinhaizhou 银海州
Yiyang 弋阳
Yizhou 宜州
Yongning 永宁
Youjiang 右江
Yu Shaojie 余少杰
Yu Zuobai 俞作柏
Yu Zuoyu 俞作豫
Yuan Wencai 袁文才
Yucai 育才
Yun Daiying 恽代英
Zhang Guotao 张国焘
Zhang Jiao 张角
Zhang Qihuang 张其湟
Zhang Shenfu 张申府
Zhang Yunyi 张云逸
Zhao Shijun 赵世俊
Zhuang 壮 (僮)
Zuojiang 左江

Bibliography

Chinese Language Sources

Bai Chongxi 白崇禧. "Guangxi jinhou de zhengzhifangzhen he women dui guojia de zeren" 广西今后的政治方针和我们对国家的责任 (The Future Political Policies of Guangxi and Our Duties to the Nation). October 14–15, 1932. In *WCSLZJ*, 575–576.

———. "Zuoyoujiang zhengzhi shicha baogao" 左右江政治视察报告 (A Field Report about the Political Situation in the Left River and Right River Region). October 23, 1932. In *ZYJGMSLHB*, Vol. 3, 141–144.

———. *Bai Chongxi huiyilu* 白崇禧回忆录 (The Memoirs of Bai Chongxi). Beijing: Jiefangjun, 1987.

Bai Xianjing 白先经, ed. *Hongqijun Hongbajun yinglie zhuan* 红七军红八军英列传 (Biographies of the Martyrs of the Seventh and Eighth Red Armies). Beijing: Jiefangjun, 1991.

Bai Yaotian 白耀天. *Nong Zhigao: Lishi de xingyun'er yu qi'er* 侬智高：历史的幸运儿与弃儿 (Nong Zhigao as a Favored and Abandoned Son of History). Beijing: Minzu, 2006.

Ban Feng 班锋 and Luo Zhaowen 罗昭文. "Liao Yuanfang" 廖源芳. In *ZGGXDSRWZ*. Vol. 1 (1992), 202–211.

Benteng de Zuoyoujiang 奔腾的左右江 (The Rolling Torrents of the Left and Right Rivers). Nanning: Guangxi renmin, 1980.

Bi Mengping 闭梦平. "Wo zai Donglan disanjie jiangxisuo renjiao qianhou" 我在东兰第三届讲 习所任教前后 (Recollections about My Days Teaching at the Third Class of Donglan Institute of Peasant Movement). In *WCSLZJ*, 364–365.

Blagodatov, Aleksei Vasilevich 勃拉戈达托夫. *Zhongguo geming zhaji: 1925–1927* 中国革命 札记： 1925–1927 (Notes on the Chinese Revolution: 1925–1927). Zhang Kai, trans. Beijing: Xinhua, 1985.

BSD (Baiseshi dang'anguan 百色市档案馆 Baise Municipal Archives). 083-002-0013, "Baqun waichu youli" 拔群外出游历 (Wei Baqun's Excursion).

———. 083-002-0013, "Wei Baqun bianxian" 韦拔群变仙 (Wei Baqun Changes Himself into a Celestial Being).

———. 083-002-0013, "Wei Baqun tongzhi de gushi" 韦拔群同志的故事 (Stories about Comrade Wei Baqun).

———. 083-002-0013, "Teyamiao de mimi" 特牙庙的秘密 (Secrets about the Teya Temple).

———. 083-002-0017-004, "Baqun de qizi he ernu" 拔群的妻子和儿女 (Wei Baqun's Wives and Children).

———. 083-002-0017-005, "Hongse nuyoujiduiyuan: Weilieshi de airen Huang Xiumei tongzhi" 红色女游击队员：韦烈士的爱人黄秀梅同志 (A Red Female Guerilla Fighter: Martyr Wei Baqun's Wife Huang Xiumei).

———. 084, "Wei Libo zhi Liu Pinqing" 韦礼伯致刘聘卿 (Wei Libo's Letter to Liu Pinqing), 1927.

Cao Yuwen 曹裕文 and Lu Jiaxiang 卢家翔. *Xinguixi yu Zhongguo gongchandang* 新桂系与中国共产党 (The New Guangxi Clique and the CCP). Nanning: Guihai luncong zazhishe, 1994.

Cen Jianying 岑建英. "Guangxi Baise de yanbang" 广西百色的烟帮 (The Opium Caravans of Baise, Guangxi). *GXWSZLXJ*, 3 (1963), 155–160.

Chen Bomin 陈伯民, Ya Sumin 牙苏民 and Qin Kongxian 覃孔贤. "Donglanxian dangwu baogao" 东兰县党务报告 (A Report about the KMT Affairs in Donglan). *Zhongguo guomindang Guangxisheng di'erci daibiaodahui rikan* 中国国民党广西省第二次代表大会日刊 (Journal of the Second Congress of the Guangxi Branch of the KMT), March 13, 1927. In *WCSLZJ*, 76–77.

Chen Gongbo 陈公博. *Kuxiaolu: Chen gongbo huiyi, 1925–1936* 苦笑录：陈公博回忆，1925至1936 (Moments of Wry Smiles: Memoirs of Chen Gongbo, 1925–1936). 1939. 2 vols. Hong Kong: University of Hong Kong Centre of Asian Studies Occasional Papers and Monographs, No. 36, 1979.

Chen Guopei 陈国培 and Lu Xiuxiang 陆秀祥. "Beishang Jiangxi he canjia fanweijiao douzheng de huiyi" 北上江西和参加反'围剿'斗争的回忆 (Recollections about the March to Jiangxi and the Struggles against the Extermination Campaigns). In Lu Xiuxiang ed., 1990, 336–338.

Chen Guoying 陈国英. "Zai shizhang he zhengwei shenbian gongzuo de rizi" 在师长和政委身边工作的日子 (Memories of the Days When I Worked for Wei Baqun and Chen Hongtao). 1987. In *WCSLZJ*, 447–450.

Chen Hanming 陈寒鸣. "Lun jindai zhongguo wuzhengfu zhuyi sichao" 论近代中国无政府主义思潮 (Anarchism in Modern China). Xueshuo lianxian 学说连线 http://www.xslx.com/Html/sxgc/200408/6950.html.

Chen Haoren 陈豪人. "Qijun qianwei baogao" 七军前委报告 (Report from the Front Committee of the Seventh Red Army). January 1930. In *ZYJGMGJD*, Vol. 1, 158–167.

———. "Qijun gongzuo zongbaogao" 七军工作总报告 (A General Report about the Activities of the Seventh Red Army). March 9, 1931. In *ZYJGMGJD*, Vol. 1, 358–381.

Chen Hongtao 陈洪涛. "Dao Baqun tongzhi" 悼拔群同志 (Mourn for Comrade Baqun). October 1932. In *WCSLZJ*, 225.

Chen Mianshu 陈勉恕. "Guangxi Donglan nongmin yundong zhi shiji zhuangkuang" 广西东兰农民运动之实际状况 (A True Account of the Peasant Movement in Donglan of Guangxi). *Nongmin yundong* (Wuhan), 22 & 23. April 1927. In *WCSLZJ*, 47–57.

Chen Rukai 陈儒楷. "Donglan shiyan zhuanmai gongdian gaikuang" 东兰食盐专卖公店概况 (The Government Monopoly on Salt in Donglan). *Donglan wenshi ziliao* 东兰文史资料, 2(1987), 18–21.

Chen Ruzhen 陈儒珍. "Chen Ruzhen zizhuan" 陈儒珍自传 (An Autobiography of Chen Ruzhen). 1952. In *WCSLZJ*, 679–680.

Chen Shidu 陈仕读. "Huiyi Mian'e binggongchang" 回忆免俄兵工厂 (Memories of the Mian'e Arsenal). *Donglan wenshi ziliao* 东兰文史资料, 1 (1985), 24–25.

———. "Fanji Huang Shouxian dui nongsuo de pohuai" 反击黄守先对农所的破坏 (To Counter Huang Shouxian's Attack on Donglan Institute of Peasant Movement). In Lu Xiuxiang, ed., Donglan nongmin yundong, 1921–1927, 1986, 179–182.

Chen Xiewu 陈协五. "Chenbuzhang yanshuogao" 陈部长演说稿 (Director Chen's Speech). 1926. In Lu Xiuxiang, ed., 1986, 74–78.

———. "Guangxi Donglan nongmin zhi can'an" 广西东兰农民之惨案 (The Atrocities against the Peasants of Donglan, Guangxi). *Nongmin yundong* (Guangzhou), No. 6 & 7. September 7 & 14, 1926. In *WCSLZJ*, 39–46.

Chen Xinde 陈欣德. "Wei Baqun" 韦拔群. In Hu Hua 胡华, ed., *Zhonggong dangshi renwu zhuan* 中共党史人物传, Vol. 12, 183–216. Xi'an: Shanxi renmin, 1983.

———. "Zongshu" 综述 (Introduction). In *ZYJGMGJD*, Vol. 1, 1–42.

———. "Zuoyoujiang geming genjudi de tudigeming yundong" 左右江革命根据地的土地革命运动 (The Land Revolution in the Left River and Right River Revolutionary Base Area). In *ZYJGMGJD*, Vol. 2, 1080–1093.

———. "Wei Baqun" 韦拔群. In *ZGGXDSRWZ*, Vol. 1 (1992), 244–260.

———. "Huang Fangri" 黄昉日. In *ZGGXDSRWZ*, Vol. 1 (1992), 324–332.

———. "Lei Tianzhuang" 雷天壮. In *ZGGXDSRWZ*, Vol. 4 (2004), 74–78.

———. "Li Qian" 李谦. In *ZGGXDSRWZ*, Vol. 4 (2004), 447–454.

Chen Yung-fa 陈永发. "Zhengzhi kongzhi he qunzhong dongyuan: Eyuwan sufan" 政治控制与群众动员：鄂豫皖肃反 (Political Control and Mass Mobilization: The Purge at Eyuwan). *Dalu zazhi* 大陆杂志, 86(1), 20–38; 86(2), 19–30; 86(3), 24–33. 1993.

Chen Zhenwei 陈祯伟. "Xishanxing" 西山行 (A Journey to the Western Mountains). In Hechi ribaoshe, ed., 1990, 43–44.

Chen Zuncheng 陈遵诚. "Dengzhengwei zai Enlong" 邓政委在恩隆 (Political Commissar Deng Xiaoping in Enlong). *Tiandong wenshi ziliao* 田东文史资料, Vol. 1 (1987), 22–31.

———. "Teng Guodong" 滕国栋. In Lan Tian and Huang Zhizhen, eds., 1992, 382–385.

———. "Yang Jinmei" 杨金梅. In *ZGGXDSRWZ*, Vol. 4 (2004), 455–457.

Cheng Siyuan 程思远. *Zhenghai mixin* 政海秘辛 (Inside Stories of the Political World). Haerbin: Beifang wenyi, 1991.

Chenshi zongqin luntan 陈氏宗亲论坛. "Jinian Baise qiyi diyihao lingdaoren Chen Haoren tongzhi danchen yibai zhounian" 纪念百色起义第一号领导人陈豪人同志诞辰100周年 (Commemorate the 100th Birthday of Comrade Chen Haoren—the Number One Leader of the Baise Uprising). http://bbs.chens.org.cn/showtopic.asp?TOPIC_ID=14953&Forum_ID=37

Chiang Kai-shek 蒋介石. "Jiangzhuxi zhonggao Li Mingrui dian quanwen" 蒋主席忠告李明瑞电全文 (Chairman Chiang Kai-shek's Advice for Li Mingrui). *Gongpingbao* 公评报, October 5, 1929. In *ZYJGMSLHB*, Vol. 3, 37–38.

Dai Xiangqing 戴向青. "Lun ABtuan he Futian shibian" 论A B团和富田事变 (The Anti-Bolshevik Corps and the Futian Incident). *Zhonggong dangshi yanjiu* 中共党史研究, 1989(1), 24–29.

Deng Baqi 邓拔奇. "Deng Baqi gei Zhonggong Youjiang tewei ji ershiyishi shiwei xin" 邓拔奇给中共右江特委及二十一师师委信 (Deng Baqi's Letter to the Right River Special Committee of the CCP and the CCP Committee of the 21st Division). June 15, 1931. In *ZYJGMGJD*, Vol. 1, 415–420.

———. "Muqian Guangxi de zhengzhi xingshi" 目前广西的政治形势 (The Current Political Situation in Guangxi). August 1, 1931. In *ZYJGMGJD*, Vol. 1, 421–428.

———. "Baqi guanyu Guangxi gongzuo baogao" 拔奇关于广西工作报告 (Deng Baqi's Report about the CCP Work in Guangxi). September 1, 1931. In *ZYJGMGJD*, Vol. 1, 429–435.

Deng Xiaoping 邓小平. "Qijun gongzuo baogao" 七军工作报告 (A Report about the Activities of the Seventh Red Army)." April 29, 1931. In *ZYJGMGJD*, Vol. 1, 392–411.

———. "Wo de zishu" 我的自述 (An Account of My Life). 1968. http://hetai2.blog.hexun.com/40777325_d.html.

———. "Fazhan zhongri guanxi yao kande yuanxie" 发展中日关系要看得远些 (We Should Take a Long Term Perspective in Developing Sino-Japanese Relations." March 15, 1984. In *Deng Xiaoping wenxuan* 邓小平文选 (Selected Works of Deng Xiaoping), Vol. 3, 31–32. Beijing: Renmin, 1993.

Diqijun yuandan tekan 第七军元旦特刊. "Junfachu yinianlai gongzuo zhi gaikuang" 军法处一年来工作之概况 (The Work of the Military Court in the Past Year). 1932. In *ZYJGMGJD*, Vol. 2, 948.

Donglan nongmin yundong 东兰农民运动 (The Donglan Peasant Movement). Guilin: Guangxi shifan xueyuan zhengzhixi, 1978. Unpublished manuscript.

Donglan xianzhi 东兰县志 (Donglan Gazette). Vol. 1. 1960. Unpublished manuscript.

Donglan xianzhi 东兰县志 (Donglan Gazette). Nanning: Guangxi renmin, 1994.

Donglanxian geming weiyuanhui 东兰县革命委员会. "Guangxi Donglanxian geming weiyuanhui zuidi zhenggang cao'an" 广西东兰县革命委员会最低政纲草案 (Draft Minimum Political Program of the Revolutionary Committee of Donglan County in Guangxi). October 1929. In *ZYJGMGJD*, Vol. 1, 93–96.

Donglanxian nongmin xiehui 东兰县农民协会 (The Donglan Peasant Association). "Kuaiyou daidian" 快邮代电 (An Express Letter to the Public). May 1926. In *WCSLZJ*, 30–31.

Donglanxian Suwei'ai 东兰县苏维埃. "Muqian xuanchuan biaoyu" 目前宣传标语 (Slogans for Current Use). August 1, 1930. In *ZYJGMGJD*, Vol. 1, 319–321.

Fan Honggui 范宏贵 and Gu Youshi 顾有识, et al. *Zhuangzu lishi yu wenhua* 壮族历史与文化 (History and Culture of the Zhuang People). Nanning: Guangxi minzu, 1997.

Fang Daheng 方大恒 and Zou Wensheng 邹文生. "Zuoyoujiang geming genjudi de sufan baowei gongzuo" 左右江革命根据地的肃反保卫工作 (The Work on Purging Internal Enemies in the Left River and Right River Revolutionary Base Area). In *ZYJGMGJD*, Vol. 2, 1124–1133.

Gao Hua 高华. "Su ABtuan shijian de lishi kaocha" 肃AB团事件的历史考察 (A Historical Analysis of the Purge of the Anti-Bolshevik Corps). *Ershiyi shiji* 二十一世纪, No. 54 (August, 1999), 60–71.

Gao Yaoguang 高瑶光. "Chen Mianshu ersanshi" 陈勉恕二三事 (Some Recollections about Chen Mianshu). In Lu Xiuxiang, ed., 1986, 186–195.

Gong Chu 龚楚. *Wo yu hongjun* 我与红军 (I and the Red Army). Hong Kong: South Wind Publishing Co., 1954.

Gong Sheng 共声. "Huang Songjian" 黄松坚. In Bai Xianjing, ed., 1991, 235–248.

Gongpingbao 公评报. "Guiren shu Yu Zuobai shidazui" 桂人数俞作柏十大罪 (The People of Guangxi Believe that Yu Zuobai Has Committed Ten Crimes). October 8, 1929. In *ZYJGMSLHB*, Vol. 3, 34–35.

———. "Yan Dezhong fu Wu wu Li Mingrui" 颜德忠赴梧晤李明瑞 (Yan Dezhong Came to Wuzhou to Meet with Li Mingrui). December 26, 1929. In *ZYJGMSLHB*, Vol. 3, 48.

Gu Zuyu 顾祖禹. *Dushi fangyu jiyao* 读史方舆纪要 (Essentials of China's Historical Geography). Beijing: Zhonghua shuju, 2005.

Guangdong shengwei 广东省委. "Yuesheng dui qijun qianwei de zhishixin" 粤省对七军前委的指示信 (Directives from the Guangdong Provincial Committee of the CCP to the Front Committee of the Seventh Red Army). December 25, 1929. In *ZYJGMGJD*, Vol. 1, 139–145.

Guangxi geming douzheng huiyilu 广西革命斗争回忆录 (Memories of the Revolutionary Struggles in Guangxi). 2 volumes. Nanning: Guangxi renmin, 1981 and 1984.

Guangxi Gongbao 广西公报. "Shengfu xuanhong gouji Weifei Baqun ji Chen Hongtao deng bugao" 省府悬红购缉韦匪拔群及陈洪涛等布告 (Announcement of the Provincial Government about Offering Bounty for Bandit Wei Baqun, Chen Hongtao and Others), No. 32. May 21, 1931. In *WCSLZJ*, 546.

Guangxi minjian wenxue yanjiuhui 广西民间文学研究会, ed. *Dadan youmaqi: Zuoyoujiang geming lingdaoren gushi chuanshuo* 大胆有马骑：左右江革命领导人故事传说 (The Daring Ones Will Have Horses to Ride: Stories about the Leaders of the Left River and Right River Revolution). *Guangxi minjian wenxue congkan* 广西民间文学丛刊, No. 11. Nanning, 1984.

Guangxi minzheng yuekan 广西民政月刊. "Donglanxian diyici quanshu tuanwu huiyilu" 东兰县第一次全属团务会议录 (Minutes from the First Meeting of Militia Leaders of Donglan). *Guangxi minzheng yuekan*, 1(1). January 1928. In *ZYJGMSLHB*, Vol. 3, 15–17.

———. "Minzhengting dianfu Donglan xianzhang jubao gaixian houbeiduizhang Huang Shaoxian souhuo nifei paijipaodan qingxing yang zhuanling jiajiang you" 民政厅电复东兰县长据报该县后备队长黄绍先搜获逆匪迫击炮弹情形仰转令嘉奖由 (Telegram from the Department of Civil Affairs to the Magistrate of Donglan about Citing Commander of Reserve Unit Huang Shaoxian for Helping Discover the Mortar Shells of the Bandits). No. 7. June 1932. In *ZYJGMSLHB*, Vol. 3, 97.

Guangxi shaoshuminzu shehui lishi diaochazu 广西少数民族社会历史调查组, ed. *Guangxi zhuangzu zizhiqu Donglanxian Zhonghe renmingongshe Donglitun shehuilishi diaocha baogao* 广西壮族自治区东兰县中和人民公社东里屯社会历史调查报告 (A Report on Field Research about the History and Society of Dongli Village of Zhonghe Commune, Donglan County, Guangxi Zhuang Autonomous

Region). Nanning: Zhongguo shehui kexueyuan minzu yanjiusuo Guangxi shaoshuminzu shehui lishi diaochazu, 1964.

Guangxi tewei 广西特委. "Guangxi dang zhengzhi renwu jueyi'an" 广西党政治任务决议案 (Resolution about the Political Tasks of the CCP in Guangxi). September 13, 1929. In *ZYJGMGJD*, Vol. 1, 51–63.

Guangxi xinhai gemingshi yanjiuhui 广西辛亥革命史研究会, ed. *Minguo Guangxi renwu zhuan* 民国广西人物传 (Biographies of Prominent Figures of Guangxi during the Republican Era), Vol. 1. Nanning: Guangxi renmin, 1983.

Guangxisheng Donglanxian nongmin xiehui 广西省东兰县农民协会. "Kuaiyou daidian" 快邮代电 (A Telegram to the Public). May 1926. In *WCSLZJ*, 30–31.

Guangxisheng minzhengting 广西省民政厅. *Guangxi gexian gaikuang* 广西各县概况 (The Counties of Guangxi). Nanning: Dacheng yinshuguan, 1934.

Guangxisheng nonghui choubeichu 广西省农会筹备处. "Nongmin yundong de celue" 农民运动的策略 (The Strategies of the Peasant Movements). In *WCSLZJ*, 86–87.

Guangxisheng nongminbu 广西省农民部. "Guangxisheng nongminbu gongzuo baogao" 广西省农民部工作报告 (Report of the Department of Peasant Affairs of the Guangxi Provincial Government). 1927. In *ZYJGMSLHB*, Vol. 2, 42–59.

Guangxisheng zhengfu 广西省政府. "Guangxisheng zhengfu dui Donglan nong'an zhi jingguo" 广西省政府对东兰农案之经过 (A Report on How the Guangxi Provincial Government Has Handled the Dispute over the Donglan Peasant Movement). *Zhongguo guomindang guomin gemingjun diqijun tebiedangbu banyuekan* 中国国民党国民革命军第七军特别党部半月刊, No. 11. December 15, 1926. In *ZYJGMSLHB*, Vol. 3, 2–4.

———. "Guangxisheng zhengfu ruidian ju renmin chengkong Donglan gequ nonghui bufa xingwei bing chi gaixian nongminxiehui su zunzhao danggang qieshi zhengli wen" 广西省政府锐电据人民呈控东兰各区农会不法行为并饬该县农民协会速遵照党纲切实整理文 (In Response to Accusations about the Illegal Activities of the Peasant Associations of Donglan the Provincial Government Ordered the Peasant Associations to Reform their Behavior According to the KMT Program). July 1, 1927. In *ZYJGMSLHB*, Vol. 3, 5–6.

———. "Guangxisheng zhengfu xunling minzheng sifa liangting jiang Huang Shouxian qian zai Donglanxian zhishi rennei yin lan'an suoshou zhi chufen chexiao wen" 广西省政府训令民政司法两厅将黄守先前在东兰县知事任内因兰案所受之处分撤销文 (A Directive from the Guangxi Provincial Government about Revoking the Verdict for Former Magistrate Huang Shouxian of Donglan). *Guangxisheng zhengfu gongbao* 广西省政府公报, No. 49. October 11, 1927. In *ZYJGMSLHB*, Vol. 3, 8–9.

———. "Guangxisheng zhengfu xunling ge xianzhang ge jingtingju an ju Tiannan qingxiang zongban Liu Rifu cheng yiding shangge gouji shouyao feidang Wei Baqun deng yangji yiti xieji wuhuo gui'an xunban wen [fu shangge]" 广西省政府训令各县长各警厅局案据田南清乡总办刘日福呈议定赏格购缉首要匪党韦拔群等仰即一体协缉务获归案训办文 [附赏格] (Guangxi Provincial Government's Order to County Governments and Local Police about Offering Bounties for Capturing Leading Bandit Wei Baqun and His Followers). December 12, 1927. In *ZYJGMSLHB*, Vol. 3, 12–13.

———. "Guangxisheng zhengfu xunling di 37 hao" 广西省政府训令第三七号 (Directive Number 37 of the Guangxi Provincial Government). *Guangxisheng zhengfu gongbao*, No. 59.January 21, 1928. In *ZYJGMSLHB*, Vol. 3, 14–15.

———. "Guangxisheng zhengfu yudian" 广西省政府鱼电 (A Telegram from the Guangxi Provincial Government). *Guangxisheng zhengfu gongbao* 广西省政府公报, No. 66. April 1, 1928. In *ZYJGMSLHB*, Vol. 3, 22–23.

———. "Guangxisheng zhengfu zhiling di 439 hao" 广西省政府指令第四三九号 (Directive Number 439 of the Guangxi Provincial Government). *Guangxisheng zhengfu gongbao*, No. 66. April 1, 1928. In *ZYJGMSLHB*, Vol. 3, 20–22.

Guo Hongtao 郭洪涛. *Guo Hongtao huiyilu* 郭洪涛回忆录 (The Memoirs of Guo Hongtao). Beijing: Zhonggong dangshi, 2004.

GXWSZLXJ [Guangxi wenshi ziliao xuanji] 广西文史资料选辑 (Collections of Cultural and Historical Materials about Guangxi). 38 volumes. Nanning: Guangxi Zhuangzu zizhiqu zhengzhi xieshang huiyi wenshi ziliao bianjizu, 1961–1990.

GXZZD [Guangxi Zhuangzu zizhiqu dang'anguan] 广西壮族自治区档案馆 (Archives of the Guangxi Zhuang Autonomous Region). L4/1/11-1, "Guangxisheng zhengfu kuaiyou daidian" 广西省政府快邮代电 (A Telegram to the Public from the Guangxi Provincial Government). June 15, 1927.

———. L4/1/11-4, "Wei Baqun he Huang Daquan" 韦拔群和黄大权 (Wei Baqun and Huang Daquan). August, 1929.

Han Jianmeng 韩建猛. "Ya Sumin" 牙苏民. In *ZGGXDSRWZ*. Vol. 4 (2004), 343–350.

He Bingfen 何炳芬. "Ning Peiying" 宁培瑛. In *ZGGXDSRWZ*, Vol. 1 (1992), 74–81.

He Jiarong 何家荣. "Huiyi hongbajun" 回忆红八军 (Recollections about the Eighth Red Army). 1985. In *ZYJGMGJD*, Vol. 2, 867–888.

He Weidian 何伟典. ed. *Donglanxian diming zhi* 东兰县地名志 (Place Names of Donglan). Donglan: Donglanxian diming bangongshi, 1988.

Hechi ribao 河池日报. "Qinbo: zhongqing zhongyao de laohongjun" 覃波，钟情中药的老红军 (Qin Bo: An Old Red Army Fighter Who Loves Herbal Medicine). April 2, 2009.

Hechi ribaoshe 河池日报社, ed. *Zhuixun hongqijun zuji* 追寻红七军足迹 (Trace the Footsteps of the Seventh Red Army). Nanning: Guangxi renmin, 1990.

Hong Bo 洪波. "Hong Bo gei Zhonggong zhongyang de baogao [diyihao]" 洪波给中共中央的报告 [第一号] (Hong Bo's First Report to the CCP Central Committee). April 30, 1932. In *ZYJGMGJD*, Vol. 1, 436–437.

Hongqijun 红七军. "Tudi geming" 土地革命 (Land Revolution). December 21, 1929. In *ZYJGMGJD*, Vol. 1, 129–135.

———. "Qianwei tonggao diqihao" 前委通告第七号 (Bulletin No. Seven of the Front Committee of the Seventh Red Army). September 19, 1930. In *ZYJGMGJD*, Vol. 1, 342–348.

———. "Hongqijun zai Baise xie de biaoyu" 红七军在百色写的标语 (Slogans Left by the Seventh Red Army in Baise). In *ZYJGMSLHB*, Vol. 2, 91.

———. "Hongqijun zai Hechi xie de biaoyu" 红七军在河池写的标语 (Slogans Left by the Seventh Red Army in Hechi). In *ZYJGMSLHB*, Vol. 2, 172–177.

Hu Bingqiong 胡炳琼. "Yuanzhu Donglan de nongyou" 援助东兰的农友 (Support the Peasant Friends in Donglan). June 6, 1926. In *WCSLZJ*, 34–35.

Hua Cheng 华成. "Ma Junwu" 马君武. In Guangxi xinhai gemingshi yanjiuhui, ed., 1983, 23–32.

Hua Gang 华岗. *Zhongguo dageming shi* 中国大革命史 (History of the Great Revolution of China), Shanghai: 1931. Reprinted by Beijing: Wenshi ziliao, 1982.

Huang Bin 黄赟. "Donglan faxian yi shenqi rongdong, luyou kaifa qianjing kanhao" 东兰：发现一神奇溶洞 旅游开发前景看好 (A Miraculous Cave Discovered in Donglan Has the Potential of Being Developed into a Tourist Attraction). Guangxi daxuesheng cunguanwang 广西大学生村官网 May 7, 2010. http://hcdxscg.com/news/html/?371.html.

Huang Bingdian 黄炳钿. "Jiang, Gui zhengduo yapianyan shui de yimu" 蒋、桂争夺鸦片烟税的一幕 (An Episode in the Confrontation between Chiang Kai-shek and the Guangxi Leaders over Taxes from the Opium Trade). In *GXWSZL*, 3 (1963), 52–54.

Huang Bingli 黄炳利. "Jisheng xiangche Donglan cheng" 机声响彻东兰城 (The Roar of Machines Reveberates through the County Seat of Donglan). In Hechi ribaoshe, ed., 1990, 45–46.

Huang Chao 黄超. "Gensui Bage naogeming" 跟随拔哥闹革命 (Follow Elder Brother Ba into the Revolution). *Guangxi geming douzheng huiyilu*, Vol. 1 (1981). In *WCSLZJ*, 345–351.

———. "Dui Hongqijun jianli yishu de jidian yijian" 对红七军《简历》一书的几点意见 (Some Opinions on *A Brief History of the Seventh Red Army*). In Qin Wenliang, ed., 1988, 227–229.

Huang Chao 黄超, Huang Huiliang 黄惠良, and Tan Qingrong 谭庆荣. "Shaizi tuidi" 筛子退敌 (Defeat the Enemy with a Sifter). In *Huiyi Wei Baqun*, 51–54.

Huang Chaoying 黄超英 and Guan Lixiong 关立雄. "Chen Xiewu" 陈协五. In *ZGGXDSRWZ*, Vol. 2 (1995), 156–161.

Huang Chengshou 黄成授. "He Jiannan" 何建南. In *ZGGXDSRWZ*, Vol. 1 (1992), 119–129.

Huang Dakun 黄大昆. "Diexue liuqiangu: Li Zhengru lieshi zhuanlue" 喋血流千古—李正儒烈士传略 (Forever a Great Hero: A Brief Biography of Martyr Li Zhengru). In *Baise diqu dangshi ziliao: renwu* 百色地区党史资料：人物, Vol. 2 (1992), 25–28.

———. "Li Zhengru" 李正儒. In *ZGGXDSRWZ*, Vol. 4 (2004), 443–446.

Huang Feng 黄锋. "Weishi sandai kang wokiu" 韦氏三代抗倭寇 (Three Generations of the Weis Fought against the Japanese Pirates). *Donglan wenshi* 东兰文史, 4 (2001), 112–115.

Huang Guangwei 黄光伟. "Huang Bangwei lieshi mu beiwen" 黄榜巍烈士墓碑文 (The Epitaph for Martyr Huang Bangwei). 1923. In Lu Xiuxiang, ed., 1986, 69.

Huang Guoguang 黄国光. "Huang Zhifeng" 黄治峰. In *ZGGXDSRWZ*, Vol. 1 (1992), 286–295.

Huang Hanji 黄汉纪 and Huang Yulu 黄语录. "Tan Tongnan" 谭统南. In *ZGGXDSRWZ*, Vol. 3 (1997), 42–47.

Huang Hanzhong 黄汉钟. "Qingchao keju zhidu zai Donglan" 清朝科举制度在东兰 (The Qing Dynasty Civil Service Examinations in Donglan). *Donglan wenshi ziliao* 东兰文史资料, 1 (1985), 1–7.

———. "Yinhaizhou gaikuang" 银海州概况 (About Mountain Yinhaizhou). *Donglan wenshi ziliao* 东兰文史资料, 1 (1985), 77–81.

———. "Wei Baqun guju Dongli" 韦拔群故居东里 (Dongli: Wei Baqun's Birth Place). *Donglan wenshi ziliao* 东兰文史资料, No. 1 (1985), 82–85.

———. "Tingsi zhanyi hou de shangyuan jiuhu" 亭泗战役后的伤员救护 (Rescue and Treat the Wounded Soldiers after the Battle at Tingsi). *Donglan wenshi* 东兰文史, Vol. 4 (2001), 104–105.

———. "Donglan shanhou weiyuanhui zhenxiang" 东兰善后委员会真相 (The Truth about the Donglan Reconstruction Committee). *Donglan wenshi*, No. 4 (2001), 144–146.

Huang Hanzhong 黄汉钟 and Chen Baxian 陈霸先. "Yucai gaodeng xiaoxue yange gaikuang" 育才高等小学沿革概况 (A History of the Yucai Advanced Elementary School). *Donglan wenshi* 东兰文史, No. 4 (2001), 170–174.

Huang Hanzhong 黄汉钟 and Chen Rukai 陈儒楷. "Chen Shusen qiren qishi" 陈树森其人其事 (Chen Shusen the Man and His Deeds). In *Donglan wenshi ziliao* 东兰文史资料, No. 2 (1987), 46–50.

Huang Hongyi 黄鸿翼(?). *Weishizhang Baqun lingdao Donglan geming* 韦师长拔群领导东兰革命 (Division Commander Wei Baqun Led the Donglan Revolution). Vol. 2. Unpublished manuscript.

Huang Huanmin 黄唤民. "Disanjie nongjiangsuo shenghuo pianduan" 第三届农讲所生活片段 (Some Recollections about Life in the Third Class of Donglan Institute of Peasant Movement). In *WCSLZJ*, 359–363.

———. "Pubumie de huoyan" 扑不灭的火焰 (An Unextinguishable Fire). In *ZYJGMGJD*, Vol. 2, 914–918.

Huang Huanying 黄焕英. "Bage jiao tian kai" 拔哥叫天开 (Elder Brother Ba Ordered the Sky to Open Its Door). In Guangxi minjian wenxue yanjiuhui, ed., 1984, 141–144.

———. "Bianlong" 变龙 (Wei Baqun Changed into a Dragon). In Guangxi minjian wenxue yanjiuhui, ed., 1984, 242–246.

Huang Jiashi 黄家仕. "Yi qingsuan Wei Longfu he sanda Donglancheng" 忆清算韦龙甫和三打东兰城 (Settling Accounts with Wei Longfu and the Three Attacks on the County Seat of Donglan). In Lu Xiuxiang, ed., 1986, 165–169.

Huang Jinqiu 黄金球. "Huiyi di'erjie nongjiangsuo funuban" 回忆第二届农讲所妇女班 (Recollections about the Women's Group of the Second Class of Donglan Institute of Peasant Movement). In Lu Xiuxiang, ed., 1986, 199–202.

Huang Jinqiu 黄金球 and Lu Xiuxiang 陆秀祥. "Huiyi zai Nonglao maimi song Xishan" 回忆在弄劳买米送西山 (Recollections about Purchasing Rice at Nonglao for Transporting to the Western Mountains). In Lu Xiuxiang, ed., 1990, 310–312.

Huang Jishu 黄继树. *Baibing chengfei: 1949 nian dao 1952 nian de jiaofei wangshi* 败兵成匪： 1949 年到 1952 年的剿匪往事 (From Defeated Soldiers to Bandits: The Extermination of the Bandits from 1949 to 1952). Beijing: Wenhua yishu, 2011.

Huang Juping 黄举平. "Donglan geming genjudi de jianli" 东兰革命根据地的建立 (The Creation of the Donglan Revolutionary Base Area). 1976. In Lu Xiuxiang, ed., 1990, 137–142.

———. "Lieningyan" 列宁岩 (The Lenin Cave). In *Huiyi Wei Baqun*, 68–80.

———. "Chen Hongtao tongzhi xunnanji" 陈洪涛同志殉难记 (An Account of Comrade Chen Hongtao's Death). 1985. In *ZYJGMGJD*, Vol. 2, 906–913.

Huang Juping 黄举平 and Xie Fumin 谢扶民. "Yi Donglan baodong" 忆东兰暴动 (Memories of the Donglan Revolt). In Ou Jiwen, ed., 2007, 135–136.

Huang Longxing 黄龙星 and Gao Wanzhang 高万章. "Liao Mengqiao" 廖梦樵. In *ZGGXDSRWZ*, Vol. 1 (1992), 47–49.

Huang Maotian 黄茂田. "Wei Baqun rudang shijian de kaozheng" 韦拔群入党时间的考证 (Dating Wei Baqun's Entry into the CCP). 1981. In *WCSLZJ*, 483–486.

Huang Meilun 黄美伦. "Dengzhengwei laidao Wuzhuan" 邓政委来到武篆 (Political Commissar Deng Xiaoping Came to Wuzhuan). 1981. In *ZYJGMGJD*, Vol. 2, 682–686.

———. "Donglan geming chuqi de funu yundong pianduan" 东兰革命初期的妇女运动片断 (Some Recollections about the Women's Movement during the Early Years of the Donglan Revolution. In *Guangxi geming douzheng huiyilu*, Vol. 2 (1984), 94–99.

———. "Bage yinwo zoushang geminglu" 拔哥引我走上革命路 (Elder Brother Ba Guided me onto the Revolutionary Path). In Lu Xiuxiang, ed., 1986, 183–185.

———. "Shuangfeng feilai" 双凤飞来 (Double Pheonixes Fly Over). *Donglan wenshi ziliao* 东兰文史资料, 2 (1987), 62–67.

———. "Huiyi Wei Jing fu Xianggang huibao" 回忆韦菁赴香港汇报 (Memories of Wei Jing's Departure for Hong Kong to Report to the Party). In Lu Xiuxiang, ed., 1990, 274–275.

———. "Bage he Sange dai wo zoushang geminglu" 拔哥和三哥带我走上革命路 (Elder Brother Ba and Brother Shuxiang Guided Me onto the Revolutionary Path). *Dangdai Guangxi* 当代广西, No. 23 (December 2009), 18.

Huang Mingzheng 黄明政. "Dengzhengwei guanxin shangbingyuan" 邓政委关心伤病员 (Political Commissar Deng Xiaoping Cared about Wounded and Sick Soldiers). 1994. In Ya Zukun and Wei Jiabo, eds., 2005, 11–13.

Huang Naiwen 黄乃文. "Chen Bomin zhuanlue" 陈伯民传略 (A Brief Biography of Chen Bomin). *Donglan wenshi* 东兰文史, 4 (2001), 58–62.

Huang Rong 黄荣 and Huang Yuyang 黄语扬. "Deng Xiaoping yu Wei Baqun" 邓小平与韦拔群 (Deng Xiaoping and Wei Baqun). *Dangdai Guangxi* 当代广西, No. 14 (2004, 7, 30). In Ya Zukun and Wei Jiabo, eds., 2005, 1–8.

Huang Qifeng 黄奇峰. "Shizha Eguo dan" 试炸俄国弹 (A Trial Explosion of a Russian Bomb). In Guangxi minjian wenxue yanjiuhui, ed., 1984, 131–133.

Huang Ruhai 黄如海 and Fang Sunzhen 方孙振. "Huang Xiaopeng" 黄肖彭. In *ZGGXDSRWZ*, Vol. 4 (2004), 232–236.

Huang Runsheng 黄润生. "Qu Guangzhou diliujie nongjiangsuo xuexi qianhou de huiyi" 去广州第六届农讲所学习前后的回忆 (Recollections about the Events around My Attendance at the Sixth Class of Guangzhou Institute of Peasant Movement). 1974, 11, 26. In Lu Xiuxiang, ed., 1986, 231–233.

Huang Shaohong 黄绍竑. "Quansheng zhengzhi gaikuang" 全省政治概况 (The Political Situation of Guangxi). *Xin Guangxi* 新广西, 3(10). February 21, 1929. In *ZYJGMSLHB*, Vol. 3, 29–30.

———. Siyi'er shibian qianhou wo qinshen jingli de huiyi 四一二事变前后我亲身经历的回忆 (My Personal Experience of the April 12th Incident). *Guangxi wenshi ziliao*, No. 7 (1978), 1–42.

———. Siyi'er shibian guanyu Guangxi fangmian cailiao de buchong 四一二事变关于广西方面材料的补充 (Supplementary Information about the April 12th Incident in Guangxi). *Guangxi wenshi ziliao*, No. 7 (1978), 43–49.

———. *Huang Shaohong huiyilu* 黄绍竑回忆录 (The Memoirs of Huang Shaohong). Nanning: Guangxi renmin, 1991.

Huang Songjian 黄松坚. "Hongqijun zhuli beishang yihou" 红七军主力北上以后 (After the Departure of the Main Force of the Seventh Red Army). 1981. In *ZYJGMGJD*, Vol. 2, 898–905.

———. "Gongxian zhuozhu fengfan yongcun" 贡献卓著风范永存 (Outstanding Contributions, An Everlasting Model). *Renmin ribao* 人民日报, October 21, 1982.

———. "Hong21shi gaibianwei dulishi hou de douzheng" 红21师改编为独立师后的斗争(Struggles after the Reorganization of the Twenty-first Division into the Independent Division). In Wei Xinyin, ed., 1999, 162–174.

———. "Sanlu nongjun weigong Fengshan xiancheng" 三路农军围攻凤山县城 (Three Routes of Peasant Army Attacked the County Seat of Fengshan). In Wei Xinyin, ed., 1999, 136–139.

———. "Guanyu Hongqijun junji wenti de huiyi" 关于红七军军纪问题的回忆 (Recollections about the Discipline of the Seventh Red Army). 1985. In Wei Xinyin, ed., 1999, 144–151.

———. "Wo zai Youjiang xiayou de huodong ji liangci fu Shanghai huibao gongzuo de qingkuang" 我在右江下游的活动及两次赴上海汇报工作的情况 (My Activities in the Lower Reaches of the Right River and My Two Trips to Shanghai for Reporting to the Party). In Wei Xinyin, ed., 1999, 177–217.

Huang Xianfan 黄现璠, Gan Wenjie 甘文杰, and Gan Wenhao 甘文豪. *Wei Baqun pingzhuan* 韦拔群评传 (A Critical Biography of Wei Baqun). Guilin: Guangxi shifan daxue, 2008.

Huang Xianfan 黄现璠, Huang Zengqing 黄增庆, and Zhang Yimin 张一民. *Zhuangzu tongshi* 壮族通史 (A History of the Zhuang People). Nanning: Guangxi minzu, 1988.

Huang Xiang 黄相. "Yexi Nalutun" 夜袭那绿屯 (A Night Attack on the Nalu Village). In Guangxi minjian wenxue yanjiuhui, ed., 1984, 169–172.

Huang Xuchu 黄旭初. "Guangxi Li Bai Huang yu qingdang zhi yi" 广西李白黄与清党之役 (Li Zongren, Bai Chongxi, and Huang Shaohong of Guangxi and the Purge of the Communists in 1927). *Chunqiu* 春秋, No. 108 (1962).

———. "Wei Baqun luan Donglan huo Guangxi shimo" 韦拔群乱东兰祸广西始末 (An Account of How Wei Baqun Brought Calamities to Donglan and Guangxi). *Chunqiu* 春秋, 187 (1965).

Huang Yingjun 黄英俊. "Bai Hanyun" 白汉云. In Lu Xiuxiang, Huang Jianping and Huang Yingjun, eds., 1988, 76–91.

———. "Huang Shuxiang" 黄书祥. In Lu Xiuxiang, Huang Jianping and Huang Yingjun, eds. 1988, 92–110.

———. "Huang Daquan" 黄大权. In Lu Xiuxiang, Huang Jianping and Huang Yingjun, eds., 1988, 111–123.

———. "Huang Daquan" 黄大权. In *ZGGXDSRWZ*. Vol. 1 (1992), 315–323.

———. "Wei Baqun lieshi huaxiang zhimi" 韦拔群烈士画像之谜 (The Mystery about Wei Baqun's Portrait). *Dangshi bolan* 党史博览, 2003(3), 50–51.

———. "Wei Jing" 韦菁. In *ZGGXDSRWZ*, Vol. 4 (2004), 514–520.

Huang Yiping 黄一平. "Hongqijun chuchuang shiqi de ruogan zhengce" 红七军初创时期的若干政策 (Some Policies of the Seventh Red Army during Its Early Days of Existence). In *ZYJGMGJD*, Vol. 2, 687–694.

Huang Yucheng 黄羽成. "Gongchandang xingzhengzuzhi neimu qingkuang" 共产党行政组织内幕情况 (The Inside Stories about the CCP Organization). 1934. In *ZYJGMGJD*, Vol. 2, 1004–1021.

Huang Yulu 黄语录, ed. *Zhongguo gongchandang Guangxi Zhuangzu zizhiqu Donglanxian zuzhishi ziliao, 1926–1987* 中国共产党广西壮族自治区东兰县组织史资料, 1926–1987 (History of the CCP Organizations in Donglan County of the Guangxi Zhuang Autonomous Region, 1926–1987). Nanning: Guangxi renmin, 1994.

———. "Donglan jiefang jishi" 东兰解放纪实 (An Account of the Liberation of Donglan). *Donglan wenshi* 东兰文史, No. 5 (2004), 1–12.

Huang Yumei 黄玉美. "Chongpo laolong gangeming" 冲破牢笼干革命 (Break the Cage to Join the Revolution). In *Guangxi geming douzheng huiyilu*, Vol. 2 (1984), 100–108.

Huang Yushan 黄雨山. "Hongqijun shenghuo huiyi" 红七军生活回忆 (Memories of Life in the Seventh Red Army). 1984. In *ZYJGMGJD*, Vol. 2, 744–749.

———. "Huiyi Donglan nongmin yundong jiangxisuo" 回忆东兰农民运动讲习所 (Recollections about Donglan Institute of Peasant Movement). In Lu Xiuxiang, ed., 1986, 170–178.

Huang Zenong 黄泽农. "Huiyi Guode nongmin xiehui de douzheng lichen" 回忆果德农民协会的斗争历程 (Recollections about the Struggles of the Peasant Association of Guode). In Yu Xinshun, ed., 2003, 566–570.

Huang Zheng 黄征. "Huiyi Youjiang chiweijun shi'erlian" 回忆右江赤卫军十二连 (Memories of the Twelfth Company of the Right River Red Guards). In *ZYJGMGJD*, Vol. 2, 750–754.

Huang Zhengxiu 黄正秀. "Zai xian nongmin xiehui gongzuo de huiyi" 在县农民协会工作的回忆 (Recollections about My Days Working for the Donglan Peasant Association). In *WCSLZJ*, 352–354.

Huang Zhiping 黄志平, ed. *Hongtu zhi hun: Donglan yingxiong pu* 红土之魂：东兰英雄谱 (The Soul of the Red Earth: Heroes of Donglan). Nanning: Guangxi Zhonggong dangshi xuehui, 2003.

Huang Zhizhen 黄志珍. "Huang Boyao" 黄伯尧. In *ZGGXDSRWZ*, Vol. 2 (1995), 144–150.

Huiyi Wei Baqun 回忆韦拔群 (Recollections about Wei Baqun). Nanning: Guangxi renmin, 1979.

Jiang Huang 蒋晃. *Donglan xianzheng jiyao* 东兰县政纪要 (Records of the Political Affairs of Donglan). Guilin: Guangxi shengli Guilin zhiyexuexiao yinshuachang, 1947.

Jiang Maosheng 姜茂生. *Qianli lailong* 千里来龙 (From a Faraway Place Comes the Dragon). Fuzhou: Fujian renmin, 1985.

蒋永敬. *Baoluoting yu Wuhan zhengquan* 鲍罗廷与武汉政权 (Mikhail Borodin and the Wuhan Government). Taipei: Zhongguo xueshu zhuzuo jiangzhu weiyuanwei, 1963.

Jiang Yuli 蒋于里 and Chen Shichang 陈世长. "Dashiji" 大事记 (Chronicle of Events). In *ZYJGMGJD*, Vol. 2, 1257–1282.

Junshi tongxun 军事通讯. "Dui Guangxi hongjun gongzuo buzhi de taolun" 对广西红军工作布置的讨论 (Discussions about the Tasks of the Red Army in Guangxi). January 1930. In *ZYJGMGJD*, Vol. 1, 174–199.

Junshi yuekan 军事月刊. "Canmouchu gongzuo gaikuang" 参谋处工作概况 (A Report of the Work of the Staff Office). No. 1. November 30, 1932. In *ZYJGMSLHB*, Vol. 3, 114–115.

Lan Guixiang 蓝桂祥 and Huang Shiping 黄世平. "Lan Maocai" 蓝茂才. In *ZGGXDSRWZ*, Vol. 2 (1995), 122–128.

Lan Handong 蓝汉东 and Lan Qixuan 蓝启渲. "Zhanyou shenqing" 战友深情 (Deep Love for Comrades). In Guangxi minjian wenxue yanjiuhui, ed., 1984, 105–109.

———. *Wei Baqun* 韦拔群. Beijing: Zhongguo qingnian, 1986.

Lan Huaichang 蓝怀昌 and Li Dehan 李德汉. *Renmin qunzhong de lingxiu Wei Baqun* 人民群众的领袖韦拔群 (Wei Baqun: A Leader of the People). Beijing, Zhongguo qingnian, 2009.

Lan Leibin 蓝磊斌. "Wei Baqun xiangpian zhi mi" 韦拔群相片之谜 (The Mystery of a Photo of Wei Baqun). *Guangxi wenshi* 广西文史, 2009(3), 77–80.

Lan Qixuan 蓝启渲. "Huang Bangwei" 黄榜巍. In *ZGGXDSRWZ*, Vol. 4 (2004), 1–7.

Lan Qixuan 蓝启渲 and Lan Baoshi 蓝宝石. "Huang Zhifeng" 黄治峰. In Bai Xianjing, ed.,1991, 258–277.

Lan Qixuan 蓝启渲 and Su Xing 苏醒. "Wei Baqun tongzhi rudang shijian kaozheng" 韦拔群同志入党时间考证 (Research Notes about When Wei Baqun Joined the CCP). *Geming renwu* 革命人物, 1987 (1), 30–34.

Lan Tian 蓝天. "Chen Hongtao" 陈洪涛. In *ZGGXDSRWZ*, Vol. 1(1992), 273–285.

———. "Youjiang geming genjudi de fanweijiao douzheng" 右江革命根据地的反'围剿'斗争 (Struggles against the Extermination Campaigns in the Right River Revolutionary Base Area). 1992. In *WCSLZJ*, 494–508.

Lan Tian and Huang Zhizhen 蓝天、黄志珍, eds. *Zhongguo gongnong hongjun Youjiang dulishi* 中国工农红军右江独立师 (The Right River Independent Division of the Chinese Red Army). Nanning: Guangxi renmin, 1992.

Lan Tianli 蓝天立. "Hongyang Baqun jingshen, cujin kexue fazhan" 弘扬拔群精神 促进科学发展 (Carry forward the Baqun Spirit to Promote Scientific Development). In Li Li, ed., 2009, 7–14.

Lei Jingtian 雷经天. "Guangxi de Suwei'ai yundong" 广西的苏维埃运动 (The Soviet Movement in Guangxi). 1945. In *ZYJGMGJD*, Vol. 2, 600–614.

———. "Yan Min zai Guangxi geming douzheng shilue" 严敏在广西革命斗争事略 (A Brief Account of Yan Min's Revolutionary Activities in Guangxi). 1959. In *ZYJGMGJD*, Vol. 2, 825–828.

Lei Rongjia 雷荣甲, Chen Yeqiang 陈业强 and Jin Kaishan 金开山. "Lei Peihong" 雷沛鸿. In Guangxi xinhai gemingshi yanjiuhui, ed., 1983, 33–37.

Lei Xiaocen 雷啸岑. *Sanshinian dongluan zhongguo* 三十年动乱中国 (Three Decades of Chaos in China). Hong Kong: Yazhou, 1955.

Li Changshou 李长寿. "Baise qiyi he hongjun zai Baise" 百色起义和红军在白色 (The Baise Uprising and the Red Army in Baise). *Baise shizhi* 百色史志, 1 (1985), 1–13.

———. "Echeng zhanshi shihua" 鹅城战事史话 (A Military History of Baise). *Baise shizhi* 百色史志, 4 (1988), 33–49.

Li Dehan 李德汉. "Huang Shixin" 黄世新. In *ZGGXDSRWZ*, Vol. 2 (1995), 95–100.

Li Fuhua 李府华. "Lei Peitao" 雷佩涛. In *ZGGXDSRWZ*, Vol. 1 (1992), 14–16.

Li Guoxiang and Yang Chang 李国祥、杨昶. eds. *Mingshilu leizuan: Guangxi shiliao juan* 明实录类纂 广西史料卷 (Classified Records about Guangxi from the Annals of the Ming Dynasty). Guilin: Guangxi shifan daxue, 1990.

Li Guozhou 黎国轴. *Lun Wei Baqun* 论韦拔群 (Essays on Wei Baqun). Nanning: Guangxi renmin, 1989.

Li Guozhou 黎国轴 and Yan Yongtong 严永通. "Bage de gushi" 拔哥的故事 (Stories about Elder Brother Ba). In Guangxi minjian wenxue yanjiuhui, ed., 1984, 114–126.

———. *Wei Baqun zhuan* 韦拔群传 (A Biography of Wei Baqun). Guilin: Guangxi shifan daxue, 1989.

Li Huaqing 李华清. "Yi hongqijun junyi chuzhang Wu Qingpei tongzhi" 忆红七军军医处长吴清培同志 (My Memories of Comrade Wu Qingpei, Head Doctor of the Seventh Red Army). In Ou Jiwen, ed., 2007, 260–263.

Li Jiaxian 李家诜. "Zizhijun zhanling Nanning hou Guangxi de jumian" 自治军占领南宁后广西的局面 (The Situation in Guangxi after the Occupation of Nanning by the Autonomous Army). In *GXWSZLXJ*, Vol. 3 (1963), 135–142.

Li Li 黎丽, ed. *Wei Baqun jingshen lun* 韦拔群精神论 (On the Spirit of Wei Baqun). Beijing: Jiefangjun, 2009.

Li Qishi 李其实, et al. "Guanyu Guangxi de zuzhiqingkuang, gongnong geming yundong ji dui jinhou gongzuo yijian" 关于广西的组织情况、工农革命运动及对今后工作意见 (A Report about the CCP Organization, Revolutionary Movements of the Workers and Peasants in Guangxi, and Suggestions about our Future Work). February 7, 1928. In *WCSLZJ*, 83–84.

Li Shiyao 黎式尧 and Tang Renji 唐人基. "Chen Bomin xianzhang zai Hechi" 陈伯民县长在河池 (Magistrate Chen Bomin in Hechi). *Hechi wenshi* 河池文史, No. 1 (1987), 71–77.

Li Tianxin 李天心. "Sanshiliupo douzheng jishi" 三十六坡斗争纪实 (An Account of the Struggles at Sanshiliupo). In *ZYJGMGJD*, Vol. 2, 919–927.

Li Tianyou 李天佑. "Huiyi Baise qiyi" 回忆百色起义 (Memories of the Baise Uprising). 1959. In *ZYJGMGJD*, Vol. 2, 597–599.

Li Xiang 李翔. "1897–1927 nian 'guomingeming' gainian yanbian kaoshi" 1897–1927 年"国民革命"概念演变考释 (The Evolution of the Concept of 'National Revolution' from 1897 to 1927). *Yunnan shehui kexue* 云南社会科学, 2008 (2), 140–144.

Li Xianxian 黎先贤 and Lu Xiuxiang 陆秀祥. "Beishang Jiangxi hou de pianduan huiyi" 北上江西后的片断回忆 (Some Recollections about the Events after We Left Hechi for Jiangxi). In Lu Xiuxiang, ed., 1990, 332–335.

Li Xiulang 李修琅. ed. *Huang Shuxiang geming shengya* 黄书祥革命生涯 (Huang Shuxiang's Revolutionary Activities). Nanning: Guangxi minzu, 2009.

Li Yanfu 李彦福, Wei Wei 韦卫 and Huang Qihui 黄启辉. "Zuoyoujiang geming genjudi de jiaoyu shiye" 左右江革命根据地的教育事业 (The Education System in the Left River and Right River Revolutionary Base Area). In *ZYJGMGJD*, Vol. 2, 1143–1155.

Li Zhuoren 黎灼仁, Ye Xueming 叶学明 and Lu Yuan 卢渊. "Zuoyoujiang geming genjudi de caizheng jingji jianshe" 左右江革命根据地的财政经济建设 (Financial and Economic Reconstruction of the Left River and Right River Revolutionary Base Area). In *ZYJGMGJD*, Vol. 2, 1094–1103.

Li Zongren 李宗仁 and Tang Degang （Tong Te-kong）唐德刚. *Li Zongren huiyilu* 李宗仁回忆录 (The Memoirs of Li Zongren). Nanning: Guangxi shifan daxue, 2005.

Liang Baowei 梁宝渭. "Dui Wei Baqun haopingruchao qianxi" 对韦拔群'好'评如潮浅析 (An Analysis of the Reasons for the Favorable Comments on Wei Baqun). In Li Li, ed., 2009, 243–250.

Liang Hanming 梁汉明, He Guang 何光 and Huang Wencai 黄文彩. "Li Zhihua" 李植华. In *ZGGXDSRWZ*, Vol. 1 (1992), 115–118.

Liang Lieya 梁列亚. "Gaizao Guangxi tongzhihui de chengli jiqi douzheng" 改造广西同志会的成立及其斗争 (The Founding of the Association for Reforming Guangxi and Its Struggles). *GXWSZLXJ*. Vol. 6 (1963), 150–174.

Liang Tingwang 梁庭旺. *Zhuangzu wenhua gailun* 壮族文化概论 (An Introduction to the Zhuang Culture). Nanning: Guangxi jiaoyu, 2000.

Liang Yaodong 梁耀东. "Chen Gutao" 陈鼓涛. In *ZGGXDSRWZ*, Vol. 4 (2004), 531–535.

Liao Lei. 廖磊. "Chedi suqing gongfei Wei Baqun banfa" 彻底肃清共匪韦拔群办法 (Methods of Exterminating Communist Bandit Wei Baqun). 1932. In *WCSLZJ*, 597–599.

———. "Jinhou Dongfeng shanhou banfa ji minzhong ying nuli yaodian" 今后东凤善后办法及民众应努力要点 (Methods for Future Reconstruction of Donglan and Fengshan and Tasks for the People of Donglan and Fengshan). 1932. In *WCSLZJ*, 600–604.

Liao Mengqiao 廖梦樵. "Gei Donglan xianzhang Huang Shouxian yifeng gongkai de xin" 给东兰县长黄守先一封公开的信 (An Open Letter to Magistrate Huang Shouxian of Donglan County). June 8, 1926. In *WCSLZJ*, 36–37.

Liao Ruizhen 廖瑞珍 and He Detang 何德唐. "Wo suo zhidao de Liao Lei" 我所知道的廖磊 (My Memories of Liao Lei). *Luchuan wenshi ziliao* 陆川文史资料, No. 1 (1985), 65–71.

Lin Jinghua 林经华. "Liao Lei zai kangzhanzhong de yiduan gushi" 廖磊在抗战中的一段故事 (Some Stories about Liao Lei during the War against the Japanese Invasion). *Luchuan wenshi ziliao* 陆川文史资料, 10 (1999), 101–103.

Lin Jinwen 林锦文, ed. *Guangzhou nongmin yundong jiangxisuo ziliao xuanbian* 广州农民运动讲习所资料选编 (Selected Materials about Guangzhou Peasant Movement Institute). Beijing: Renmin, 1987.

Lingyun wenshi ziliao 凌云文史资料. "Lingyun renmin fandui tongzhizhe de douzheng" 凌云人民反对统治者的斗争 (The Struggles of the People of Lingyun against the Rulers). No. 4 (1989): 4–5.

Liu Chuanzeng 刘传增. "Liao Lei he xinsijun lingdao tongzhi" 廖磊和新四军领导同志 (Liao Lei and the Commanders of the New Fourth Army). *Luchuan wenshi ziliao* 陆川文史资料, 4 (1988), 25–31.

Liu Lidao 刘立道. "Zhang Qihuang" 张其锽. In Guangxi xinhai gemingshi yanjiuhui, ed., 1983, 104–108.

Liu Lin 柳林. "Jiankufendou de Zhuangzu funu Huang Meilun." 艰苦奋斗的壮族妇女黄美伦 (Huang Meilun: A Hardworking and Perservering Zhuang Woman). *Youjiang ribao* 右江日报, March 7/9/11/13/15, 1957.

Liu Xifan 刘锡蕃. *Lingbiao jiman* 岭表纪蛮 (The Barbaric Groups in Southern China). Shanghai: Shangwu inshuguan, 1934.

Liu Yanzhi 刘延智. "Donglan dali wajue hongyang hongse ziyuan" 东兰大力挖掘弘扬"红色"资源 (Donglan Makes Great Efforts at Exploiting and Promoting Its

"Red" Resources). Donglan dangjianwang 东兰党建网, October 12, 2007. http://www.71dj.gov.cn/ReadNews.asp?NewsID=2697.

Long'anxian zhengxie wenshiwei 隆安县政协文史委. "Liang Di" 梁砥. In *ZGGXDSRWZ*, Vol. 4 (2004), 50–52.

Lu Jinlun 陆锦仑. "Baise zhongxue lieshi zhiduoshao" 百色中学烈士知多少 (The Number of Martyrs from the Baise High School). *Baise shizhi* 白色史志, Vol. 3 (1988), 19–22.

———. "Guan Chonghe" 关崇和. In *ZGGXDSRWZ*, Vol. 4 (2004), 380–386.

Lu Julie 陆炬烈. "Yu Shaojie" 余少杰. In *ZGGXDSRWZ*, Vol. 1 (1992), 82–88.

Lu Xianling 陆现灵. "Huiyi cantong liangjianshi" 回忆惨痛两件事 (My Recollections of Two Painful Events). *Donglan wenshi ziliao* 东兰文史资料, 2 (1987), 30–37.

Lu Xing 卢行. "Deng Xiaoping zai Guangxi" 邓小平在广西 (Deng Xiaoping in Guangxi). In *ZYJGMGJD*, Vol. 2, 1031–1054.

Lu Xiuxiang 陆秀祥, ed. *Donglan nongmin yundong, 1921–1927* 东兰农民运动, 1921–1927 (The Donglan Peasant Movement: 1921–1927). Nanning: Guangxi minzu, 1986.

———. "Wei Baqun" 韦拔群. In Lu Xiuxiang, Huang Jianping and Huang Yingjun, eds., 1988, 1–52.

———. "Lu Haoren" 陆浩仁. In Lu Xiuxiang, Huang Jianping and Huang Yingjun, eds., 1988, 138–160.

———. "Deng Xiaoping zai Donglan" 邓小平在东兰 (Deng Xiaoping in Donglan). In Ya Zukun and Wei Jiabo, eds., 2005, 31–38.

———, ed. *Donglan geming genjudi* 东兰革命根据地 (The Donglan Revolutionary Base Area). Donglan: Zhonggong Donglan xianwei dangshi bangongshi, 1990.

———. "1929 nian Donglan renkou kaozheng" 1929 年东兰人口考证 (A Study of Donglan's Population in 1929). In Lu Xiuxiang, ed., 1990, 402–403.

Lu Xiuxiang 陆秀祥, Huang Jianping 黄建平 and Huang Yingjun 黄英俊, eds. *Zhonggong Donglan dangshi renwu zhuan* 中共东兰党史人物传 (Biographies of Prominent Figures in the History of the Communist Movement in Donglan). Donglan: Zhonggong Donglan xianwei dangshi bangongshi, 1988.

Lu Xiuxuan 陆秀轩. "Dadao Wei Longfu, Ganzou Meng Yuanliang" 打倒韦龙甫 赶走蒙元良 (Overthrow Wei Longfu and Expel Meng Yuanliang). In *Huiyi Wei Baqun*, 61–67.

———. "Shuqi yiqi zhengjiu nongmin" 竖起义旗拯救农民 (Raise the Banner of Righteousness to Rescue the Peasants). In *WCSLZJ*, 290–293.

Lu Xiuxuan 陆秀轩 and Huang Juping 黄举平. *Youjiang xinghuo* 右江星火 (Sparks along the Right River). 1956.

Lu Yongke 卢永克. "Youjiang geming de bozhongren Wei Baqun" 右江革命的播种人—韦拔群 (Wei Baqun: the Man Who Sowed the Seeds of Revolution in the Right River Region). In *Huiyi Wei Baqun*, 89–95.

Lu Yongke 卢永克 and Huang Yingjun 黄英俊. "Huang Shuxiang" 黄书祥. In *ZGGXDSRWZ*, Vol. 1 (1992), 306–314.

Luchuan wenshi ziliao 陆川文史资料. Nos. 8 & 9. Luchuan: Zhengxie Luchuanxian weiyuanhui wenjiaoweiti wenshi weiyuanhui, 1994–1995.

Luo Huo 罗活. "Diqijun di'ershisishi diqishi'ertuan yinianlai gongzuo baogao" 第七军第二十四师第七十二团一年来工作报告 (Report about the Work of the

Seventy-second Regiment, the Twenty-fourth Division of the Seventh Army). 1932. In *ZYJGMSLHB*, Vol. 3, 272–274.

Luo Rikuai 罗日块. "Huiyi Weishizhang xisheng qianhou" 回忆韦师长牺牲前后 (Recollections about the Last Days of Division Commander Wei Baqun). 1976. In *WCSLZJ*, 461–463.

Luo Xiulong 罗秀龙. "Huang Wentong" 黄文通. In *ZGGXDSRWZ*, Vol. 4 (2004), 536–539.

Ma Yin 马寅, ed. *Zhongguo shaoshu minzu,* 中国少数民族 (Ethnic Minorities of China). Beijing: Renmin, 1984.

Mao Mao 毛毛. *Wode fuqin Deng Xiaoping* 我的父亲邓小平 (My Father Deng Xiaoping). Volume 1. Beijing: Zhongyang wenxian, 1993.

Ming Yuezhong 明月中. "Xueran Lanzhong xiaoyuan" 血染兰中校园 (Killings at Donglan High School). *Donglan wenshi* 东兰文史, 5 (2004), 138–151.

Mo Fengxin 莫凤欣. "Liao Lei" 廖磊. In Guangxi xinhai gemingshi yanjiuhui, ed., 1983, 114–119.

Mo Li 磨力. "Yici nanwang de baogaohui" 一次难忘的报告会 (An Unforgettable Lecture). In *Huiyi Wei Baqun*, 102–106.

Mo Shujie 莫树杰. "Lin Junting" 林俊廷. In Guangxi xinhai gemingshi yanjiuhui, ed., 1983,109–113.

Mo Wenhua 莫文骅. *Huiyi hongqijun* 回忆红七军 (My Recollections about the Seventh Red Army). Nanning: Guangxi renmin, 1962.

———. "Huiyi Wei Baqun tongzhi" 回忆韦拔群同志 (Recollections about Comrade Wei Baqun). In *Huiyi Wei Baqun*, 7–13.

———. *Mo Wenhua huiyilu* 莫文骅回忆录 (The Memoirs of Mo Wenhua). Beijing: Jiefangjun, 1996.

Mo Yingzhong 莫应忠. "Chen Bomin Hechi jishi" 陈伯民河池纪事 (Chen Bomin in Hechi). *Donglan wenshi* 东兰文史, 4 (2001), 48–57.

Nanning minguo ribao 南宁民国日报. "Li Ruixiong diancheng tongjiao Donglan gongfei qingxing" 李瑞熊电呈痛剿东兰共匪情形 (Li Ruixiong's Telegram about the Extermination Campaign in Donglan). May 17, 1932. In *ZYJGMSLHB*, Vol. 3, 82–83.

———. "Shengfu yi yiwanyuan gouji zhi gongfei Wei Baqun beishengqin" 省府以一万元购缉之共匪韦拔群被生擒 (Communist Bandit Wei Baqun for Whom the Provincial Government Has Offered a Bounty of 10,000 Silver Dollars Is Captured Alive). May 19, 1932. In *ZYJGMSLHB*, Vol. 3, 85.

———. "Gongfei Wei Baqun beiqin zhengshi" 共匪韦拔群被擒证实 (The Capture of Communist Bandit Wei Baqun Confirmed). May 19, 1932. In *ZYJGMSLHB*, Vol. 3, 85.

———. "Raoluan Donglan zhi feigong yinmou" 扰乱东兰之匪共阴谋 (The Communist Bandits' Scheme for Disrupting Donglan). June 14, 1932. In *ZYJGMSLHB*, Vol. 3, 90–91.

———. "Donglan zhi zhenzai fenji qingxing" 东兰之赈灾分济情形 (The Relief Work in Donglan). June 15, 1932. In *ZYJGMSLHB*, Vol. 3, 91.

———. "Shengfu ling cui Dongfeng chouyi shanhou banfa" 省府令催东凤筹议善后办法 (The Provincial Government Urged Donglan and Fengshan to Come Up with Plans for Reconstruction). June 28, 1932. In *ZYJGMSLHB*, Vol. 3, 97–98.

———. "Gedi fugongfenzi ruxi xiecong zhunyu zixin" 各地附共分子如系胁从准予自新 (Communist Supporters Who Are Accomplices under Duress Are Offered Amnesty). September 27, 1932. In *ZYJGMSLHB*, Vol. 3, 112–113.

———. "Baifuzongzuo ling jiang gaifei shouji jiesong laiyong xuan zhongshang gouji gongfei Huang Daquan dengwen" 白副总座令将该匪首级解送来邕悬重赏购辑共匪黄大权等文 (Deputy Commander in Chief Bai Chongxi Ordered that Bandit Wei Baqun's Head Be Brought to Nanning; The Provincial Government Offered a Large Bounty for Communist Bandit Huang Daquan). October 25, 1932. In *WCSLZJ*, 583–584.

———. "Dongfeng jiaofei ji shanhou jinkuang" 东凤剿匪及善后近况 (Recent Developments about the Extermination and Reconstruction in Donglan and Fengshan). December 6, 1932. In *ZYJGMSLHB*, Vol. 3, 176–178.

———. "Xiezhihui tan Dongfeng qingkuang" 谢指挥谈东凤情况 (Commander Xie's Remarks on the Situation in Donglan and Fengshan). December 6, 1932. In *ZYJGMSLHB*, Vol. 3, 164–166.

———. "Gongfei Wei Baqun yunie Chen Hongtao beiqin zongbu ling jie se xunban" 共匪韦拔群余孽陈洪涛被擒总部令解色讯办 (Communist Bandit Wei Baqun's Accomplice Chen Hongtao Captured; The Headquarters Ordered that Chen Be Taken to Baise for Interrogation). December 14, 1932. In *WCSLZJ*, 609–610.

———. "Dongfeng shanhou weiyuanhui zuijin gongzuo qingkuang" 东凤善后委员会最近工作情况 (Recent Work of the Donglan-Fengshan Reconstruction Committee). December 15, 1932. In *ZYJGMSLHB*, Vol. 3, 169–170.

———. "Weifei Baqun zhi tewu duizhang jiuqin yu Chen Hongtao yibing jie Baise xunban" 韦匪拔群之特务队长就擒与陈洪涛一并解百色讯办 (The Commander of Wei Baqun's Special Assignment Unit Has Been Captured and Will Be Taken to Baise along with Chen Hongtao). December 15, 1932. In *WCSLZJ*, 611–612.

———. "Chenfei Hongtao deng jing zai se qiangjue" 陈匪洪涛等经在色枪决 (Bandit Chen Hongtao and Others Executed in Baise). December 27, 1932. In *WCSLZJ*, 615.

Nanning wanbao 南宁晚报. "Zhezhang heying shang guozhen you Wei Baqun ma" 这张合影上果真有韦拔群吗？ (Is Wei Baqun Really in this Group Photo?). March 30, 2010.

Ning Xianbiao 宁显标. "Hongshuihegu de gushi" 红水河谷的故事 (Stories about the Red Water River Valley). Nandan zhengxie wang 南丹政协网, 2006-10-31. http://www.hccppcc.com/zx_nd/comment.php?Articleid=614.

Nong Qizhen 农其振. "Zuojiang geming yundong pianduan huiyi" 左江革命运动片段回忆 (Some Recollections about the Revolutionary Activities in the Left River Region). In *ZYJGMGJD*, Vol. 2, 889–892.

Ou Jiwen 区济文, ed. *Guangxi hongjun* 广西红军 (The Red Armies in Guangxi). Nanning: Guangxi xinsijun lishi yanjiuhui, 2007.

Ou Zhengren 欧正人. *Ma Junwu zhuan* 马君武传 (A Biography of Ma Junwu). Nanning: Zhengxie Guangxi Zhuangzu zizhiqu weiyuanhui wenshiziliao yanjiushi, 1982.

Ou Zhifu 欧致富. "Yi Wei Baqun tongzhi dui Fengyi yidai nongmin yundong de yingxiang" 忆韦拔群同志对奉议一带农民运动的影响 (Recollections about

Wei Baqun's Influence on the Peasant Movement of the Area around Fengyi). In *Huiyi Wei Baqun*, 55–60.

Pan Qixu 潘其旭. "Gexian Liu Sanjie de chansheng shi gexu xingcheng de biaozhi" 歌仙刘三姐的产生是歌圩形成的标志 (The Rise of Folksong Fairy Third Sister Liu Signaled the Coming of Age of Folksong Fairs). In Tang Zhengzhu 唐正柱, ed., *Hongshuihe wenhua yanjiu* 红水河文化研究 (Studies on the Cultures of the Red Water River Region), 529–552. Nanning: Guangxi renmin, 2001.

Peng Pai 彭湃. "Haifeng nongmin yundong" 海丰农民运动 (The Haifeng Peasant Movement). 1926. In *Peng Pai wenji* 彭湃文集, 101–186. Beijing: Renmin, 1981.

———. "Huaxian tuanfei cansha nongmin de jingguo" 花县团匪惨杀农民的经过 (An Account of How the Bandits of the Huaxian County Militia Massacred the Peasants). September 1926. In *Peng Pai wenji*, 207–257.

———. "Wei Wuhua nongyou ku yisheng" 为五华农友哭一声 (Weeping for Our Peasant Friends in Wuhua County). October 1926. In *Peng Pai wenji*, 263–270.

———. "Shige shiyishou" 诗歌十一首 (Eleven Poems). 1921–1927. In *Peng Pai wenji*, 330–337.

Peng Yuanzhong 彭源重. "Wei Baqun budang xianzhang" 韦拔群不当县长 (Wei Baqun Refused to Take the Position of County Magistrate). In Tang Nonglin, ed., 1994, 9–10.

Qin Caiwu 覃彩五. *Donglan tongshi* 东兰痛史 (The Painful History of Donglan). 1934–1935. Vol. 2. In *ZYJGMSLHB*, Vol. 3, 221–266.

Qin Chengqin 覃承勤. "Bage shuo Yaohua" 拔哥说瑶话 (Elder Brother Ba Spoke the Yao Language). In Guangxi minjian wenxue yanjiuhui, ed., 1984, 133–135.

———. "Bage hui fei" 拔哥会飞 (Elder Brother Ba Could Fly). In Guangxi minjian wenxue yanjiuhui, ed., 1984, 220–221.

Qin Guohan 覃国翰. "Gaobie: Yi zai Hechi zhengbian zhong de Wei Baqun tongzhi" 告别—忆在河池整编中的韦拔群同志 (Farewell: Recollections about Comrade Wei Baqun during the Reorganization at Hechi). 1981. In *WCSLZJ*, 410–414.

———. "Honghe jilang" 红河激浪 (The Rolling Waves of the Red Water River). In Yu Xinshun, ed., 2003, 562–565.

Qin Guohan 覃国翰, Huang Chao 黄超 and Tan Qingrong 谭庆荣. "Geming zhandou youyi" 革命战斗友谊" (Friendship Forged During Revolutionary Struggles). In *Guangxi geming douzheng huiyilu*, Vol. 2 (1984), 162–164.

Qin Huaru 覃华儒. "Lu Tao zhuanlue" (A Brief Biography of Lu Tao). In *GXWSZL*. Vol. 21 (1984), 1–17.

Qin Jian 覃健. "Fu Pingma lingqiang qianhou" 赴平马领枪前后 (Memories of Our Journey to Pingma to Receive Weapons). 1959. In Lu Xiuxiang, ed., 1990, 171–172.

Qin Jiancai 覃建才. "Wei Longfu shuhunji" 韦龙甫赎魂记 (An Account of How Wei Longfu Redeemed His Soul). In Guangxi minjian wenxue yanjiuhui, ed., 1984, 189–192.

———. "Wei Baqun bian hu le" 韦拔群变虎了 (Wei Baqun Changed into a Tiger). In Guangxi minjian wenxue yanjiuhui, ed., 1984, 192–196.

Qin Jianping 覃剑萍. "Kenhuang zhimian" 垦荒植棉 (Open Wasteland to Plant Cotton). In Tang Nonglin, ed., 1994, 148–149.

———. “Tonggu zhixiang” 铜鼓之乡 (The Land of Bronze Drums). In Tang Nonglin, ed., 1994, 171–72.

———. “Wei Zhengbao san dai kangwo jianqigong” 韦正宝三代抗倭建奇功 (The Outstanding Service Performed by Wei Zhengbao, His Son and Grandson in the War against the Japanese Pirates). *Wenshi chunqiu* 文史春秋, 36 (1995, No. 5), 31–32.

Qin Liankui 覃联魁. “Donglan dangzuzhi jianshe he fanweijiao douzheng” 东兰党组织建设和反‘围剿’斗争 (The Creation of CCP Organizations in Donglan and the Struggles against the Extermination Campaigns).1959. In Lu Xiuxiang, ed., 1986, 218–225.

Qin Shaokuan 覃绍宽. “Jiuping he zhadan” 酒瓶和炸弹 (Liquor Bottles and Bombs). In Guangxi minjian wenxue yanjiuhui, ed., 1984, 144–146.

Qin Shimian 覃士冕. “Yi Donglan geming laodong xiaoxue” 忆东兰革命劳动小学 (Memories of the Donglan Revolutionary Workers Elementary School). 1984. In *ZYJGMGJD*, Vol. 2, 772–778.

Qin Wenliang 覃文良. *Donglanxian geming yingming lu* 东兰县革命英名录 (A Name List of the Revolutionary Heroes of Donglan). *Donglan wenshi ziliao*, 3 (1988).

Qin Yingji 覃应机. *Xiaoyan suiyue* 硝烟岁月 (Warring Years). Beijing: Zhonggong dangshi, 1991.

Qin Yingji 覃应机, Huang Songjian 黄松坚 and Huang Rong 黄荣. “Zhuoyue de gongchanzhuyi zhanshi Wei Baqun” 卓越的共产主义战士韦拔群 (Wei Baqun: An Outstanding Communist Fighter). *Guangxi ribao* 广西日报, October 19, 1982. In *ZYJGMGJD*, Vol. 2, 655–664.

Qin Yingji 覃应机, et al. “Hongjun de youxiu zhihuiyuan, dangde zhongzhen zhanshi” 红军的优秀指挥员、党的忠贞战士 (An Outstanding Commander of the Red Army and a Loyal Fighter of the Party). In *ZYJGMGJD*, Vol. 2, 636–645.

Qin Yingwu 覃应物. “Huang Shouxian de kechi xiachang” 黄守先的可耻下场 (Huang Shouxian’s Disgraceful End). *Donglan wenshi ziliao* 东兰文史资料, No. 2 (1987), 9–17.

———. “Chen Hongtao xiaozhuan” 陈洪涛小传 (A Brief Biography of Chen Hongtao). *Donglan wenshi* 东兰文史, 4 (2001), 44–47.

Qiu Jie 邱捷 and He Wenping 何文平. “Minguo chunian Guangdong de minjian wuqi” 民国初年广东的民间武器 (Private Weapons in Guangdong during the Early Republican Era). *Zhongguo shehui kexue* 中国社会科学, 2005 (1), 178–190.

Rao Kai 饶开. “Bai Chongxi chongshang guoshu” 白崇禧崇尚国术 (Bai Chongxi Promoted Martial Arts). In Guangxi wenshi yanjiuguan 广西文史研究馆, ed., *Bagui xiangxielu* 八桂香屑录 (Anecdotes about Guangxi), 12–14. Shanghai: Shanghai shudian, 1992.

Ruan Xiaoxian 阮啸仙. “Quanguo nongmin yundong de xingshi jiqi zai guomingeming zhong de diwei” 全国农民运动的形势及其在国民革命中的地位 (The Peasant Movement: Its Current Situation and Its Role in the National Revolution.” August 19, 1926. In *Ruan Xiaoxian wenji* 阮啸仙文集 (Collected Works of Ruan Xiaoxian), 277–298. Guangzhou: Guangdong renmin, 1984.

Shaosheng 韶生 et al. “Cifu, yanshi: yi fuqin Huang Songjian” 慈父、严师：忆父亲黄松坚 (Loving Father, Strict Teacher: Memories of Our Father Huang Songjian). In Wei Xinyin, ed., 1999, 369–373.

Sheng Ming 盛明. "Wuzhengfu zhuyi zai Sichuan de liuchuan" 无政府主义在四川的流传 (The Spread of Anarchism in Sichuan). *Sichuan dangshi* 四川党史, 1995(3), 45–49.

Shuang Cai 双才. "Zhide zhuyi de Donglan nongmin yundong" 值得注意的东兰农民运动 (The Donglan Peasant Movement Deserves Our Attention). 1926. In *WCSLZJ*, 32–33.

Shi Hua 时花. "Guangxi gongchandang de guoqu ji xianzai" 广西共产党的过去及现在 (The Past and Present of the CCP in Guangxi). *Xiandai shiliao* 现代史料, 1(11). 1932. In *WCSLZJ*, 621–624.

Su Changxian 苏长仙. "Paodan yepa Wei Baqun" 炮弹也怕韦拔群 (Even Artillery Shells Are Afraid of Wei Baqun). In Guangxi minjian wenxue yanjiuhui, ed., 1984, 205–207.

Su Guanchang 粟冠昌. *Guangxi tuguan zhidu yanjiu* 广西土官制度研究 (Studies on the System of Indigenous Hereditary Lords of Guangxi). Nanning: Guangxi minzu, 2000.

Su Xing 苏醒. "Qin Daoping" 覃道平. In *ZGGXDSRWZ*, Vol. 1 (1992): 296–300.

Tan Qingrong 谭庆荣. "Wo dang nongjun jiaotong de huiyi" 我当'农军'交通的回忆 (Recollections about My Days as a Messenger for the Peasant Army). In Lu Xiuxiang, ed., 1986, 212–215.

Tang Ling 唐凌. "Qingchao tongguang shiqi Guangxi renkou wenti chutan" 清朝同光时期广西人口问题初探 (A Preliminary Study on the Population of Guangxi during the Tongzhi and Guangxu Era of the Qing Dynasty). In Zhong Wendian, ed., *Jindai Guangxi shehui yanjiu* 近代广西社会研究 (Studies on Modern Guangxi Society), 285–301. Nanning: Guangxi renmin, 1990.

Tang Nonglin 唐侬麟, ed. *Guihai yizhu* 桂海遗珠 (Cultural and Historical Notes about Guangxi). Shanghai: Shanghai shudian, 1994.

Tang Shishu 唐士书 and Shen Gengzhi 申耕智. "Hongqijun de yiyao weisheng gongzuo" 红七军的医药卫生工作 (The Medical System of the Seventh Red Army). In *ZYJGMGJD*, Vol. 2, 1156–1162.

Tang Songqiu 唐松球. "Yan Min" 严敏. In *ZGGXDSRWZ*, Vol. 1 (1992), 130–138.

Tian Shulan 田曙岚. *Guangxi luxingji* 广西旅行记 (An Account of My Travels in Guangxi). Shanghai: Zhonghua shuju, 1935.

Wang Jinxia 王锦侠 and Chen Youming 陈幼明. "Chen Mianshu" 陈勉恕. In *ZGGXDSRWZ*, Vol. 1 (1992), 376–388.

Wang Lintao 王林涛. "Lei Jingtian" 雷经天. In Hu Hua 胡华, ed., *Zhonggong dangshi renwu zhuan* 中共党史人物传, Vol. 20, 346–360. Xi'an: Shanxi renmin, 1984.

Wang Lintao 王林涛, Cheng Zongshan 程宗善 and Lin Weicai 林为才. "Chen Hongtao" 陈洪涛. In Hu Hua, ed., *Zhonggong dangshi renwu zhuan* 中共党史人物传, Vol. 7 (1983): 206–224. Xi'an: Shanxi renmin, 1983.

Wang Luyong 汪路勇. "Guangzhou nongmin yundong jiangxisuo de chuangban jiqi lishigongji" 广州农民运动讲习所的创办及其历史功绩 (The Creation and Achievements of Guangzhou Peasant Movement Institute). *Fujian dangshi yuekan* 福建党史月刊, 2005(2), 39–41.

Wang Yanyi 王延义. "Wei Baqun lieshi yongyuan huozai women xinzhong: Wei Baqun lieshi Tougu zai Wuzhou chutuji" 韦拔群烈士永远活在我们心中：韦拔群烈士头骨在梧州出土记 (Martyr Wei Baqun Will Forever Live in Our Heart: An

Account of the Excavation of Martyr Wei Baqun's Skull in Wuzhou). *Wuzhou wenshi ziliao* 梧州文史资料, No. 11 (1986), 19–21.

Wang Yushu 王玉树. "Wang Yushu guanyu qibajun qingxing baogao" 王玉树关于七、八军情形报告 (Wang Yushu's Report about the Situation of the Seventh and Eighth Red Armies). 1930, 8, 22. In *ZYJGMGJD*, Vol. 1, 327–331.

WCSLZJ [Wei Baqun, Chen Hongtao shiliao zhuanji] 韦拔群、陈洪涛史料专辑 (A Special Collection of Historical Materials on Wei Baqun and Chen Hongtao). Nanning: Zhonggong Guangxi Zhuangzu zizhiqu dangshi yanjiushi, 2006.

WCYZJHXJ [Wei Baqun Chen Hongtao yizuo he jianghua xuanji] 韦拔群 陈洪涛 遗作和讲话选辑 (Selected Writings and Speeches of Wei Baqun and Chen Hongtao). Donglan: Zhonggong Donglan xianwei dangshi ziliao zhengji bangongshi, 1984.

Wei Baqun 韦拔群. "Anwei qinren ge" 安慰亲人歌 (A Song to Console My Loved Ones). In *WCSLZJ*, 221.

———. "Xiaoshi ershou" 小诗二首 (Two Short Poems). In *WCSLZJ*, 222.

———. "Shige shishou;" "Shange shiwushou" 诗歌十首; 山歌十五首 (Ten Poems; 15 Folksongs). In *WCYZJHXJ*, 70–87.

———. "Geming daodi" 革命到底 (Carry the Revolution Through to the End). In *Benteng de Zuoyoujiang*, 22.

Wei Baqun 韦拔群 et al. "Jinggao tongbaoshu" 敬告同胞书 (To the Compatriots). In *WCSLZJ*, 26–27.

Wei Chengzhu 韦成珠, Li Dingzhong 李鼎中 and Qin Maocai 覃茂才. "Huang Shuxiang zai Nama geming huodong pianduan" 黄书祥在那马革命活动片断 (Some Memories of Huang Shuxiang's Activities in Nama). *Mashan wenshi ziliao* 马山文史资料, 1(1986), 21–26.

Wei Chun 韦春. "Fengbei, yili zai renmin xinzhong" 丰碑，屹立在人民心中 (A Monument in the Hearts of the People). In Hechi ribaoshe, ed., 1990, 51–52.

Wei Dingxin 韦鼎新 and Lu Xiuxiang 陆秀祥. "Beishang Jiangxi hou de qinshen jingli" 北上江西后的亲身经历 (My Personal Experiences after Leaving Hechi for Jiangxi). In Lu Xiuxiang, ed., 1990, 324–331.

Wei Guoqing 韦国清. "Yingfan yongcun" 英范永存 (An Immortal Model). *Minzu tuanjie* 民族团结, 1982(10). In *ZYJGMGJD*, Vol. 2, 650–654.

Wei Hanchen 韦汉臣. "Jianguoqian Donglan fazhan shaoshuminzu jiaoyu gaikuang" 建国前东兰发展少数民族教育概况 (The Development of Education for the Minority Groups in Donglan before the Liberation). *Donglan wenshi* 4 (2001), 183–186.

Wei Jie 韦杰. "Sanci jian Bage" 三次见拔哥 (My Three Meetings with Elder Brother Ba). In *Huiyi Wei Baqun*, 41–50.

Wei Qiang 韦强. "Huang Bangcheng" 黄榜呈. In Lu Xiuxiang, Huang Jianping and Huang Yingjun, eds., 1988, 64–75.

Wei Qinglan 韦庆兰 and Huang Chaoyin 黄超荫. "Chen Mengwu" 陈孟武. In *ZGGXDSRWZ*, Vol. 4 (2204), 169–172.

Wei Qirong 韦崎嵘. "Huang Fangri" 黄昉日. In Lu Xiuxiang, Huang Jianping and Huang Yingjun, eds., 1988, 124–137.

———. "Huang Fangri" 黄昉日. In Bai Xianjing, ed., 1991, 585–591.

Wei Qirong 韦崎嵘 and Huang Jianping 黄建平. "Chen Bomin" 陈伯民. In *ZGGXDSRWZ*. Vol. 1 (1992), 139–147.

Wei Ronggang 韦荣刚. "Wei Hanchao" 韦汉超. In *ZGGXDSRWZ*, Vol. 2 (1995), 14–18.

Wei Ruilin 韦瑞霖. "Lu Rongting" 陆荣廷. In Guangxi xinhai gemingshi yanjiuhui, ed., 1983, 48–60.

———. "Mo Rongxin" 莫荣新. In Guangxi xinhai gemingshi yanjiuhui, ed., 1983, 71–79.

Wei Shiba 韦仕拔. "Husong Dengzhengwei ji wo beishang de huiyi" 护送邓政委及我北上的回忆 (Recollections about Escorting Political Commissar Deng Xiaoping and Making the Journey to Jiangxi). In Lu Xiuxiang, ed., 1990, 249–251.

Wei Shilin 韦仕林. "Du'an nongmin yundong de xingqi" 都安农民运动的兴起 (The Rise of the Peasant Movement in Du'an). In Yu Xinshun, ed., 2003, 560–561.

Wei Shukui 韦树奎. "Meng Bumen qiren qishi" 蒙卜门其人其事 (The Story of Meng Pumen). *Donglan wenshi* 4 (2001), 196–205.

Wei Tianfu, 韦天富 ed. *Donglanxian minzheng zhi* 东兰县民政志 (History of the Civil Administration in Donglan). Donglan: Donglanxian renmin zhengfu minzhengju and Donglanxian difangzhi bangongshi, 2001.

———. "Yu Zuobai yu Donglan geming ersanshi" 俞作柏与东兰革命二三事 (Yu Zuobai and Some of His Connections with the Donglan Revolution). *Donglan wenshi* 东兰文史, 4 (2001), 70–72.

———. "Donglan weishi tusi de xingshuai" 东兰韦氏土司的兴衰 (The Rise and Fall of the Wei's Who Served as the Hereditary Lords of Donglan). *Donglan wenshi*, 4 (2001), 116–131.

Wei Tianfu 韦天富 and Tan Lu 谭律. "Wei Baqun yunan qianhou" 韦拔群遇难前后 (An Account of Wei Baqun's Death). *Donglan wenshi* 东兰文史, 4 (2001), 32–38.

Wei Tingzhang 韦廷章. ed. *Fengshan xianzhi* 凤山县志 (Fengshan Gazette). Nanning: Guangxi renmin, 2008.

Wei Wenjun 韦文俊 and Ma Yongquan 马永全, eds. *Donglan geyao ji* 东兰歌谣集 (A Collection of Folksongs from Donglan). Donglan: Donglanxian minjianwenxue jichengxiaozu, 1987.

Wei Xianzhi 韦显知. "Chen Liya" 陈立亚. In *ZGGXDSRWZ*, Vol. 4 (2004), 63–68.

Wei Xinyin 韦信音 ed. *Qingsong gaojie: Huang Songjian shiliao zhuanji* 青松高洁：黄松坚史料专辑 (As Noble and Unsullied as the Pines: A Special Collection of Historical Materials on Huang Songjian). Nanning: Guangxi renmin, 1999.

Wei Xinyin 韦信音 and Huang Yongsheng 黄邕生. "Huang Songjian zhuanlue" 黄松坚传略 (A Brief Biography of Huang Songjian). In Wei Xinyin, ed., 1999, 399–427.

Wei Xiukang 韦秀康. "Wei Rong" 韦荣. In Bai Xianjing, ed., 1991, 659–667.

Wei Zhihua 韦志华. "Lu Tao" 卢涛. In *ZGGXDSRWZ*. Vol. 3 (1997), 258–264.

Wei Zhihong 韦志虹, Wu Zhongcai 吴忠才 and Gao Xiong 高雄 eds. *Baise qiyi renwuzhi* 百色起义人物志 (Biographies of the Prominent Figures in the Baise Uprising). Nanning: Guangxi renmin, 1999.

Wei Zhongquan 韦仲权 and Lu Xiuxiang 陆秀祥. "Huiyi hongjun he chiweidui zai Beihe de huodong" 回忆红军和赤卫队在北荷的活动 (Recollections about the Activities of the Red Army and Red Guards at Beihe). In Lu Xiuxiang, ed., 1990, 296–299.

Wenshizu 文史组. "Sanda Donglan cheng" 三打东兰城 (The Three Attacks on the County Seat of Donglan). *Donglan wenshi ziliao* 东兰文史资料, 1 (1985), 26–35.

———. "Donglanxian geming lieshi lingyuan" 东兰县革命烈士陵园 (The Donglan Cemetery of Revolutionary Martyrs). *Donglan wenshi ziliao* 东兰文史资料, No. 1 (1985), 86–92.

———. "Donglan nongyun zhong de fuyun gaikuang" 东兰农运中的妇运概况 (A Brief Account of the Women's Movement in the Donglan Peasant Movement). *Donglan wenshi* 东兰文史, 4 (2001), 94–96.

———. "Wei Huchen zhuanlue" 韦虎臣传略 (A Brief Biography of Wei Huchen). *Donglan wenshi*, 4 (2001), 132–133.

Wenshiwei 文史委. "Wenhua dageming zai Donglan fasheng he fazhan de zhuyao shiji" 文化大革命在东兰发生和发展的主要事记 (Major Events in the Evolution of the Cultural Revolution in Donglan). *Donglan wenshi* 东兰文史, 5 (2004), 176–180.

Wu Delin 吴德林. "Dui Donglan nongyun de jidian huiyi" 对东兰农运的几点回忆 (Some Recollections about the Donglan Peasant Movement). In Lu Xiuxiang, ed., 1986, 239–247.

———. "Huiyi Weishizhang yu Hongjun Youjiang dulishi" 回忆韦师长与红军右江独立师 (Recollections about Division Commander Wei Baqun and the Youjiang Independent Division of the Red Army). In Lu Xiuxiang, ed., 1990, 199–217.

Wu Delin 吴德林 and Huang Hanzhong 黄汉钟. "Kuixinglou gaikuang" 魁星楼概况 (The Tower of Literary Stars). *Donglan wenshi ziliao* 东兰文史资料, 1 (1985): 71–76.

Wu Xi 吴西. "Quzhe de lichen" 曲折的历程 (A Tortuous Journey). 1981. In *ZYJGMGJD*, Vol. 2, 835–841.

Wu Zhongcai 吴忠才, Huang Yuanzheng 黄远征 and Chen Xinde 陈欣德. *Baise qiyi shigao* 百色起义史稿 (A History of the Baise Uprising). Guilin: Guangxi shifan daxue, 2004.

Wuzhou minguo ribao 梧州民国日报. "Liaojunzhang dushi jiao Dongfeng gongfei" 廖军长督师剿东凤共匪 (General Liao is Commanding his Troops to Exterminate the Communist Bandits in Donglan and Fengshan). September 20, 1932.

———. "Xuanshang ji gongfei shouyao" 悬赏缉共匪首要 (Bounties Offered for Leading Communist Bandits." October 5, 1932.

———. "Baifuzuo you Baise zhuanfu Donglan" 白副座由百色转赴东兰 (Deputy Commander Bai Chongxi Leaves Baise for Donglan). October 10, 1932.

———. "Liaojunzhang zai Dongfeng ban shanhou" 廖军长在东凤办善后 (General Liao Is Directing the Reconstruction of Donglan and Fengshan). October 26, 1932.

———. "Dongfeng shanhou weiyuanhui chengli" 东凤善后委员会成立 (The Committee for Reconstructing Donglan and Fengshan Organized). November 3, 1932.

———. "Chenfei Hongtao bujiu ke jiuqin" 陈匪洪涛不久可就擒 (Bandit Chen Hongtao Can Be Captured Soon). November 9, 1932.

———. "Weifei shouji shizhong hou yanmai" 韦匪首级示众后掩埋 (Bandit Wei Baqun's Head Buried after a Public Display). November 20, 1932.

———. "Fengshan chihuo diaocha" 凤山赤祸调查 (A Report about the Calamities the Communists Have Caused in Fengshan). November 21, 1932. In *ZYJGMSLHB*, Vol. 3, 156–162.

Xie Fumin 谢扶民. *Wei Baqun* 韦拔群. Beijing: Gongren, 1958.

———. "Yi Youjiang chiweijun zongzhihui Huang Zhifeng" 忆右江赤卫军总指挥黄治峰 (Memories of Huang Zhifeng: Commander in Chief of the Red Guards of the Right River Region). 1959. In *ZYJGMGJD*, Vol. 2, 673–681.

———. "Baqun tongzhi zhandou de yisheng" 拔群同志战斗的一生 (Comrade Wei Baqun as a Lifetime Revolutionary). In *Huiyi Wei Baqun*, 14–32.

Xie Fumin 谢扶民, Yuwen 宇文 and Qian Shengfa 钱生发. *Wei Baqun* 韦拔群, 2 vols. Shanghai: Shanghai renmin meishu, 1978.

Xie Shenghua 谢生桦. "Duiyu Guangxi Donglan nongmin beinan de wogan" 对于广西东兰农民被难的我感 (Some Reflections on the Sufferings of the Peasants in Donglan of Guangxi). 1926. In *WCSLZJ*, 60–63.

Xiong Hongming 熊红明 and Yang Zijian 杨子健. "Wei Baqun lieshi beihai'an zhenpoji" 韦拔群烈士被害案侦破记 (An Account of How the Case of Wei Baqun's Murder Was Solved). *Nanguo zaobao* 南国早报, November 13, 2009.

Xu Shu 许述. "Zhu De rudang de yibosanzhe" 朱德入党的一波三折 (The Twists and Turns Zhu De Experienced When Applying for the CCP Membership). *Dang de wenxian* 党的文献, 135 (2010, No. 3), 118–119.

Ya Guohua 牙国华. "Jidian de huiyi" 几点的回忆 (Some Recollections). In Lu Xiuxiang ed., 1990, 304–309.

Ya Meiyuan 牙美元. "Diyici gemingzhanzheng shiqi guonei ge renmintuanti ji gejierenshi zhiyuan Donglan nongminyundong de huiyi" 第一次革命战争时期国内各人民团体及各界人士支援东兰农民运动的回忆 (Recollections about How People's Organizations and Personalities of all Circles from the Entire Country Supported the Peasants of Donglan during the First Civil War). *Donglan wenshi ziliao*, 1 (1985), 18–23.

———. "Huiyi dageming he tudigeming shiqi Donglan shehui zhi'an gaikuang" 回忆大革命和土地革命时期东兰社会治安概况 (Recollections about Public Security in Donglan during the First United Front and the Land Revolution). *Donglan wenshi ziliao*, 1 (1985), 44–48.

———. "Donglanxian sufu caijing gaikuang" "东兰县苏府财经概况" (The Financial Conditions of the Donglan Soviet Government). In Lu Xiuxiang, ed., 1990, 228.

———. "Genjudi liuxing gequxuan" 根据地流行歌曲选 (Selected Popular Songs in the Revolutionary Base Areas). In Lu Xiuxiang, ed., 1990, 404–406.

———. "Geming xianzhang Chen Mianshu" 革命县长陈勉恕 (Chen Mianshu the Revolutionary Magistrate). *Donglan wenshi* 东兰文史, 4 (2001), 73–76.

———. "Guixi junfa tongzhi shiqi de Donglan tanguan haoshen" 桂系军阀统治时期的东兰贪官豪绅 (The Corrupt Officials and Evil Gentry of Donglan during the Rule of the Guangxi Clique). *Donglan wenshi*, 4 (2001), 136–143.

Ya Meiyuan 牙美元 and Chen Shidu 陈仕读. "Wei Baqun jianli geming wuzhuang de huiyi" 韦拔群建立革命武装的回忆 (Our Recollections about How Wei Baqun Created the Revolutionary Armed Force). *Donglan wenshi ziliao*, 1 (1985), 54–61.

Ya Meiyuan 牙美元 and Qin Yingwu 覃应物. "Yi Chen Hongtao tongzhi" 忆陈洪涛同志 (Memories of Comrade Chen Hongtao). *Donglan wenshi* 东兰文史, 4 (2001), 40–43.

Ya Yuanbo 牙远波. "Wei Baqun deng jinggao tongbao chengwen, fabu shijian kao" 韦拔群等《敬告同胞》成文、发布时间考 (Dating the Writing and Distribution of "To the Compatriots" by Wei Baqun and Others). *Hechi shizhuan xuebao* 河池师专学报, 21 (3), 30–32. 2001.

———. "Wei Baqun tongzhi rudang shijian zai kaozheng" 韦拔群同志入党时间再考证 (Further Discussions on When Comrade Wei Baqun Joined the CCP). *Hechi shizhuan xuebao* 《河池师专学报》, 23(1),76–78. 2003.

Ya Zukun 牙祖坤 and Wei Jiabo 韦加波, eds. *Deng Xiaoping yu Donglan* 邓小平与东兰 (Deng Xiaoping and Donglan). Nanning: Donglanxian geming laoqu jianshe cujinhui, 2005.

Yan Heng 阎衡. "Yan Heng tongzhi guanyu diqijun de baogao" 阎衡同志关于第七军的报告 (Comrade Yan Heng's Report about the Seventh Red Army). April 4, 1931. In *ZYJGMGJD*, Vol. 1, 382–391.

Yang Dongquan 杨冬权. "Deng Xiaoping he Wei Baqun" 邓小平和韦拔群 (Deng Xiaoping and Wei Baqun). 2004. In Ya Zukun and Wei Jiabo, eds., 2005, 17–19.

Yang Shaojuan 杨绍娟. "Zuoyoujiang geming genjudi de funu yundong" 左右江革命根据地的妇女运动 (The Women's Movement in the Left River and Right River Revolutionary Base Area). In *ZYJGMGJD*, Vol. 2, 1111–1123.

Yang Shiheng 杨士衡 and Qin Jiancai 覃建才. "Cenxunwang" 岑逊王 (King Cenxun). In Nong Guanpin 农冠品 and Cao Tingwei 曹廷伟, eds., *Zhuangzu minjian gushi xuan* 壮族民间故事选 (Selected Folk Stories of the Zhuang People), vol. 1, 20–22. Nanning: Guangxi renmin, 1982.

Yang Wenke 杨文科. "Cedong shahai wo hongqijun Wei Baqun shizhang de zuifan Chen Dibo luoru fawang" 策动杀害我红七军韦拔群师长的罪犯陈的伯落入法网 (Criminal Chen Dibo Who Plotted the Murder of Division Commander Wei Baqun of the Seventh Red Army Has Been Arrested). *Rongshui wenshi ziliao* 融水文史资料, 5 (1989), 124–127.

Yang Xiangchao 杨相朝. "Lingyunxian Sicheng Zhuangzu yehun xisu" 凌云县泗城壮族夜婚习俗 (Holding Marriage Ceremonies at Midnight: A Custom of Sicheng in Lingyun). In Tang Nonglin, ed., 1994, 146–147.

Yang Yexing 杨业兴 and Huang Xiongying 黄雄鹰, eds. *Youjiang liuyu Zhuangzu jingji shigao* 右江流域壮族经济史稿 (An Economic History of the Zhuang People in the Right River Region). Nanning: Guangxi renmin, 1995.

Ye Jizhuang 叶季壮. "Dui Wei Baqun tongzhi de jidian huiyi" 对韦拔群同志的几点回忆 (Some Memories of Comrade Wei Baqun). In *Huiyi Wei Baqun*, 1–6.

Youjiang Suwei'ai zhengfu 右江苏维埃政府. "Youjiang Suwei'ai zhengfu kouhao" 右江苏维埃政府口号 (Slogans of the Right River Soviet Government). December 1929. In *ZYJGMGJD*, Vol. 1, 146.

———. "Gongnongbing shizi keben" 工农兵识字课本 (Literacy Textbook for Workers, Peasants and Soldiers). Vols. 1–2. In *ZYJGMSLHB*, Vol. 2,136–150.

———. "Tudifa zanxing tiaoli" 土地法暂行条例 (Provisional Regulations of the Agrarian Law). May 1, 1930. In *ZYJGMGJD*, Vol. 1, 265–269.

———. "Gonggen tiaoli" 共耕条例 (Regulations about Collective Farming). May 15, 1930. In *ZYJGMGJD*, Vol. 1, 271–274.

Yu Xinshun 庾新顺. "Zuoyoujiang diqu de nongmin wuzhuang douzheng" 左右江地区的农民武装斗争 (The Armed Struggles of the Peasants in the Left River and Right River Region). In *ZYJGMGJD*, Vol. 2, 1055–1069.

———. "Zuoyoujiang geming genjudi de dangzuzhi" 左右江革命根据地的党组织 (The CCP Organizations in the Left River and Right River Revolutionary Base Area). In *ZYJGMGJD*, Vol. 2 (1989), 1163–1181.

———. "Yu Zuoyu" 俞作豫. In Bai Xianjing, ed., 1991, 157–170.

———. "Deng Baqi" 邓拔奇. In *ZGGXDSRWZ*, Vol. 1 (1992), 229–242.

———, ed. *Zuoyoujiang geming genjudi renwuzhi* 左右江革命根据地人物志 (Biographies of Prominent Figures of the Left River and Right River Revolutionary Base Area). Nanning: Guangxi renmin, 1998.

———, ed. *Dang de chuangjian he dageming shiqi de Guangxi nongmin yundong* 党的创建和大革命时期的广西农民运动 (Peasant Movements in Guangxi during the Period of the Founding of the CCP and the First United Front). Nanning: Guangxi renmin, 2003.

———. "Liang Liudu" 梁六度. In *ZGGXDSRWZ*, Vol. 4 (2004), 53–62.

Yu Xinshun 庾新顺 and Ban Feng 班锋. "Hengli Hongjunyan lieshi" 恒里红军岩烈士 (Martyrs at the Red Army Cave of Hengli). In *ZGGXDSRWZ*, Vol. 4 (2004), 562–569.

Yuan Renyuan 袁任远. "Cong Baise dao Xianggan" 从百色到湘赣 (From Baise to Xianggan). 1961. In *ZYJGMGJD*, Vol. 2, 621–635.

Yuan Renyuan 袁任远 and Mo Wenhua 莫文骅. "Guanyu Guangxi suwei'ai yundong yu hongjun diqijun zongjie de yijianshu" 关于广西苏维埃运动与红军第七军总结的意见书 (Our Opinions on the Soviet Movement in Guangxi and the Final Report about the Seventh Red Army). In Ou Jiwen, ed., 2007, 77–79.

Yun Daiying 恽代英. "Gei Zhonggong zhongyang de baogao" 给中共中央的报告 (A Report to the CCP Central Committee). October 24, 1927. In *WCSLZJ*, 82.

Zeng Qiqiang 曾启强, ed. *Zhongguo gongchandang Donglan lishi* 中国共产党东兰历史 (History of the Communist Movement in Donglan). Beijing: Zhonggong dangshi, 2007.

———. *Zhongguo zaoqi nongmin yundong lingxiu Wei Baqun* 中国早期农民运动领袖韦拔群 (Wei Baqun: An Early Peasant Movement Leader of China). 2nd edition. Donglan: Zhonggong Donglan xianwei dangshi yanjiushi, 2010.

ZGGXDSRWZ [Zhonggong Guangxi dangshi renwu zhuan] 中共广西党史人物传 (Biographies of Prominent Figures in the History of the Communist Movement in Guangxi). Five Volumes. Nanning: Guangxi renmin, 1992–2004.

Zhang Xiushan 张秀山. *Wode bashiwu nian* 我的八十五年 (My Eighty Five Years of Life). Beijing: Zhonggong dangshi, 2007.

Zhang Yunyi 张云逸. "Baise qiyi yu hongqijun de jianli" 百色起义与红七军的建立 (The Baise Uprising and the Birth of the Seventh Red Army). 1958. *Xinghuo liaoyuan* 星火燎原, Vol. 1 (1997), 410–420.

———. "Xuexi Wei Baqun tongzhi" 学习韦拔群同志 (Learn from Comrade Wei Baqun). 1962. In *Huiyi Wei Baqun*, front page.

Zhang Yunyi zhuan bianxiezu 张云逸传编写组. *Zhang Yunyi zhuan* 张云逸传. Beijing: dangdai zhongguo, 2012.

Zhao Bingzhuang 赵秉壮. "Diyige lai Enlongxian jianli gongchandang zuzhi de Yu Shaojie" 第一个来恩隆县建立共产党组织的余少杰 (Yu Shaojie: The Founder of the CCP Organization in Enlong County). *Tiandong wenshi ziliao* 田东文史资料, 1 (1987), 33–42.

———. "Lu Jizhang" 陆矶彰. In *ZGGXDSRWZ*, Vol. 1 (1992), 8–9.

Zhen 真. "Muqian zhuyao de renwu" 目前主要的任务 (Our Primary Tasks at the Present). December 18, 1929. In *ZYJGMGJD*, Vol. 1, 121.

Zhong Wendian 钟文典, ed. *Ershi shiji sanshi niandai de Guangxi* 二十世纪三十年代的广西 (Guangxi in the 1930s). Guilin: Guangxi shifandaxue, 1992.

Zhonggong Donglan xianwei dangshi bangongshi 中共东兰县委党史办公室. "Guanyu jinggao tongbaoshu fabiao shijian de kanfa" 关于'敬告同胞'书发表时间的看法 (Our Views on the Dating of "To the Compatriots"). In Lu Xiuxiang, ed., 1986, 281–284.

Zhonggong Dongfeng xianwei 中共东凤县委. "Zhonggong Dongfeng xianwei tonggao" 中共东凤县委通告 (Annoucement of the Dongfeng County Committee of the CCP). 1930. In *ZYJGMGJD*, Vol. 1, 349–354.

Zhonggong Guangdong shengwei 中共广东省委. "Zhonggong Guangdong shengwei gei Guangxi tewei zhishixin" 中共广东省委给广西特委指示信 (Directives from the

Guangdong Provincial Committee of the CCP to the Guangxi Special Committee of the CCP). November 19, 1929. In *WCSLZJ*, 101–103.

Zhonggong Guangxi tewei 中共广西特委. "Guangxidang zhengzhi renwu jueyi'an" 广西党政治任务决议案 (The Resolution about the Political Tasks of the Guangxi Branch of the CCP). September 13, 1929. In *ZYJGMGJD*, Vol. 1, 51–63.

———. "Zhonggong Guangxi tewei gei Guangdong shengwei de xin" 中共广西特委给广东省委的信 (A Letter from the Guangxi Special Committee of the CCP to the Guangdong Provincial Committee of the CCP). October 20, 1929. In *WCSLZJ*, 92–96.

Zhonggong Guangxi Zhuangzu zizhiqu wenyuanhui dangshi yanjiushi 中共广西壮族自治区委员会党史研究室, ed., *Guangxi jiaofei ji* 广西剿匪记 (An Account of the Extermination Campaigns against the Bandits in Guangxi). Beijing: Zhonggong dangshi, 2008.

Zhonggong zhongyang 中共中央. "Muqian nongyun jihua" 目前农运计划 (Our Current Plan about the Peasant Movement). November 15, 1926. In *WCSLZJ*, 67–68.

———. "Zhongyangju baogao" 中央局报告 (Report of the CCP Central Bureau). December 5, 1926. In *WCSLZJ*, 69–70.

———. "Zuijin nongmin douzheng de jueyi'an" 最近农民斗争的决议案 (Resolution about Recent Peasant Struggles). August 1927. In Zhongyang dang'anguan 中央档案馆, ed., *Zhonggong zhongyang wenjian xuanji* 中共中央文件选集, Vol. 4, 294–297. Beijing: Zhonggong zhongyang dangxiao, 1989.

———. "Nongmin yundong jueyi'an" 农民运动决议案 (Resolution on the Peasant Movement). July 9, 1928. In Zhongyang dang'anguan, ed., *Zhonggong zhongyang wenjian xuanji*, Vol. 4, 354–366.

———. "Zhonggong zhongyang gei Guangdong shengwei zhuan qijun qianwei de zhishi" 中共中央给广东省委转七军前委的指示 (Directives of the CCP Central Committee for the Front Committee of the Seventh Red Army Sent through the Guangdong Provincial Committee of the CCP). March 2, 1930. In *ZYJGMGJD*, Vol. 1, 218–248.

———. "Zhonggong zhongyang gei junwei nanfang banshichu bingzhuan qijun qianwei zhishixin" 中共中央给军委南方办事处并转七军前委指示信 (Directives from the CCP Central Committee to the Southern Office of the Central Military Committee and the Front Committee of the Seventh Red Army). June 167, 1930. In *ZYJGMGJD*, Vol. 1, 315–317.

Zhongguo qingnian bao 中国青年报. "Donglanxian guanfang huiying tiaoshui laoren guiqiu zhengfu xiulu shijian" 东兰县官方回应"挑水老人跪求政府修路"事件 (Donglan County Government's Response to the Incident Involving Old Villagers Who Knelt Down and Begged the Government to Build Road while on Their Way to Carry Water). *Zhongguo qingnian bao*, March 28, 2010.

Zhonghua Suwei'ai gongheguo 中华苏维埃共和国. "Zhonghua Suwei'ai gongheguo linshi zhongyang zhengfu bugao" 中华苏维埃共和国临时中央政府布告 (Bulletin of the Provisional Government of the Chinese Soviet Republic). November 1931. In *WCSLZJ*, 205.

Zhongyang fangwentuan diyi fentuan lianluozu 中央访问团第一分团联络组. *Guangxi Donglanxian diwuqu (Zhonghequ) minzu gaikuang* 广西东兰县第五区（中和区）民族概况 (Ethnography of the Fifth District [Zhonghe District] of Donglan County, Guangxi Province). 1951 (A).

———. *Guangxi Donglanxian Xishanqu minzu gaikuang* 广西东兰县西山区民族概况 (Ethnography of the Western Mountains District of Donglan, Guangxi). 1951 (B).

Zhongyang ribao 中央日报. "Gui shengwei shengtao Yuni Zuobai jiefa Yuni huo Gui zuizhuang" 桂省委声讨俞逆作柏揭发俞逆祸桂罪状 (Members of the Guangxi Provincial Committee of the KMT Condemned Traitor Yu Zuobai for Causing Calamities for Guangxi). *Zhongyang* ribao, October 15, 1929. In *ZYJGMSLHB*, Vol. 3, 40–42.

Zhou Enlai 周恩来. "Guanyu yijiuersi zhi yijiuerliu nian dang dui Guomindang de guanxi" 关于1924 至 1926 年党对国民党的关系 (On the Relations between Our Party and the Nationalist Party from 1924 to 1926), 1943. In *Zhou Enlai xuanji* 周恩来选集, Vol. 1, 112–124. Beijing: Renmin, 1980.

Zhou Jizhong 周继忠. "Xishan tuwei ji" 西山突围记 (Breaking out of the Encirclement around the Western Mountains). In *Huiyi Wei Baqun*, 119–124.

Zhu Hongyuan 朱浤源. *Cong bianluan dao junsheng: Guangxi de chuqi xiandaihua, 1860–1937* 从变乱到军省：广西的初期现代化， 1860–1937 (From Social Upheaval to Military Rule: The Early Modernization of Guangxi, 1860–1937). Taipei: Zhongyang yanjiuyuan jindaishi yanjiusuo zhuankan, 76 (1995).

Zhu Wanli 祝万里. "Zhuangzu weixing qiyuan sanshuo" 壮族韦姓起源三说 (Three Theories about the Origins of the Family Name Wei of the Zhuang People). *Wenshi chunqiu* 文史春秋, 10 (1995, No. 3), 50–51.

Zhu Xi'ang 朱锡昂. "Zhu Xi'ang gei zhongyang xunshiyuan he Guangdong shengwei de baogao" 朱锡昂给中央巡视员和广东省委的报告 (Zhu Xi'ang's Report to the Inspector of the CCP Central Committee and the Guangdong Special Committee of the CCP). January 27, 1929. In Lan Yingbo and Deng Lineng, eds., *Guangxi geming lishi wenjian huiji* 广西革命历史文件汇集 (Collected Historical Documents about the Revolution in Guangxi). 1982.

Zhu Zhongyu 朱仲玉. *Wei Baqun* 韦拔群. Beijing: Zhonghua shuju, 1959.

Zong Ying 宗英, et al. *Wei Baqun lieshi de gushi* 韦拔群烈士的故事 (Stories about Martyr Wei Baqun). Beijing: Zuojia, 1959.

ZYJGMGJD [Zuoyoujiang geming genjudi] 左右江革命根据地 (The Left River and Right River Revolutionary Base Area). Two volumes. Beijing: Zhonggong dangshi ziliao, 1989.

ZYJGMSLHB [Zuoyoujiang geming shiliao huibian] 左右江革命史料汇编 (Collected Historical Sources about the Revolution in the Left River and Right River Region). Three volumes. Zuoyoujiang geming lishi diaochazu 左右江革命历史调查组, 1978.

English Language Sources

Alitto, Guy. *The Last Confucian: Liang Shu-ming and the Chinese Dilemma of Modernity.* Berkeley, CA: University of California Press, 1979.

Anderson, James. *The Rebel Den of Nung Tri Cao: Loyalty and Identity along the Sino-Vietnamese Frontier.* Seattle: University of Washington Press, 2007.

Averill, Stephen C. *Revolution in the Highlands: China's Jinggangshan Base Area.* Rowman & Littlefield Publishers, 2006.

Barlow, Jeffrey G. "The Zhuang Minority Peoples of the Sino-Vietnamese Frontier in the Song Period." *Journal of Southeast Asian Studies*, 18(2), 1987, 250–269.

———. "The Zhuang Minority in the Ming Era." *Ming Studies*, 28 (1989), 15–45.

Benton, Gregor. *Mountain Fires: The Red Army's Three-Year War in South China, 1934–1938.* Berkeley, CA: University of California Press, 1992.

Bianco, Lucien. *Origins of the Chinese Revolution, 1915–1949.* Stanford, CA: Stanford University Press, 1971.

———. *Peasants Without the Party: Grassroots Movements in Twentieth-Century China.* Armonk, New York: M. E. Sharpe, 2001.

———. *Wretched Rebels: Rural Disturbances on the Eve of the Chinese Revolution.* Cambridge, MA and London: Harvard East Asian Monographs, 2009.

Billingsley, Phil. *Bandits in Republican China.* Stanford, CA: Stanford University Press, 1988.

Chang Kuo-tao (Zhang Guotao). *The Rise of the Chinese Communist Party: The Autobiography of Chang Kuo-tao.* Two volumes. Lawrence: University Press of Kansas, 1971–72.

Chen Yung-fa. "The Futian Incident and the Anti-Bolshevik League: The 'Terror' and CCP Rovolution." *Republican China*, Vol. XIX, No. 2 (April 1994), 1–51.

Chesneaux, Jean. *Peasant Revolts in China, 1840–1949.* W. W. Norton & Company, Inc., 1973.

Cohen, Paul, A. *History in Three Keys: The Boxers as Event, Experience, and Myth.* New York: Columbia University Press, 1997.

DeFronzo, James. *Revolutions and Revolutionary Movements.* 4th Edition. Boulder, Colorado: Westview Press, 2011.

Derlik, Arif. *The Origins of Chinese Communism.* New York: Oxford University Press, 1989.

———. *Anarchism in Chinese Revolution.* Berkeley: University of California Press, 1993.

Esherick, Joseph W. "Ten Theses on the Chinese Revolution." In Jeffrey N. Wasserstrom, ed., *Twentieth-Century China: New Approaches*, 37–65. New York: Routledge, 2003.

Faure, David. "The Yao Wars in the Mid-Ming and Their Impact on Yao Ethnicity." In Pamela Kyle Crossley, Helen F. Siu, and Donald S. Sutton, eds., *Empire at the Margins: Culture, Ethnicity, and Frontier in Early Modern China*, 171–189. Berkeley, CA: University of California Press, 2006.

Forster, Keith. "Localism, Central Policy, and the Provincial Purges of 1957–1958: The Case of Zhejiang." In Timothy Cheek and Tony Saich, eds., *New Perspectives on State Socialism in China*. Armonk, NY: M. E. Sharpe, 1997.

Friedman, Edward. *Backward toward Revolution: The Chinese Revolutionary Party*. Berkeley, CA: University of California Press, 1974.

Galbiati, Fernando. *Peng Pai and the Hai-Lu-Feng Soviet*. Stanford, CA: Stanford University Press, 1985.

Goodman, David, S. G. *Deng Xiaoping and the Chinese Revolution: A Political Biography*. London & New York: Routledge, 1994.

Guo Xiaolin. *State and Ethnicity in China's Southwest*. Leiden/Boston: Brill, 2008.

Han, Xiaorong. *Chinese Discourses on the Peasant, 1900–1949*. Albany: State University of New York Press, 2005.

———. "Localism in Chinese Communist Politics Before and After 1949—The Case of Feng Baiju." *Chinese Historical Review*, 11(1), 23–56. 2004.

Hartford, Kathleen, and Steven M. Goldstein, eds. *Single Sparks: China's Rural Revolutions*. Armonk, NY: M. E. Sharpe, INC. 1989.

Hayford, Charles. *To the People: James Yen and Village China*. New York: Columbia University Press, 1990.

Ho, Ping-ti. *The Ladder of Success in Imperial China: Aspects of Social Mobility, 1368–1911*. New York: John Wiley & Sons, 1964.

Hofheinz, Roy, JR. *The Broken Wave: the Chinese Communist Peasant Movement, 1922–1928*. Cambridge, MA: Harvard University Press, 1977.

Hutchings, Graham. "The Troubled Life and After-Life of a Guangxi Communist: Some Notes on Li Mingrui and the Communist Movement in Guangxi Province before 1949." *China Quarterly*, No. 104 (1985), 700–708.

Isaacs, Harold R. *The Tragedy of the Chinese Revolution*. Stanford, CA: Stanford University Press, 1961. 2nd revised edition.

Johnson, Chalmers A. *Peasant Nationalism and Communist Power: The Emergence of Revolutionary China, 1937–1945*. Stanford, CA: Stanford University Press, 1962.

Kaup, Katherine Palmer. *Creating the Zhuang: Ethnic Politics in China*. Boulder, Colo.: Lynne Rienner, 2000.

Kroeber, Clifton B. "Theory and History of Revolution." *Journal of World History*, Vol. 7, No. 1 (1996), 21–40.

Kuhn, Philip A. *Origins of the Modern Chinese State*. Stanford: Stanford University Press, 2002.

Kurtz, Marcus J. "Understanding Peasant Revolution: From Concept to Theory and Case." *Theory and Society*, No. 29 (2000), 93–124.

Lary, Diana. "Communism and Ethnic Revolt: Some Notes on the Chuang Peasant Movement in Kwangsi 1921–31. *The China Quarterly*, No. 49 (1972), 126–135.

———. *Region and Nation: The Kwangsi Clique in Chinese Politics, 1925–1937*. London and New York: Cambridge University Press, 1974.

———. "A Zone of Nebulous Menace: The Guangxi/Indochina Border in the Republican Period." In Diana Lary, ed. *The Chinese State at the Borders*, 181–197. Vancouver: University of British Columbia Press, 2007.

Levich, Eugene William. *The Kwangsi Way in Kuomintang China, 1931–1939*. Armonk, New York: M. E. Sharpe, 1997.

Levine, Marilyn A. *The Found Generation: Chinese Communists in Europe during the Twenties*. Seattle: The University of Washington Press, 1993.

Li Jui. *The Early Revolutionary Activities of Comrade Mao Tse-tung*. White Plains, NY: M. E. Sharpe, 1977.

Mao Zedong. "Report on the Peasant Movement in Hunan." In Staurt Shram, ed., *Mao's Road to Power*. Vol. 2, 429–464. Armonk: NY: M. E. Sharpe, 1994.

Marks, Robert. *Rural Revolution in South China: Peasants and the Making of History in Haifeng County, 1570–1930*. Madison: University of Wisconsin Press, 1984.

McAleavy, Henry. *Black Flags in Vietnam: The Story of a Chinese Intervention*. London: Allen & Unwin, 1968.

McDonald, Angus W. *Urban Origins of Rural Revolution: Elites and the Masses in Hunan Province, China, 1911–1927*. Berkeley, CA: University of California Press, 1978.

Meisner, Maurice. *Li Ta-chao and the Origins of Chinese Marxism*. Cambridge, MA: Harvard University Press, 1967.

———. *Mao Zedong: A Political and Intellectual Portrait*. Cambridge; Malden, MA: Polity, 2007.

North, Robert and Xenia Eudin, *M. N. Roy's Mission to China: The Communist-Kuomintang Split of 1927*. Berkeley, CA: University of California Press, 1963.

Perry, Elizabeth. *Rebels and Revolutionaries in North China, 1845–1945*. Stanford, CA: Stanford University Press, 1980.

Rowe, William. *Saving the World: Chen Hongmou and Elite Consciousness in Eighteenth-Century China*. Stanford, CA: Stanford University Press, 2001.

———. *Crimson Rain: Seven Centuries of Violence in a Chinese County*. Stanford, CA: Stanford University Press, 2007.

Rue, John E. *Mao Tse-tung in Opposition, 1927–1935*. Stanford: Stanford University Press, 1966.

Schoppa, Keith R. *Blood Road: The Mystery of Shen Dingyi in Revolutionary China*. Berkeley, CA: University of California Press, 1995.

Schwartz, Benjamin. *Chinese Communism and the Rise of Mao*. Cambridge, MA: Harvard University Press, 1951.

Selden, Mark. *The Yenan Way in Revolutionary China*. Cambridge, MA: Harvard University Press, 1971.

Sheel, Kamal. *Peasant Society and Marxist Intellectuals in China: Fang Zhimin and the Origin of a Revolutionary Movement in the Xinjiang Region*. Princeton: Princeton University Press, 1989.

Sheridan, James E. *China in Disintegration: The Republican Era in Chinese History, 1912–1949*. New York: The Free Press, 1975.

Short, Philip. *Mao: A Life*. New York: Henry Holt, 2000.

Shram, Stuart. *Mao Tse-tung*. Harmondsworth: Penguin, 1966.

Skinner, G. William. "Introduction: Urban and Rural in Chinese Society." In Skinner, G. William, ed., *The City in Late Imperial China*. Stanford: Stanford University Press, 1977.

———. "Introduction: Urban Development in Imperial China." In Skinner, G. William, ed., *The City in Late Imperial China*. Stanford: Stanford University Press, 1977.

Skocpol, Theda. *States and Social Revolutions: A Comparative Analysis of France, Russia, and China*. Cambridge: Cambridge University Press, 1979.

Spence, Jonathan. *God's Chinese Son: The Taiping Heavenly Kingdom of Hong Xiuquan*. New York: W. W. Norton & Company, 1996.

———. *Mao Zedong*. New York: Lipper/Viking, 1999.

Terrill, Ross. *Mao: A Biography*. Stanford, CA: Stanford University Press, 1999.

U, Eddy. "Third Sister Liu and the Making of the Intellectual in Socialist China." *The Journal of Asian Studies*, No. 69 (2010), 57–83.

Van De Ven, Hans, J. *From Friends to Comrades: The Founding of the Chinese Communist Party, 1920–1927*. Berkeley, CA: University of California Press, 1991.

Vogel, Ezra. *Deng Xiaoping and the Transformation of China*, 15–28. Belknap Press of Harvard University Press, 2011.

Wakeman, Frederick, Jr. "Rebellion and Revolution: The Study of Popular Movements in Chinese History." *The Journal of Asian Studies*, Vol. 36, No. 2 (1977), 201–237.

Walder, Andrew G. and Yang Su. "The Cultural Revolution in the Countryside, Scope, Timing and Human Impact." *The China Quarterly*, No. 173 (2003), 74–99.

Wou, Odoric, Y. K. *Mobilizing the Masses: Building Revolution in Henan*. Stanford, CA: Stanford University Press, 1994.

Wu Tien-wei. "A Review of the Wuhan Debacle: The Kuomintang-Communist Split of 1927." *Journal of Asian Studies*, 29(1), 1969.

Yang, Benjamin. "The Making of a Pragmatic Communist: The Early Life of Deng Xiaoping, 1904–1949." *China Quarterly*, No. 135 (1993), 444–456.

Yeh Wen-hsin. *Provincial Passages: Culture, Space, and the Origins of Chinese Communism*. Berkeley, CA: University of California Press, 1996.

Zarrow, Peter. *China in War and Revolution, 1895–1945*. London: Routledge, 2005.

———. *Anarchism and Chinese Political Culture*. New York: Columbia University Press, 1990.

Zheng Chaolin. *An Oppositionist for Life: Memoirs of the Chinese Revolutionary Zheng Chaolin*. Gregor Benton, trans. Atlantic Highlands, N.J.: Humanities Press, 1997.

Index